Popular Romance in Iceland

Popular Romance in Iceland

*The Women, Worldviews, and Manuscript
Witnesses of Nítíða saga*

Sheryl McDonald Werronen

LONDON AND NEW YORK

First published in 2016 by Amsterdam University Press Ltd.

Published 2025 by Routledge
4 Park Square, Milton Park, Abingdon, Oxon OX14 4RN
605 Third Avenue, New York, NY 10158

Routledge is an imprint of the Taylor & Francis Group, an informa business

ISBN: 9789089647955 (hbk)
ISBN: 9781041184478 (pbk)
ISBN: 9781003701712 (ebk)
NUR 635

Cover illustration: Reykjavík, National and University Library of Iceland, MS JS 27 fol., f. 306r (*c.* 1662-67). The opening of *Nítíða saga*, copied by Magnús Þórólfsson (with initials by Hannes Gunnlaugsson), probably for Magnús Jónsson í Vigur. Used with permission.

Cover design: Coördesign, Leiden

DOI: 10.5117/9789089647955

For Product Safety Concerns and Information please contact our EU representative:
GPSR@taylorandfrancis.com
Taylor & Francis Verlag GmbH, Kaufingerstraße 24, 80331 München, Germany

Table of Contents

Part II Romance Characters

List of Figures

Manuscript Abbreviations

Add.	Additional manuscript
AM	Den arnamagnæanske håndskriftsamling
ÍB	Safn Hins íslenska bókmenntafélags
ÍBR	Handritasafn Reykjavíkurdeildar Hins íslenska bókmenntafélags
JS	Jón Sigurðsson
Lbs	Handritasafn Landsbókasafn–Háskólabókasafn Íslands
Nks	Den nye kongelige samling
Papp.	Pappers-Handskrifter
Perg.	Pergaments-Handskrifter
Rask	Rasmus Rask
SÁM	Stofnun Árna Magnússonar á Íslandi

Acknowledgements

This book grew out of research I undertook at the University of Leeds from 2009-2013. The idea to carry out a detailed study of *Nítíða saga* was formed after reading a number of medieval Icelandic romances for the first time, at the suggestion of Alaric Hall. Needless to say, *Nítíða saga* caught my eye as a particularly enjoyable romance, not least because of its strong female lead. The prospect of working with a text surviving in so many hand-written paper copies, and which so relatively few people had studied before me, was also exciting. The invaluable support of both Alaric Hall and Catherine Batt during my time at Leeds helped me to navigate the many paths of inquiry I found before me in such an ambitious project; their insightful readings of early drafts were crucial in sharpening my arguments. Likewise, the critical readings of my work by Alan V. Murray and Matthew James Driscoll improved it further, and Shaun F.D. Hughes' thorough review of a late draft of the book helped to tighten everything up while highlighting areas meriting more detailed discussions.

My ideas were also regularly challenged and developed at conferences, including the annual medieval gatherings held at Leeds and Kalamazoo, and especially at the small conference in Freiburg, Germany, 'Dreams of Fame and Honor', on late medieval Icelandic prose fiction in autumn 2010; as well as the International Saga Conference in Aarhus, Denmark in 2012. At Leeds, and later in Canterbury when shaping my research into the book in its present form, I was fortunate enough to have the support of friends, colleagues, and family from around the world – you know who you are, though you are too many in number to name here!

I received financial support for my research from the Social Sciences and Humanities Research Council (SSHRC) of Canada from 2011-2013, and a grant from the Viking Society for Northern Research Support Fund in 2011 allowed me to visit Iceland to undertake further training in Icelandic palaeography and codicology, and to study in person most of the manuscripts preserving *Nítíða saga*. To this end, I would also like to thank the staff of the Stofnun Árna Magnússonar and the Landsbókasafn in Reykjavík, who very kindly brought out manuscript after manuscript for me to consult. The staff of Den Arnamagnæanske Samling in Copenhagen were equally accommodating when I visited in 2012.

Some of the material in one of the case studies in Chapter 1 was first published in *Digital Philology: A Journal of Medieval Cultures*, volume 1, issue 2, December 2012, pages 303-18; and my text and translation of *Nítíða saga* included in this book's Appendix are also based on versions previously published in the journal *Leeds Studies in English*, new series volume 40 (2009), pages 119-46.

   A final word of thanks is due to Simon Forde and others at Amsterdam University Press, along with Tuomo Fonsén and the other editors of the Turku Centre for Medieval and Early Modern Studies series Crossing Boundaries, for their help and guidance throughout the process of seeing this work through to publication.

Introduction

er og ei audsagt med öfrodre tungu i utlegdumm veralldarinnar, so
mõnnum verde skemtelegt, hvor fõgnudur vera munde i midiumm
heimenum af sliku hoffolke samannkomnu[1]

(it is also not easily said with an unlearned tongue in the outer regions of
the world, so that it might be entertaining for people, what joy might be
in the middle of the world when such courtiers come together)

It is tempting to think of Iceland in the Middle Ages as sitting somewhat
uneasily on the 'outer regions of the world'. While it had first existed as an
independent Commonwealth without a monarch, Iceland became subject to
the control of Norway in 1262 and just over a century later became part of the
larger Kalmar Union. While the communities inhabiting this small island
in the middle of the Atlantic were clearly different from their Scandinavian
neighbours in terms of their history, literature, and eventually also their
language, at the height of the Middle Ages Iceland was drawn into the
mainland European community with which Nordic monarchs were keenly
interacting. With its landscape of farmsteads instead of towns and, in its
Commonwealth days, its decentralized government structured around a
federation of chieftains instead of kings, Iceland in many ways had far less
in common with the rest of medieval Europe than did Norway or Denmark.[2]
It is no wonder, then, that the author of a romance called *Nítíða saga*[3] – a
text written in Iceland, probably sometime during the fourteenth century
– would appear to situate Iceland at the fringes of the world. But, as we
will see throughout this book, the culture and literature of late medieval
Iceland was not as isolated from medieval European ideas and ideals as this
excerpt might lead us to believe, taken at face value. Likewise, we will see
that Iceland's language was not such an *ófróður tunga* 'unlearned tongue'
as the author here suggests.

While the marginality or non-marginality of Iceland is certainly not a
new line of enquiry in itself, it has yet to be considered in very much detail

1 'Nitida saga', ed. by Loth, p. 36.
2 On the historical background see e.g. Gunnar Karlsson, *Iceland's 1100 Years*; Helgi Þorláksson,
'Historical Background', pp. 136-54.
3 The convention is to treat this name, whether in its Latinate form – *Nitida* – or its modern
Icelandic reflex – *Nítíða* (pronounced 'NEE-tee-the') – as an indeclinable noun.

from the vantage point of late medieval Icelandic romance (*riddarasögur*), which has until recently been a genre of Icelandic literature left to the margins in favour of the better known family sagas (*Íslendingasögur*) and legendary sagas (*fornaldarsögur*).[4] It is only relatively recently that romances composed in Iceland (those not translated from other European vernaculars) have become the primary subjects of academic study, and the number of medieval Icelandic romances translated into modern languages, including English, also still remains far too small. Many texts still await a proper edition, let alone a translation, although progress is now being made.[5] *Nítíða saga* is one such Icelandic romance that has been little studied, and yet is deeply concerned with such questions of Iceland's place within the wider world at the end of the Middle Ages – and also in early modern times, in the story's many younger post-Reformation versions. *Nítíða saga* is also, even more, concerned with the question of what it means to *be* a romance in Iceland. In its questioning, the saga challenges many of the boundaries that come along with genre classification.

The occasional passing reference to *Nítíða saga* appears in some early twentieth-century scholarship,[6] but it was largely unstudied until the publication of Agnete Loth's edition (never meant to be comprehensive) in 1965,[7] and the *Bibliography of Old Norse–Icelandic Romances* twenty years later.[8] For the next twenty-five years limited analysis of *Nítíða saga* has appeared in a number of works on Icelandic romance, but not usually in much detail.[9]

---

4   For an overview of this see Driscoll, 'Late Prose Fiction', pp. 190-204 (esp. pp. 196-97); Ármann Jakobsson, *Illa fenginn mjöður*, pp. 171-72.

5   The legendary sagas in Hermann Pálsson and Edwards, trans., *Seven Viking Romances*, and the efforts of O'Connor, trans., *Icelandic Histories and Romances*, have contributed good translations; however, many less well known romances remain untranslated. Alaric Hall's recent call for translations and his collaborative translations of two romances are efforts that are beginning to address this need. See Hall, 'Translating the Medieval Icelandic Romance-Sagas'; Hall, Richardson, and Haukur Þorgeirsson, '*Sigrgarðs saga frækna*'; Hall and others, '*Sigurðar saga fóts*'.

6   Some mentions are generally dismissive, e.g. Finnur Jónsson, *Den oldnorske og oldislandske litteraturs historie*, pp. 112-13. Others are more favourable, but it is still only noted in passing, e.g. Leach, *Angevin Britain and Scandinavia*; Schlauch, *Romance in Iceland*; Wahlgren, 'The Maiden King in Iceland', pp. 10-13, *passim*.

7   'Nitida saga', ed. by Loth, pp. 1-37.

8   Kalinke and Mitchell, *Bibliography of Old Norse–Icelandic Romances*. *Nítíða saga*'s entry here is primarily valuable for its list of extant manuscripts (pp. 85-86).

9   Bibire, 'From *riddarasaga* to *lygisaga*', pp. 55-74; Driscoll, 'Þögnin mikla', pp. 157-68; Driscoll, '*Nitida saga*', p. 432; Glauser, *Isländische Märchensagas*; Kalinke, 'The Misogamous Maiden Kings of Icelandic Romance', pp. 47-71; Kalinke, 'The Foreign Language Requirement in Medieval Icelandic Romance', pp. 850-61; Kalinke, 'Norse Romance (Riddararsögur)', pp. 316-63; Kalinke,

In 2009 the saga was translated (from Loth's edition), into English,[10] and in the same year was the sole subject of a chapter of Ármann Jakobsson's introductory volume on Icelandic literature.[11] The greatest strides, however, have been made much more recently, with *Nítíða saga* being discussed in detail, as an atypical Icelandic romance. In Jóhanna Katrín Friðriksdóttir's 2013 monograph on women in Old Norse literature, *Nítíða saga* is presented as an example of 'proto-feminism' that subverts the misogynistic norms exhibited in other Icelandic romances.[12] Likewise, Geraldine Barnes notes the saga's unconventional reorientation of world geography in her 2014 monograph entirely dedicated to Icelandic romances,[13] and Werner Schäfke cites the main character as an example of the regendering of masculine nobility.[14] In this book, I consider and develop these most recent ideas further to show how *Nítíða saga* consciously questions many of the norms and expectations of medieval Icelandic romance. Through the examination of various aspects of the text, from its relationships with other romances to its depiction of the world and the many characters – notably the women – populating it, I will discuss how *Nítíða saga* interrogates and complicates the genre with which it has been associated, to produce a unique medieval romance worldview. In addition to these critical readings of the text itself, I will explore the post-medieval manuscript witnesses of the saga and the different versions these resulted in, often exhibiting their own contemporary worldviews. Because this is still a relatively obscure saga, the full text and English translation are included in an appendix, but a synopsis highlighting some of the main areas I focus on in this book will not now be out of place.

'Riddarasögur, Fornaldarsögur, and the Problem of Genre', pp. 77-91; Kalinke, *King Arthur*; Kalinke, *Bridal-Quest Romance*; Driscoll, *The Unwashed Children of Eve*; Barnes, 'Travel and *translatio studii*', pp. 123-39; van Nahl, *Originale Riddarasögur*. The saga was the focus of an Icelandic BA thesis in the early 1990s, which until more recently was the only work to focus primarily on this romance (Guðbjörg Aðalbergsdóttir, 'Nítíða saga: Meykóngur í aðalhlutverki', and the resulting article Guðbjörg Aðalbergsdóttir, 'Nítíða og aðrir meykóngar'). Geraldine Barnes's 2006 International Saga Conference paper was the next to take the text as its main subject (Barnes, 'Margin vs. Centre').

10   McDonald, '*Nítíða saga*'. This was the first translation of this text out of Old Norse.
11   Ármann Jakobsson, *Illa fenginn mjöður*, pp. 171-79.
12   Jóhanna Katrín Friðriksdóttir, *Women in Old Norse Literature*, pp. 107-33.
13   Barnes, *The Bookish Riddarasögur*, pp. 35-40.
14   Schäfke, *Wertesysteme*, pp. 220-23.

Synopsis

Nítíða saga begins by describing the maiden-king (*meykóngur*) Nítíða, who rules France (*Frakkland*) alone. Her characterization might have led a medieval audience to expect the saga to be a typical maiden-king romance in which male suitors are violently rejected by the female sovereign, but this is the first of many expectations surrounding Icelandic romance that this saga does not fulfil. After Nítíða's introduction she travels from Paris to Apulia to visit her foster mother Egidía, and from there she ventures to the remote island Visio, from which she brings back stones (*náttúrusteinar*), apples, and herbs with magical properties. In this way, in anticipation of the challenges she will face later in the story, Nítíða is equipped with objects that may prove helpful in much the same way that the male protagonists of other Icelandic romances find or are given magical aids. Returning to Apulia, Nítíða asks for her foster brother Hléskjöldur to accompany her back to France to help defend her kingdom, and this foster sibling partnership, in parallel with Nítíða's recent acquisition of magical objects, further solidifies her characterization as this romance's protagonist.

After these first scenes, the saga introduces the remaining principal characters, many of whom exist simply to pursue Nítíða in marriage, in the tradition of an Icelandic bridal-quest romance: Ingi of Constantinople (*Miklagarður*, lit. 'great city') and his sister Listalín; Soldán of Serkland and his sons Logi, Vélogi, and Heiðarlogi; and Livorius[15] of India and his sister Sýjalín. Ingi is the first to travel to France and ask for Nítíða's hand, and she immediately refuses, as is typical of a haughty maiden-king, but while the rejection hurts Ingi's pride, the saga here does not follow the convention whereby the unwanted suitor is abused, and he leaves without sustaining any physical wounds. Ingi next meets the mysterious figure Refsteinn (lit. Fox Stone), who agrees to aid him in retaliation; they return to France and Ingi abducts Nítíða and brings her back to Constantinople. Once there, Nítíða escapes with the help of one of her supernatural stones, which transports her back to France. Nítíða's escape enhances her reputation as a cunning opponent. After this second humiliation, Ingi meets another mysterious helper, Slægrefur (lit. Sly Fox), who also sails with him back to France. Nítíða, seeing this in her magical stones, which give

---

15   While this is the generally accepted form of this character's name, in the manuscript AM 529 4to, the copy text for Loth's edition, the form found is *Livorinus* or *Liforinus* (with an extra \<n>). I use the form *Livorius* throughout this study, and use it instead of *Liforinus* even when translating Icelandic in which that form of the name appears, as in for example Chapter 4 below.

her supernatural vision as well as the ability to fly or teleport, prepares to outwit Ingi again by giving a servant woman her own appearance and making herself invisible, again facilitated by the magic objects obtained from Visio. Ingi arrives, abducts the disguised woman, and returns with her to Constantinople. Ingi's sister Listalín becomes suspicious of this 'maiden-king', and confronts her, while Ingi, hidden, listens. The woman reveals the truth, and in a rage, Ingi tears off her dress, causing the magical disguise to wear off as well. This scene epitomizes another major theme that surfaces throughout the saga, that of women's agency, power, and psychologies in the midst of the inherently masculine world of bridal-quest and maiden-king romance: it is not only that Nítíða again outwits Ingi, but that his sister is the one who considers the possibility of deceit, and that the feelings and emotions of the servant woman are highlighted as much as Nítíða's concern to outwit her suitor.

Nítíða saga next looks to two of Soldán's sons, Vélogi and Heiðarlogi, who sail to France demanding that Nítíða marry one of them. Again, Nítíða foresees their arrival in her supernatural stones, and fortifies her castle in preparation. When the brothers arrive, Hléskjöldur tricks them, one by one, into approaching the castle, where they and their armies are killed. In its violence, this episode in one sense seems to follow the conventions of an aggressive maiden-king story more closely than Ingi's previous encounters with Nítíða in that these suitors from Serkland are killed. However, the scene is not the equivalent of a failed bridal-quest because the brothers do not even manage to address Nítíða in person, but must go through her foster brother proxy, due to their characterization as an Other threat, who must be eliminated. Significantly and potentially somewhat problematically for modern readers, in the saga these characters' deaths in no way mar Nítíða's character, but rather work to reinforce her position as the saga's hero.

After this interlude, the saga turns to Livorius of India, who encounters a dwarf who is willing to help him on his quest to marry Nítíða – by this point in the story she is renowned for her ability to outwit her suitors. Livorius and the dwarf sail to France and manage to bring Nítíða back to India. Once there, she again escapes with a supernatural stone and this time brings Livorius's sister Sýjalín with her back to France in retaliation for her own abduction. While their relationship may not have begun on amicable terms, the two women become good friends, and the saga highlights the support Sýjalín shows Nítíða, developing further the theme of female concerns and perspectives touched on previously. Now Soldán, eager to avenge his sons' deaths, gathers an army and sets off for France by sea with his remaining son Logi. Seeing their plans in her supernatural stones, Nítíða sends Hléskjöldur with her navy to meet them and fight at sea, away from France. After a two-day battle, Livorius arrives unexpectedly and defeats Soldán in single combat. Hléskjöldur defeats Logi, and Livorius brings him home to India to heal his wounds before sending him back to France. This point marks the beginning of Livorius's portrayal as a positive and caring character, in contrast to the more negative, aggressive suitor of the earlier episodes.

Livorius then travels to Småland for advice from his aunt Alduria, who suggests he return to France in disguise, stay the winter in Nítíða's household, and get to know her personally, through the exercise of courtly manners. Taking his aunt's advice, he gains Nítíða's confidence during his stay, disguised as a prince named Eskilvarður. In the spring, Nítíða asks him to look into her magical stones, where they see throughout the world, which is depicted in three parts. In this scene, the saga's presentation of world geography is comprehensive, yet also rather unconventional. The geographical descriptions are interspersed with dialogue between Eskilvarður and Nítíða, who claims to be unable to find Livorius of India anywhere in the world. Nítíða then dramatically reveals that she saw through Livorius's disguise as soon as he arrived, and knows he is standing there with her. Livorius then proposes to Nítíða, who accepts, and their wedding is set for autumn.

Ingi hears of this and, still angry and humiliated, gathers an army against France. Upon arrival, Livorius meets Ingi and offers a settlement on behalf of Nítíða. Ingi prefers to fight, and will not give up until he agrees to single combat with Livorius, who confidently names Nítíða as the winner's prize. Ingi is seriously injured, but Livorius graciously spares his life and asks his sister Sýjalín to heal Ingi. Sýjalín and Ingi then fall in love, and Nítíða's foster brother Hléskjöldur is also offered as a match for Ingi's sister Listalín. The saga ends with a lavish triple wedding, after which the couples return to their kingdoms. *Nítíða saga* ends by relating how Nítíða and Livorius's son succeeds them as ruler of France.

Women and Worldviews

As is evident from the synopsis, *Nítíða saga* negotiates a number of themes and the representation and significance of the saga's characters is particularly important in demonstrating these. The roles of women are of central concern, not only because the story is named after a woman, but because of the other female characters represented throughout the story, and their many relationships, both with other women and with male characters. The characterization and presentation of women are prime examples of how this saga challenges the norms of Icelandic romance, by rejecting the widespread formula identified and discussed by Marianne Kalinke in her 1990 monograph *Bridal-Quest Romance in Medieval Iceland*: the male hero, his companions, and their quest for a bride (or brides), often including the woman's humiliation, if not outright abuse. *Nítíða saga* instead cultivates a worldview that not only accepts women as men's equals in marriage and rulership, but hones in on their actions, words, and skills as more than stock characteristics. In addition to this, the saga's vision of the medieval world these characters inhabit also demonstrates a quite literal 'worldview', with the extensive geographical reach that Nítíða holds. This opens up questions of how the saga's Icelandic author and audiences understood their relationship with Continental Europe, as seen through the lens of romance literature. The chivalric sagas of Iceland, while recognizably romances (adopting and adapting foreign plots and motifs), are still quite different to those of medieval England or France. Considering these differences, and especially in light of *Nítíða saga*'s own differences to other Icelandic romances, will shed light on issues of late medieval (as well as post-Reformation) identity.

Nítíða saga is a type of saga that can be categorized using a variety of terminology. A now seldom used term is *lygisaga* (lie-saga), once popular in earlier scholarship because of these sagas' inclusion of non-realistic – i.e. obviously fictional – plots and motifs.[16] This genre label reveals the negative attitude once commonly held towards such romances, dismissed as almost worthless because they 'lie', when compared to other types of sagas, notably the *Íslendingasögur* (sagas of Icelanders, or, family sagas), which have been deemed more serious and historical representations of Icelandic life.[17] Other, less pejorative genre descriptors include 'native' or 'indigenous' *riddarasaga* (chivalric or knights' saga), to avoid confusion with the separate group of translated *riddarasögur* – European romances (particularly French) translated into Old Norse at the court of the Norwegian King Hákon Hákonarson

16   Andrews, 'The Lygisögur', pp. 255-63; Barnes, 'Romance in Iceland', pp. 266-86; Bibire, 'From *riddarasaga* to *lygisaga*'; Driscoll, 'Late Prose Fiction'; Driscoll, 'The Oral, the Written, and the In-Between', pp. 193-220; Driscoll, 'Traditionality and Antiquarianism in the Post-Reformation *Lygisaga*', pp. 84-99; Foote, 'Sagnaskemtan: Reykjahólar 1119', pp. 65-83; Jakob Benediktsson, 'Lygisögur'; Glauser, 'Lygisaga', p. 398; Kalinke, 'Norse Romances (Riddarasögur)', pp. 316-63.
17   See e.g. Andersson, *The Icelandic Family Saga*; Jones, 'History and Fiction in the Sagas of Icelanders', pp. 285-306; Vésteinn Ólason, 'The Icelandic Saga as a Kind of Literature', pp. 27-48; Vésteinn Ólason, 'Family Sagas', pp. 101-18.

in the thirteenth century.[18] Within the romance genre we find two other subgroups and *Nítíða saga* has also been associated with both. While on some levels it can be said to be a 'maiden-king' and 'bridal-quest' romance,[19] this romance is, as I have already mentioned, not a typical member of either type, concerning not a hero's exploits in search of a bride, but a potential bride's exploits to keep herself from marrying.

In this book, I have tried to avoid referring to the texts I discuss as 'indigenous/native Icelandic romance' and 'popular romance', as I feel these are potentially problematic terms. The distinction between romances that are 'native' or 'indigenous' and those that are 'translated' is of course significant,[20] but in this book, I prefer, following Loth in her collection of editions, simply to refer to the so-called 'indigenous' *riddarasögur* that shape my discussions as 'Icelandic', or 'late medieval Icelandic', romances. They were written in Iceland, using the Icelandic (West Norse) language, for Icelanders. It is worth re-evaluating the dichotomy of translated vs. indigenous Icelandic romance, and it is in order to take a step towards forming a sharper critical vocabulary in this field that I wish to put it to one side in the present work. However, I do also find it useful occasionally to refer to *Nítíða saga* and its peers as 'popular' romance, in the sense of 'well-known' or 'widely-read' literature, rather than necessarily 'appealing to the masses' or 'non-elite'.[21] At the end of the Middle Ages, the audiences and authors of these romances can certainly be understood as elite: the literate, including not only the clergy, but also wealthy educated landowners and aristocrats.[22] After the Middle Ages the copyists and audiences of Icelandic romances spread as this 'popular', secular literature was no longer read and enjoyed as openly as before the Reformation, following

---

18   On the translated romances see Barnes, 'Some Current Issues in Riddararsögur-Research', pp. 73-88; Barnes, 'The *Riddarasögur*: A Medieval Exercise in Translation', pp. 403-41; Glauser, 'Romance (Translated *riddarasögur*)', pp. 372-87; Kalinke, *King Arthur*; Kalinke and Barnes, 'Riddarasögur', pp. 528-33. Most recent is Sif Rikhardsdottir's *Medieval Translations and Cultural Discourse*, studying various aspects of translation into Old Norse, including those from Middle English.

19   See Kalinke, *Bridal-Quest Romance*, and my discussion of her definitions in Chapter 4; and Sif Ríkharðsdóttir, 'Meykóngahefðin í riddarasögum', pp. 410-33. On bridal-quest in other medieval literature see Bornholdt, *Engaging Moments*.

20   Barnes, 'Romance in Iceland', pp. 266-86; Kalinke, 'Norse Romances'; Kalinke and Barnes, 'Riddarasögur', pp. 528-33.

21   For work on the increasingly established field of medieval English popular romance, see e.g. McDonald, ed., *Pulp Fictions of the Middle Ages*; Putter and Gilbert, eds., *The Spirit of Medieval English Popular Romance*; Lacy, 'The Evolution and Legacy of French Prose Romance', pp. 167-82.

22   Barnes, *The Bookish Riddarasögur*, pp. 183-85.

strong Church disapproval. It is then that late medieval Icelandic romance can be understood also as popular in the former sense,[23] for despite their discouragement in official circles, romances like *Nítíða saga* became as well-loved and widespread as ever.

Manuscript Witnesses

The manuscripts that preserve *Nítíða saga* are many, and in fact almost all of those known survive from after the Icelandic Reformation of 1550. The ways in which this originally medieval story continued to be told and retold in early modern times, and even up to the beginning of the twentieth century, are lines of enquiry just as interesting, and important, as the close reading of the text itself. Looking at some of the different manuscripts from different post-medieval periods allows us to see that not all Icelanders enjoyed the same *Nítíða saga* – the text, popular as it was, was never accessed through print, but always as the product of a scribe's copying, from another manuscript, or sometimes even from memory. This allows us also to question what really constitutes the text under consideration when it survives in such diverse forms, and to reveal the differences of outlook and worldview that each version of this medieval romance suggests its scribes and readers may have held.

While one of the manuscripts preserving *Nítíða saga* contains this text alone – Reykjavík, Landsbókasafn–Háskólabókasafn Íslands, MS ÍB 312 4to (1726) – the saga is usually transmitted along with romances and other types of literature alike. There are, furthermore, a few romances that *Nítíða saga* can consistently be found with in manuscript. Therefore, in addition to discussing some of the physical manuscripts and the different versions of the medieval saga they transmitted, I also consider some of the intertextual connections that *Nítíða saga* demonstrates with other medieval Icelandic romances that share themes, demonstrate literary connections, or were transmitted together in manuscript.[24] Throughout this book I compare and

23 Driscoll, *The Unwashed Children of Eve*, pp. 1-33.

24 See the following catalogues, which list the texts contained in the manuscripts: British Library, *Catalogue of Additions to the Manuscripts in the British Museum in the Years MDCCCLIV-MDCCCLXXV*; British Library, *Catalogue of Additions to the Manuscripts, 1756-1782*; Gödel, *Katalog öfver Kongl. Bibliotekets fornisländska och fornnorska handskrifter*; Kalinke and Mitchell, *Bibliography of Old Norse-Icelandic Romance*; Kommissionen for det Arnamagnæanske Legat, *Katalog over den Arnamagnæanske Handskriftsamling*; Kommissionen for det Arnamagnæanske Legat, *Katalog over de Oldnorsk-Islandske Håndskrifter*; Lárus H. Blöndal, Grímur M. Helgason, and

contrast *Nítíða saga* with other Icelandic 'maiden-king' romances, focusing mainly on *Clári saga*,[25] *Dínus saga drambláta*,[26] *Nikulás saga leikara*,[27] and *Sigurðar saga þǫgla*.[28] *Nikulás saga leikara* by far occurs most frequently with *Nítíða saga*, and half the time it does it appears directly before or after, suggesting that they were often transmitted together. *Dínus saga drambláta* is the next most frequently co-occurring with *Nítíða saga* in manuscript, and is also occasionally adjacent. These three texts were transmitted together as a group in at least one manuscript, Stockholm, Kungliga biblioteket–Sveriges nationalbiblioteket, MS Papp. 4to nr. 31 (1650×1689), containing these three texts, along with one other,[29] only. Various other sagas occur multiple times in *Nítíða saga*'s manuscripts, but these are the most significant. However, in addition to high co-occurrence in manuscript, the number of parallels in plot and motif shared with *Nítíða saga* are also important factors that suggest strong relationships among texts and the usefulness of comparing them. In this way may be added both *Sigurðar saga þǫgla* – which despite only co-occurring in manuscript with *Nítíða saga* a couple of times, shares more motifs with it than any other text,[30] and *Clári saga*, which also shares important motifs and, as we will see especially in Chapter 2, seems to have inspired *Nítíða saga*'s author.

Organization and Conventions

This book is in two parts. In the first, comprising three chapters, I discuss some of the metatextual issues already raised here, as well as the way in which *Nítíða saga* sets out the romance world in which the story takes place.

Ögmundur Helgason, *Handritasafn Landsbókasafns*; Páll Eggert Ólason, *Skrá um handritasöfn Landsbókasafnsins*; Stefán Einarsson, 'Safn Nikulásar Ottensons í Johns Hopkins Háskólabókasafninu í Baltimore, Md.', pp. 157-72.

25 *Clári saga*, ed. by Cederschiöld.

26 *Dínus saga drambláta*, ed. by Jónas Kristjánsson. This edition provides two redactions of the saga; I here refer to the older version (pp. 1-94), which is dated to the fifteenth century (p. lxiv).

27 Wick, 'An Edition and Study of Nikulás saga Leikara'. This edition provides two redactions of the saga; I refer to the longer redaction (pp. 62-161), the oldest manuscripts of which date to the seventeenth century; the saga itself may however be much older than this.

28 'Sigurðar saga þǫgla', ed. by Loth. This edition is of the longer redaction of the saga, and is based on the oldest manuscript survivals, which date roughly to the end of the fourteenth century. For more on the two redactions and their relationship, see Driscoll, ed., *Sigurðar saga þǫgla*.

29 The fourth text is a fragmentary life of St Eustace, known in Iceland as *Plácidus saga*.

30 See Boberg, *Motif-Index of Early Icelandic Literature*.

In Chapter 1 I consider the saga's manuscript context, from its late medieval origins to one of its youngest rewritings in the early twentieth century, in order to shed light on the textual diversity of the surviving manuscript witnesses. Discussing this medieval text's post-Reformation reception and transformation through three case studies will also illuminate some of the differences of worldview evident in these different versions. In Chapter 2 I discuss the saga's intertextual relationships through the analysis of a motif important to this and other romances, and through two case studies that highlight *Nítíða saga*'s relationships with *Clári saga* and *Nikulás saga leikara*. In Chapter 3 I analyse aspects of the saga's setting through a close reading of *Nítíða saga*'s unique depiction of world geography and the distinctions maintained between private and public spaces, in order better to understand the way in which this romance situates Iceland in relation to the rest of the known world.

In the second part of this book, also of three chapters, I discuss *Nítíða saga*'s characters and their various relationships. These analyses are primarily through close readings of the edited text, although I also consider, as a means of comparison, some of the other post-Reformation manuscript versions that survive, and which I will have touched on earlier in the book. In Chapter 4 I focus on the depiction of the saga's female hero, including perspectives on gender and power; I also look at the characterization and actions of Nítíða's main rivals. In Chapter 5 I consider the characterization of the saga's other female figures and how their depiction reinforces Nítíða's position as the saga's hero, while also demonstrating the importance of elite women's relationships. In Chapter 6 I end by exploring the role of the saga's anonymous narrator as another character who guides the audience through the story, and in doing so, further illustrates some of the aspects of the worldviews I discuss in other chapters, but from different perspectives.

This book sets out to show, through close readings of the saga as literature and through material philological considerations of some of the variant early modern and later versions of this originally medieval romance, how *Nítíða saga* explores and negotiates the genre of Icelandic romance, and raises questions of Icelandic worldview and identity, both locally and in relation to the wider world. In the process, this book introduces to a wider audience some of the hitherto little-known relationships among Icelandic romance manuscripts and texts, and illuminates Icelandic attitudes towards literature and literacy in the late medieval and early modern periods. In all of this I aim to demonstrate how *Nítíða saga*, as a late medieval Icelandic romance, engages with and questions the norms of the genre and the nature of the society in which it was produced, and to show how this text, significantly, crosses the boundaries of periodization, popular in medieval as well as early modern Iceland – though copied and recopied, written and rewritten, its hold over Icelandic imaginations remained strong across time and place.

All translations of original language quotations are my own unless otherwise noted. I have decided to normalize the names of characters and places across textual versions in my discussions, so that regardless of the form in any given manuscript, I always refer to Nítíða and Livorius, for the sake of consistency. Further to this, I use the form Nítíða (instead of Nitida) because this is the form the name takes in most modern Icelandic scholarship. I feel it more appropriate to use modern orthography for this saga and its title character, though medieval in their origin, primarily because I discuss the saga over time: it seems to me no more anachronistic to use modern spelling than it would be to retain the fifteenth-century spelling popularized by Loth's single, and far from exhaustive, edition. Apart from this, when quoting from *Nítíða saga* and other works in either edited or manuscript form, I have not modified or normalized my quotations, and when quoting directly from unedited manuscripts, I have endeavoured to use semi-diplomatic transcriptions, following the individual orthography of each manuscript as closely as possible, but expanding abbreviations using italics and parentheses in order to keep the texts easily readable for those less familiar with unnormalized Icelandic.

Part I
Romance Contexts

1 Manuscript Witnesses

Different Versions, Different Worldviews

Nítíða saga survives in sixty-five known manuscripts ranging in date from the end of the Middle Ages to the beginning of the twentieth century, making it arguably one of the most popular of all the late medieval Icelandic romances. Kalinke and Mitchell's *Bibliography of Old Norse–Icelandic Romances* provides a list of sixty-five manuscript witnesses for this saga,[1] but its transmission history is more complex than this might suggest. While one of the manuscripts in the *Bibliography*'s list actually contains a poetic *rímur* rather than a prose version of the story,[2] there is also at least one further manuscript not listed, Lbs 3625 4to (1800s, with a number of leaves missing from the middle), which also once contained *Nítíða saga*. Its table of contents lists *Nítíða saga* between two other romances, *Nikulás saga leikara* and *Þjalar-Jóns saga*, and a later owner's hand has added in the margin that the text is now 'vantari bókina' (missing from the book).[3] However, as not all manuscripts include lists of their contents, it is very likely that the saga once also appeared in many more manuscripts, which are now fragmentary or simply lost altogether.

Moreover, as well as the many witnesses of *Nítíða saga* in prose, there are also a significant number of extant *rímur* manuscripts, which are very rarely mentioned in scholarship dealing with romances in general, let alone *Nítíða saga* in particular,[4] and these are just as important to this story's transmission history as its prose versions. There are at least twenty-four additional manuscript witnesses of verse *Nítíða rímur* cycles, and from these, there exist at least eight different versions of the story.[5] Combining the known saga and *rímur* manuscripts, then, there are today at least ninety separate witnesses of the Nítíða story in verse and prose, spanning approximately

1 Kalinke and Mitchell, *Bibliography of Old Norse–Icelandic Romances*, pp. 85-86.

2 London, British Library, MS Add. 24,973 8vo (1824).

3 Lbs 3625 4to, f. 1ʳ. See also Wick, 'An Edition and Study of Nikulás saga Leikara', p. 261.

4 The only mentions of *Nítíða rímur* are in Driscoll, *The Unwashed Children of Eve*, p. 11 (only a passing reference); Finnur Sigmundsson, *Rímnatal*, p. 360 (a reference work); and Hughes, 'The Re-emergence of Women's Voices in Icelandic Literature', p. 123, which, following Finnur Sigmundsson, notes the one possibly female author of a set of *Nítíða rímur*, again, only in passing. No critical analyses have been done on any of these sets of *rímur*, and studies of *rímur* in general, especially in English, are relatively few.

5 Driscoll, *The Unwashed Children of Eve*, p. 11; Finnur Sigmundsson, *Rímnatal*, I, 356-60.

five hundred years. Unfortunately, it is impossible to discuss all of these, given the scope of the present work and the sheer number of extant texts. In this book I will, therefore, as a whole and in this chapter, continue in the tradition of focusing on the prose saga rather than the *rímur*, in an attempt to manage such a vast corpus of material. This chapter will not only draw attention to the textual variation in *Nítíða saga*'s manuscript tradition, which is not yet widely known,[6] but it will also serve as a background on which to anchor my analysis of the story in later chapters that focus on the one version that is most readily accessible, while still taking into account the variation discussed here. While to study the *rímur* in detail would involve a different type of investigation than the present study permits, I do make reference to them because they are important not merely for their own sake as further examples of variations of the Nítíða story, but also because they prove important to understanding some of the manuscripts of prose versions. While the *rímur* are based on the earlier prose versions of *Nítíða saga* – as far as we know the saga survives earlier than any *rímur* and it is common for *rímur* to rewrite prose sagas[7] – it is also likely that some of the many post-medieval prose versions derive not from earlier prose versions, but are adapted from *rímur*.[8] I will discuss this further later in this chapter.

Although only one version of *Nítíða saga* is generally known among scholars of Icelandic romance, in Iceland from the late Middle Ages and early modern period onwards there were many versions. Each time the story was written down – and we know it was written down many times over, throughout the island – it took on a new form, however slight were the differences from its exemplar. As Bernard Cerquiglini has put it in his influential work *In Praise of the Variant*: 'variance is the main characteristic of a work in the medieval vernacular [...]. This variance is so widespread and constitutive that [...] one could say that every manuscript is a revision, a version'.[9] While Cerquiglini's examples are generally taken from medieval French texts, his assertions are also especially applicable to Icelandic literature, with its incredibly rich manuscript culture, both medieval and post-medieval. In the discussions that follow considering the variety of

---

6   The version of the Nítíða story known today in academia is the prose text starting with AM 529 4to and ending with AM 537 4to, published in Loth's *Late Medieval Icelandic Romances*. My recent translation of the saga into English also reinforces the prominence of this version, as it is based on Loth's edition (McDonald, '*Nítíða saga*', pp. 119-44).

7   Jorgensen, 'Rímur', pp. 536-37.

8   Hughes, 'Late Secular Poetry', pp. 205-22; Jorgensen, 'The Neglected Genre of Rímur-Derived Prose', pp. 187-201.

9   Cerquiglini, *In Praise of the Variant*, pp. 37-38.

Nítíða texts surviving from Iceland, we will see how, as Stephen Nichols has stated, '[i]f we accept the multiple forms in which our artefacts [i.e. manuscripts] have been transmitted, we may recognize that medieval culture did not simply live with diversity, it cultivated it'.[10] While, again, I do not have the space here to discuss all surviving versions of the Nítíða story – although that would make a fascinating study – I will present three case studies to demonstrate in some detail the variety of versions of this medieval story, and what they can reveal about the individuals who copied and read them at different times and places in Iceland. This chapter will show how through the active engagement with the saga text that is required in the act of not merely copying but revising and even rewriting the text, Icelanders valued and enjoyed this saga, making it popular, and making it their own.[11]

As I have already mentioned, sixty-five manuscripts preserve prose versions of *Nítíða saga*, making it the third most popular out of thirty-four late medieval Icelandic romances if we consider their numbers of manuscript survivals, following *Mágus saga jarls* (75 manuscripts) and *Jarlmanns saga ok Hermanns* (71 manuscripts). While the number of manuscripts surviving from Iceland is quite high overall, it is still possible that even these numbers are only a fraction of what may actually have been produced, disseminated, read, and enjoyed in medieval and early modern Scandinavia, as well as later perhaps in Europe and North America, where Icelandic immigrants settled

---

10   Nichols, 'Introduction', pp. 8-9.

11   For an overview of the significance of analysing manuscripts and the value of recognizing the presence of different versions through material philological methodologies and from a specifically Old Norse–Icelandic perspective, see Driscoll, 'The Words on the Page', pp. 85-102; Haugen, 'The Spirit of Lachmann, the Spirit of Bédier'; Wolf, 'Old Norse – New Philology', pp. 338-48; and Hansen, 'The Icelandic *Lucidarius*, Traditional and New Philology', pp. 118-25. An earlier call for the consideration of post-medieval alongside medieval manuscripts is in Blaisdell Jr., 'The Value of the Valueless', pp. 40-46. In addition to Cerquiglini and Nichols, for further consideration of material philology more generally, see also Nichols, 'Why Material Philology?', pp. 10-30; Nichols, 'Philology and its Discontents', pp. 113-41; and the other articles in the 1990 issue of *Speculum*, especially Fleischman, 'Philology, Linguistics, and the Discourse of the Medieval Text', pp. 19-37; and Wenzel, 'Reflections on (New) Philology', pp. 11-18. The Canterbury Tales Project also provides an interesting parallel in which the entire manuscript tradition of Chaucer's *Tales* is taken into account and analysed – see Robinson, 'The History, Discoveries, and Aims of the Canterbury Tales Project', pp. 126-39. Two relatively early studies of medieval Icelandic romances also refer to the manuscript tradition of some of the romances they study: van Nahl includes a brief chapter at the end of *Originale Riddarasögur*, pp. 197-200; and Glauser discusses manuscript evidence and variety in *Isländische Märchensagas*, pp. 78-100; both works mention *Nítíða saga*, but only Glauser discusses its variation in manuscript, however briefly (pp. 82-84).

from the nineteenth century onwards, often bringing their books with them.[12] At least two manuscripts containing *Nítíða saga* did reach North America,[13] but it is certainly possible that others, as yet undocumented, also made it there. A relatively recent and well-known example is that of the eighteenth-century manuscript known as *Melsted's Edda* (SÁM 66), which in the nineteenth century was brought from Iceland to, ultimately, an Icelandic settlement in Saskatchewan, Canada. The manuscript was donated back to Iceland in 2000.[14] Even more recently, Katelin Parsons has discovered a number of Icelandic manuscripts in libraries in Manitoba, Canada, many of which contain Icelandic romances.[15] It has been suggested that in total, the manuscripts surviving today account for roughly 7-8 percent of what may have actually once existed, with the figure at likely no more than 10 percent.[16] With this in mind, *Nítíða saga*'s popularity and ongoing significance in Icelandic culture should by no means be overlooked. There has been some work on post-medieval saga popularity and reception in Iceland and abroad,[17] but the post-medieval reception and manuscript filiation of *Nítíða saga* in particular has been studied very little, although I have elsewhere very roughly grouped the manuscripts together,[18] and considered variation in the story as it is preserved in the oldest manuscripts.[19]

12   Driscoll, *The Unwashed Children of Eve*, pp. 71-73; Gunnar Karlsson, *Iceland's 1100 Years*.

13   Baltimore, MD, The Johns Hopkins University Library, Nikulás Ottenson Collection, MS 100, Nr. 17 (1853) and Ithaca, NY, Cornell University Library, Fiske Icelandic Collection, Ic F75 A125 (1824). The latter manuscript arrived in America after being purchased from a London, England second-hand bookseller in 1915, and how it came to be in London is uncertain (Þórunn Sigurðardóttir, *Manuscript Material, Correspondence and Graphic Material in the Fiske Icelandic Collection*, p. 37).

14   Gísli Sigurðsson, 'Melsted's Edda', pp. 179-84.

15   Parsons, 'The Great Manuscript Exodus?'.

16   Haugen, 'On the Birth and Death of Medieval Manuscripts'; Ommundsen, 'Books, Scribes, and Sequences in Medieval Norway'; Neddermeyer, 'Möglichkeiten und Grenzen einer quantitativen Bestimmung der Buchproduktion im späten Mittelalter', pp. 23-31; Frederiksen, 'Dansksprogede bøger fra middelalderen', pp. 154-62; Åström, 'Manuscripts and Bookprinting in Late Medieval Scandinavian and in Early Modern Times', pp. 1067-75; Cisne, 'How Science Survived', pp. 1305-07. See Wilson, *The Lost Literature of Medieval England*, for discussion of English texts' survivals.

17   Driscoll, *The Unwashed Children of Eve*; Glauser, 'The End of the Saga', pp. 101-41; Helgason, 'Continuity? The Icelandic Sagas in Post-Medieval Times', pp. 64-81; Malm, 'The Nordic Demand for Medieval Icelandic Manuscripts', pp. 101-07; O'Donoghue, *Old Norse–Icelandic Literature*, pp. 106-48; Springborg, 'Antiqvæ historiæ lepores', pp. 53-89; Wawn, 'The Post-Medieval Reception of Old Norse and Old Icelandic Literature', pp. 320-37. For a study of another medieval text's post-medieval manuscripts see Hast, *Pappershandskrifterna till Harðar saga*.

18   McDonald Werronen, 'Transforming Popular Romance on the Edge of the World', pp. 24-55.

19   McDonald Werronen, 'Two Major Groups in the Older Manuscript Tradition of *Nítíða saga*', pp. 75-94.

This chapter provides an overview of three different versions of *Nítíða saga* through discussion of three manuscripts in which the story is preserved. I will consider textual variation first and foremost (and will sometimes compare each version with the best known, edited version described in the introduction's synopsis), but will also touch on the manuscripts' geographical origins, information about their owners and scribes, and their composition and physical properties. The three manuscript versions date from three different post-Reformation periods (the seventeenth, eighteenth, and twentieth centuries), and two of them are from nearly as far away from each other geographically speaking, as is possible in Iceland. Overall, I will highlight the importance of recognizing and remembering the inherent instability of any given medieval text, as it is inevitably reworked and rewritten as it is copied from manuscript to manuscript. As Judy Quinn states in her introduction to *Creating the Medieval Saga*,

> To a significant degree, for those producing manuscripts in Iceland [...], retelling and recasting seem to have been the mainstay of tradition: it is only when the text becomes an artefact, for whatever religious, cultural or commercial reasons, that verbatim copying becomes the dominant mode of transmission, albeit that is the mode most familiar to us, having prevailed across the centuries since the widespread use of the printing press.[20]

Of course this is the case not only for the literature of medieval Iceland, but also for medieval literature elsewhere in Europe, but it is worth stressing here nonetheless. Because medieval literature essentially '*is* variance' exemplified,[21] it will be useful to consider *Nítíða saga* in the later chapters of this book within its complex manuscript context, even if that cannot be fully understood at present, and to interrogate the very notion of what constitutes a text and what contributes to its (in)stability. Considering *Nítíða saga*'s wider manuscript context can only further enrich our understanding of the originally medieval story and its implications for medieval Icelandic society, such as the role of literature and literacy in familial and other social contexts. Looking at different post-medieval versions here will help to keep in mind, in later chapters, that the version discussed and analysed is only one of many.

---

20 Quinn, 'Introduction', pp. 16-17.
21 Cerquiglini, pp. 77-78.

Different Versions

The oldest surviving manuscript preserving parts of *Nítíða saga* is a single-leaf vellum fragment from the end of the fifteenth century, which is now kept in Stockholm, Kungliga biblioteket–Sveriges nationalbiblioteket, MS Perg. 8vo nr. 10 VII. Two other vellums survive, both from the sixteenth century and both kept in the Árni Magnússon Institute in Reykjavík.[22] These are AM 529 4to, which ends defective but is the primary manuscript used by Agnete Loth in her diplomatic edition of *Nítíða saga*; and AM 567 4to XVIII, which is a fragment only consisting of two leaves and which Loth uses to note variants in the edition. In my first case study below, that of JS 166 fol. (1679), I chose to focus on one of the relatively early manuscripts in which the saga is preserved in full, in order to consider a single, continuous narrative – something that cannot be done if one considers the edited text. Though dating from 1679 and written on paper, firmly in the post-medieval Icelandic scribal tradition, the text preserved in JS 166 fol. is one of the earliest complete versions of the saga.

I consider manuscripts from the medieval period up until the end of the seventeenth century 'earlier' (comprising the traditional Icelandic periodization of both pre-Reformation and post-Reformation humanist renaissance), and manuscripts from the beginning of the eighteenth century to the twentieth I consider 'later' (comprising the period of popular dissemination that took place after the humanist renaissance). While arbitrary, this is motivated by two factors. First, the earliest *Nítíða saga* manuscript is only from the end of the medieval period, which is also an arbitrary cut-off point, as the European Middle Ages are generally considered over by the end of the fifteenth century. However, the Protestant Reformation in Iceland, formally complete in 1550, indicates an Icelandic Middle Ages extending until at least the mid-sixteenth century. This brings us to my second reason for my division of the manuscripts into earlier and later, that medieval scribal practices, as we will see in detail shortly, continued in Iceland throughout the early modern period and beyond – far longer than in most of the rest of Europe.[23] This echoes the fact that published versions of medieval texts are often to some extent arbitrary, and may not

22   The Arnamagnæan Manuscript Collection, named after the Icelandic scholar and collector of manuscripts Árni Magnússon (1663-1730) and containing some 3000 items, is now split between the Institute in Reykjavík and its sister Institute in Copenhagen. All of the Arnamagnæan manuscripts (shelfmarks abbreviated AM) referred to in this book are kept in Reykjavík, unless otherwise indicated.

23   See e.g. Margrét Eggertsdóttir, 'From Reformation to Enlightenment', p. 174 ff.

even always be based on single manuscript attestations or indeed medieval manuscripts.[24]

By far the greatest number of prose *Nítíða saga* manuscripts has survived from the nineteenth century. Almost half of the surviving *Nítíða saga* manuscripts were written sometime in the 1800s, and this should not be surprising considering the proximity of that century to our own (fewer manuscripts may have been lost), and considering the rising access to literacy, falling costs of materials in some cases, and population growth, to name only a handful of factors. Additionally, the composing and reciting of sagas had not yet begun to decline as rapidly as happened in the twentieth century, from which only seven manuscripts survive, all dating from the first part of the 1900s. From the eighteenth century, fourteen manuscripts (close to a quarter of the total) survive, which, again, is not to say that *Nítíða saga* was less popular then than in the nineteenth century, but that more eighteenth-century manuscripts may have been lost.

In the discussion that follows my aim is not to make definitive claims about which manuscripts were copied from which, but rather to propose broader trends, and ultimately to focus on only a few manuscripts and the versions they preserve.[25] In analysing the manuscripts to discover different versions of the saga, I began by transcribing selected passages (the beginning, end, and the section in which the geography of the world is described) and then recording and comparing variants. In addition to these longer passages, I recorded all manuscript variants of personal and place names, and made groupings according to those variations. I chose to compare these passages and names because of their diagnostic potential: a variation on a name, for example, seems to provide evidence of the relatedness (or unrelatedness) of the manuscripts that do or do not include that variation. Whereas with nouns, scribes can rely on both their exemplars and context clues to establish their readings, for names, and especially unfamiliar non-Icelandic names, scribes would need to rely most heavily on their exemplars, increasing their chances of misunderstanding these names – and we will see examples of this below. I also considered much broader terms for comparison, such as the basic structure of the story and the physical size of the manuscripts. I found that the story as it is told

---

24 McDonald, '*Nítíða saga*', p. 121.
25 For a more detailed description of the relationships among the manuscripts, including diagrams, see McDonald Werronen, 'Two Major Groups in the Older Manuscript Tradition of *Nítíða saga*', pp. 75-94; and McDonald Werronen, 'Transforming Popular Romance on the Edge of the World', pp. 24-55.

in the manuscripts is presented in two basic ways: either all of the most important characters are introduced successively and the plot then skips back and forth among them to present their adventures (and this is the slightly more common structure); or the main characters are introduced as the plot progresses, so that, for example, Livorius, although he is a crucial character, is not mentioned at all until the major adventures concerning the other suitors have already concluded.

Considering the physical size of manuscripts, the majority are quartos, with only five larger folios and eighteen smaller octavos. The folio manuscripts are all from the seventeenth or eighteenth centuries, while the quartos span the sixteenth century to the twentieth, and the octavos range from the fifteenth century to the twentieth, but, not surprisingly, more of the octavos are from later. The folios are relatively early, from a time when Icelandic sagas were being rediscovered and appreciated in Scandinavia, and copied accordingly for show and as high-status texts, which, while not very portable, are very legible since their size allowed a large, clear script to be used.[26]

Manuscript scribes and locations of origin are often difficult to pin down with certainty, as many scribes did not leave colophons, and even when they did it is not always possible to match names, dates, and locations with precision, especially place names from earlier times. Nevertheless, I have been able to obtain scribal and/or geographical information for thirty-five of the manuscripts, relying on colophons, and where these are not included, catalogues and editions, in order to localize these manuscripts. More might be localized through further study of the physical manuscripts themselves, i.e. their codicology, palaeography, and marginalia, but such an exhaustive analysis is, again unfortunately, outside the scope of this book. My findings presented here must, therefore, remain somewhat limited. Despite this, patterns have emerged from plotting the locations of origin I have found onto a map. The most striking pattern shows one group of textually similar manuscripts that were produced relatively late, in eastern Iceland (see Figure 1), which I will discuss in greater detail in my third case study.

The following studies are meant to be examples that are, in their individuality, representative of the transformations that *Nítíða saga* underwent after the medieval period from which the story originates; all three studies show different textual versions. While the three cases are all different and show a variety of changes and modifications to the text that separate

---

26 Springborg, 'Antiqvæ historiæ lepores', pp. 53-89. See also Hall and Parsons, 'Making Stemmas with Small Samples', fig. 15.

Figure 1   Map of Manuscript Locations

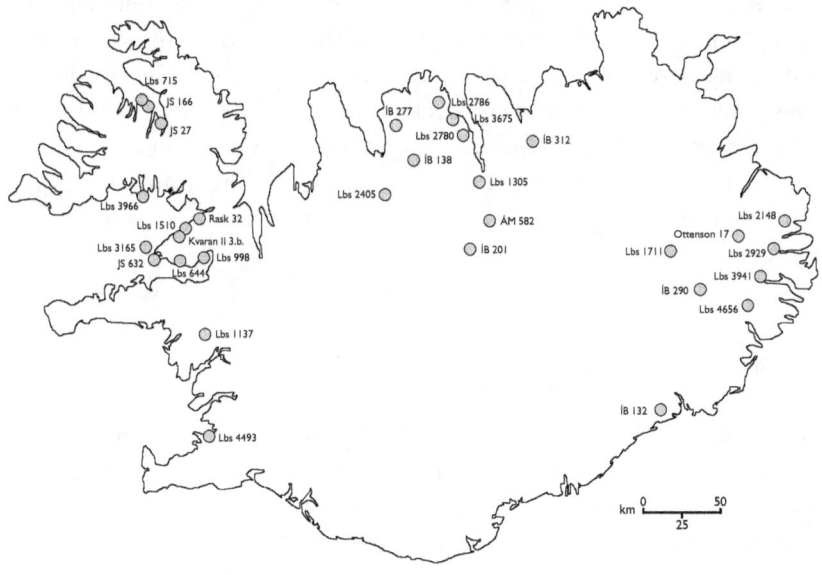

these versions into different groups, their value is as three examples among many, from which a larger textual and cultural history surrounding *Nítíða saga* may be imagined. These studies provide a taste of the rich variation not only in the medieval story, but also in the people who caused this variation to occur – the scribes, listeners, readers, and other members of the reading communities within which post-medieval manuscript culture thrived. A recent doctoral thesis by Davíð Ólafsson includes a case study of the nineteenth-century Icelandic scribe Sighvatur Grímsson as an example of one man who became a prolific copyist by taking advantage of his circumstances to educate himself and supplement his livelihood through commissioned scribal projects. This detailed case study has as its foundation microhistorical methodology,[27] which is usually employed in the study of individual figures in history, with the understanding that one detailed example is potentially more valuable than a more conventional broader approach to writing history. As Giovanni Levi states in an essay explaining the value and practice of microhistory, 'The unifying principle of all microhistorical research is the belief that microscopic observation will

---

27   Davíð Ólafsson, 'Wordmongers', pp. 17, 36. See also Ginzburg, 'Microhistory', pp. 10-35; Levi, 'On Microhistory', pp. 97-119.

reveal factors previously unobserved'.[28] However, this principle can also be applied to the study of objects, such as the concrete physical manuscript book, and the more abstract literary text. The following studies will not only demonstrate *Nítíða saga*'s textual variation and manuscript context from a material philological perspective, but will also combine with this a microhistorical approach that sees the saga audiences through the story's adaptability and the notion of the text, the work of literature, as a figure in history appearing and reappearing at each instance of copying and recopying.

JS 166 fol.

My first case study is of the version of the saga preserved in the early modern manuscript Reykjavík, Landsbókasafn–Háskólabókasafn Íslands, MS JS 166 fol.,[29] which was written during the winter of 1678-79 by a single scribe named Þórður Jónsson (fl. 1667-1693).[30] He lived at Strandsel, a farm situated in Strandseljavík on the south side of Ísafjarðardjúpur to the south of Æðey in the Ögurhreppur area of Norður-Ísafjarðarsýsla, a district in the Icelandic Westfjords (see JS 166 on the maps in Figure 1, above, and the detail in Figure 2, below).[31] While relatively little is known about Þórður at present, he was an important member of the scribal community surrounding the landowner, scholar, and manuscript patron Magnús Jónsson í Vigur (1637-1702) in the late seventeenth century.[32] Many of the paper leaves of JS 166 (including a significant number of those in which *Nítíða saga* is copied) have been damaged, both from wear and tear and trimming, and in a number of places missing text has been added by a later hand, identified as that of Páll Pálsson (1806-1877) from Reykjavík.[33] Our copyist Þórður Jónsson was also the scribe of at least a handful of other late seventeenth-century

28 Levi, p. 101.

29 See also McDonald, 'Variance Uncovered', which is based on the present case study.

30 'Þórður Jónsson', *Handrit.is*, National and University Library of Iceland.

31 Árni Magnússon and Páll Vídalín, *Jarðabók*, VII: *Ísafjarðar- og Strandasýsla*, pp. 196-97. The farm was still inhabited in the nineteenth century; see Jón Johnsen, *Jarðatal á Íslandi*, p. 200, entry #187.

32 Further study of Þórður Jónsson and his connections form part of my current research on the scribal networks fostered by Magnús í Vigur, the results of which will be published in due course (the research has been funded by a Marie Skłodowska-Curie Actions Individual Fellowship from the European Commission, grant agreement H202-MSCA-IF-2014-654825).

33 Páll Eggert Ólason, *Íslenskar æviskrár*, IV, 136-37; 'Páll Pálsson stúdent', *Handrit.is*, National and University Library of Iceland.

manuscripts. All housed in the same institution as JS 166, these include JS 6 4to, a copy of the Icelandic law code known as *Jónsbók*; JS 12 fol., a compilation of saga literature including other *riddarasögur* and *fornaldarsögur* (the manuscript's elaborate title page calls it *Florilegium Historicum, það er einn fagur aldingarður ýmislegra frásagna [...]* (A Historical Anthology, that is, a lovely orchard of various stories [...]); JS 148 4to, a copy of bishops' records; JS 641 4to, a *Sögubók* (book of sagas) of seven romances and an eighth copied by a different scribe), and another *Nítíða saga* manuscript, Lbs 715 4to, which also contains *riddarasögur* and *fornaldarsögur*. Þórður Jónsson was also the scribe of at least one manuscript now in London, British Library, MS Add. 4857 fol., which likewise mainly contains romances.

In JS 166, *Nítíða saga* is the fifth of eight sagas. Those preceding it are *Trójumanna saga* (an Icelandic translation of the matter of Troy), *Vilmundar saga viðutan*, and *Rémundar saga keisarasonar* (both Icelandic romances). Those following it are *Hálfdanar saga Eysteinssonar, Hálfdanar saga Brönufóstra* (both *fornaldarsögur*), and *Orms þáttur Stórólfssonar* (an *Íslendingaþáttur*, that is, a short tale of Icelanders). This variety of texts make rather normal company for *Nítíða saga*, showing it was transmitted along with a range of other types of stories, and even suggesting that our modern ideas about genre and saga classification could be quite foreign to a medieval or early modern system of textual classification. *Nítíða saga* is divided into thirteen chapters in this manuscript, and there are a number of simple sketches of faces enclosed within the first letter of some of the chapters, for example, within the initial <N> of *Nú* (now).[34] Sketches also occur in the manuscript's other texts. A colophon following *Nítíða saga* gives the date Þórður completed it: 'þann 7. *febrúarii anno* 1679'.[35] Nearly all the other texts in the manuscript contain similar colophons. These dates throughout the manuscript demonstrate that it was copied throughout the winter months, in a process of copying commonly undertaken in farmhouse communities where the reading aloud of sagas from manuscripts, *sagnaskemmtun* (saga-diversion), was part of the entertainment and activities enjoyed during the *kvöldvaka* (evening-wake).[36]

In JS 166 *Nítíða saga* is roughly 6600 words, a bit longer than the edited version included in the appendix, which as a composite of two manuscripts runs to about 5700 words. While the romance is largely similar in both

---

34 JS 166 fol., ff. 182ʳ, 183ʳ, 186ʳ, 187ʳ, 189ʳ.
35 JS 166 fol., f. 190ʳ.
36 Magnús Gíslason, *Kvällsvaka*, 'Läsning', pp. 95-100; Davíð Ólafsson, 'Wordmongers', pp. 118-22, 154-58; Driscoll, *The Unwashed Children of Eve*, pp. 38-46, 73.

versions, sometimes even verbatim, in JS 166 many of the key episodes and
descriptions are extended and include more details. One part of the story
where this is most readily apparent is at the end of the romance, from the
wedding celebrations onwards. In JS 166 the triple wedding festivities are
much lengthier than in the edition[37] – fleshed out with more details of both
the celebration and the narrator's perception of it. The scene first describes
the elaborate celebrations themselves:

> Hefiast nu upp þesse þriu ʙrullaup, j upp hafe Augusti ᴍänadar, og stödu
> yfer allann þann ᴍänud, med miklumm prÿs og veralldar blöma, þar var
> fagurlega eted & ᴅrucked, allz konar wÿn og beste ᴅryckur, sem kiender
> voru hier ä nordur løndumm, & ønnur ᴅÿr mät fæda, med huørskinz
> bestu krä∫summ & friddum til reÿdd. þar voru allra handa leÿkur framdur
> þar var ʙurttreÿd & ᴛurniment. Riddarar og ᴊungkiærar ridu vt fyrir sÿnar
> vnnustur, þar voru framdar allra handa hliöd færa lystir, sumer skiemta
> sier med fräsøgumm, sumer med ᴀnnallumm og vÿsinda bökumm, enn
> þar sem kongarner geingu, var breÿdtt nidur pell og purpure, og kostuleg
> klæde.[38]

(These three weddings now begin at the start of the month of August, and
they lasted the whole month with great ceremony and worldly glory. There
was lovely eating and drinking, all sorts of wine and the best drinks, as
were known here in northern lands, and other costly foods provided, with
each of the best delicacies and lovely things carried out. There were all
sorts of games performed, there was bohourt[39] and tournament; knights
and young men rode out for their lovers. There were performed musical
arts of all sorts. Some were amused with stories, some with annals and
learned books. And there where the kings walked was spread down costly
fabric, cloth of purple, and valuable raiment.)

37   The episode in AM 537 4to reads: 'hefiast nu þesse þriu brudkaup i upphafe augusti manadar
og yfir stendur allan þann manud med miklumm veralldarpris og blöma, þar var fallega eted
og fagurlega drucked med allskins matbunade og dïrustu drickiumm, þar var allskins skemtun
framinn i burtreidumm og hliodfæraslætte, enn þar sem kongarner geingu var nidurbreidt pell
og purpure og heidurleg klæde' ('Nitida saga', ed. by Loth, pp. 35-36).
38   JS 166 fol., ff. 189ᵛ-190ʳ.
39   The term *burtreið* is translated here not as 'joust' but as 'bohourt', the now generally obsolete
English descendant of the medieval French *béhourd, bohort*, from which the Old Norse *burtreið*
ultimately derives (perhaps via German), even though it is doubtful whether the distinction
between bohourt (mass tourney among teams of knights with blunted weapons) and joust
(combat between individual knights) was understood in Scandinavia and Iceland. Thanks to
Alan V. Murray for drawing this to my attention.

Here, all aspects of the wedding celebrations and entertainment are noted, and the variety of entertainment in particular, is far greater here than in the other version. There are more specific descriptions of the food and drink available, the types of people participating in tournaments, and that some people sought entertainment from different types of books. The distinction between *frásögn*, *annáll*, and *vísinda-bók* is especially noteworthy as an explicit comment on literature itself, indicating that these are the types of texts appropriate for entertainment at the most important and extravagant of royal celebrations, and that stories, annals, and learned books go hand in hand with tournaments, feasting, and other courtly pastimes, while also hinting at what may have been appropriate at an Icelandic (rather than French) marriage feast.[40] This contrasts, for example, with an earlier mention of Livorius, disguised as the prince Eskelvarður, having entertained Nítíða and Sýjalín with 'morgumm dæmesøgumm' (many edifying stories),[41] which suggests that this other type of literature or entertainment – the *dæmisaga* – while suitable for elite consumers like the maiden-king of France, belongs primarily in homely and familiar settings, at the hearth during winter, rather than at high court during official summer ceremonies. All of these references to literature and learning combined show its overall importance in the romance world of the saga. This also complements Nítíða's characterization early on as 'vel vite borinn sem hinn lærdaste klerkur, þui hün kunne þar 10. tüngur sem adrir kunnu ei nema eina' (as knowledgeable as the most learned scholar, that she knew ten languages when others knew only one),[42] and other romances' general preoccupation with learning.[43] In AM 529, Nítíða's introduction is similar: 'suo buen at viti sem hinn frodasti klerkur. og hinn sterkasti borgarveggur mætti hun giora med sinu viti yfer annara manna vit og byrgia suo vti annara ræd. og þar kunni hun .x. ræd er adrer kunnu eitt' (as endowed with knowledge as the wisest scholar, and she could make the strongest castle-wall through an intellect above other people's, and she could also outwit the counsel of others, so much that she knew ten answers when others knew one).[44] However, the differences, especially the seeming confusion of 'ten languages' with 'ten answers', demonstrate further that these manuscripts represent two distinct versions

---

40 For other examples of Icelandic points of view being introduced into courtly settings see Hughes, 'Aspects of Courtly Literature in the Riddarasögur', pp. 11-12.

41 JS 166 fol., f. 188ʳ.

42 JS 166 fol., f. 181ᵛ.

43 Divjak, *Studies in the Traditions of Kirialax Saga*; Kalinke, 'The Foreign Language Requirement'.

44 'Nitida saga', ed. by Loth, p. 4.

of the saga, as the differences are too complex to be simply scribal error. The subtle distinctions seen in JS 166 between different types of written material, as well as the sense that linguistic skill, literature, and literacy are important themes in the text are not present in the edited version, which at this point in the saga instead highlights cleverness as a more prominent theme. Whether these differences reflect different medieval versions or whether they can be attributed to the changing tastes of Icelanders in the intervening years is uncertain.

In addition to elaborations on the wedding scene, the narrator's voice appears briefly when mention is made of expensive and possibly exotic food (*sem kiender voru hier ä nordur løndumm* [as were known here in northern lands]). The mention is off-hand, but acknowledges, importantly, that the narrator is a member of a different geographical community than that which he describes in the text, something that is only really apparent with the inclusion of the adverb *hier* (here). But even without this adverb, specifying northern lands suggests a narrator (or scribe) who is aware of his Icelandic, northern audience, even if he does not characterize himself as such. The narrator is not yet concerned with commenting on the subject of his story, but emphasis is placed on northern lands, in a similar way to the northern focus that is evident in the edited version of the romance, which I mentioned breifly at the beginning of this book, and will discuss further in Chapters 3 and 6. The focus of this passage is, so far, on description and reinforcement of courtly norms and expectations through feasts and celebrations, with the sole interpretive aspect mentioned in passing.

The description now continues from the magnificent celebrations to a much more interpretive viewpoint, showing the narrator's relationship with the material related to the audience:

> verdur ei alltt skẏrtt m*ed* öþiælgre tungu, huørsu mikill fagnadur vered mun hafa ä *þeim* Døgum*m* J øndueige heimsin*n*z, hjä slẏku hoffölke. Stendur nu Brullauped m*ed* mikille glede þessa heimz, & Dẏrlegre skiemtan, af høfdinglegre tilfeyngiu, sem nög er til j þuilẏkum*m* stødumm. En*n* af þui ad þessa heimz glede lẏdur skiött, og ei sẏst Brullaups glaum*ur*, þä *var* Brullauped wtdrucked, og høfding*iar* wtleẏster m*ed* störum*m* giøfum*m* gulle og Gym*m*steinum*m*, perlum*m* og dẏrgripum*m*, skildest þesse hoflẏd*ur* med bestu vinattu.[45]

(All is not clear with a clumsy tongue, how great rejoicing might be had in those days in the throne of the world, near such courtiers. Now the wedding stands with great joy of this world, and splendid amusement, from courtly provisions, as is sufficient in such a place. And because this world's joy passes quickly, and not least the merriment of a wedding, then the wedding was concluded, and the nobles led out with great gifts of gold and jewels, pearls and precious jewels, these courtiers parted with the best friendship.)

In this half of the passage, description becomes secondary to commentary, inverting that relationship set out earlier. More is said in this version of the commentary than in other versions, with small additions to the text. Further, even where the message is essentially identical in the two manuscript versions, it is relayed with different diction. To give only a few examples, JS 166's *ei alltt skÿrtt* is used for AM 537's *ei audsagt*; it is *öþialgre tungu* for *öfrode tungu*; and *øndueige heimsinnz* (repeating exactly the phrase used at the saga's opening) for *midiumm heimenum*. Further, the addition of *ä þeim døgumm* (in those days) works to distance the story temporally, whereas in other versions the distance implied in the corresponding section is simply spatial. Despite focusing on the transitory nature of celebrations like the triple wedding, the passage still emphasizes the importance of the occasion and the relationships fostered through it – those present leave *med bestu vinattu* (with the best friendship).

Perhaps the most striking difference in this version, present also in a number of other textually similar manuscripts from the Icelandic Dales and Westfjords (see below, and Figure 2), is a small expository passage in the closing remarks of the text after the weddings have been described, where the narrator explicitly connects *Nítíða saga* to *Nikulás saga leikara*:

Livorius kongur & meykongur stÿrdu Franns vel & lengi. þau ättu sier ägiæt born 4. sonu & 2. dætur. Rÿgardur hët þeirra ellste son, eptter mödur födur sÿnum, er sÿdann stÿrde Fracklande med allann heidur og sæmd, enn hannz son hët Fhaustus, er vann Ungaria med her skyllde & seigät fornar Bækur ad hann hafe vered fadir Nicula/sar leÿkara, er vmm sÿdir eignadest Döttir kongsinnz af Grycklande Walldemarz, huor ed [sic] hiet Dormä huoruim kvennkoste hann näde medur med brøgdumm [...], sem seigir j søgu hannz.[46]

(King Livorius and the maiden-king ruled France long and well. They had excellent children: four sons and two daughters. Their eldest son was called Rígarður, after his mother's father, and he ruled France with all honour. And his son was called Faustus, who won Hungary by harrying, and old books say that he had been the father of Nikulás leikari, who at last married the daughter of Walldemar king of Greece, who is called Dormä, whom he got as a match through tricks [...], as it says in his story.)

This intertextual reference must be an established part of the manuscript versions most similar to that in JS 166, considering that it was not included here in order to provide a smooth transition to the following text: as we know, *Nikulás saga leikara* does not appear in JS 166 at all, though it does in other manuscripts containing the same version, which I list at the end of this case study. Making Nítíða and Livorius the great-grandparents of Nikulás leikari sets a firm connection between the two texts. From this evidence one can suggest that these romances were considered related in certain aspects of theme, style, or characterization, or a combination of these, by those who heard or read them, or at least by those who copied them. I will explore the relationship between these two texts in further detail in Chapter 2.

This type of specific genealogical connection between different texts seems relatively uncommon in Icelandic romance. Two of the only other examples occur in the younger recension of *Jarlmanns saga ok Hermanns*, where that text links itself to *Konráðs saga keisarasonar*,[47] and in the long redaction of *Sigurðar saga þǫgla*, which connects itself to *Flores saga ok Blankiflur*.[48] Apart from the very specific intertextual connection, this ending quotation also demonstrates once more the importance of literary culture, books, and the act of reading or being read to, when it specifies that the story of Nikulás leikari is known from *fornar bækur* (old books). Just as books and stories are mentioned at the weddings and elsewhere in this version, here they reinforce the connection between sagas and their characters, the ancient books validating what is written in contemporary seventeenth-century Iceland, all literary conventions aside.

After this, at the very end of the text in JS 166, the saga is brought to a close and in so doing provides a final characterization of Nítíða, which is also a key aspect of this version. After stating that none of their other children's names are known, the narrator says, 'Og liükumm vier hier med

47   Rydberg ed., *Jarlmanns saga ok Hermanns i yngre handskrifters redaktion*.
48   'Sigurðar saga þǫgla', ed. by Loth, pp. 99-102.

þessa søgu, af Nitedä frægu & hennar breÿtelegumm brøgdumm' (And we end here this saga, of Nítíða the Famous and her various tricks).[49] Unlike in other versions, which we will see below, here Nítíða really does have the last word. Livorius is not mentioned again, and this is not just another mention of Nítíða's name, but one last opportunity to round out this character. Here, Nítíða's prominent role is seen through to the very end, and the audience is told to remember Nítíða as a trickster, which considering the preceding explicit connection to Nikulás leikari, who is called such because he is a trickster and uses magic, is even more appropriate. I deal with this in further detail in the following chapter on *Nítíða saga*'s intertextual relationships.

In JS 166, once the saga is ended, there is one more noteworthy addition where the voice of the scribe is foregrounded, in a verse in rhyming couplets unique to this manuscript:

Hafe þeir þøck er hlÿddu,
& mä'led og gamaned[50] þrÿddu.
Lesaran<um> Launist
enn Langmælge riemst.
Sætur og seggia lid,
sitied allur j Gudz frid,
Eg þesse öska & bid,
ä' þad halldest vid.[51]

(May those who listened be thanked,
and the speech and entertainment exhausted.
May the reader be rewarded
and longwinded talk diminish.
Women and company of men,
remain, all of you, in God's peace.
I wish this and pray
that it prevails.)

Here the scribe, Þórður Jónsson, speaks directly to his audience in the first person. Similar verses also appear after the other sagas in this manuscript,

49   JS 166 fol., f. 190ʳ. Other manuscripts preserving largely the same version add one further sentence to this ending. Copenhagen, Den Arnamagnæanske Samling, MS Rask 32, for example, adds 'med so voxnu nidurlæge' (with such an augmented conclusion), f. 35ʳ.
50   MS 'gamaded'.
51   JS 166 fol., f. 190ʳ.

and are not an uncommon feature of Icelandic romance manuscripts in general. Glauser provides examples from romances including *Dínus saga dramblála, Jarlmanns saga ok Hermanns*, and *Rémundar saga keisarasonar*, and also suggests that some manuscripts favour these types of formulaic endings ('Schlußformeln'), while other manuscripts (of the same sagas) end their texts differently, confirming the involvement of the scribe in shaping the text.[52] This final verse not only shows the voice of the scribe, but shows through the specific mention of listeners (*þeir [...] er hlÿddu*) that the environment in which this saga was enjoyed was that of a community and not an individual: this instance of copying was for it reading aloud and communal enjoyment, not just as a record of the text, nor for personal study.

To consider now a different part of the *Nítíða saga* version of JS 166, in terms of the geographical picture presented there, it is actually slightly shorter than in some other versions. When Nítíða and Livorius, disguised as Eskelvarður, look into her magical stones (*náttúrusteinar*), the world is divided into thirds, and many lands are named, although fewer than in the edited version. When they see Europe, it is 'alla Frackland, Gasconia, Hispania, Galicia,[53] Flandren, & nær verande slot, lønd & þiöder, þar byggiande' (all France, Gascony, Spain, Galicia, Flanders, and present castles, lands, and people dwelling there).[54] When they see the 'Nordur älfu heimsinnz' (the northern part of the world), the only places specified are 'Noreg, Danmørk, Eingland, & øll ønnur er þar lyggia, & hann visse einginn Deyle ä' (Norway, Denmark, England, and all others which lay there, and which he knew nothing of).[55] This covers the basic Nordic countries while leaving room for a mental addition of others known by the audience, being suggestive of *øll ønnur* without having to name any definitive locations. And when the 'Austur älfu heimsinnz' (eastern part of the world) is seen, mention is made of 'Indiäland, Falstnia,[56] Asia, Serkland, & øll lønd Austur og sudur vnder bruna belltted, þar sem ecki er bygt' (India, Palestine, Asia, Serkland, and

---

52 Glauser, *Isländische Märchensagas*, pp. 86-92.

53 This explains AM 537's *Hallitiam*, which has not been identified satisfactorily before (e.g. Barnes's '?Helvetia', *The Bookish Riddarasögur*, p. 38). Further, in an encyclopaedic text that lists all the countries in the three regions of the world *Galicia* also occurs adjacent *Hispania* (Kålund, *Alfrœði íslenzk*, III, p. 72). As I have noted above and will be evident in the remaining two case studies below, *Galicia* appears consistently in other manuscript versions, while *Hallitia* never does. For another example of scribal error identified through textual comparison of names see McDonald, 'Variance Uncovered', p. 314.

54 JS 166 fol., f. 188ʳ.

55 JS 166 fol., f. 188ʳ.

56 This is a corruption of *Palestina* (Palestine), which is present in AM 529/537 and other groups.

all lands east and south under the burning belt, which is uninhabited),[57] with the significant inclusion of *sudur* (south) in the designation of the region. In the edited version, for example, there is no mention of the south either as a direction or as a region. While *øll lønd* (all lands) in addition to those named are again evoked, they are less concrete than in the north, as a point is made not to say that Livorius knows of other lands, perhaps rather ironically considering that is the general region – east and south, classified as one region here – from which this Indian character comes. But again, the focus returns to the lands of the north with the addition of information concerning the location in which Livorius's aunt resides: 'ei er hann j Svÿa løndumm nie Sv<iþjod> hiä Aldÿnu frænd konu sinne [...]' (he is neither in Swedish lands nor Sweden near his kinswoman Aldína).[58] The apparent distinction between Sweden and Swedish lands is also not present in some other groups (though it does echo the distinction sometimes made between *Svíþióð* and *Svíþióð hinn kalda*, which I note in Chapter 3), but is consistent with its focus on the North and the many different lands and people within that region.

To bring this first case study to a close it is worth mentioning the eleven other manuscripts that preserve textually similar versions of *Nítíða saga* to that considered here in JS 166. They are, from oldest to youngest, AM 567 4to XVIII (1500s), AM 568 4to (1600×1650), Lbs 715 4to (1670-80), Lbs 644 4to (1730-31), Rask 32 (1750×1799), ÍB 116 4to (1786-94), JS 632 4to (1799-1800), Lbs 1137 8vo (1800s), Lbs 998 4to (1860), Lbs 3966 4to (1870-71), and Lbs 3165 4to (1870-71). In each of these manuscripts, the text is written with the more common story structure, and, significantly, make explicit reference to *Nikulás saga leikara* at the end.[59] The texts in this group also all begin by saying 'Hier mega unger menn heyra hystoriu og fagra fräsøgu' (Here young people can hear a history and beautiful narrative),[60] with minor variations such as the addition of an adjective or switching of the word order, as in 'agiæta fräsøgu & fagra historiu' (excellent narrative and beautiful history).[61] The most important parts of this phrase are the words *hér* and *historia*, which only ever appear in this context in this group of manuscript versions. Furthermore, and finally, the location of origin is known for nearly all of

---

57 JS 166 fol., f. 188ʳ.
58 JS 166 fol., f. 188ʳ.
59 In Lbs 715 4to the ending has not survived, but based on other similarities to this group it seems safe to consider that had the ending survived, reference to *Nikulás saga leikara* would be present there as well.
60 JS 166 fol, f. 181ᵛ.
61 Reykjavík, Landsbókasafn–Háskólabókasafn Íslands, MS ÍB 116 4to, f. 93ʳ.

Figure 2   Map of Manuscripts from the Dales and Westfjords

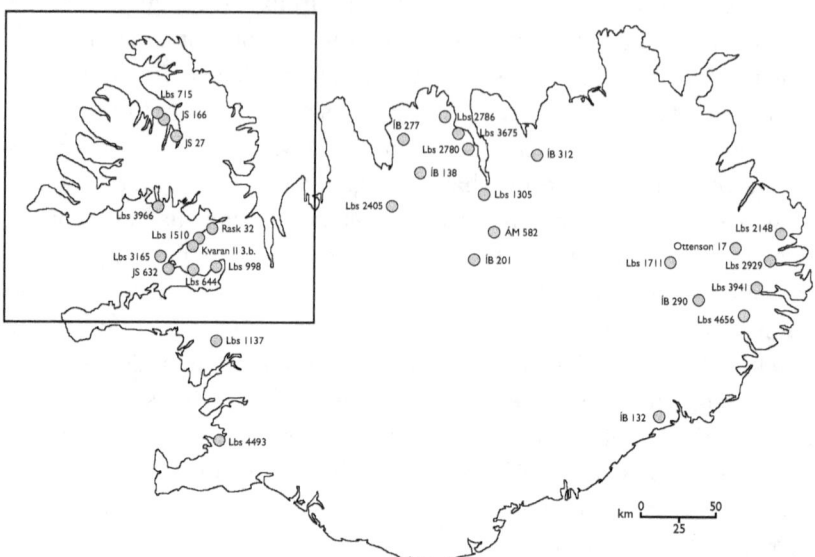

these manuscripts, which come from the north-western areas of Iceland, both the Westfjords and Dales,[62] as illustrated in Figure 2.

Overall, the version of *Nítíða saga* preserved in JS 166 is an interesting variation on the better known version edited from the manuscripts AM 529 and AM 537. While JS 166 contains a longer story overall, some episodes are still briefer, such as in the portrayal of geography, but even here the text shows significant alteration, and deliberate and meaningful differences, just as much as those changes that result in the text's length. As demonstrated in JS 166, this version of the story puts its focus on literature, textual reception, and literacy as a cultural phenomenon, as we have seen in its references not merely to stories and tales within the romance and its extra-textual closing verse, but to different types of physical books, the acts of reading and listening, and the implication in the saga and in Þórður Jónsson's verse, that enjoying stories is a shared social experience through which communities can be built and maintained.

---

62   On localization, cf. Stefán Einarsson, 'Heimili (skólar) fornaldarsaga og riddarasaga', p. 272. On the grouping of these manuscripts, cf. Jónas Kristjánsson, ed., *Dínus saga drambláta*, pp. vii-xlvi; Spaulding, pp. 93-110; Hall and Parsons, 'Making Stemmas with Small Samples'; Zitzelsberger, 'The Filiation of the Manuscripts of *Konráðs saga keisarasonar*', pp. 145-76, for *Konráðs saga*.

Add. 4860 fol.

My second case study moves from the seventeenth century to the eighteenth with London, British Library, MS Add. 4860 fol., which contains a version of *Nítíða saga* much closer to the edited text from AM 529 and AM 537, than in JS 166. There are, however, differences that merit its consideration here; moreover, this manuscript preserves a previously unstudied version of the romance. Add. 4860 is also an Icelandic manuscript with an interesting provenance that has led it ultimately to Britain as part of the British Library's Banks Collection. It was, along with a number of other manuscripts, given to the British Museum by Sir Joseph Banks (1743-1820). Better known as a botanist and explorer alongside Captain James Cook,[63] Banks also visited Iceland in 1772 (primarily to observe and collect samples of the local flora), and took back with him about thirty manuscripts in 1773. Banks also had manuscripts sent to him from Iceland upon his return to England in subsequent years up to 1781.[64] It is uncertain into which of these two categories Add. 4860 falls, and as the manuscript contains no scribal notations revealing any dates, the precise date of this version of *Nítíða saga* is uncertain beyond being from the later eighteenth century based on manuscript's palaeography and the possibility that it may have been specially commissioned for Banks. In any case it can have been copied no later than 1781. The manuscript is a large folio written in one very legible hand throughout, and with very few abbreviations. There are also clearly defined chapters, page headings, and plenty of white space in the margins. If it was not commissioned especially for Banks, then it must have been prepared as a display copy for a wealthy Icelander at a slightly earlier date. In his study of Banks's visit to Iceland, Halldór Hermannsson states that Banks 'was anxious to get printed books and manuscripts', and that in addition to being given 'a copy of every book which lately had been printed at [the Church-run press at] Hólar', Banks was also in contact with 'Bjarni Pálsson, the surgeon general, who lived at Nes not far from Hafnarfiord, and received from him as gifts various natural objects, antiquities, and books'.[65] This may mean that the manuscript was copied somewhere in or around Hafnarfjörður in south western Iceland (where Banks visited), if it was not brought there later. The latter possibility is equally likely considering the incredible textual similarities with the version of *Nítíða saga* in Reykjavík,

---

63 See e.g. Lyte, *Sir Joseph Banks*.
64 Halldór Hermannsson, *Sir Joseph Banks and Iceland*, p. 15.
65 Halldór Hermannsson, p. 13.

Landsbókasafn–Háskólabókasafn Íslands, MS JS 27 fol.,[66] another large book of sagas copied in *c.* 1662-67, which originated in the Westfjords, many miles north of Hafnarfjörður (see Figure 2).[67] Alternatively, Add. 4860 could just as easily have been copied from an intermediary manuscript itself copied from JS 27. While it is unfortunate that we cannot determine precisely how Banks came to acquire Add. 4860 or the exact location in which it was copied, it is nevertheless fascinating that it has become part of the earliest history of British interest in Nordic literature.

Nítíða saga is divided into seventeen chapters in Add. 4860 – four more than in JS 166 – and is the manuscript's opening text. Following it are *Drauma-Jóns saga, Viktors saga og Blávus, Hálfdanar saga Brönufóstra, Flores saga kongs og sona hans, Hrólfs saga Gautrekssonar, Bragða Mágus saga, Partalópa saga, Hrólfs saga kraka, Friðþiófs saga Þorsteinssonar, Álaflekks saga, Tiódels saga, Dínus saga dramblóta,* and *Vilmundar saga viðutann,* that is, a wide selection of legendary and romance sagas, which again are not surprising or at all out of place with *Nítíða saga.* Some of these, such as *Drauma-Jóns saga, Hrólfs saga Gautrekssonar,* and especially *Dínus saga dramblóta* as noted above, occur regularly with *Nítíða saga* in a variety of manuscripts. The composition of this manuscript with such a wide range of *riddarasögur* and *fornaldarsögur* shows that its patron was interested in obtaining, either for him or herself, or for someone else, a volume entirely comprised of these popular texts, which while many of them contain elements of fantasy, were worth owning and reading. This collection is representative of the type of literature still widely popular and frequently read in eighteenth-century Iceland.

Add. 4860 preserves a slightly shorter rendition of *Nítíða saga* than the edited version. Details that fleshed out the story and added depth in JS 166, and details that embellish the edited version, are set aside in favour of a more streamlined tale. Instead of the elaborately described festivities that are usually recounted as the saga comes to a close, the weddings here take place in the space of a sentence:

---

66 Jónas Kristjánsson says that '*Add. 4860* mun skrifað nálægt 1800. Það virðist vera komið frá glötuðu handriti sem verið hefur náskylt A² [= JS 27 fol.]' (Add. 4860 was written close to 1800. It seems to come from a lost manuscript that was closely related to A² [= JS 27 fol.]), *Dínus saga dramblóta,* p. xxxii.

67 This lavish manuscript (featured on the cover of the present study) was probably among those commissioned by Magnús Jónsson í Vigur. The texts were copied by Magnús Þórólfsson (d. 1667), and the decorative initials by Hannes Gunnlaugsson (1640-1686) (see Jónas Kristjánsson, 'Hannes Gunnlaugsson braut stafina', pp. 89-96).

Nu geingur meykongur framm og lætur búa virduglega veitslu og fúllgio-
rast þessi kaup. fara þaug nú heim í Miklagard Ingi kongur og Svíalyn,
enn Hlieskiolldur giftist Listalín, enn Livorius kongur og Nitida hin fræga
untust leingi og vel þokti Livorius kongur hinn mest hofdinge og var vin
sæll hvar sem hann kom framm og lukum vier svo þessari sögu.[68]

(Now the maiden-king goes forth and prepares a worthy feast and
completes these dealings. King Ingi and Svíalyn now travel home to
Constantinople, and Hlieskiolldur marries Listalín, and King Livorius and
Nitida the famous love each other very well. King Livorius was thought
the best leader and was popular wherever he went forth. And so we end
this saga.)

This very short and pointed conclusion is in sharp contrast to that discussed
above, and conspicuously missing here is any reference to worldly transience, which is often highlighted as a notable feature of *Nítíða saga*,[69] and
which I will discuss in later chapters. Considering that nothing elaborate
had been described, however, it makes sense that this element is missing,
with only passing mention of a typically vague *virðulega veislu* (worthy
feast). Add. 4860 presents a much simpler picture of European royalty,
without any of the elaborate foods, entertainment, decorations, or gifts
that are so carefully described in other versions.

Also significant, however, is this text's focus on Livorius at the end,
with Nítíða all but out of the picture entirely. Livorius certainly has the
last word here – the couple's children are not even mentioned – yet in
the final words no reference is made to any character as the saga's focus;
it is simply *þessi saga* (this saga), rather than 'the saga of Nítíða and/or
Livorius'. But it is also significant that Livorius is here called *höfðingi* (head,
leader, chieftain).[70] While *kóngur* (king) is also used as part of his name
in his personal title, *höfðingi* is used to describe his role in the society
and culture he governs, something not found in the earlier edited version.
Whereas the word *höfðingi* appears in the *Nítíða saga* of AM 529 and AM
537 some eight times, it is always used of nameless vassals within Nítíða's
kingdom, who are sometimes recognized as lesser kings or advisors; but
none of the main characters, least of all Livorius, is called by this term.

---

68   Add. 4860 fol., f. 16ᵛ.
69   Barnes, 'Margin vs. Centre', p. 111; Barnes, 'Romance in Iceland', p. 272; Driscoll, 'Late Prose
Fiction', p. 202; Driscoll, 'Nitida saga', p. 432.
70   Gudbrand Vigfusson, *An Icelandic-English Dictionary*, p. 306.

Its use in Add. 4860, however, gives this excerpt a very Icelandic feel, and brings the saga's foreign characters, plot, and action, centred in Europe and the East, back home to Iceland. The Icelandic word *höfðingi* is used for example in the *Íslendingasögur* to designate chieftains. This sense has been retained to the present day,[71] meaning that the images associated with it in the eighteenth century likely included some sort of old chieftain, if that was not still its exclusive meaning at the time of this manuscript's production. Of course, *kóngur* is also an Icelandic word, but its use here is different than that of *höfðingi*; it is a far more common, and even expected, element of naming royalty in romances (and equally does not appear as often in the *Íslendingasögur* unless referring to specific foreign monarchs, not Icelandic chieftains). This difference, especially when in other versions the text ends with reference to *Livorius kóngur*, thus makes the appearance of *höfðingi* here remarkable. In an entirely different, subtle way, the focus of the story still, at the very last, directs the audience's focus back on Iceland and its history. Perhaps it also glances back with an aim to encourage the audience – whether that audience is conceived by the scribe as Icelandic or English, plural (a household or community) or singular (Joseph Banks alone) – to reconsider what it means to be European, Icelandic, or whatever community, national or local, to which one might belong.

If we consider now the portrayal of geography in this version of the saga, we see that the locations mentioned in the scene where Nítíða and Livorius look into the *náttúrusteinar* (magic stones) are divided into three separate regions seen on three occasions, and that the place names show interesting variations compared to those in other versions. The first time Nítíða and Livorius look, they see 'Frackkland, Galisiam, Provinciam, Bravenam,[72] Spaniam og Galliam, Agyptum, Frísland, Frankaríki, Flandur, Normandi, Skotland, Grikkland' (France, Galicia, Provence, Ravenna, Spain and Gaul, Egypt, Frisia, the Frankish Kingdom, Flanders, Normandy, Scotland, Greece).[73] As in some other versions, including the edition, this part of the world is not given any kind of title, and the number of places named is similar as well (unlike the mention of far fewer in JS 166). However, with the addition of Egypt, this part of the world, seen all at once, cannot so easily be classified as a coherent geographical unit like Europe, as is possible in other versions – the locations grouped together here are, in reality, all over

---

71   Modern Icelandic *höfðingi*: '1. leader, chief, chieftain; 2. aristocrat; 3. generous person' (*Íslensk-Ensk Orðabók*, ed. by Sverrir Hólmarsson, Sanders, and Tucker.

72   This is likely an error, for *Ravenam*, as in AM 537.

73   Add. 4860 fol., f. 13ᵛ.

the place. The form of the word *Agyptus* is also significant.[74] Instead of using an Icelandic form of the name (compare *Egiptaland*, from which derives the Modern Icelandic country name), the form matches the Latinate character of the other locations in the list, and therefore contributes to the learned character indicated by this passage. Interestingly though, the forms *Flandur* and *Normandi* have not been given (pseudo) accusative endings, becoming less Latinate here than they appear in some other versions. In for example AM 537, these appear as *Flandren* and *Norðmandiam*, the latter simultaneously more nordicized with the form *norð-* and also more Latinized with the ending *-am*. Another unusual addition to this list, in contrast with the usual *Frackkland* (France), is *Frankaríki*. While there is no indication as to how these two should be distinguished, if at all, the latter could be seen as a clarified form of *Francia* (found in Icelandic geographical treatises), to show it is a kingdom (*ríki*).[75] Along with the preservation of Latinate endings in this list, the name suggests either old medieval roots for this version despite the manuscript's much younger age, or, alternatively a conscious desire to present the text as archaic.

The second time the characters look into the magic stones they see 'Norduráfúna alla, Noreg, Island, Færeyar, Sudureyar, Svíþióð, Danmork, Irland, Eingland og morg lond on*n*ur sem han*n* hafdi eí deili á' (All the northern part, Norway, Iceland, the Faroes, the Hebrides, Sweden, Denmark, Ireland, England, and many other lands that he [Livorius] did not know).[76] This part of the world is called 'the north', and these places easily justify this title, despite the exclusion of some places named in AM 537 like Orkney and Shetland – further indicating that Add. 4860 is a somewhat shorter version of the story. At the third look, 'Meykóngur vendur þá upp einum steini siáandi þá í austúr alfú veralldarin*n*ar, Indialand, Palestínam, Asíam, Grickland og oll lond út undir heimsskautid, jafnvel Brunabelltid siálft þad sem ecki er biggt' (The maiden-king then held up a stone, seeing then in the eastern part of the world, India, Palestine, Asia, Greece, and all lands out past the corner of the world, including the Burning-Belt [torrid zone] itself, which is uninhabited).[77] Serkland is here excluded from the list of eastern lands, and Greece is listed instead, and for the second time, perhaps indicating a perception of its belonging both to the eastern and

---

74 Cf. Kålund, *Alfræði íslenzk*, III, p. 72.

75 Cf. Kålund, *Alfræði íslenzk*, III, p. 72. The inclusion of both place names relating to France may also suggest that the compiler of this manuscript might not have had any precise understanding of the country's location.

76 Add. 4860 fol., ff. 13ᵛ-14ʳ.

77 Add. 4860, fol., f. 14ʳ.

the western world, acting as a bridge between the two, in the way that
Constantinople was often thought of in medieval Icelandic romance.[78] Also
interesting is the inclusion of the phrase *lönd út undir heimsskautið* (lands
out past the corner of the world) within this eastern/southern group, as
this phrase is used in other versions to describe the location of the island
Visio, said to be located somewhere near the northernmost regions. In the
beginning of this version Visio is also located, 'útundan*n* Svíþióð hin*ni*
kolldu ut undir heims skautinu' (out past Sweden the Cold, out past the
corner of the world).[79] There appears, therefore, to be somewhat less of an
emphasis on the northern lands here than in other versions, although the
text's depiction of geography is maintained, which may indicate the scribe's
interest in geography and learning, or which may be merely a remnant of
an earlier scribe's interests carried over from this manuscript's exemplar.

Five other manuscripts contain versions of *Nítíða saga* similar to that in
Add. 4860, all of which employ the dominant story structure and none of
which makes reference to *Nikulás saga leikara*. Four are more closely related
to each other than to Add. 4860, and include the manuscripts used as the
sources for the saga's edition: AM 529 4to (1500s) and AM 537 4to (1600×1650),
as well as Perg. 8vo nr. 10 VII (1450×1499) and the single leaf Reykjavík,
Landsbókasafn–Háskólabókasafn Íslands, MS ÍB 201 8vo (1650×1699). As
already mentioned, there is one manuscript, JS 27 fol. (*c.* 1662-67) that contains a version so similar to that in Add. 4860 that it is almost certain that
it is somehow involved in the production of Add. 4860. While some of these
manuscripts are localizable, no obvious patterns or clusters are evident (see
Figure 1 above). The known locations of origin cover four separate regions,
including the Westfjords and the north of Iceland, relatively near to the
episcopal seat of Hólar. This range of distribution is more or less typical of
manuscript circulation in early modern Iceland.[80]

To conclude this second case study, the version of *Nítíða saga* in Add.
4860 is shorter than some other versions, and particularly if we compare
it directly to the version seen above in JS 166. In addition to producing a
streamlined version of the story by excluding non-essential information or
deciding not to elaborate on certain descriptions and scenes, the variety
of other, relatively small, changes that are made, such as emphasizing the

---

78 Divjak, *Studies in the Traditions of Kirialax Saga*, pp. 240-47.

79 Add. 4860 fol., f. 2^r.

80 Springborg identifies these (and other) areas as early modern Icelandic scribal centres
('Antiqvæ historiæ lepores', pp. 57-81). See also Hall and Parsons, 'Making Stemmas with Small
Samples', fig. 14.2.

role of Livorius at the end instead of Nítíða, or de-emphasizing the focus from the north in the description of the world, are employed deliberately, in order to shift slightly some of the focal points of the text that are exhibited in other versions. While there remains a focus on Icelandic identity, it is subtler than in other versions and the question is approached from different perspectives. The identity and sense of community in general, as well as specifically in terms of that of Icelanders, thus emerge in this version as important themes.

Lbs 3941 8vo

In my final case study of this chapter, I will consider Reykjavík, Landsbókas-afn–Háskólabókasafn Íslands, MS Lbs 3941 8vo, one of the manuscripts from the Eastfjords of Iceland, and one of the youngest manuscripts in which *Nítíða saga* survives, from only the first half of the twentieth century. I chose this manuscript primarily because it is so young, but also because its version of *Nítíða saga* shows important variations in the text that are very different to those of the other versions considered so far in this chapter. While the scribe is unknown, an owner's name, Hindrik Líndal, is written in pencil on the inside front cover of the manuscript. Another owner of the manuscript was Einar Guðmundsson (1888-1975), who was born on Skáleyjar in western Iceland but lived most of his life (after his marriage in 1920) in Reyðarfjörður, eastern Iceland;[81] he sold the manuscript on 26 October 1970.[82] After opening with *Nítíða saga*, which is divided into eleven chapters (again, unlike JS 166's thirteen and Add. 4860's seventeen), this manuscript contains four other texts: first is *Sagan af Ríkarði Ríkarðssyni*, a comic folktale;[83] and *Saga af Tístran Róbertssyni og Indiönu Mógúlsdóttur*, a romance composed after the Reformation, not to be confused with the much better-known translated romance *Tristrams saga og Ísöndar* or indeed the Icelandic adaptation of that translation, *Tristrams saga og Ísöddar*. Following these are the manuscript's final two texts, *Holta-Þóris saga*, a 'modern' *Íslendingasaga* first published in 1876, and *Króka-Refs saga*, a medieval *Íslendingasaga*. These are slightly less common companions for *Nítíða saga* than those seen in the other case studies but the late date of the manuscript accounts

81 Þorsteinn Jónsson and Halldór B. Kristjánsson, eds., *Eylenda*, I, p. 345.
82 'Lbs 3941 8vo', *Handrit.is*, National and University Library of Iceland.
83 This saga is also preserved in Lbs 2099 8vo ('Lbs 3941 8vo', *Handrit.is*, National and University Library of Iceland).

for this. The entire manuscript is written in one clear hand with almost no abbreviations, and the choice (and length) of texts may to some extent have been influenced by the writing support available, a small ruled notebook.

Overall, in Lbs 3941 the text of *Nítíða saga* is even more condensed than the version we have just seen in Add. 4860. Superfluous details are stripped away, and some of the details that seem to make the saga so interesting in other versions are altered here. It is, of course, also possible that the relative isolation of this version in eastern Iceland and the prospect that it could have derived from a verse *rímur* version of the prose saga led to this version of the story developing without these details from the beginning, rather than a scribe consciously choosing to eliminate them to produce a more streamlined story. In any case, this very late version of the romance can be read as one more example of the process of the redaction of a medieval text. The product is itself very much still the medieval story, renewed for new audiences in the early twentieth century. The saga in Lbs 3941 is only about 3700 words, by far the shortest text under consideration in this chapter. Again beginning our analysis with the saga's end, the way in which *Nítíða saga* concludes in Lbs 3941 is a good example of the brevity (and possibly the deliberate contraction) of some parts of this version. The saga ends very succinctly, though it is not as sparse as the conclusion in Add. 4860. Here, in a matter of only a few phrases, Listalín, the sister of King Ingi, is sent for, and the weddings are prepared, before all of the newlywed couples return to their respective kingdoms:

> Var þá sent eftir Listalín, og kom hún <til> Frakklands[84] á tilteknum tíma, með veglegu föruneyti. Var svo búist við öllum þessum brúðkaupum, og var þá allvel drukkið með alls konar skemtun, en er veislan var úti, voru allir útleiddir með gjöfum í gulli og silfri. Hléskjöldur sigldi heim til Grikklands, og settist þar að ríki. Ingi og Svíalín fóru til Indíalands og stýrðu því ríki til dauðadags. Liforius og Nididá stýrðu Frakklandi meðan þau lifðu, og áttu son sem Rikarður hét, og tók hann við ríki eftir foreldra sína. Lúkum vér svo sögunni af meykónginum Nididá og Líforíus konungi.[85]

> (Then Listalín was sent for, and she arrived in France at the specified time, with a splendid entourage. All these weddings were prepared, and

---

84 I have emended the text as the manuscript does not include the preposition *til* (to, or, here, in), which would be expected.
85 Lbs 3941 8vo, ff. 18ʳ-18ᵛ.

then all was fulfilled with all types of entertainments, and when the feast was over, all were led out with gifts of gold and silver. Hléskjöldur sailed home to Greece, and set up his kingdom there. Ingi and Svíalín travelled to India and ruled that kingdom until their deaths. Livorius and Nitida ruled France while they lived, and had a son called Rikarður, and he took up the kingdom after his parents. Thus we end the saga of the maiden-king Nitida and king Livorius.)

As in Add. 4860, the elaborate details somewhat self-consciously included in the other versions discussed above are left out of this description of the weddings. Instead, the scribe relies merely on a vague reference to *alls konar skemtun* (all types of entertainment) and *gjafar í gulli og silfri* (gifts of gold and silver), which adequately suggests the richness of the celebrations without itemizing them. Interestingly, in this version the new couples sail back to rule the women's home kingdoms, rather than the men's. Hléskjöldur, who has married Listalín, goes to rule Greece, perhaps because the name of his mother Ydía's realm was never specified from the beginning – in other versions Hléskjöldur and Listalín rule over *his* homeland Apulia. As Listalín's brother, though, Ingi might be expected to travel home to rule Greece with his new wife Svíalín, but instead goes to her homeland, India – AM 537 and most other versions have this pair ruling Ingi's kingdom in Constantinople (equivalent to this version's Greece, see below), and leave India, perhaps implying that it will be combined with France into an empire.[86] In Lbs 3941 each kingdom previously associated with a major character is ruled by one of the couples at the end. The saga closes with a brief report of Nítíða and Livorius: France is ruled as a single kingdom, completing the pattern of men travelling to co-rule women's lands, yet it is Livorius, not Nítíða, with whom the saga closes, mirroring their treatment at the end of the edited version and that in Add. 4860.

Differences in the geography of the saga can be seen in the main representation of the world, which has been analysed in each of the previous versions discussed, and which I will also address for Lbs 3941 momentarily, but geographical difference is also evident in small changes elsewhere throughout the text. For example, when Nítíða travels to visit Ydía, who is in this version *not* characterized as Nítíða's foster mother but simply as the mother of Hléskjöldur, her journey is *yfir fjallgarð einn* (over a

---

86 Exceptionally, in a couple of other versions in Reykjavík, Landsbókasafn–Háskólabókasafn Íslands, MSS ÍBR 47 4to and JS 56 4to, Livorius sends his son to rule India for him while he rules France with Nítíða.

mountain-range),[87] instead of by sea, as in other manuscripts. In fact, in the other versions examined, characters always travel by ship, making Nítíða's overland journey to Ydía's unnamed realm here even more exceptional. Other small changes in this version include the name of the island Visio and its ruler Virgilius, which are instead 'einni eyju er Viktoría heitir, henni ræður jarl sá er Vigerlíus heitir' (an island which is called Viktoria, over which rules that earl called Vigerlius).[88] The father of Ingi and Listalín is likewise different: he is Februárius, who *stjórnaði Grikklandi* (governed Greece),[89] instead of the Hugon of Constantinople found elsewhere, with the once evocative Virgilius (see Chapter 3) reduced to a meaningless, if foreign sounding name.

When Nítíða has Livorius look into the magical stones at different world regions, the extent to which Lbs 3941 is condensed compared to other versions is further evident. The scene is much briefer than those already discussed but despite this, it also demonstrates striking variations:

> Nididá tók einn steininn, og bað hann líta í, þau sáu þá um alla ~~Norður~~ Suður álfuna, og allar þær þjóðir, er þar voru í. [...] Hún tók þá annan stein, sáu þau þá um alla Vestur álfuna [...]. Hún tók þá upp þriðja steininn, sáu þau þá um alla austur álfuna, útnes og leynivoga, og jafnvel Bruna velli, sem ekki er bygt.[90]

> (Nididá took a stone, and asked him to look into it; then they saw over all the southern region, and all the people who were there. [...] She then took another stone; then they saw over all the western region [...]. She then took up the third stone; then they saw over all the eastern region, outlying headlands and hidden coves, and also the Burning Field, which is uninhabited.)

The most significant difference here is how the world is divided into three: instead of the unusual trio of Europe, the North, and the East that is demonstrated in the edited version and JS 166, we see here a different, though hardly more conventional division into the South, the West, and the East – surprisingly, the North is not mentioned at all. It is perhaps significant that the manuscript shows 'North' initially written instead of 'South', but

87   Lbs 3941 8vo, f. 1ᵛ.
88   Lbs 3941 8vo, f. 2ʳ.
89   Lbs 3941 8vo, f. 3ᵛ.
90   Lbs 3941 8vo, ff. 16ʳ-16ᵛ.

then crossed out. Perhaps this is evidence of a deliberate change in the depiction of geography from what was written in the scribe's exemplar, or a change from another version of *Nítíða saga* with which the scribe is familiar. This would make sense if the scribe had previous knowledge of a different version that came from outside of eastern Iceland, but was working from an eastern Iceland exemplar, considering that the other texts surviving in eastern Iceland manuscripts, mentioned below, also include the South as the first geographical region mentioned in this scene. Also significantly, specific lands and kingdoms are not named within these regions in this manuscript. Whereas in the other versions seen earlier in this chapter each time a region is mentioned the countries that constitute those regions are listed, in this version it is merely the name of the region that is given, further showing the streamlined nature of the version. Clearly knowledge of the world and its geography is not a priority for the scribe with whom this version originates. There is no need for him or her to display an acute awareness of lands located far from (or even near to) Iceland, nor is Iceland explicitly and consciously situated within the world in the way it is in other versions. This is not to say, however, that in Lbs 3941 *Nítíða saga* does not use geography with care, as many changes seem to be made deliberately, especially the exclusion of a northern or European region in the passage just seen, in favour of a world divided into southern, western, and eastern regions. This way of organizing the medieval saga world results in a bold statement that at once acknowledges that the medieval picture of the world is wholly different from the modern, and distances Iceland, medieval and modern, from the saga's action, without ever mentioning it or noting the details of geography so heavily emphasized in other versions. With the difference in setting emphasized in this way, the saga also more consciously becomes a piece of literature, a work of fiction that does not take place in the reality of its audience, even if most of the few place names that remain in this version are recognizable. It is almost as if by the mid-nineteenth century, when similar versions seem to have come into being in the Icelandic Eastfjords (the first manuscript containing a similar version is Reykjavík, Landsbókasafn–Háskólabókasafn Íslands, MS Lbs 1711 8vo, from 1848), Icelanders, while still actively and enthusiastically appreciating medieval romances like *Nítíða saga*, are now more aware of this aspect of such texts – their origin in the medieval world that now is such a distant part of the past, chronologically, even if culturally, medieval Iceland was still in relatively close proximity to the nineteenth-century Iceland out of which this version emerged. Thus without commenting on books, literacy, and literature in the direct manner that some earlier versions do, as seen above, this late version, through its increased and accentuated geographical distance from its Icelandic audience (mirroring the chronological distance between the original and the present audience), also facilitates reflection on the nature of the text and the relationship between literature and society.

There are at least seven other manuscripts containing versions of *Nítíða saga* textually similar to that preserved in Lbs 3941 and all housed in the same institution. The oldest of these, as just noted, dates to only just before the mid-nineteenth century: Lbs 1711 8vo (1848), Lbs 2152 4to (1850×1899), ÍB 290 8vo (1851), Lbs 3510 8vo (1851×1899), Lbs 4656 4to (1859-60), Lbs 2148 4to (1863), Lbs 2929 4to (1888). It is quite likely that the versions in these manuscripts derive from a verse *rímur* version of *Nítíða saga*, considering that they begin radically differently from the other older versions discussed above, and also because the version first appears at such a late date. In each manuscript, the saga uses the less common story structure introducing one character only after completing the adventures of the previous, and in each manuscript the saga opens with the phrase *æruverðugir sagna skrifarar* (venerable saga writers). While the opening words may simply be formulaic, this phrase could also be indicative of a *rímur* origin, with the idea of composition and scribal tradition immediately brought to the forefront, instead of (as in other versions) the subject of the story itself being composed.

In some of these manuscripts (i.e. Lbs 3491, along with Lbs 2148, Lbs 4656, Lbs 1711, and ÍB 290) the saga uses certain names not found in other versions, such as naming Nítíða's smith *Bonius* (and similar variants) instead of *Hippolytus* or simply leaving him unnamed. In other manuscripts, however, there is reference to some of the characters of *Nikulás saga leikara* at the end, but without explicitly connecting the two romances. Nikulás and his father Fástus are mentioned, but the princess Dorma and her father Valdimar are not. The intertextual reference here (i.e. Lbs 4656), then, is not as developed as it is in JS 166's version and that in the related manuscripts discussed in my first case study. Further, whereas Fástus is made a grandson of Nítíða and Livorius in JS 166, in these young manuscripts he is, rather, listed as another of their sons: '4a Syne og 2. Dætur og hiet firste Sonur þeirra Rýgardur Sem styrde Frakklande eptir fodur sin*um*. An*n*ar son þeirra hiet Fástus, vard ha*n*n kongur í Ungarýa' (four sons and two daughters and called their first son Rygard, who ruled France after his father. Another son of theirs was called Fástus; he became king in Hungary).[91] The inclusion of this reference

---

91   Lbs 4656 4to, p. 78.

Figure 3   Map of Manuscripts from the Eastfjords

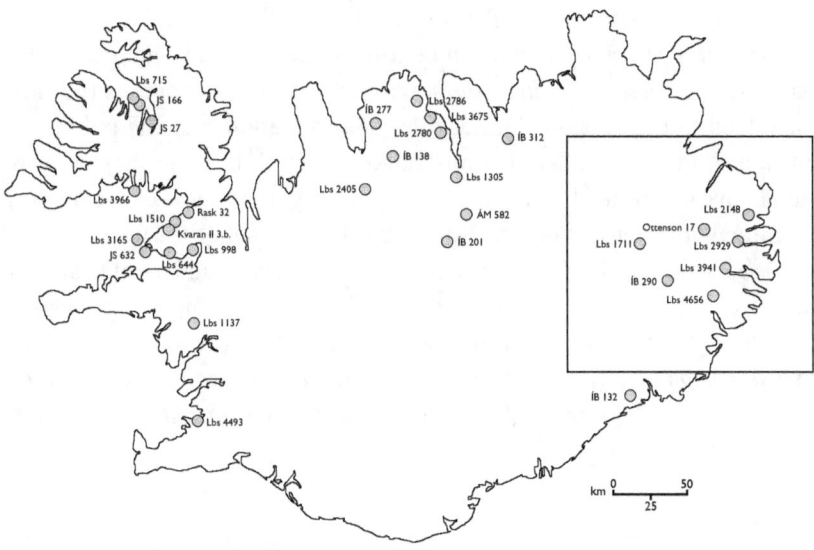

suggests the possibility that a text from the first version discussed (like that of JS 166) may have also, probably indirectly, influenced this group.

In terms of the geographical origins of Lbs 3941 and those that seem to be related to it, as mentioned briefly already, those manuscripts for which scribal information is known all originate in eastern Iceland (see Figure 3). Davíð Ólafsson has discussed evidence for a 'vivid scribal community' thriving in nineteenth-century Breiðdalur,[92] one of the places in eastern Iceland where some of these *Nítíða saga* manuscripts originate. It is also plausible that the other manuscripts containing similar versions also originate in this region, considering how textually tightly knit this group seems to be.

It is also fortunate that we are able to see such a clear picture of the origin of most of these manuscripts, seeing as such little information is known about the provenance of many of the earlier manuscripts mentioned earlier in this chapter. Additionally, one of the manuscripts I have not been able to consult (Baltimore, MD, Ottenson Collection MS 100, Nr. 17) is known to have originated in Ekkjufell in the Eastfjords – it would not be surprising to discover that the version of *Nítíða saga* contained in this manuscript is similar to that in this final case study. In fact, I would consider it highly

---

92   Davíð Ólafsson, 'Wordmongers', pp. 115-16 (p. 116). See also Parsons, 'The Great Manuscript Exodus?'.

improbable for it to contain a vastly different version, as no manuscripts preserving other versions of the saga come from anywhere near to this cluster in the Eastfjords (see Figure 1 above).

Overall, in the early twentieth-century manuscript Lbs 3941 we see a pared-down version of *Nítíða saga*, without many of the details that are includeed in the versions found in JS 166, Add. 4860, and the published edition. And, as has been demonstrated, although it is the shortest version I have examined here, it does not fail to negotiate some of the themes prominent in other versions, such as social identity, though the way in which this is accomplished is different. While the story may be understated and its messages subtle, that it was recorded in such a way, at a time so much closer to our own than those of the other versions preserving the romance, speaks to *Nítíða saga*'s continual relevance throughout the ages – its appearance may change with (or throughout) time, but its essence remains appealing to its readers and listeners.

Conclusions

In this chapter I have considered how the many manuscripts in which *Nítíða saga* survives preserve different – and sometimes vastly divergent – versions, and that some of these versions can be identified as corresponding to geographical regions such as western and eastern Iceland. I have discussed how the saga's transmission and reception was far more complicated than simply the repeated copying of a single text. From evidence of the saga being read aloud once copied down and enjoyed in a group setting seen in JS 166, to signs of the specific, careful copying of some manuscripts for (perhaps exclusively) presentation purposes seen in Add. 4860, to the possibility of a very different version of the text resulting from a later date and geographic isolation seen in Lbs 3941, *Nítíða saga* not only survived, but thrived throughout Iceland in a variety of milieux and a variety of versions, for hundreds of years after its debut in the Middle Ages, and this popularity and success is reflected in its diverse manuscript context. While in each version the text is continually recognizable as *Nítíða saga*, the variation evident among even some of the earliest manuscript witnesses demonstrates that the plot, character names, and structure were more fluid than has been previously recognized in research on the saga. The accidental differences among versions in the textual history of the saga continue to point to a story the substance of which remains constant. In the chapters that follow, in order to understand more fully such a well-received and popular late medieval Icelandic romance I will analyse it in greater detail, from various points of departure, beginning with the following chapter's discussion of the romance's relationships with other texts, and the way in which readers would have encountered it alongside other, equally treasured stories.

2 Intertextuality

Communicating with Other Romances

In the previous chapter I considered some of the different textual versions of *Nítíða saga* as preserved in manuscript form – versions of a romance that was created, enjoyed, and re-created both in the Middle Ages and in later centuries. With the context of its manuscript variation in mind, I will now consider another contextual aspect, that is, its intertextual relationships with other Icelandic romances. As an originally medieval Icelandic romance, *Nítíða saga* was not composed in isolation,[1] and as I will demonstrate in this chapter, it was in dialogue not only with the wider romance genre in general, but also with other individual texts in particular, which, both on their own and together in groups of texts containing similar themes and stories, were equally valued by medieval and early modern Icelanders. It is some of these intertextual relationships on which this chapter focuses, in order to understand better how *Nítíða saga* may have been viewed and valued in relation to other popular, secular texts available in Iceland.

It would be too great a task to enumerate and analyse an exhaustive list of intertextual connections in *Nítíða saga* considering the richly diverse literary context from which it emerged. To begin to appreciate the complexity of the relationships among *Nítíða saga* and other romances – and to understand the different approaches one might take in analysing these connections – we can consider the number of motifs shared by *Nítíða saga* and Icelandic romances, as listed in Inger Boberg's *Motif-Index of Early Icelandic Literature*, as well as the manuscripts in which romances co-occur in Kalinke and Mitchell's *Bibliography of Old Norse–Icelandic Romances*.[2] The scope of this chapter is restricted to two main case studies that highlight the relationship between *Nítíða saga* and two Icelandic romances, *Nikulás saga leikara* and *Clári saga*. These case studies will demonstrate not only some of

---

1   General studies of the medieval Icelandic romance milieu can be found in Barnes, 'Romance in Iceland', pp. 266-86; Bibire, 'From *riddarasaga* to *lygisaga*', pp. 55-74; Driscoll, 'Late Prose Fiction', pp. 190-204; Einar Ólafur Sveinsson, '*Viktors saga ok Blávus*: Sources and Characteristics', pp. cix-ccix; Glauser, *Isländische Märchensagas*; Kalinke, *Bridal-Quest Romance*; Kalinke, 'Norse Romance (Riddarasögur)', pp. 316-63; Kalinke, 'Riddarasögur, Fornaldarsögur, and the Problem of Genre', pp. 77-91; Torfi H. Tulinius, 'Íslenska rómansan', pp. 218-44.

2   See also studies that explore specific romances and their relationships in detail, e.g. Hallberg, 'A Group of Icelandic "Riddarasögur" from the Middle of the Fourteenth Century', pp. 8-53.

the similarities and differences between these texts, but also the dialogue into which the author of *Nítíða saga* may consciously have entered with them. Alongside these two case studies, I will begin the chapter by touching upon some of *Nítíða saga*'s more general relationships with other romances by discussing one of its most important motifs – the *náttúrusteinar* (magical stones) and their use – in order to situate the text in its wider context of romances, which often employ similar strategies to negotiate and fulfil the norms of the genre. The chapter will therefore provide an overview of some of the most important and interesting intertextual relationships that *Nítíða saga* demonstrates, and it will end by also touching on *Nítíða saga*'s intertextuality through time and in different versions of the text, drawing on some of the findings of the first chapter. We will see how dialogue with other romances is an integral part of this medieval Icelandic romance, which to some extent also worked to reinforce its popularity in the post-Reformation period.

Shared Motifs in *Sigurðar saga þǫgla*, *Gibbons saga*, and *Nítíða saga*

Integral to *Nítíða saga*'s plot is the motif of the *náttúrusteinar* (literally 'nature-stones' or 'power-stones',[3] but clearly signifying 'supernatural' or 'magical' stones – my preferred translations). These stones are a major source of power, which Nítíða uses intelligently to outwit her suitors. They are a typical example of the useful magical objects often found by or given to the heroes of Icelandic romances;[4] in *Nítíða saga* their physical form is never described, making it unclear whether they are more like precious stones and jewels, or rocks and pebbles, or what colours or other physical traits they might have.[5] In the simplest terms, the *náttúrusteinar* enable Nítíða to know in advance the movements of her enemies, while also providing a

---

3   Gudbrand Vigfusson, *An Icelandic-English Dictionary*, p. 449.
4   Boberg, *Motif-Index of Early Icelandic Literature*, section D 'Magic' (pp. 54-93), esp. D1300-1599 'Function of Magic Objects' (pp. 67-79) and D1600-1699 'Characteristics of Magic Objects' (pp. 79-82); Johanterwage, 'The Use of Magic Spells and Objects', pp. 446-53; Matyushina, 'Magic Mirrors, Monsters, Maiden-kings', pp. 660-70; Schlauch, pp. 42-43, 76, 119-48; Wahlgren, 'The Maiden King in Iceland', pp. 51-60 (esp. p. 53, where *Nítíða saga* and *Nikulás saga leikara* are given as prime examples of the use of magical stones). I discuss further the implications of these stones for Nítíða's characterization in Chapter 3; Lecouteux, *A Lapidary of Sacred Stones*, pp. 232-35 discusses magic stones in Icelandic narratives including *Nítíða saga*.
5   While *Nítíða saga* does not describe the stones, an Icelandic version of the lapidary of Marbod of Rennes (*c.* 1035-1123), in the manuscript AM 194 8vo (1387) speaks of, in Old Norse,

means of escape. These stones have three specific functions: to allow Nítíða to see throughout the world,[6] to render her invisible,[7] and to transport her back to France after being abducted.[8] The *náttúrusteinar* motif is present in other late medieval Icelandic romances, and *Sigurðar saga þögla* is a good example. It is a bridal-quest romance, in which the hero Sigurður of Saxony pursues and eventually overcomes (though magic and violence) the maiden-king Sedentiana of France, who had earlier humiliated his brothers in their bridal quest. This romance shares five motifs with *Nítíða saga*: D1317.12 'Magic stone gives warning', H217.1 'Decision of victory by single combat or holmgang of who is to marry girl', K1812.3 'Prince disguises as another prince to woo princess', R111.1.9 'Princess (maiden) rescued from undesired suitor', and T311.4 'Maiden queen prefers to fight instead of marrying. She usually scorns or even kills her suitors or sets them difficult tasks'.[9]

In *Sigurðar saga þögla*, the maiden-king's use of supernatural stones is markedly similar to the manner in which they are used in *Nítíða saga*. Major parallels can be seen in both maiden-kings' use of their respective magical stones to enhance their understanding, particularly through vision. In *Sigurðar saga þögla*, the stones allow Sedentiana to observe what is happening in different parts of the world, just as Nítíða does with her stones. Each time the stones are mentioned in *Sigurðar saga þögla*, emphasis is placed on seeing and vision – and therefore knowledge – as the result of looking *into* them: 'er hunn lijtur j hann sier hun og ueit huat uid ber j þessare alfu heimsinns. og huern mann þeckir hun at nafni og ætt huersu sem hann breytir sier ath yfirlitum' (when she looks into it [the stone] she sees and knows what occurs in this region of the world, and she recognizes each person by name and family [and] how he so changes himself in appearance).[10] Another passage similarly states: 'veit eg giorla at þetta er sanninnde af minne steinna natturu og fullum uijsdome þuiat mier mæ eckj æ ouart koma huat sem uid ber j þessarj alfu heimsins' (I know precisely that this is the truth from my supernatural stones full of wisdom, because I must not be ignorant about what occurs in this region of the world).[11] While Sedentiana's ability to see through people's disguises is explicitly attributed to her magic

'náttúrusteinar' – such a resource could have been available to the author or scribes of *Nítíða saga* (Kålund, ed., *Alfræði íslenzk*, I, 77-83).

6   'Nitida saga', ed. by Loth, pp. 6, 14-15, 22.

7   'Nitida saga', ed. by Loth, p. 15.

8   'Nitida saga', ed. by Loth, pp. 13, 24-25.

9   Boberg, *Motif-Index of Early Icelandic Literature*, pp. 68, 150, 180, 230, 249.

10 'Sigurðar saga þögla', ed. by Loth, p. 191. Cf. 'Nitida saga', ed. by Loth, pp. 14-15, 22.

11 'Sigurðar saga þögla', ed. by Loth, pp. 181-82.

stone, in *Nítíða saga* the maiden-king can also see through the disguise of her suitor Livorius, though her intuition is not attributed to the stones. The intense focus on vision in *Sigurðar saga þǫgla* (and on intuition based on vision) is also important in *Nítíða saga*. In both romances, it is through these characters' passive use of the *náttúrusteinar* their vision becomes panoptic and omniscient: rather than merely being able to see into the distance or in one direction, Nítíða and Sedentiana, through the stones, can see in all directions equally well, whenever they wish to, and the people being watched do not know that they are under surveillance. In *Sigurðar saga þǫgla*, Sedentiana's stones also have the ability to reveal the truth about events that have already taken place: 'Lijtur nu j sinn natturustein. ser nu og þeckir gerla ath þetta hefir uerit Sigur(dur) þǫgle er nær henni hefir legit' (Now she looks into her supernatural stone and sees and recognizes precisely that it has been Sigurður the Silent who has lain with her).[12] Additionally, Sedentiana elsewhere attributes her knowledge to her stones: 'þæ uissa eg þegar af mijnum uiturleik og natturusteine' (then I knew immediately from my wisdom and magic stones).[13] These properties are not evident in Nítíða's stones, nor is there any indication that they may have been in other versions. While it is possible that at some point more properties were attributed to the *náttúrusteinar* in *Nítíða saga* and subsequently lost, it is more likely that in *Sigurðar saga þǫgla* these properties were added. Both romances are from sometime in the fourteenth century, but the shorter redaction of *Sigurðar saga þǫgla* – that which has been considered possibly closer to an original[14] – has been dated to the second half of the fourteenth century.[15] Significantly, this shorter version does *not* contain any magic stones at all, meaning that they were added to the longer redaction, perhaps because of a new understanding of the stones gained from *Nítíða saga*. Considering also, for example, what could be called the rather indiscriminate inclusion of many place names in the long redaction of *Sigurðar saga þǫgla* as I discuss in the following chapter, the insertion of this motif along with them would not be surprising. Overall, the *náttúrusteinar* motif in *Sigurðar saga þǫgla* shows links to *Nítíða saga* in its essentially passive, vision-centred use of the stones. In this manifestation of the motif, there is nothing that the maiden-king must *do* in order to gain knowledge and supernatural vision from the

12 'Sigurðar saga þǫgla', ed. by Loth, p. 210.
13 'Sigurðar saga þǫgla', ed. by Loth, p. 245.
14 *Sigurðar saga þǫgla*, ed. by Driscoll, pp. lxxxix-xcii; Einar Ólafur Sveinsson, '*Viktors saga ok Blávus*: Sources and Characteristics', p. cxxxvii.
15 *Sigurðar saga þǫgla*, ed. by Driscoll, p. lxvi.

stones, except merely to look into them. In this way the *náttúrusteinar* here resemble magic mirrors and other magical objects associated with seeing,[16] and both Keren H. Wick and more recently Ármann Jakobsson have settled on such an interpretation on the stones in *Nítíða saga*.[17] However, this association with seeing and vision is not the only attribute of *Nítíða saga*'s *náttúrusteinar*, and the motif, when considered in relation to other texts, can be read to reveal another interpretation.

Gibbons saga is a notable example of an alternative reading of the *náttúrusteinar* motif. It is another fourteenth-century maiden-king romance, in which the hero Gibbon of France falls in love and has a child with both the fairy mistress Gríka of Greece, and the maiden-king Florentia of India.[18] Whereas in *Sigurðar saga þǫgla* the focal point of the motif was passive vision for a passive outcome (intellectual knowledge), in *Gibbons saga*, the motif is employed to increase the maiden-king's active power. Near the beginning of *Gibbons saga*, Gríka uses a magic stone to gain control over Gibbon: 'hun tekr þa einn natturu stein ok bregdr yfir hofud honum' (then she takes a supernatural stone and waves it over his head).[19] Here, Gríka's active use of the stone is highlighted, and a similar scene occurs later in the text, after the maiden-king Florentia gives her magic stone to another woman: 'tak minn natvrru steinn [...] hvn geingr ok ap<t>r kemr færrandi drottningv steninn frvin stendr þa vpp ok bregdr þessvm steini yfir hofvd kongs s(yni)' ('take my supernatural stone' [...]. She goes and comes back bringing the queen's stone. Then the woman stands up and waves the stone over the prince's head).[20] In both quotations, it is the women's actions that are crucial rather than their passive use of a magical object. These scenes showcase the use of *náttúrusteinar* as indicative of female power and male powerlessness.[21] Instead of being affected by the magical properties of the stones and using these properties to their advantage as in *Sigurðar saga þǫgla*, the women here harness the stones' power by physically brandishing them, more akin to practising magic than simply using the

16   Johanterwage, 'The Use of Magic Spells and Objects', pp. 446-53; Matyushina, 'Magic Mirrors, Monsters, Maiden-kings', pp. 660-70.

17   Ármann Jakobsson, *Illa fenginn mjǫðr*, p. 179; Wick, 'An Edition and Study of Nikulás saga Leikara', pp. 212-13.

18   The saga exists in two versions; for a discussion of its origins and relationship to other types of romance see Kalinke, 'Scribe, Redactor, Author', esp. pp. 189-93.

19   *Gibbons saga*, ed. by Page, p. 8.

20   *Gibbons saga*, ed. by Page, p. 44.

21   Cf. the discussion of male anxieties about female power and their need for subjugation in many Icelandic romances in Jóhanna Katrín Friðriksdóttir, *Women in Old Norse Literature*, pp. 116-26.

objects. The action reinforces power and thus reinforces female power and prominence instead of male power and superiority. The diction used to convey this action of practicing magic in *Gibbons saga* is, significantly, almost identical to the manner in which Nítíða's three active uses of her *náttúrusteinar* are conveyed in the saga as she escapes, first from Earl Virgilius and subsequently from Kings Ingi and Livorius: 1) 'm(ey)kongur tok nu eirn nætturu stein og bra yfer skipit og haufud þeim avllum' (the maiden-king now took a supernatural stone and waved it over the ship and all their heads);[22] 2) 'bregdur hun einum steine yfer hofud sier' (she waves a stone over her head);[23] and 3) hun bra þää steininum vpp ẏfer haufud þeim bàdum' (then she waved the stone up over both their heads).[24] The three key words here are *bregða*, *yfir*, and *höfuð*, which are used each time in both *Nítíða saga* and *Gibbons saga*, suggesting that the motif's appearance in these texts is not merely coincidental. What is significant is not simply the fact that magic stones are used, but that they are specifically waved over people's heads for their powers to be enacted. Another key word is, of course, *(náttúru)stein*. Where *Nítíða saga* here only uses the word *stein* in quotation 3, it is specified as one of her *náttúrusteinar* from Visio in the preceding sentence, and in quotation 2 the stone is immediately qualified as one obtained from Visio. It seems clear that there is a relationship between these romances in their active use of this motif, and also between them and *Sigurðar saga þögla*. While all three texts employ the motif of supernatural stones, there are two main ways in which it is manifested, and *Nítíða saga* appears to be the bridge between them, presenting the *náttúrusteinar* in both active and passive use. The text therefore demonstrates, through Nítíða's power and influence, the dual use of a single motif, and while there is clearly a relationship between *Nítíða saga* and both *Gibbons saga* and *Sigurðar saga þögla*, and a larger relationship among all three romances, it is difficult to discern exactly which text(s) influenced the other(s). Considering that *Nítíða saga* exhibits two rather different uses of this motif, it also seems plausible for its author to have drawn on at least one, if not both, of the other texts. In addition to the texts considered so far, this motif also appears in *Nikulás saga leikara*, whose relationship with *Nítíða saga* can be much more clearly defined, and which I discuss in greater depth in this chapter's second case study. Before doing so, I will consider *Nítíða saga*'s relationship with *Clári saga*.

22 'Nitida saga', ed. by Loth, p. 7.
23 'Nitida saga', ed. by Loth, p. 13.
24 'Nitida saga', ed. by Loth, p. 24.

Nítíða saga Drawing on *Clári saga*

Clári saga is romance whose plot can be summarized as a bridal quest in which Prince Clárus of Saxony falls in love with Princess Séréna of France. His attempts to woo her are unsuccessful, as she mocks his efforts and even has him whipped. At one point in the story Clárus disguises himself to try to get the princess, but without success. It is not until Clárus and his teacher Pérus trick Séréna's maidservant Tecla into helping them that Clárus is able to get to Séréna. Clárus eventually marries her after he and Pérus subject her to further violent and humiliating abuse, ostensibly in return for her earlier scornful actions. A moralizing ending warns women to respect and obey their husbands and fiancés. There has been more study of *Clári saga* than the other texts discussed above,[25] and it is the romance usually understood to be that from which the maiden-king motif in late medieval Icelandic romance originates.[26] It is for this wide reaching influence on other romances that I chose it to compare with *Nítíða saga*. *Clári saga* is classified as a maiden-king saga entirely based on Séréna's personality and actions, as she is never once called *meykóngur* or *kóngur* in the text (neither by herself nor by the narrator). Although Séréna is incredibly cruel to her suitors compared to Nítíða's far lesser degree of hostility, the two sagas, if not their 'maiden-kings', are certainly related to each other. This has been acknowledged for many years. Paul Bibire has suggested that *Nítíða saga* is a deliberate response to *Clári saga* and therefore a departure from the motif of the ruthlessly cruel romance maiden-king.[27] The present case study will develop further this basic understanding of the relationship between the two texts by examining both their style and examples of shared Latin and Low German vocabulary.

Bibire, in his assessment of the links between *Clári saga* and *Nítíða saga*, points primarily to connections between the names of the protagonists. Both names are based on Latin adjectives meaning 'shining' (*clarus* and

---

25 Recent scholarship on the saga includes Kalinke, '*Clári saga*: A Case of Low German Infiltration', pp. 5-25; Kalinke, 'Table Decorum and the Quest for a Bride in *Clári saga*', pp. 51-72; Hughes, '*Klári saga* as an Indigenous Romance', pp. 135-63. Additionally, major works in older scholarship include Jakobsen, *Studier i Clarus saga*; and the analytical introduction in *Clári saga*, ed. by Cederschiöld, pp. ix-xxxviii.

26 Driscoll, 'Late Prose Fiction', p. 202; Kalinke, *Bridal-Quest Romance*, pp. 98-107.

27 Bibire, 'From *riddarasaga* to *lygisaga*', pp. 67, 70. Cf. Guðbjörg Aðalbergsdóttir, 'Nítíða og aðrir meykóngar', pp. 49-55. *Nítíða saga* has even been labelled 'proto-feminist' (Jóhanna Katrín Friðriksdóttir, *Women in Old Norse Literature*, pp. 127-30), again in response and comparison to *Clári saga*. See also Chapter 4.

nitidus).[28] In addition to this, Bibire notes that the name *Eskilvarður* is the false identity assumed by both Livorius in *Nítíða saga* and Clárus in *Clári saga*, when they visit the respective maiden-kings.[29] Unfortunately, this is about as far as most analyses of the relationship between these two texts goes. Jóhanna Katrín Friðriksdóttir considers both romances as parts of 'an ongoing discourse about marriage and gender roles in medieval Iceland', with the 'ruthlessly patriarchal' *Clári saga* at one end of the spectrum and *Nítíða saga*, interrogating the former's norms, at the other.[30] I would, however, like to explore this relationship in more detail, and with an awareness of the differing styles of these texts. Whereas *Clári saga* is not only an overtly moralizing romance, which also refers to Christianity throughout the story, *Nítíða saga* does not: religion is not among the romance's concerns.[31] However, without making Christianity an aspect of *Nítíða saga*'s plot, the vocabulary used to convey the story exhibits a strong Latin influence, and a noticeably clerical style is used throughout. This is something also characteristic of *Clári saga*,[32] and points to both texts being written in a similar milieu, with a clerical author or early scribe. E.F. Halvorsen classifies the style of *Clári saga* as that of the late court style, which imitates Latin syntax and can be quite complex, and which Jónas Kristjánsson calls the 'younger florid style', which he argues is, in combination with the 'older court style' characteristic of late medieval Icelandic romances.[33] He illustrates this point using *Viktors saga ok Blávus*, but others, such as *Nítíða saga*, can certainly be characterized similarly. Jónas Kristjánsson notes that the basic traits of this learned style are 'the present participle used in the active sense' and 'the frequent use of the past participle used in apposition to a noun',[34] both of which occur regularly in both *Nítíða saga* and *Clári saga*. This section will first examine these stylistic features and the shared Latin vocabulary between the sagas, before moving on to discuss other aspects of these sagas' intertextual relationship.

I would like first to emphasize that the character of Nítíða ought to be directly compared, as hero, to Clárus, rather than to the cruel maiden-king

---

28   Bibire, 'From *riddarasaga* to *lygisaga*', pp. 67, 70.
29   Bibire, 'From *riddarasaga* to *lygisaga*', p. 67.
30   Jóhanna Katrín Friðriksdóttir, *Women in Old Norse Literature*, pp. 128-29.
31   Cf. Barnes, *The Bookish Riddarasögur*, p. 115.
32   Blaisdell, Jr., 'Some Observations on Style in the *riddarasögur*', pp. 87-94; Halvorsen, *The Norse Version of the Chanson de Roland*; Jakobsen, *Studier i Clarus saga*, pp. 33-40; Jónas Kristjánsson, 'The Court Style', pp. 431-40; Tannert, 'The Style of *Dínus saga drambláta*', pp. 53-62.
33   Jónas Kristjánsson, 'The Court Style', p. 440.
34   Jónas Kristjánsson, 'The Court Style', p. 437.

Séréna (whose name is also of equivalent meaning, that is 'clear' or 'bright', see below), with whom she is more usually compared, as I discuss further in Chapter 4. These female characters are arguably very different, and the principal roles enjoyed by Nítíða and Clárus links them more easily than gender links Nítíða and Séréna. Considering the adjectives *clarus* and *nitidus* as a pair seems especially deliberate and is telling, even when there are many female romance characters with names suggestive of refulgence or brightness, like Alba in *Valdimars saga*, Albína and Lúcíana in *Sigurðar saga þǫgla*, and Fulgida in *Viktors saga ok Blávus*.[35] Most importantly, however, is that one of the meanings of *clarus* is 'celebrated, illustrious, famous', in addition to 'clear, bright, shining'.[36] This appears previously to have gone unnoticed. With this in mind, the author of *Nítíða saga* may have named Nítíða *hin frœga* (the famous) with an eye to strengthening the link between her character and Clárus, and thus between the two sagas as a whole, even if these connections might be lost on audiences without a detailed knowledge of Latin, or indeed without knowledge of both saga texts. Interestingly, *Clári saga* and *Nítíða saga* appear together in manuscript far less often than might be expected – only one of the sixty-five surviving manuscripts (Reykjavík, Landsbókasafn–Háskólabókasafn Íslands, MS ÍB 138 4to, from the second half of the eighteenth century) transmits them together. We can still, however, see the potential play on names as evidence that *Nítíða saga*'s author was educated and well acquainted with Latin. In *Clári saga*, however, the primary meaning of the protagonist's name *is* to do with brightness, and the text goes to the trouble of explaining the name: 'Réttliga ok viðrkvæmiliga fekk hann þat nafn – því at "clárús" þýðiz upp á várt mál "bjartr" – sakir þess, at í þann tíma var engi vænni maðr í verǫldu með hold ok blóð' (Rightly and fittingly did he have that name – because 'clárús' means in our language 'bright' – for in that time there was no better man of flesh and blood in the world).[37] The explicatory note, one of the only of its kind in the Icelandic romances,[38] indicates that the saga's intended audience would most likely be unfamiliar with Latin. This of course does not preclude the possibility of *Nítíða saga*'s author naming Nítíða *hin frœga* with Clárus in mind, for whatever was the primary meaning in *Clári saga* does not necessarily matter when considering either saga's audience and the variety of interpretative possibilities. But complicating the matter further, even the

35 Driscoll, 'Late Prose Fiction', p. 109.
36 Lewis and Short, *A Latin Dictionary*, p. 349.
37 *Clári saga*, ed. by Cederschiöld, p. 2.
38 Barnes, *The Bookish Riddarasögur*, p. 74.

name of *Clári saga*'s maiden-king, Séréna, has connotations similar to Clárus and Nítíða, as it derives from Latin *serenus* (clear, fair, bright, serene).[39] The similarity in name may thus provoke careful readers to re-evaluate their expectations and interpretations of both characters, but particularly their understanding of Nítíða: why should Séréna's portrayal in *Clári saga* be so radically different from that of Nítíða, notwithstanding their similar names and characterization as maiden-kings? I address this question in further detail in Chapter 4, but this type of provocation and interrogation of the conventions of Icelandic romance is an important part of *Nítíða saga*. As a final point on names, it is somewhat unusual for a male romance hero to have such a Latinate name as Clárus: the heroes of Icelandic romance more often have vernacular names like Sigurður, no matter where they are meant to be from,[40] though in *Nítíða saga*, Livorius' name is also Latinate, even if it cannot be connected to any particular Latin word – it is the implied style and form of the name that in this case matters more than its meaning.

Clári saga also shares genre-specific vocabulary with *Nítíða saga*. The preceding examples of Latinate style and vocabulary, as well as those now following (including Low German examples), attest to this and show how both texts draw on the established vocabulary of romance in Icelandic and how the style of *Clári saga*, as an earlier romance, may have influenced *Nítíða saga*. In addition to Latinate names, a further, more general Latin influence can also be seen in both *Clári saga* and *Nítíða saga*. *Clári saga* has a distinctive clerical style, including a number of Latin expressions that have been translated directly into Icelandic. For example, the narrator frequently interjects the saga with phrases like *hvat meira*, which have been identified as Icelandic renderings of Latin phrases like *quid multa*, and detailed in earlier studies.[41] While it does not make use of these types of Latin phrases in particular, *Nítíða saga* (the edited text of roughly 5500 words) does contain forty-three present participle constructions (ending in -*andi*), thirty-four of which are examples of a Latinate syntactic structure characteristic of learned style.[42] The first of these, for example, appears early on in a description of Nítíða's crown: 'eiʀn haukur [...], breidandi sina vængi

39   Lewis and Short, *A Latin Dictionary*, p. 1678.
40   Driscoll, 'Late Prose Fiction', p. 109.
41   *Clári saga*, ed. by Cederschiöld, p. xx; Jakobsen, *Studier i Clarus saga*, pp. 34-35.
42   Barnes, 'The *riddarasögur* and Mediæval European Literature', p. 155; Blaisdell Jr., 'Some Observations on Style in the *riddarasögur*', p. 90; Hughes, '*Klári saga* as an Indigenous Romance', pp. 142-43; Jónas Kristjánsson, 'The Court Style', pp. 437-38; see also Tannert, 'The Style of *Dínus saga drambláta*', esp. p. 57.

framm' (a hawk [...], spreading its wings forward).[43] The rest are distributed throughout the saga 'to create a state of being and duration',[44] and propel the action forward. Other loan words of obviously Latin origin in *Nítíða saga* are *karbunculus* (carbuncle), with a Latin nominative ending rather than the alternative Icelandicized form *karbunkli*;[45] *lileam* (lily), inflected as a Latin accusative; *purpuri* (cloth of purple); and *púsa* (wife, spouse, from Latin *sponsa* via French),[46] which shows no unusual inflection. And yet the Latin nature of these words is not necessarily especially noteworthy, as such words are not rare in Icelandic romances. While they nevertheless lend an exotic or learned air, these words would not necessarily strike the medieval Icelandic reader as particularly marked.[47]

Nítíða saga's relationship with *Clári saga* goes deeper than a similarity in the meaning of names and the general use of a Latinate, clerical style. There are further lexical similarities, and the metaphorical use of the word *gimsteinn* (jewel) is the prime example, which again, is not a parallel that has been previously noted. In both texts the word is used to describe beautiful women as they are introduced, though they are not the main characters – Séréna's handmaiden Tecla in *Clári saga* and Princess Sýjalín of India in *Nítíða saga*. In *Clári saga*: 'Bæði var hon listug ok fǫgr með heiðrligri málsnild ok myndi þykkja hit kurteisasta konungsbarn, ef eigi hefði þvílíkr gimsteinn legit í annat skaut, sem var Séréna konungsdóttir' (She was both skilled and beautiful with honourable eloquence and would seem the most courteous princess, if such a jewel might not have lain in another garment's fold, that is, Princess Séréna);[48] in *Nítíða saga*: 'hvn var suo væn og listug at hun mundi forpris þott hafa allra kuenna j veraulldvnni. ef ei hefdi þvilikur gimsteinn hiä verit sem Nitida hin fræga' (she was so beautiful and skilled that she would have been thought to be most prized

---

43 'Nitida saga', ed. by Loth, p. 4.
44 Kalinke, 'Scribe, Redactor, Author', p. 184.
45 Gudbrand Vigfusson, *An Icelandic-English Dictionary*, p. 331.
46 Gudbrand Vigfusson, *An Icelandic-English Dictionary*, p. 480.
47 'Karbunculus' or 'karbunkuli stein' appears also in *Flóres saga og Blankiflúr*, *Clári saga*, *Karlamagnúss saga*, *Máguss saga jarls*, *Rémundar saga keisarasonar*, *Sigurðar saga frœkna*, and *Þiðriks saga af Bern*. See also Lecouteux, *A Lapidary of Sacred Stones*, pp. 87-90. 'Purpuri' is common in many romances, including *Clári saga*, *Sigurðar saga frœkna*, and *Viktors saga ok Blávus*, and 'púsa' appears in translated romances like *Strengleikar* (where the word is first recorded in Old Norse), *Partalopa saga*, and *Erex saga*; Icelandic romances like *Rémundar saga keisarasonar* and *Saulus saga ok Nikanors*; and also religious literature like *Maríu saga* (*Ordbog over det norrøne prosasprog* <http://dataonp.hum.ku.dk>).
48 *Clári saga*, ed. by Cederschiöld, p. 12.

of all the women in the world, if nearby there had not been such a jewel as Nítíða the Famous).[49]

The editor Cederschiöld interprets the *gimsteinn* in *Clári saga* literally, as part of Séréna's embellished clothing,[50] but Shaun Hughes argues that the sense is metaphorical, and, particularly, legal in nature:

> The term að leggja í skaut is a legal term referring to the casting lots which were marked and placed in the lap or fold (*skaut*) of a garment from which they would be drawn by some third person. [...] The term is used here metaphorically to indicate that it was not to fall to Tecla's lot to be drawn for the honor of being considered the most elegant and accomplished young woman in the realm, that being reserved for the Princess Serena.[51]

The sense is certainly also metaphorical in *Nítíða saga*, but the legal aspect has been lost, forgotten, or deliberately omitted by the scribe. The phrase *ef ei(gi) hefði þvílíkr gimsteinn* (if not had [been] such a jewel) is too specific to have occurred in both romances coincidentally, and it seems obvious to me as further evidence that *Nítíða saga*'s author knew and actively drew on *Clári saga*. This use of figurative language could also have further significance, in terms of grouping texts together based on known medieval Icelandic centres of text production. Peter Hallberg notes the metaphorical use of *gimsteinn* in the religious texts *Nikolaus saga*, *Michaels saga*, and *Guðmundar biskups saga*, and suggests that this group may have been composed by a single author, Bergr Sokkason (fl. early fourteenth century), a man who was likely to have been influenced by the Dominican Jón Halldórsson (*c.* 1275-1339), the possible author of *Clári saga*.[52] In addition to these examples, the *Dictionary of Old Norse Prose* yields more examples of this type of metaphorical use of *gimsteinn*, listed alphabetically by saga title.

---

49 'Nitida saga', ed. by Loth, p. 9.

50 *Clári saga*, ed. by Cederschiöld, p. 12, note.

51 Hughes, '*Klári saga* as an Indigenous Romance', pp. 140-41.

52 Hallberg, 'A Group of Icelandic "Riddarasögur"', pp. 18, 24 (n. 28). However, Hallberg does posit that Bergr Sokkason wrote *Clári saga* as well, and not Jón Halldórsson (pp. 13-14, 20-21). On the metaphorical use of *gimsteinn*, see Hallberg, 'Imagery in Religious Old Norse Prose Literature', p. 120-70. See also Johansson, 'Bergr Sokkason och Arngrímur Brandsson', pp. 181-97.

Gibbons saga

> vænleikr systr hans var sem duft e(dr) dumba hia þessvm gimsteini[53]
> (the beauty of his sister was as dust or mist next to this jewel)

Hungrvaka

> Þorláki byskupi, er at réttu má segjask geisli eða gimsteinn heilagra[54]
> (Bishop Þorlákr, who rightly might be said to be a sunbeam or a most
> holy jewel of the saints)

Katerine saga

> hinn skiærazti gimsteinn allra kvinna i heiminum[55]
> (the most shining jewel of all the women in the world)

Guðmundar biskups saga

> er svá opt líkist gimsteininum Thome Kantuariensi[56]
> (who so often resembles the jewel Thomas of Canterbury)

> sem hinn bjartasti gimsteinn ok geisli skínandi sólar[57]
> (as the brightest jewel and shining beam of sun)

Mariu saga

> Martein gimstein kennimanna[58]
> (Martein, jewel of priests)

Martinus saga byskups

> kalladr af allri cristni gemma sacerdotum, þat þydiz gimsteinn
> kennimanna[59]
> (called of all Christendom *gemma sacerdotum*, which means jewel
> of priests)

---

53 *Gibbons saga*, ed. by Page, p. 11.
54 'Hungrvaka', ed. by Jón Helgason, p. 115.
55 'Katerine saga', ed. by Unger, I, p. 407.
56 'Guðmundar biskups saga', ed. by Jón Sigurðsson, Gubrandur Vigfússon and others, p. 109.
57 'Guðmundar biskups saga', ed. by Jón Sigurðsson, Gubrandur Vigfússon and others, p. 175.
58 Unger, ed., *Mariu saga*, p. 190.
59 'Martinus saga byskups III', ed. by Unger, I, pp. 641-42.

Marthe saga ok Marie Magdalene

See her liosan lampa heimsins ok skinanda guds gimstein med
gǫfugligri birti Mariam Magdalenam[60]
(see here the clear lamp of the world and the shining jewel of God with
noble brightness, Mary Magdalene)

Michaels saga

gimsteinn allra meyia[61]
(jewel of all maidens)

Nikolaus saga

Her skinn liosi biartara, hverir heilagleiks gimsteinar riktu med
frabærri fegrd i gofugligum anda Nicholai erkibyskups[62]
(Here shines brighter than a light, how the jewels of holiness reigned
with great beauty in the noble spirit of Archbishop Nikolaus)

Ólafs saga Trygvassonar

guds gimstæin oftnefndan Olaf konung[63]
(God's jewel, the said King Ólaf)

Apart from the similarity to *Clári saga*, the closest phrasing to that in *Nítíða
saga* is in *Katerine saga*'s 'allra kvinna i heiminum' (cf. 'allra kvenna í veröldunni'). *Michaels saga*'s 'allra meyja', in comparing the Virgin Mary, is also
close. This manner of comparing women to precious jewels seems likely to
have first appeared in the religious texts and later influenced the romance
authors or scribes; this reinforces the possibility that romances like *Clári
saga* and even *Nítíða saga* were composed in a religious environment. Stefán
Einarsson asserts that *Clári saga*, along with *Gibbons saga* and *Viktors saga
ok Blávaus*, was probably written at Skálholt (Iceland's southern bishopric),
but that *Nítíða saga*, and others including the maiden-king romances *Dínus
saga drambláta* and *Hrólfs saga Gautrekssonar*, came from the wealthy
farm Reykhólar; additionally, he places *Sigurður saga þǫgla* at the centre
of learning at Oddi in southern Iceland.[64] Even if *Nítíða saga* was composed
at a secular location, the clear influence of Latin and vernacular religious

---

60 'Marthe saga ok Marie Magdalene', ed. by Unger, I, p. 530.
61 'Michaels saga', ed. by Unger, I, p. 701.
62 'Nikolaus saga II', ed. by Unger, II, p. 109.
63 'Ólafs saga Tryggvasonar', ed. by Guðbrandur Vigfusson and Unger, p. 515.
64 Stefán Einarsson, 'Heimili (skólar) fornaldarsaga og riddarasaga', p. 272.

style points to an educated, widely read, and religious author, whether professionally religious in holy orders or a religiously educated layman. Geraldine Barnes notes that Icelandic romances, albeit translated ones in particular, sometimes bear strong resemblance to Icelandic saints' lives,[65] an observation that further supports the possibility that both romance and religious literature emerged from similar environments and even perhaps from similar authors and translators. Further investigations into these religious literary-cultural environments and, especially, more research involving the reading of Icelandic romances against Icelandic saints' lives and other religious writing would surely be important and useful areas of study, which unfortunately fall outside the scope of this book. It must suffice to say that future research will undoubtedly uncover previously unnoticed cross-genre connections that at present can only be inferred in the case of *Nítíða saga*.

Not only does *Nítíða saga* show Latin vocabulary and style, but it also contains Low German vocabulary. In this, too, it is similar to *Clári saga*. Kalinke explains a number of *Clári saga*'s Low German loans,[66] and some of these also occur in *Nítíða saga*, such as *hof* (courtly), *kukl* (magic), *klók* (cunning), *mekt* (power), *skari* (entourage), and *stað* (place).[67] In addition to these, the word *ævintýr* (narrative, or, exemplum), coming ultimately from French, is another possible example of Low German influence.[68] Again, whereas many of these words do appear in other Icelandic romances, their presence in *Nítíða saga* alongside so many other clear parallels with *Clári saga* can serve as further evidence to reinforce *Nítíða saga*'s response to and mirroring of *Clári saga*. There are hints of not just a surface dialogue between the two texts, but a rich and deep-seated conversation effected by a complex echoing of vocabulary to produce in *Nítíða saga* a truly informed and conscious interplay with *Clári saga*. Low German vocabulary in both romances also suggests the possibility of an even more specific relationship between these texts' authors. Jón Halldórsson, the bishop mentioned

---

65 Barnes, 'The *riddarasögur* and Mediæval European Literature', pp. 155-58. For more on the relationship between religious and secular texts and genres, see Kalinke: *The Book of Reykjahólar*, esp. pp. 3-44.

66 Kalinke, '*Clári saga*: A Case of Low German Infiltration', pp. 5-25.

67 Hughes, '*Klári saga* as an Indigenous Romance', pp. 144-45; Kalinke, '*Clári saga*: A Case of Low German Infiltration', pp. 14-18; and de Vries, *Altnordisches etymologisches Wörterbuch*, pp. 318, 333, 383, 484, 682. See also Braunmüller, 'Language Contacts in the Late Middle Ages and in Early Modern Times', pp. 1222-33; Veturliði Óskarsson, *Middelnedertyske Låneord i islandsk Diplomsprog*.

68 Veturliði Óskarsson, *Middelnedertyske Låneord i islandsk Diplomsprog*, p. 346.

above to whom *Clári saga* is often attributed, writes in an identifiable style, which includes Low German and Norwegian vocabulary.[69] It is uncertain whether *Nítíða saga* was composed or copied by someone whose Icelandic vocabulary contained these words because he (or she) had read widely enough to encounter them consistently in other texts of a similar genre or style (such as *Clári saga*), or whether the author or scribe may have originally been from or spent a substantial amount of time in an area in which Low German was spoken, as Jón Halldórsson did in the Hanseatic port of Bergen, Norway.[70] Having considered some of the influences that *Clári saga* very likely had on *Nítíða saga*, I now turn to how *Nítíða saga* likewise influenced the composition of *Nikulás saga leikara*, another Icelandic romance.

Nikulás saga leikara Drawing on *Nítíða saga*

Nikulás saga leikara is a little-studied Icelandic romance, but, as I aim to show in this case study, one almost certainly influenced by *Nítíða saga*. While its earliest manuscript attestations are only from the first half of the seventeenth century, evidence has been found to suggest that *Nikulás saga leikara* originated in the Middle Ages, despite its exclusively post-Reformation witnesses. A table of contents on folio 28[v] of the fifteenth-century Stockholm, Kungliga biblioteket–Sveriges nationalbiblioteket, MS Perg. fol. nr. 7 'seems to include the letters ...lafe leikara, suggesting the presence of Nikuláss saga leikara'.[71] The saga is also not widely available for study; despite existing in sixty manuscripts (indicating an overall popularity comparable to that of *Nítíða saga*), the only English translation appears in Keren H. Wick's 1996 doctoral thesis,[72] and there are only two Icelandic-language editions, published in 1889,[73] and in 1912,[74] the latter being 'a direct copy' of the former 'in all but the finer points of orthography'.[75] The saga does appear a handful of times in the *Motif-Index*

69 Hughes, '*Klári saga* as an Indigenous Romance'; Jakobsen, *Studier i Clarus saga*, pp. 17-22, 43-104; Kalinke, '*Clári saga*: A Case of Low German Infiltration'; Sigurdson, 'The Church in Fourteenth-Century Iceland', pp. 53-65.

70 Hughes, '*Klári saga* as an Indigenous Romance', pp. 137-38, 145; Kalinke, '*Clári saga*: A Case of Low German Infiltration', pp. 24-25.

71 Sanders, ed., *Tales of Knights*, p. 17 (see also pp. 14, 21).

72 Until the thesis was recently digitized and made available online it was largely unknown.

73 *Nikulás saga leikara* (Winnipeg, 1889).

74 *Sagan af Nikulási konungi leikara*.

75 Wick, 'An Edition and Study of Nikulás saga Leikara', p. 58, n. 9.

of Early Icelandic Literature,[76] is mentioned in Erik Wahlgren's thesis on the figure of the maiden-king (though he ultimately dismisses this saga),[77] and has a brief entry in Rudolf Simek and Hermann Pálsson's dictionary,[78] but it seems, still, that few people are aware of *Nikulás saga leikara* as a late medieval Icelandic romance, and that this is the reason for its scholarly neglect.

In her thesis, Wick's analysis of the saga is arguably limited by her reading of it as a family drama, after the frameworks of Derek Brewer and Bruno Bettelheim.[79] She defends this approach on the grounds that the saga is 'a tale read and listened to by families'.[80] While the purpose of the present case study is not to offer a new interpretation of *Nikulás saga leikara*, but rather to highlight its intertextual relationship with *Nítíða saga*, I will, at times, offer readings of the text alternative to, or in greater detail than, those Wick provides. Additionally, as *Nikulás saga leikara* is not well known, a brief synopsis will not be out of place before continuing. The saga follows the adventures of the Hungarian king Nikulás, who acquires the nickname *leikari* (trickster) because he practises magic.[81] His foster father Svívari suggests he marry Dorma, the daughter of King Valdimar of Constantinople (and who is introduced as a maiden-king). On behalf of Nikulás, Svívari travels there to ask for her hand, unsuccessfully. Eventually Nikulás goes himself, disguised as the merchant Þórir. As Þórir he gains Valdimar's approval, woos Dorma, and takes her back to Hungary to marry, without her father's knowledge, but not against her will. After their marriage, Dorma is abducted back to Constantinople through sorcery, but in the end she is rescued by Nikulás, who then makes peace with her father. The saga is thus structured somewhat unusually for a romance, in that it does not end with a wedding but with a feast of reconciliation instead, the nuptials having taken place roughly in the middle of the story.

Nikulás saga leikara and *Nítíða saga* contain several identical or near-identical phrases and sentences. Many of these similarities of diction are likely no more than evidence that the two texts are a part of a wider Icelandic romance tradition for which specific vocabulary came to be used

---

76 Boberg, *Motif-Index of Early Icelandic Literature*, cites the 1912 Reykjavík edition.

77 Wahlgren 'The Maiden King in Iceland', pp. 18-19, 63, and *passim*.

78 Simek and Hermann Pálsson, *Lexikon der nordischen Literatur*, p. 279.

79 Brewer, *Symbolic Stories*, and Bettelheim, *The Uses of Enchantment*.

80 Wick, 'An Edition and Study of Nikulás saga Leikara', p. 196.

81 Wahlgren mistranslates this nickname, calling him instead 'Nikulás the Sportsman' ('The Maiden King in Iceland', p. 18).

as a matter of course, as discussed above with *Clári saga*.[82] If *Nítíða saga* were read in detail against other romances that co-occur in manuscript and share similar themes,[83] it is likely that some of the same stock phrases and descriptions would appear as they do here. However, other shared phrases point to a more specific relationship between *Nikulás saga leikara* and *Nítíða saga*. It is, though, worth beginning by mentioning some examples of genre-specific vocabulary shared by these texts, before focusing on more specific examples of phrases and ideas that were possibly borrowed from one text to the other. While I will not be taking into account variations in different manuscripts in this case study, and while the manuscript on which the greater part of the version of *Nítíða saga* to be discussed is based is late medieval (AM 529, 1500s), that from which quotations from *Nikulás saga leikara* are taken is slightly later (Copenhagen, Det Kongelige Bibliotek, MS Nks 331 8vo, 1600s): if both versions were medieval (or both post-medieval), the evidence available may be different, but this need not be an issue, especially considering the role the seventeenth-century manuscript AM 537 plays in the edition of *Nítíða saga*, alongside the slightly earlier AM 529. I have, essentially, chosen to compare standardized and edited versions of each text.

An example of similar phrasing results from the romances' origins in similar cultural and stylistic environments. Some prime examples of similar lexis concern Dorma's physical description: she is described in nearly the same way as Nítíða, and female beauty more generally is also pictured in similar terms: 'føgur sem rösa huÿt sem lilia' (beautiful as a rose, white as a lily),[84] and 'øllum ʙlöma og fegurd' (in full bloom and beauty);[85] and in *Nítíða saga*, similarly, 'lios og riod j andliti þuilikast sem en rauda rosa væri samtemprad vid sniohuita lileam',[86] and 'aull fegurd og blomi'.[87] This manner of description was also common in other medieval Icelandic romances and a conventional way of describing female characters in continental romance.[88] The diction is general enough to be expected of a romance, but

82   Blaisdell, 'Some Observations on Style in the *riddarasögur*', pp. 87-94; Jónas Kristjánsson, 'The Court Style', pp. 431-40; Matyushina, 'On the Imagery and Style of the *Riddarasögur*'.

83   *Dínus saga drambláta* would make another very apt comparison: see Tannert, 'The Style of *Dínus saga drambláta*', pp. 53-62.

84   Wick, 'An Edition and Study of Nikulás saga Leikara', p. 124. Translations of this text are based on those provided by Wick in her thesis.

85   Wick, 'An Edition and Study of Nikulás saga Leikara', p. 93.

86   'Nitida saga', ed. by Loth, p. 3.

87   'Nitida saga', ed. by Loth, p. 18.

88   Kölbing, ed., *Elis saga ok Rosamundu*, p. 136; *Partalopa saga*, ed. by Præstgaard Andersen, p. 118. This was adopted from European (specifically French) romance, as noted in Kalinke, *King*

because *Nítíða saga* employs it, it is possible that the author of *Nikulás saga leikara* also chose to do so.

In addition to these loose resemblances, sometimes both texts do use identical phrases. The quotations listed below (found in both sagas; see specific references in the footnotes) are also used in similar contexts in both texts. Such similarities could be coincidental, but may also be evidence of borrowing between texts: 'j þessar aalffur heimsens' (in this region of the world),[89] 'fullur (vpp) af golldrum og giorningum' ([all] full of sorcery and witchcraft),[90] and 'er menn hafa spurn af / sem eg hefi spurn af' (that people have had a report of / that I have had a report of).[91] A final example of lexical similarity between these texts, likely attributable to their shared romance vocabulary, occurs when Nikulás enters Dorma's tower and sees elaborate murals depicting many stories painted there, an image probably borrowed from *Clári saga*. After describing the murals in some detail, the narrator comments on the difficulty of describing what he sees. In *Nítíða saga* the narrator makes a similar comment after describing the triple wedding scene, as already noted in Chapter 1, and while the phrasing in each text is different, both comments convey the same sense of feigned inadequacy, on the part of the author or narrator, to describe the scenes. It is in comparisons like this that we begin to see the possibility of intertextual connections reaching deeper than the examples considered thus far might suggest. Both narrators here project anxieties that either they themselves (as unlearned people) or the language they write in (an unlearned tongue) are not sufficiently equipped to describe the scenes at hand. In *Nikulás saga leikara*: 'var þad af meÿrra hagleÿk giørt enn eirn fäfrödur madur kunne ordum til ad koma' (it was made of finer workmanship than any unlearned man can begin to relate);[92] and in *Nítíða saga*: 'er og ei audsagt med öfrodre tungu i utlegdumm veralldarinnar' (And it is not easily said with an unlearned tongue in the outer regions of the world).[93] Both texts employ essentially the same word, meaning 'unlearned' or 'ignorant', though they take the slightly different forms *fáfroður* (lit. little-learned) and *ófroður* (lit. unlearned). The means of communicating these messages and the

---

Arthur, pp. 94-95, and *Bridal-Quest Romance*, pp. 72-74.

89 'Nitida saga', ed. by Loth, p. 30; Wick, 'An Edition and Study of Nikulás saga Leikara', p. 82.

90 'Nitida saga', ed. by Loth, p. 8; Wick, 'An Edition and Study of Nikulás saga Leikara', p. 110. This phrase is also used in *Rémundar saga keisarasonar*, another late medieval Icelandic romance with similar themes (*Rémundar saga keisarasonar*, ed. by Broberg, p. 96).

91 'Nitida saga', ed. by Loth, p. 5; Wick, 'An Edition and Study of Nikulás saga Leikara', p. 103.

92 Wick, 'An Edition and Study of Nikulás saga Leikara', p. 125.

93 'Nitida saga', ed. by Loth, p. 36.

similarity of the messages themselves suggest that they may have been inspired by or borrowed from one to the other. These comments by the narrator can also of course be seen as conventional humility topoi, which were common in medieval literature, and which I discuss in Chapter 6. The striking similarity of the vocabulary, however, suggests that this is not just a coincidental correspondence. These similarities, while employed within the expected romance vocabulary and conventions, are close enough to suggest a deeper relationship between the two sagas.

There is further evidence of a richer intertextual connection between *Nítíða saga* and *Nikulás saga leikara*. Whereas *Nítíða saga* has many female characters, all of whom play important roles (as I will discuss in Chapters 4 and 5), in *Nikulás saga leikara* only one female character is named and the only other women mentioned at all are the mothers of Dorma and Nikulás, both of whom are anonymously referred to only as their husband's queen, and a Christian princess whom Nikulás saves from an evil Saracen in a self-contained episode within the romance.[94] The difference between the texts in terms of their representation of women nevertheless reveals something of the relationship between them. Dorma, the only named female character in this romance, shares certain characteristics with Nítíða. When Nikulás visits Dorma, disguised as the merchant Þórir, she recognizes him in a way similar to when Nítíða sees through Livorius's disguise: 'eigi þurftu nikuläs kongur ad diliast firer mier, þuÿad firsta sinne, er eg þig leÿt j høll fødur mÿnz, þekta eg ydur ökiendann' (King Nikulás, you do not need to conceal yourself from me, because the first time when I looked on you in my father's hall, I knew you without being taught).[95] Compare this, then, to *Nítíða saga*: 'Liv(orius) kongur' seger hun, 'legg aff þier dular kufl þinn, hinn fyrsta dag er þu komst kiennda eg þig' ('King Livorius', she says, 'remove your cloak of disguise. I knew you the first day you came').[96] Dorma, like Nítíða, addresses the man by name, tells him not to disguise himself, and reveals she knew him immediately: in both texts this revelation combines the same pieces of information and proceeds in the same order. This piece of direct speech is much more likely to be a direct borrowing than an accidental similarity. Unlike in *Nítíða saga*, however, no explanation is provided in *Nikulás saga leikara* as to how Dorma knows Nikulás's true identity – it is not through the *náttúrusteinar*, which in this saga are not even associated with Dorma, but with the protagonist, Nikulás, as I will discuss shortly. In terms of her

---

94 Wick, 'An Edition and Study of Nikulás saga Leikara', pp. 116-17, 162-63.
95 Wick, 'An Edition and Study of Nikulás saga Leikara', pp. 125-26.
96 'Nitida saga', ed. by Loth, p. 31.

characterization, Dorma is introduced as a typical maiden-king:[97] 'hen*nar* bädu m*arger* k*ongar og* k*on*gasin*er* ägiæt*er. og* feÿngu all*er* sneÿpu, *og* vor*u* sum*er* drepn*er* en*n* sum*er* flÿdu' (Many famous kings and princes asked to marry her. And all suffered disgrace and some were killed, but some fled).[98] Nikulás later reinforces this characterization when he shows concern at the suggestion he marry Dorma.[99] But when she is actually encountered in person, her positive opinion of and behaviour towards Nikulás suggests that her characterization as a maiden-king might better be understood as a blind motif,[100] borrowed to give the saga the feel of a maiden-king romance, without developing the characters in ways that would see this motif through. In this respect, *Nikulás saga leikara*, like *Nítíða saga*, can also be considered a saga in open dialogue with the bridal-quest and maiden-king genres of Icelandic romance, responding to texts that portray women in such negative roles such as *Clári saga*. Dorma seems sensible and intelligent, not haughty, condescending, or violent, as would be expected from a maiden-king.[101] Additionally, when Nikulás succeeds in wooing Dorma, she leaves with him freely, by her own choice,[102] much more like Nítíða's ability to choose freely to marry Livorius than the outcome of any other bridal-quest romance.[103] Like *Nítíða saga*, *Nikulás saga leikara* approaches the idea of the maiden-king from an unconventional perspective, even though the end result is different in each text. Further, it is possible that the author of the one text chose to approach romance in this way as a result of reading the other, rather than both questioning romance in this way independently.

The fame and wisdom of key characters in *Nikulás saga leikara* and *Nítíða saga* are also important attributes, and demonstrate further connections between the texts. As Nítíða is renowned for her wisdom and becomes even more famous through her various stratagems, Dorma is characterized as similarly famous when Nikulás says that 'mikl*ar* søg*ur* hafa geÿngid fr*ä*

97 See Kalinke's discussions of typical maiden-kings in many Icelandic romances (*Bridal-Quest Romance*, pp. 66-108).

98 Wick, 'An Edition and Study of Nikulás saga Leikara', p. 65.

99 Wick, 'An Edition and Study of Nikulás saga Leikara', pp. 69-70.

100 Wick, 'An Edition and Study of Nikulás saga Leikara', pp. 75-77, 126-27.

101 *Sigurðar saga þǫgla*'s Sedentiania, *Clári saga*'s Séréna, and *Dínus saga drambláta*'s Philotemia are typically haughty maiden-kings. See also Kalinke, *Bridal-Quest Romance*, pp. 66-108.

102 Wick, 'An Edition and Study of Nikulás saga Leikara', p. 128.

103 Consider, for example, Clárus's domination of Séréna in *Clári saga* and Sigurðar's domination of Sedentiania in *Sigurður saga þǫgla*, as well as the forceful abduction of brides in romances like *Viktors saga ok Blávus* and *Vilhálms saga sjóðs*. For more on the treatment of women in Icelandic romances, see Jóhanna Katrín Friðriksdóttir, *Women in Old Norse Literature*, pp. 107-33.

hen*nar* vit*ur*leÿk' (many tales are told of her wisdom).[104] The kingdoms
from which these characters come are also compared with another clear
connection between the texts: Valdimar of Constantinople rules over
twenty other kings, just as Nítíða's kingdom of France comprises twenty
subsidiary kingdoms.[105] This again echoes Nítíða's characterization, but
the saga does not build on it, focusing instead on its hero Nikulás, whose
reputation is predominantly negative, as a magician or sorcerer. Nikulás is
a trickster like Nítíða, whose positive characterization depends to an extent
on her ability to outwit and trick her suitors,[106] yet for Nikulás this proves
to be a negative trait, which he is only able to overcome through disguise
and through his wisdom. That Nítíða and Nikulás should be compared
and contrasted based on their shared characterizations as tricksters is
confirmed further in those *Nítíða saga* manuscripts that make a genealogical connection between the two characters. Not only must *Nikulás saga
leikara* necessarily have been known before the earliest extant version of
the one text to link itself explicitly to the other (maybe as early as the late
fifteenth century),[107] but the connection also invites a contemporary critical
reading of the two against each other, as *Nítíða saga*'s acknowledgment of
Nikulás saga leikara's similarities indicates a dialogue between them in the
minds of their scribes and readers. While it is difficult to say precisely at
what point this connection entered the *Nítíða saga* manuscript tradition,
it seems to be rather early on, but most likely not as part of the author's
'original' text, as that would mean *Nikulás saga leikara* must be the older
romance – I would find that a difficult argument to make considering the
evidence at hand. Although this was an early development in the textual
tradition of *Nítíða saga* it is also significant that the popularity of the story
containing this intertextual narrative element declined somewhat in the
post-medieval period as other versions began to emerge and thrive, so that
by the nineteenth and twentieth centuries there were more extant versions
of the story that did not contain this connection than those that did. In
the nineteenth century there are, as far as we know, only five manuscripts
containing versions of the romance linking it to *Nikulás saga leikara*, and
fifteen containing other versions that do not connect the texts. There are
no twentieth-century manuscripts in which the stories are connected. This

---

104 Wick, 'An Edition and Study of Nikulás saga Leikara', p. 106.
105 Wick, 'An Edition and Study of Nikulás saga Leikara', pp. 64, 76, 106; 'Nitida saga', ed. by
Loth, p. 11.
106 See Chapter 4 on Nítíða's characterization.
107 See also Sanders, *Tales of Knights*.

indicates that in later centuries this connection was not important to scribes, readers, and others to whom the story was known, and that this feature was not important enough to preserve in new copies of the text, even if some of the other lexical and thematic correspondences between the romances were preserved. In the larger branch of the nineteenth- and twentieth-century eastern Icelandic manuscripts, almost all of the similarities with *Nikulás saga leikara* that are present in earlier versions are absent; as mentioned in Chapter 1, the two manuscripts from the Eastfjords do refer to *Nikulás saga leikara*, suggesting that in rare cases this connection persisted in some form. *Nikulás saga leikara* appears in *Nítíða saga*'s manuscripts more than any other saga, as mentioned earlier, strongly suggesting that they were transmitted together. While common post-medieval transmission does not necessarily mean that paired texts influenced each other and the opposite could in fact be the case, in which the texts are paired in manuscript because of their already existing (and thus maybe incidental) similarities, it does seem likeliest to conclude that *Nikulás saga leikara* was influenced and even inspired by *Nítíða saga*, and is thus a slightly younger romance. Overall, while dissimilarity between some episodes exists, the basic motifs remain the same, and are too similar to be mere coincidence.

Further evidence of borrowing from one text to the other is seen in the *náttúrusteinar* motif, which I introduced at the beginning of this chapter. Almost as equally important as the stones themselves is the way that Nítíða obtains them – from the island of Visio and the sorcerer Virgilius. More parallels with *Nítíða saga* dominate the stones' use and portrayal in *Nikulás saga leikara* than in the other texts discussed, especially concerning the manner in which they are acquired. In *Nikulás saga leikara*, Nikulás, like Nítíða, finds magical stones on an island within an island, and in both sagas the mysterious island is situated in an indeterminate northerly location. However, whereas this northern setting serves a specific purpose in *Nítíða saga*, as I will discuss in Chapter 3, it does not make much sense in *Nikulás saga leikara*. Nikulás and his men 'komu ad eÿrne eÿ sÿd vm kuelld. hun var firer bretlande' (came to an island late in the evening. It was off Britain).[108] Both islands are located in reference to a place (in *Nítíða saga* Visio is near Sweden), and whether real or imaginary, they are somewhere significantly further north than the places in which the rest of both sagas' action occurs. And while Nítíða's nautical route from Apulia

---

108 Wick, 'An Edition and Study of Nikulás saga Leikara', p. 90. In the 1912 printing, however, the island is *nálægt Grikkland* 'close to Greece' (p. 19). Cf. 'Nitida saga', ed. by Loth, p. 5: 'þesse ey liggur vt vndan Suiþiod jnni kaulldu. vt vnder heims skautid'.

past Scandinavia is, admittedly, somewhat difficult to conceptualize and map, that of Nikulás, who the saga tells us sailed past Britain from Hungary on his way to Constantinople, is so much more far-fetched that it seems indicative of the author's geographical ignorance, in sharp contrast to *Nítíða saga*'s particularly learned author. This suggests that *Nítíða saga* may have influenced and inspired *Nikulás saga leikara*'s use of the motif as the form but not the function of *Nítíða saga*'s geography is imitated. Wick considers mapping the routes that Nikulás takes on his sea-voyages from Hungary, but concludes the effort futile.[109] She also considers it problematic that Nikulás travels by sea, noting that Hungary is landlocked, evidently forgetting that medieval Hungary was a much greater kingdom than the borders of modern Hungary might suggest, and at times extended all the way to the Dalmatian coast in the west and nearly to the Black Sea in the east.[110] Alternatively, *Nikulás saga leikara*'s author could have understood the significance of the north as in general an otherworldly place where strange things can happen, and localized the episode accordingly,[111] but it seems more likely that *Nítíða saga* plays an equal if not greater role in the scene's construction.

In *Nikulás saga leikara* the descriptions of the expedition to the island are much more detailed than they are in *Nítíða saga*, and the episode is, overall, much more complex. The differences are discussed below, but comparison of phrasing begins with examples of identical or nearly identical diction, starting with the arrival at the mysterious island. In *Nikulás saga leikara*, 'hann keimur ad eÿnu störu vatne, *og* sier eirn hölma j midiu vatninu' (he comes to a large lake. And he sees an islet in the middle of the lake);[112] then, 'hann þöttist siä vm allann heÿmenn *og* vm øll lønd *og* kongaʀÿke *og* huad huer hafdist ad ä siö *og* lande (He thought he saw over all the world, and all the lands and kingdoms, and what each one did at sea and on land),[113] and 'hann þikist skinia ad þesser steynar mune hafa med sier allra handa nätturu' (He believes he understands that these stones must contain all kinds of powers).[114] In *Nítíða saga*, elements of the scene are similar: 'j þessari eyiv er vatn eitt stort. enn j vatninu er holmi,[115] 'hun sä þä vm allar hælfur

109 Wick, 'An Edition and Study of Nikulás saga Leikara', p. 205.
110 Engel, *The Realm of St Stephen*, p. 374.
111 See esp. Chapter 3, but also Chapter 4, for discussions of the conceptions of different world regions in the Icelandic romances. John Shafer's chapter on the conception of the North in Icelandic sagas is also useful: Shafer, 'Saga Accounts of Norse Far-Travellers', pp. 207-72.
112 Wick, 'An Edition and Study of Nikulás saga Leikara', p. 91.
113 Wick, 'An Edition and Study of Nikulás saga Leikara', pp. 92-93.
114 Wick, 'An Edition and Study of Nikulás saga Leikara', p. 93.
115 'Nitida saga', ed. by Loth, p. 5.

veralldarinnar. þar med konga og konga sonu og huad huer hafdest at',[116] and 'hun vnder stod af sinni visku hueria nætturu huer bar'.[117] While not all of these phrases are identical, the same sense is present in each, with at least some parallel diction. Unlike in *Nítíða saga*, where the stones collectively have three functions (discussed already above), in the shorter redaction of *Nikulás saga leikara* the ability to see other places in the world is transferred to four magical tablets of four different colours, which could also be akin to the four-cornered vessel containing the stones in *Nítíða saga*.[118] In addition to this, each specific stone has its own detailed properties and functions. Considering the style of language in these two passages, *Nikulás saga leikara* appears to use more typically native Icelandic words, phrases, and constructions, compared to the borrowed words and more learned style of *Nítíða saga*. Where *Nikulás saga leikara* uses the simple past tense *lögðu* and the common Icelandic word *heiminn*, *Nítíða saga* uses the Latinate present participle *leggjandi* and the less prosaic term *veröld*;[119] and where *Nikulás saga leikara* uses the native construction *þykist skynja*, *Nítíða saga* uses the borrowed verb *undirstanda*. Consequently, it is possible that *Nikulás saga leikara* was influenced by *Nítíða saga*, but was either written without adopting some of its learned stylistic features, or else these features have been eradicated in the course of the text's transmission.

The functions and properties of the *náttúrusteinar* are revealed to Nikulás by a mysterious helper figure, who also tells him that the stones 'eru so ägiæter griper ad önguer finnast þujlijker firer heidann hafid' (are such renowned treasures that nothing similar has been found on this side of the sea).[120] This is, again, reminiscent of Nítíða's assertion that in no place besides Visio might one find greater treasures. The interpretation continues, and the properties of the three coloured stones are listed:

> sä raudi steÿrnenn hefur þä nätturu, ef þu hefur hann ä þier j bardøgum þä fær þu sigur og alldrei verdur þier aflafätt vid huern sem þu ätt. og ei mä þier eitur granda og eÿnginn jll äløg meÿga ä þier hrÿna. enn su er nättura hinz bläa þier mä alldre kullde granda og ei ä sundi mædast ei

---

116 'Nitida saga', ed. by Loth, p. 6.

117 'Nitida saga', ed. by Loth, p. 6.

118 Wick, 'An Edition and Study of Nikulás saga Leikara', p. 245. In the longer redaction the magical mirror has three parts of three colours (p. 92). Wick interprets the vessel as a 'water-mirror' (p. 212).

119 This word is used especially with an ecclesiastical sense (Gudbrand Vigfusson, *An Icelandic-English Dictionary*, p. 699).

120 Wick, 'An Edition and Study of Nikulás saga Leikara', p. 94.

elld*ur* skada *og* eÿngin*n* fiølkÿnge. su er nätt*ur*a hinz græna steÿnsinz
ef þu lik*ur* han*n* j hendi þin*n*e þä mä eÿngin*n* siä *þig* hu*ar* sem þu ert
komen*n*. *og* þeÿm m*anni* lÿk*ur* ad allre skøpun er þu villt, *og* þeÿrar
kuin*n*u ast*er* fä er þü villt kiösa.[121]

(That red stone has the power that if you have it with you in battles,
then you will gain victory; and you will never become short of strength
whoever you are dealing with. And poison may not harm you, and no evil
spell may affect you. And this is the nature of the blue: cold may never
harm you, and you will not grow tired swimming. And fire will not scathe
you, and no magic. That is the nature of the green stone: if you enclose
it in your hand, then no one may see you wherever you have gone. And
you may adopt those human shapes for any destiny that you wish, and
obtain the love of those women whom you wish to choose.)

It is worth remembering that Nítíða's *náttúrusteinar* are not physically
described in any way, only that they are found in a vessel.[122] Such detailed
description and explanation in this text demonstrates a major difference
between *Nikulás saga leikara* and *Nítíða saga* in their use of the *náttúrusteinar* motif. While *Nikulás saga leikara* takes its time and includes
many details that might be seen as inessential (and in fact the whole scene
on the island with the stones lasts a number of pages in an edition), in
Nítíða saga the scene is narrated much more directly and concisely. Such a
dramatic difference could be explained by the fact that *Nitida saga* features
a specific, planned expedition, with the clear goal from the outset to find
supernatural stones, whereas by contrast in *Nikulás saga leikara* the stones
are found entirely by accident – the protagonist has no foreknowledge of
their existence and therefore no driving desire to seek them. The lengthy
episode features detail after detail, in an effort to heighten the tale's
sense of adventure and to make use of the fact that the audience has no
expectations as to what could happen next. The audience of *Nítíða saga*, in
contrast, has a sense of what the protagonist is looking for, and, in the most
basic sense, what could be expected from the episode. In her commentary,
Wick very briefly notes these parallels with *Nítíða saga*,[123] and also draws
attention to other similarities in passing, but without offering any thoughts
on how these similarities may have arisen. Despite these differences, the

121 Wick, 'An Edition and Study of Nikulás saga Leikara', pp. 94-95.
122 'Nitida saga', ed. by Loth, p. 6.
123 Wick, 'An Edition and Study of Nikulás saga Leikara', p. 213.

number of other similarities in the way the *náttúrusteinar* motif appears suggests that *Nikulás saga leikara*'s author took the basic structure from *Nítíða saga* and then elaborated on it to create a new and interesting, if lengthy, scene.

Conclusions

This chapter has only begun to uncover some of the intertextual relationships evident in *Nítíða saga*, from the texts like *Clári saga* that likely influenced its author, to those that may also have been influenced by it, such as *Nikulás saga leikara* and *Sigurðar saga þǫgla*. Teasing out the complex web of connections that these texts exhibit is a great task, but in this chapter I have been able to suggest some of the directions from which to begin, in presenting some of the more interesting relationships among these romances. I sought not definitively to explain *Nítíða saga*'s origin in the company of various other medieval Icelandic romances, but to understand how the text relates to certain others, in order to inform my discussions in this book's later chapters. *Clári saga*'s influence seems to have been key to the conception and development of *Nítíða saga* on a thematic level, as the latter's positive portrayal of women calls into question some of the themes and norms of romance that feature in *Clári saga*. While the relationship is clear, with these romances arguably composed in similar learned environments, in later versions of *Nítíða saga* preserved in paper manuscripts the connection to *Clári saga* becomes less pronounced, though the influence remains in basic respects like the bridal-quest and maiden-king motifs, and the intertextual dialogue evident in character names. Because *Nítíða saga* does not explicitly state the nature of of its relationship to *Clári saga* in the medieval manuscripts but rather plays off of the text, its genre classifications, and its themes, it is unsurprising that in later versions the connection between the two texts is obscured, if not lost completely, having been absorbed as an essential component of *Nítíða saga*'s fabric. In contrast, it seems that *Nikulás saga leikara*, while drawing on the themes, motifs, and vocabulary of *Nítíða saga* and other late medieval Icelandic romances, was written without some of the wider knowledge and book learning featuring in *Nítíða saga* and *Clári saga*, and evident in Latinate vocabulary, for example. The relationship between *Nikulás saga leikara* and *Nítíða saga* that was recognized by early audiences and in turn influenced the development of a version of *Nítíða saga* incorporating that detailed connection to the trickster protagonist of *Nikulás saga leikara* might even have contributed to the widespread popularity of both romances in paper copies during the centuries after the end of the Middle Ages.

What all of this suggests is that the intertextual relationships demonstrated in this chapter were present and important in *Nítíða saga* in the later Middle Ages when the text was first recorded and disseminated, and that they also played a significant part in the story's early development in differing manuscript versions. Knowledge of other Icelandic romances, and also of religious texts, seems to have shaped *Nítíða saga*'s characters, settings, and motifs, and most importantly situated the text within the literary landscape of not just Icelandic romance but also the hagiographic and other works of the almost certainly religious literary-cultural milieu in which the saga was produced and from which its author drew inspiration. Having first already discussed *Nítíða saga*'s many manuscript witnesses as evidence of its continued appreciation among Icelanders both during and after the Middle Ages in Chapter 1, and now in Chapter 2 having focused primarily on one textual witness in relation to some of the other romances enjoyed alongside it, I have so far presented mainly contextual information that will enrich the following primarily literary-analytical chapters. In the next chapter, the final one of this first part of the book, I will discuss *Nítíða saga*'s physical setting and the worldviews this exhibits – a final romance context. Through the lens of its portrayal of geography and space, I will consider how *Nítíða saga* maximizes certain similarities between Iceland and the rest of Europe and minimizes its differences to show how seamlessly the peripheral land and its people fit within Europe. I will consider the idea of Iceland becoming 'Europeanized' in its adoption, or appropriation, of a Continental form of literature (romance), taking as an example *Nítíða saga*'s uniquely Icelandic understanding of the world.

3   Setting the Scene

Geography and Space

Whereas in the previous two chapters I considered *Nítíða saga*'s manuscripts, scribes, and intertextual relationships, I now consider the saga's interest in geography and space, both of which contribute to the setting and atmosphere of the story. While I began outside of the text, looking at 'external contexts', I now move more closely to the text itself to see its 'internal contexts', but stopping short of analysing the characters, which is the subject of the second half of this book. Geography plays an important role in most medieval Icelandic romances – *Nítíða saga* is not unique in this respect – and this has long been recognized, for the Icelandic romances, practically by definition, are set away from Iceland, and away from Scandinavia. They have been defined as 'the group of sagas composed in Iceland from the late thirteenth or early fourteenth centuries onwards *which take place in an exotic (non-Scandinavian), vaguely chivalric milieu*, and are characterized by an extensive use of foreign motifs and a strong supernatural or fabulous element'.[1] Geraldine Barnes has recently discussed ways in which the Icelandic romances map these exotic romance worlds and the sources their authors drew on to do so.[2] In the past, it was partly these non-Icelandic settings that contributed to the neglect of Icelandic romances, some scholars seeing them as having little to do with Iceland.[3] But with settings reaching from Sweden to Syria and including fantastic locations such as *Nítíða saga*'s island of Visio, the geographical range presented in the Icelandic romances as a group is impressive, and by looking at the geography of romance we can consider how medieval Icelanders may have seen themselves in relation to the rest of the known world.[4] I will consider space on both a global level by looking at *Nítíða saga*'s unusual portrayal of world geography, and on a smaller scale by considering the much more typical separation of public and private space as it is represented in the text. I will first discuss how

---

1   Driscoll, 'Late Prose Fiction', p. 190, my italics.

2   Barnes, *The Bookish Riddarasögur*, pp. 31-76.

3   This is discussed in e.g. Driscoll, 'Late Prose Fiction', pp. 196-97; Kalinke, 'Norse Romances', pp. 317-17.

4   For overviews of medieval Scandinavian knowledge of geography see Simek, *Altnordische Kosmographie* (with editions of all the surviving Old Norse geographical liteature); and also Jakobson, 'Geographical Literature', p. 225; Jesch, 'Geography and Travel', pp. 119-35; Simek, 'Elusive Elysia', pp. 247-75.

Iceland views itself within Europe – insofar as 'Europe' is a useful concept when dealing with the Middle Ages – through the worldview of *Nítíða saga*. I will also consider the notion of Iceland's cultural colonization of medieval Europe through romance literature, and whether such interaction between Iceland and Europe displayed in *Nítíða saga* could be called Europeanization. Comparison with related Icelandic romances (*Clári saga, Dínus saga drambláta, Nikulás saga leikara,* and *Sigurðar saga þǫgla*) will also situate *Nítíða saga* in its literary environment, and showcase its unique developments alongside motifs and topoi incorporated from other texts, to build on our understanding of its intertextuality, which we began to consider in the previous chapter. After discussing the saga's descriptions of world geography, a detailed reading of the saga's construction of different categories of space will accompany more detailed discussions in studies of the three categories of places found in *Nítíða saga*. Before delving into the text, it will be useful first to define terms such as 'Europeanization' and 'Europe'.

Nítíða saga can be read as a text through which Icelandic society and culture enter into dialogue with the society and culture of medieval Europe. Bjørn Bandlien has used the term Europeanization in reference to the translated romances *Karlamagnús saga* and *Elis saga ok Rósamundu*. He notes that 'Although they are of French or Anglo-Norman origin, it seems promising to read these texts in their Norwegian and Icelandic setting with regard to a wider problem: the "Europeanization" of Scandinavia'.[5] This idea of Europeanization is appealing as a means to classify Scandinavian (including Icelandic) interaction with and reaction to the cultural and political developments of the European Continent, as seen through socio-cultural attitudes mediated through literature. By looking at the representation of geography in Icelandic romance, we are also looking at Icelandic appropriation and interpretation of the geography inherited from and mediated by European sources, to see how in *Nítíða saga* the author or scribe's aims to fulfil 'geographical desire' are achieved in crafting an image of the world separate and distinct from that of any of his or her sources.[6] My analyses focus not on potential sources of Icelandic writers' geographical knowledge – on that, see Barnes's recent monograph[7] – but on how world geography is variously portrayed in their texts. Silvia Tomasch's view that accurate geography is unattainable – 'Faced with irreconcilable demands

5   Bandlien, 'Muslims', p. 86.
6   Tomasch, 'Introduction', p. 2.
7   Barnes, *The Bookish Riddarasögur*.

and expectations of politics and ideality, a totally successful "writing of the world" is simply not possible' for modern (literary) historians of the Middle Ages[8] – can be said also of medieval writers of romance (and some of their post-medieval descendents), whose inclusion of geography and a set worldview necessarily reflects their own desires and ambitions, whether personal, cultural, nationalistic, or a combination of these, to assert themselves and their texts within medieval Europe.

It is easy to see how the idea of Europeanization applies to Bandlien's two examples – translated sagas with definite European sources – and to other translated romances undertaken during King Hákon Hákonarson's reign in thirteenth-century Norway. *Karlamagnús saga* 'consists of adaptations of ten different branches of the Charlemagne cycle [...] commonly presumed to have been translated independently in the thirteenth century, probably by Icelanders, [...] and then compiled into a long version as they are now preserved',[9] and some of its immediate sources are the *Chanson d'Aspremont, Chanson d'Otinel, La Chanson de Roland,* and *Le Pèlerinage de Charlemagne.*[10] *Elís saga ok Rósamundu,* however, 'derives from an incomplete version of the French *Elie de St. Gille,* translated by a certain Abbot Robert at the request of Hákon Hákonarson' and is one of the few romances to exist in a Norwegian manuscript (now at Uppsala, Universitetsbiblioteket, MS De La Gardie 4-7 fol., *c.* 1250), rather than only in Icelandic copies.[11] In order to engage with the rest of Europe, the Norwegian king sought to import influential and successful European literature, thereby taking measures to Europeanize his realm and appropriate European culture through chivalric, courtly literature.[12] That most of the translated romances exist today in Icelandic versions – almost exclusively[13] – speaks also to the notion of Europeanization on an even greater scale,[14] for Iceland was so much further removed from

---

8   Tomasch, 'Introduction', pp. 10-11.

9   Bandlien, 'Muslims', p. 86, and n. 2.

10   Kalinke and Mitchell, *Bibliography of Old Norse-Icelandic Romances,* p. 61.

11   Kalinke and Mitchell, *Bibliography of Old Norse-Icelandic Romances,* pp. 36-37.

12   Barnes, 'The *riddarasögur* and Mediæval European Literature', pp. 140-58; Bibire, 'From *riddarasaga* to *lygisaga*', pp. 56-58; Kalinke, 'Norse Romance (Riddararsögur)', pp. 320-22; McDougall, 'Foreigners and Foreign Languages in Medieval Iceland', esp. p. 233; Rasmussen, 'Translation in Medieval and Reformation Norway', pp. 629-45.

13   De La Gardie 4-7 fol., just mentioned, is the main manuscript of Norwegian provenance preserving four translated texts. There are many other Old Norse romances with known European sources existing in Icelandic manuscripts (see individual entries in Kalinke and Mitchell, *Bibliography of Old Norse–Icelandic Romances*).

14   Barnes, 'The *Riddarasögur*: A Medieval Exercise in Translation', pp. 403-41; Kalinke, 'Norse Romances', pp. 322, 332-33.

the European continent, if only geographically, than Norway. However, this mode of reading can be applied not only to sagas known to have been translated from Continental sources, but also to romances like *Nítíða saga*, composed by Icelanders. Whether translated or not, Icelandic romances are in active communication with other types of medieval romance, as a major form of entertainment in the later Middle Ages.[15] Because of their similarity, at least in genre, to stories from the Continent, the Icelandic romances also place themselves, and their authors, scribes, and audiences, in communication with the rest of Europe through literature. Just as in Europe, romance in Iceland throve.[16] While we cannot lump all forms of European medieval romance into a homogenous group with which to contrast romances from Iceland, broadly speaking, romances written in medieval France or Germany, for example, are rather more similar to each other than to their Scandinavian counterparts.[17] As only one of many examples of this, courtly love, which might be considered one of the defining characteristics of Continental romance in the Middle Ages,[18] is noticeably absent in both the Icelandic versions of Chrétien de Troyes, and the solely Icelandic compositions.[19] Bridal-quest and marriage define many Icelandic romances instead.[20]

Icelandic romance composition (just as much as other literary genres like history writing) works to situate Iceland within the late medieval European literary-cultural milieu. That Icelandic romances were well received and enjoyed by their audiences for many years after their original composition, as seen in Chapter 1, also demonstrates that Iceland's own popular literature could easily compete with imported romances.[21] Indeed, the Icelandic ro-

---

15   Heng, *Empire of Magic*; Kalinke, 'Norse Romance'; McDonald, 'A Polemical Introduction', pp. 1-21; Schlauch, *Romance in Iceland*, p. 3.

16   Driscoll, 'Late Prose Fiction', pp. 348-49.

17   Krueger, 'Introduction', pp. 1-9. The fact that this introductory volume excludes Scandinavian romance is enough to demonstrate its conception as belonging outside of medieval Europe, and to reinforce the homogeneity (whether justified or not) of romance from various other European vernaculars.

18   Krueger, 'Introduction', pp. 2-5.

19   Sif Rikhardsdottir deals with such differences in style and content through examples from *Yvain* and its Norse translation in *Medieval Translations and Cultural Discourse*, pp. 76-112. Other chapters looking at Norse translations of Marie de France's *lais* and the Middle English *Partonope of Blois* are also illuminating in this context. On translations see also Kalinke, 'Scribe, Redactor, Author'.

20   Kalinke, *Bridal-Quest Romance*; Kalinke, *King Arthur*. See also the discussion of depictions of love in Icelandic romance in Sävborg, *Sagan om kärleken*, pp. 558-89.

21   The Arthurian romances are the best example of imported popular literature in Iceland; even while Icelandic versions exist in many manuscripts, there are more indigenous non-Arthurian

mances survived much better than the translated ones.[22] Icelandic romance provided a popular literature suitable for comparison with that of other places such as England, where popular romance often functioned as a means of affirming national identity and national mythologies surrounding the country and its rulers.[23] In Geraldine Heng's words, 'romance is, in fact, a genre of the nation: a genre *about* the nation and for the nation's important fictions'.[24] One can argue that it is similar in Iceland, with romance acting as an expression of a type of elite late medieval Icelandic identity. There is little doubt that in composing romances, Icelanders actively engaged with the ideas about identity found in European romance, and evaluated themselves in relation to it, to create a literature distinct from that of Continental origin. Despite this, European influence is evident in most Icelandic romances, even in those not directly translated. Motifs and plots were borrowed and adapted,[25] and the romance form itself is imported, considering the saga types of the earlier Middle Ages,[26] which were long understood as more or less historically aware, if not factually accurate.[27] In modifying traditional elements of European romance,[28] Icelanders interacted and engaged with Continental literature without slavishly copying foreign style, which was instead adapted to a distinctly Icelandic taste; Icelandic authors could not but recognize their land's place in the world and see how that made them different.

I must briefly consider the usefulness of the term 'Europe' when speaking of the Middle Ages. Whereas some medieval Icelandic romances use 'Europe' to refer to roughly what it is today, that is, the part of the world that

---

romances that survive, demonstrating that in the end, Icelanders preferred romances of their own devising. See Kalinke, *King Arthur*; Sif Rikhardsdottir, *Medieval Translations and Cultural Discourse*.

22 Hall and Parsons, 'Making Stemmas', figs. 2, 3.

23 Heng, *Empire of Magic*, pp. 63-114; Speed, 'The Construction of the Nation in Middle English Romance', pp. 135-57; Stein, 'Making History English', pp. 97-115.

24 Heng, *Empire of Magic*, p. 113; italics original.

25 Barnes, 'Romance in Iceland', pp. 273-74; Kalinke, 'Old Norse-Icelandic Literature, Foreign Influence On', pp. 451-54; Kalinke, 'Norse Romances', pp. 348-49. Consider e.g. the faithful lion motif from Chrétien de Troyes' *Yvain*, which appears in Icelandic romances including *Sigurðar saga þögla* (see Kalinke, *King Arthur*, pp. 220-39; Boberg, *Motif-Index of Early Icelandic Literature*, B301.8 'Faithful lion follows man who saved him', B431.2 'Helpful lion', B520 'Animals save person's life' [pp. 47-48]; Barnes, 'The *riddarasögur* and Mediæval European Literature', pp. 140-58; Schlauch, p. 167).

26 Bibire, 'From *riddarasaga* to *lygisaga*', pp. 58-59.

27 Vésteinn Ólason, 'The Icelandic Saga as a Kind of Literature', pp. 27-48; Jones, 'History and Fiction in the Sagas of Icelanders', pp. 285-306. See also Chapter 6.

28 Kalinke, 'Old Norse-Icelandic Literature, Foreign Influence On', p. 453.

is neither Africa nor Asia (or the Americas),[29] might not 'Christendom' be a better designator for this region during the time in question? Christianity after all, though by no means uniform throughout the areas it reached, was perhaps the sole unifying cultural influence across such vast geographical regions. Covering diverse ethnic and linguistic groups, medieval Europe arguably stretched only as far as Christianity's influence. Christendom thus might seem a more appropriate place name than Europe, but what then of the idea of 'Europeanization'? This term does not share the same relationship with 'Christianization' as does Europe with Christendom; it would be an entirely different thing to speak of the Christianization, that is, the conversion, of Iceland. It is primarily for this reason that I prefer instead to use 'Europeanization' and 'Europe' here, while also sometimes using 'Europe' and 'Christendom' interchangeably. As the place name *Europe* was certainly known in medieval Iceland,[30] it does not seem anachronistic to me to speak of late medieval Iceland's place in and conceptualization of Europe.

While Iceland lay on the fringes of the world (as defined according to medieval European geography), a fact of which Icelanders were aware, their understanding of their marginality also necessitated an understanding of the world's centre. Culturally and politically, this was in Continental Europe; spiritually, it was in Jerusalem (or Byzantium).[31] Sverrir Jakobsson notes that 'Icelanders appropriated a world view that entailed that their own society was a marginal and peripheral one', rather than that 'of an isolated culture, as traditionally defined by anthropologists', in which marginal 'cultures tend to view themselves as the centre of the world'.[32] Thus not only do Icelanders know where they stand in relation to the 'centres', but they also recognize the part they play in the world's 'centres'. We see Icelandic interaction with Europe not merely through contact with European culture and ideas following the settlement of Iceland,[33] but in settlement itself and the subsequent literary tradition that aimed to record it[34] – recognition and remembrance of where their ancestors came from and where those places

29   Hamilton, 'The Lands of Prester John', p. 128.

30   The world is divided into three parts including Europe, in e.g. *Snorra Edda*, p. 4; *Clári saga*, p. 3; and *Dínus saga drambláta*, p. 3. See also Barnes, *The Bookish Riddarasögur*.

31   Akbari, 'From Due East to True North', pp. 19-34; Barnes, 'Byzantium', pp. 92-98; Higgins, 'Defining the Earth's Center in a Medieval "Multi-Text"', pp. 29-53.

32   Sverrir Jakobsson, 'Centre and Periphery in Icelandic Medieval Discourse', p. 918.

33   Amory, 'Things Greek and the *riddararsögur*', pp. 509-23; Barnes, 'Byzantium'; Sigfús Blöndal, *The Varangians of Byzantium*.

34   The main sources for the settlement of Iceland are *Landnámabók* and Ari Þorgilson's *Íslendingabók*, both composed in the twelfth century, along with episodes in some later *Íslendingasögur*, such as *Laxdœla saga*.

fit in the wider world. Further, we must not forget later pilgrimages from Iceland to the centres of Christianity.[35] Iceland could not easily, as a part of Christendom, be too isolated from the rest of that pan-European community, and with a worldview locating itself within Europe–Christendom, no matter how far on the edge, Iceland considered itself in dynamic dialogue and exchange with the world's centre. In considering these questions of 'Europeanization', worldview, religion, centre and periphery, and Iceland's place compared with other known localities, medieval Icelandic romance is certainly involved in the idea of 'the Europeanization of Scandinavia', which is raised in these texts. *Nítíða saga* is an especially active agent in these questions; it both prompts their debate in the sagas and is influenced by them in a reciprocal relationship between society and text, and culture and literature. I will develop this in the sections below, examining this romance's perspective on Iceland's place in Europe, and keeping in mind especially questions of Europeanization and cultural colonization through literature. After considering *Nítíða saga*'s descriptions of geography and travel in both real and imagined spaces, that is, images of global space, and what they mean in view of Iceland's geographical and political position in the late medieval world, I will also analyse the saga's depiction of space along a public-private continuum in three case studies of real and imagined places.

Global Space

Nítíða saga names thirty-one different places, which can be divided into three categories: 1) places understood to be real and which are relatively easy for modern readers to identify, 2) places understood to be real and which could be more difficult for modern readers to identify, and 3) places understood to be fantastic or unrealistic – imagined or magical locations – which are almost impossible for modern readers to identify. The first group is by far the largest, containing twenty-five locations; the second group has four; and the third group just two. I will begin this section with an overview of these places in *Nítíða saga*, followed by a brief discussion of what the saga excludes from its geography, before looking in some depth at an example of one location from each of the three groups of places in order to see how *Nítíða saga* depicts each type of location, and what this suggests about late medieval Icelanders' views about the world and their

35   Sverrir Jakobsson, 'Centre and Periphery', pp. 920-22.

place in it. Although, as mentioned in the introduction, little work has been
carried out specifically on *Nítíða saga*, Geraldine Barnes has written on
the saga's geography, interpreting the text as a 'cosmographical comedy'
centred on a struggle for power between East and West,[36] and further, as
a text whose particular geographical awareness results in a reconfiguring
of the traditional medieval cartography seen in other medieval Icelandic
romances and the encyclopaedic sources they drew on.[37] Ármann Jakobsson
has also recently discussed the saga's geography, but paints a more negative
picture of the global view represented in *Nítíða saga*, dismissing it as largely
unrealistic and therefore typical of late medieval Icelandic romances.[38] I will
consider and challenge these views in the discussions that follow.

The most significant episode demonstrating the geographical worldview
of the saga occurs in what can be called the seeing-stones scene, when Nítíða
shows Livorius her *náttúrusteinar* (supernatural stones). I have discussed
this already in relation to the different versions of the text in Chapter 1,
and as part of an important motif in Chapter 2, but I will now consider its
significance in greater detail. On three occasions, Nítíða shows Livorius
(alias Eskilvarður) three global regions in her *náttúrusteinar*. The first
time, 'meÿkongur took upp stein og bad hann j lyta, hann sä þa yffer allt
Frackland, Provintiam, Ravenam, Spaniam, Hallitiam, Friisland, Flandren,
Nordmandiam, Skottland, Grickland, og allar þær þiooder þar biggia' (The
maiden-king took up a stone and asked him to look in it. Then he saw over
all France, Provence, Ravenna, Spain, Galicia,[39] Frisia, Flanders, Normandy,
Scotland, Greece, and all the peoples who live there).[40] The second time,
'Drottning bad Eskil(vard) enn lyta j steinninn. þa sau þau nordur aalffuna alla, Noreg, Ysland, Færeÿar, Sudureyar, Orkneÿar, Svijþiod, Danmork,
Eingland, Ÿrland, og morg lond onnur, þau er hann visse eÿ skil a' (The queen
asked Eskilvarður to look into the stone. Then they saw all the northern
region, Norway, Iceland, the Faeroes, the Hebrides, the Orkneys, Sweden,
Denmark, England, Ireland, and many other lands, which he did not know
of).[41] The third time, 'meÿkongr vindur upp enn eirn stein, siande þa nu
austur aalffuna heimsins, Jndialand, Palestinam, Asiam, Serkland, og oll

36 Barnes, 'Margin vs. Centre', pp. 104-12. See also Barnes, 'Travel and *translatio studii*', pp.
138-39.
37 Barnes, *The Bookish Riddarasögur*, pp. 35-40; Barnes, 'Romance in Iceland', p. 272.
38 Ármann Jakobsson, *Illa fenginn mjöður*, p. 177.
39 See Chapter 1, as well as McDonald, 'Variance Uncovered', pp. 313-14.
40 'Nitida saga', ed. by Loth, p. 30. See Chapter 1 for the differences in JS 166 fol. in this and the
following two quotations.
41 'Nitida saga', ed. by Loth, p. 30.

onnur lond heimsins, og jafnvel umm bruna bellted, þad sem eÿ er bigt' (The maiden-king lifted up a stone, seeing then the eastern region of the world, India, Palestine, Asia, *Serkland,* and all other lands in the world, and also the burning-belt, which is uninhabited).[42] As touched on in Chapter 2, it is clear from these quotations and the details they include that Nítíða sometimes has, by means of her *náttúrusteinar,* panoptic vision. Nítíða's panoptic views of the world around her can also characterize her as participating in the often masculine-associated idea of the gaze. It is the act of looking and the knowledge this imparts on Nítíða that gives her power over her suitors and allows her to outwit them again and again. However, the people she views are, significantly, unaware of being watched and so cannot consider themselves objectified, as noted in Chapter 2. This of course changes when she shares the view from her magic stones here with Livorius, who by the end of the scene has realized his own powerlessness against her.[43] Nítíða can monitor the world as far as the stones allow her to see, and she can use this power to search for and locate anyone or anything she wants; indeed, in this scene Nítíða is ostensibly searching for Livorius, using the supernatural stones as a tool to do so. In this succession of quotations, the division of the world into three regions does not, however, correspond to the traditional medieval European tripartite division of the world into thirds consisting of Europe, Asia, and Africa,[44] a global configuration also often represented graphically by what has come to be known as a T–O Map, illustrated in Figure 4.[45]

Having an eastern orientation, T–O maps, with all land encircled by the ocean, usually placed Jerusalem at the centre of the world;[46] Asia in the east

42 'Nitida saga', ed. by Loth, p. 31.

43 For studies of the gaze in Old Norse literature see Jochens, 'Before the Male Gaze', pp. 3-29; and Larrington, '"What Does Woman Want?"', pp. 3-16. For comparison with Middle English literature see Mills, 'Seeing Face to Face', pp. 117-36.

44 Akbari, pp. 19-34; Harrison, *Medieval Space,* p. 4; Simek, *Altnordische Kosmographie,* pp. 37-43; Simek, *Heaven and Earth in the Middle Ages,* pp. 44-48; Woodward, 'Reality, Symbolism, Time, and Space in Medieval World Maps', pp. 510-21. Certainly this division is known and preserved in many Icelandic texts, including romances like *Dínus saga dramblátá,* which drew on Isidore of Seville's encyclopaedia (Barnes, *The Bookish Riddarasögur,* p. 31 ff).

45 The concept for the T–O *mappae mundi* was first introduced by Isidore of Seville in his *De natura rerum.* In Book 48, 'De partibus terrae' (Concerning the divisions of the earth), the world is divided into Europe, Asia, and Africa (*Traité de la nature,* pp. 324-27 [p. 325]).

46 Simek, *Altnordische Kosmographie,* pp. 37-43, 297-98; Simek, *Heaven and Earth in the Middle Ages,* pp. 44-48, 73-81; in *De natura rerum* Isidore does not make Jerusalem the centre of the world, but in the *Etymologies* XIV.iii.21, in his description of Palestine, he notes that Jerusalem is in the middle of Judea, 'quasi umbilicus regionis totius' (as it were the navel of the whole region) (*Isidori Hispalensis episcopi etymologiarum,* ed. by Lindsay, II, p. H5v; translation from

Figure 4   T–O Map

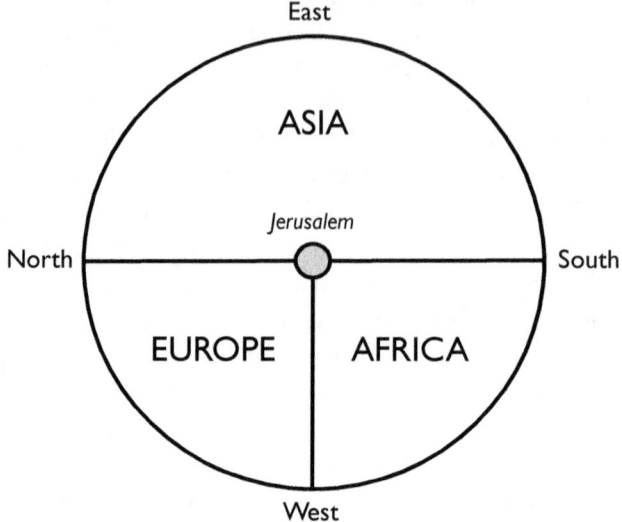

was divided from Europe in the north by the Tanais River (the Don), and from Africa in the south by the Nile; Europe and Africa were divided by the Mediterranean Sea.[47] In *Nítíða saga*, instead of this type of configuration, the first quotation showcases what could be called 'predominantly Latin Europe',[48] common to standard T–O maps, despite not being explicitly named. The second quotation presents the North (*nordur aalffuna alla*).[49] Considering the places specifically named, there is not really a better designation for this region, unless one wanted to call it 'Scandinavia', though this is not entirely appropriate as it includes England and Ireland. However, the presence of these places in some *Íslendingasögur* and *fornaldarsögur*, in a Viking Age context suggests that England and Ireland are in fact part of a wider Scandinavia than is recognized by that name today. 'The North' seems to be the most appropriate name for the region, as it easily encompasses both Scandinavia and the British Isles. The third quotation displays the East

The Etymologies of Isidore, trans. by Barney, p. 287). Woodward questions the notion that most medieval maps centred on Jerusalem throughout the Middle Ages (pp. 515-17).

47   Simek, *Altnordische Kosmographie*, pp. 37-43; Simek, *Heaven and Earth in the Middle Ages*, pp. 44-46; Woodward, p. 511.

48   Barnes, 'Margin vs. Centre', p. 110. See also Barnes, *The Bookish Riddarasögur*, p. 38.

49   On what is meant by *norður* and other directions in Old Norse, see Lindow, 'The Social Semantics of Cardinal Directions in Medieval Scandinavia', pp. 209-24; and Wanner, 'Off-Center', pp. 36-72.

(*austur aalffuna heimsins*), and what could otherwise be called Asia. Thus in *Nítíða saga* three slightly unconventional world regions are portrayed: Europe is divided into the Continent and the Northern, with Asia as the third region. Generally speaking, the naming of locations radiates outwards from France, reinforcing its position in the centre, which is explicitly stated at the beginning of the text: Nítíða 'sat j aunduegi heimsins j Fracklandi jnu goda og hiellt Páris borg' (sat on the throne of the world in France the Good, and ruled in Paris).[50]

In addition to the locations named here, elsewhere the saga mentions *Púl*, *Smáland* (both more or less equivalent with the modern regions of Apulia in Italy and Småland in Sweden, respectively), the island *Kartagia* (either Cartagena on the southern Spanish coast or Carthage on the North African coast[51]), *Mundia* (the Alps), and the somewhat indeterminate locations of *Svíþjóð hin kalda* (which I distinguish from *Svíþjóð* [Sweden]),[52] *Visio*, and *Skóga blómi*, an island within a lake on Visio. The Latinate character of many of these names is particularly interesting, as I have touched on briefly in the previous chapters: *Asia*, *Hallitia*, *Norðmandia*, *Proventia*, and *Spania*, exhibit Latin rather than Icelandic grammar (declining as accusative first declension nouns). At least in some cases, it seems likely that the author or scribe deliberately Latinized vernacular words by adding the -*am* ending, perhaps to show off. However, in other versions of *Nítíða saga*, the Latinate character of these place names is not preserved, such as in the manuscripts originating in the Dales and Westfjords of Iceland (e.g. JS 166). Some eighteenth-century manuscripts containing a different version of the story do retain the Latin endings for some place names (e.g. for *Asia*, *India*, and *Gaskonia*), while other locations (e.g. [*Hi*]*spania* and *Proventia*) are not mentioned at all. Other manuscripts such as the closely related JS 27 and Add. 4860 even add other place names to the list (e.g. *Gallia* 'Gaul'), while also substituting *Normandi* for *Norðmandia*. Interestingly, a small group of nineteenth-century manuscripts also preserve many Latinate endings, even when the place names themselves have become garbled, as in, for example, *Vardonia* (ultimately from *Gasconia*, via *Vasconia*) and *Pístilia* (ultimately from *Palestina*) both in the manuscript Reykjavík, Stofnun Árna Magnússonar í íslenskum fræðum, MS SÁM 13 (1851). Still others (including but not limited to the manuscripts from the Eastfjords of Iceland) leave

50   'Nitida saga', ed. by Loth, p. 3.
51   Barnes, 'Margin vs. Centre', p. 108.
52   *Svíþjóð hin kalda* may be the same as *Svíþjóð hin mikla*, that is, the region west of the Volga, explored by predominantely Swedish Vikings. See also n. 80 below.

off place names at this point in the text altogether, as noted in Chapter 1. Overall it seems that with the exception of SÁM 13 and related manuscripts, when *Nítíða saga* was preserved in later centuries, and perhaps especially in the east of Iceland, the text could be said to become more Icelandic, losing some of the learned prestige associated with the Latin form of some names, whereas when the saga was preserved in a handful of eighteenth- and nineteenth-century manuscripts, these characteristics, while likely no longer indicative of the prestige of the author or scribe, were kept as an original feature of the text, evidently important to those transmitting it.

However, what is strikingly missing from the edited version in this geographical episode quoted above is any reference to the Southern (or Western) regions of the world, and to Africa in particular, which, as already mentioned, would be an expected part of the world together with Europe and Asia, especially in T–O maps.[53] Of course, *Nítíða saga* makes passing reference to 'oll onnur lond heimsins, og jafnvel umm bruna bellted, þad sem eÿ er bigt', but it seems clear that no particular location is here implied, the narrator quickly passing it over without any elaboration at the most opportune time in the saga to demonstrate geographical knowledge. And while it is also true that *blámenn* ('blue-men' or 'black-men', a term usually denoting evil or barbarous people) make an appearance in King Soldán's army,[54] this does not necessarily place his kingdom Serkland anywhere in Africa;[55] on the contrary, the romance specifically situates it in the eastern part of the world. Further, this version of *Nítíða saga* mentions neither *Bláland* nor *Affrika*, and makes no comment on any aspect of Soldán's appearance.[56] It seems logical to see *blámenn* in particular making up only a small contingent of Serkland's army, and that it is for this reason that they are mentioned at all at this point in the story. Serkland, as I discuss below, seems best understood as an eastern, but still indeterminate, land

53   On Africa as a western land in Icelandic romance, see 'Vilhjálms saga sjóðs', ed. by Loth, pp. 3, 41.

54   *Nikulás saga leikara* refers to *blámenn* as enemies of the Christians in Constantinople; Wick consistently renders the term as 'Moor' in her translation ('An Edition and Study of Nikulás saga Leikara', p. 219), potentially indicating African origin. Blue-land and blue-people also appear in some Middle English romances. See Kelly, 'Blue Indians, Ethiopians, and Saracens in Middle English Narrative Texts', pp. 35-52.

55   The proper name *Soldán*, does mean 'Sultan', i.e. a Muslim emperor, and so could have carried with it associations with Africa. As early as in the thirteenth-century *Sverris saga*, the title character's maternal uncle is called Nikolás *sultan*, possibly because he served in a crusade (*Sverris saga*, p. 150).

56   See Chapter 5 for a discussion of the characters from Serkland and of Soldán's son's description.

inhabited by Saracens. Finally, even if the island Kartagia, mentioned above, does refer to Carthage, the fact that it is not specifically located in any particular region of the world means that it is not *necessarily* to be associated with Africa. General ignorance of Africa on the part of the author seems unlikely, not only considering his awareness of so many other world regions, but also considering that many other Icelandic romances, and especially those I compare with *Nítíða saga* below, mention Africa. The geographical picture that the saga paints thus comes across distinctly as a shifted version of traditional medieval cosmography. Instead of the T–O map we (and at least some of medieval Icelandic readers of romance) are accustomed to, we can here visualize the world described in *Nítíða saga* with Africa pushed off the map and a separate northern region added, with Paris supplanting Jerusalem at the centre, as illustrated in Figure 5.[57] As Barnes writes, 'This upending of medieval geographical conventions through the medium of fantasy invites its audience to rethink the implied equation between geographical distance and cultural inferiority',[58] moving Iceland closer to the world's centre and deliberately ignoring other areas of the known world.

In direct contrast to this, the romance *Dínus saga dramblata* is set exclusively in the Africa that *Nítíða saga* lacks, and two distinct kingdoms – Dínus's Egypt and Philotemia's Bláland (which may refer to Ethiopia) – are not only named, but comprise the story's main settings. In this saga, some twenty place names appear, almost all of them located in Africa and what would today be called the Middle East. No European countries are named, in a direct reversal of *Nítíða saga*'s geography. From the beginning of *Dínus saga dramblata*, we see the world divided into its traditional medieval thirds, before situating the action in Egypt: 'heiminum sie skifft j þria hlute edur parta, og heiter hinn firste sudur Hasia, enn hinn vestre Affricha, enn nordur älfann er kóllud Euröpä' (the world may be divided into three parts or divisions, and the first, in the south, is called Asia, and the west Africa, and the northern region is called Europe).[59] In the saga's first words, the reader perceives the author's knowledge of traditional medieval geography, different from the geographical reorganization evident in *Nítíða saga*. Furthermore, Paradise is located in Africa (again, according to medieval

---

57 Thanks to Werner Schäfke for suggesting the possibility of viewing the saga's geography as a variation of the traditional T–O map. The suggestion arose in discussing an early draft of this chapter, which I presented in 2009 at the International Medieval Congress in Leeds (UK).
58 Barnes, *The Bookish Riddarasögur*, p. 40.
59 *Dínus saga dramblata*, ed. by Jónas Kristjánsson, p. 3.

Figure 5   Alternative T–O Map

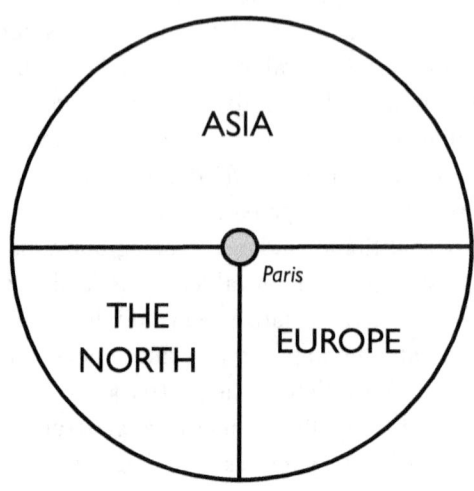

convention),[60] which, we are told, has 'og ein aa, su er Nijl heitier, ein aff þeim Paradijsar äm' (also a river, which is called the Nile, one of the rivers of Paradise),[61] in opposition to *Nítíða saga*'s localization of Visio in the far north, if Visio is considered a type of Earthly Paradise (see below). Bláland is introduced as the home of 'miog jøtnar jmissliger og blaamen bannsetter, og allskins skiesseligar skiepnur' (many different giants and cursed blue people, and all monstrous creatures), yet despite this, the realm is ruled by a king who is introduced and described in the same way as any other romance character.[62] This may be evidence of a conventional association for Africa (or at least Bláland) meeting and mixing with *Dínus saga drambláta*'s unique incorporation of African lands into the main plot on a par with traditional Icelandic romance settings, like France.[63]

As another example, *Sigurðar saga þǫgla* contains over forty geographical references – many more than *Nítíða saga* – and among these, as in *Dínus saga drambláta*, are references to Africa. The saga speaks of princes 'vtan

---

60 Relaño, 'Paradise in Africa', pp. 1-11.
61 *Dínus saga drambláta*, ed. by Jónas Kristjánsson, pp. 3-4.
62 *Dínus saga drambláta*, ed. by Jónas Kristjánsson, p. 11.
63 For further analysis of *Dínus saga drambláta* see some of the only literary scholarship on the romance in Barnes, *The Bookish Riddarasögur*, pp. 53-66 and *passim*; and Barnes, 'Cognitive Dysfunction in *Dínus saga drambláta* and *Le Roman de Perceval*', pp. 53-63.

af Affrica ʀiki' (from the kingdom of Africa),[64] and of Bláland.[65] Overall, the geographical distribution of locations named in *Sigurðar saga þǫgla* concentrates on Europe, with fewer in Asia, and the least in Africa. As noted in Chapter 2, the saga's maiden-king Sedentiana possesses magic stones in which she can see over the world, like Nítíða. Additionally, her 'alfu heimsins' (region of the world) is, like Nítíða's, Europe – and specifically France – but there is much less focus on the North in *Sigurðar saga þǫgla* than in *Nítíða saga*.[66] Instead, the saga is set, at the beginning, within the context of another romance mainly taking place in 'Kaldealande ur hinne miklu Babilon' (Chaldea in Greater Babylon);[67] and it is set, at the end, within the context of early medieval European history. In the saga's long prologue, background information connects *Sigurðar saga þǫgla* to *Flóres saga ok Blankiflúr* – or to the French original *Floire et Blancheflor* – casting Sedentiana as the daughter of the earlier text's eponymous characters.[68] Situating the maiden-king in a wider textual and historical setting suggests the importance of Christianity among the community from which the saga emerged. This romance's world is Christendom, the same Christendom, more or less, as that in which it was composed.[69] Furthermore, in *Sigurðar saga þǫgla* the world is not divided into any number of regions, as it is in *Nítíða saga* and *Dínus saga dramblátá*. Rather, the various places are mentioned throughout the text, often only in passing. The tripartite division of the world can be seen as evidence of the learned environment from which those romances showing that worldview emerge; the absence of such a device for organizing and understanding geography in *Sigurðar saga þǫgla* suggests that perhaps its author was less well educated or did not understand the medieval order of the world as well as other authors. The author or compiler of the longer redaction of *Sigurðar saga þǫgla* is known for his almost indiscriminate eclecticism,[70] and it would not be unlikely for this great number of geographical references combined with the ignorance of the Asia–Africa–Europe division of the world thus to be the product

64 'Sigurðar saga þǫgla', ed. by Loth, p. 193.
65 'Sigurðar saga þǫgla', ed. by Loth, p. 175.
66 'Sigurðar saga þǫgla', ed. by Loth, p. 182.
67 'Sigurðar saga þǫgla', ed. by Loth, pp. 101-02.
68 'Sigurðar saga þǫgla', ed. by Loth, pp. 101-02.
69 Likewise, towards the end of the text, reference is also made to the Christianization of France in order to root the saga in history: 'æ dǫgum Constantini keisara og Flouenz er kristnade Frackland og frelsade unndan heidingia valldi' (in the days of Emperor Constantine and Flóvent who converted France to Christianity and freed it from heathen power) ('Sigurðar saga þǫgla', ed. by Loth, pp. 228-29).
70 *Sigurðar saga þǫgla*, ed. by Driscoll, pp. xcviii-cxx.

simply of an insatiable desire to expand and compile plot lines, motifs, and allusions, from diverse sources. In *Sigurðar saga þǫgla*, geography appears not to situate the story, its writer, or its readers in Europe or elsewhere, but mainly functions as a display of knowledge, and perhaps only superficial knowledge at that.

In contrast to the wide-reaching array of geographical locations in *Nítíða saga* and *Sigurðar saga þǫgla*, *Clári saga* names only six places. The protagonist Clárus comes from Saxland in Europe, his teacher Pérus is from Arábía (also called Arábíaland), and Séréna is the princess of Frakkland (also called Frannz). In addition to these, *Clári saga* mentions Bláland, the homeland of Clárus's alter ego Eskelvarður, and, in passing, Erópa. Similarly, *Nikulás saga leikara* makes relatively few geographical references. The protagonist's homeland of Hungary is featured, as is that of the princess Dorma and her father Valdimar of Constantinople. From the beginning, the introduction of the king draws attention to both the geography of his and surrounding kingdoms and the integration of Christianity throughout the region: 'ha*nn* var r*ÿ*k*ur* miøg *og* vel christi*nn og* øll lønd fir*er* norda*nn* gricklandz haf' (He was very rich, and a good Christian, as were all lands north of the Mediterranean Sea).[71] Yet the Hungarian kingdom is never affiliated with any religion. Nikulás also travels to an unnamed island off the coast of Britain, and more specific Byzantine locations are named – *Gullborg* (most likely the *Porta Aurea* [Golden Gate], the southernmost fortification on Constantinople's western wall and the city's main ceremonial entrance) and *Stolpasund* (the Golden Horn, or possibly the Diplokionion,[72] an important harbour on the southeastern side of Constantinople, across from the Golden Horn). Both of these references suggest some sort of local knowledge of the city from the author's source material. Paris and France are also mentioned, but only as the saga's source (see Chapter 6). However, *Nikulás saga leikara* makes no mention of Africa, nor of much of Europe; there are no references

---

71 Wick, 'An Edition and Study of Nikulás saga Leikara', p. 64.

72 This harbour takes its name from Greek *diplokione* (double pillar); Old Norse *stólpasund* (channel of pillars) may be a direct translation, particularly as Old Norse *sund*, in addition to 'channel', can also mean 'narrow entrance', such as that of a harbour. In the context of this saga the name clearly does not refer to the Pillars of Hercules (Straits of Gibraltar), as *Stólpasund* is sometimes interpreted. The name also appears in a late medieval exemplum that Gering calls *Af Rómverska dáranum* (Of Roman Tricks), clearly referring to a harbour in Constantinople: 'til Miklagarðs kemur hann ok leggr í Stólpasund nærri keisarans bryggju' (to Constantinople he comes and puts into *Stólpasund* near the emperor's pier) (Gering, ed., *Íslendzk æventýri*, I, pp. 239-44 [p. 240]). This was later retold by Þorkell Pálsson in the eighteenth century as *Ríma af Rómverskum narra* (Rhymes of Roman Tricks), surviving in at least eight manuscripts. Thanks to Shaun Hughes for these references.

to Northern Europe, Scandinavia, or Iceland. I have already, in Chapter 2, highlighted the similarity to *Nítíða saga* in *Nikulás saga leikara*'s use of Britain as a marker for the fantastic North, in parallel to *Nítíða saga*'s Sweden the Cold as a marker on the way to the fantastic island Visio, and concluded that this demonstrates *Nikulás saga leikara*'s author's attempt to emulate *Nítíða saga*. *Nikulás saga leikara*, like *Clári saga*, is not as concerned with using geography to map worldviews or to address questions of belonging and identity, or even of showing off a scribe's learning, in the way that *Nítíða saga* is, along with *Sigurðar saga þǫgla* and *Dínus saga drambláta*. Instead of using geography to set its scenes, *Nikulás saga leikara* seems more concerned with conveying meaning through the depiction of religion, both implicitly as in the quotation just mentioned and explicitly in the portrayal of Christian triumph over non-Christian adversaries.[73]

Of course it is by no means essential for a scribe or especially a reader to know the precise, real location of any of the places a romance mentions; the more important question is, rather, *why* so many (or in some cases so few) place names are included in these texts. The displays of geography serve different functions in different texts (a scribe or author showing off in *Sigurðar saga þǫgla* as opposed to perhaps a scribe wanting to create a realistic setting in *Dínus saga drambláta* by focusing on local African geography), and provide interesting contrasts with that in *Nítíða saga*, with its scribe or author's interest in demonstrating the proximity of Iceland to the rest of Europe. Having considered the overall cosmographical worldview of this romance and compared it to those of related texts, I will now delve deeper into examples of the three different types of places that *Nítíða saga*'s geography encompasses.

---

73 Christianity and its heathen opposition are quite unselfconsciously incorporated into the text, and it is Nikulás (from religiously neutral Hungary) who showcases this rather than Christian Valdimar or anyone else from Constantinople. In a dramatic and religiously elaborate exorcism scene, Nikulás (disguised as the merchant Þórir) calls on God to free a Christian princess from a heathen *blámaðr*: 'nu skulum vier kalla ä nafn gudz. og bidia þess ad hann veÿte þeÿm riddara nockra hiälp og huggan. enn þessi skeÿti er vÿgd af .5. Biskupum. [...] þä tök þórer kaupmadur bogann, [...] og signdi sig j nafne heÿlagra þrennÿngar, hann gi ørdi kross firer øruaroddinum. og nu bendi hann bogann, og mællte nu skÿt eg ør þessare j nafne faudur og sonar og heilags anda. hann saung vers ÿr däuÿdz psalltara ä medann ørinn var ä flugenne' ('Now we shall call on God's name, and ask this that he offer the knight some help and comfort. And this arrow is blessed by five bishops'. [...] Then Þórir the merchant took the bow, [...] and signed himself in the name of the Holy Trinity. He made a cross over the arrow's point, and now he bent the bow, and said, 'Now I shoot this arrow in the name of the Father, and Son and Holy spirit'. He sang a verse out of David's psalms while the arrow was in flight) (Wick, 'An Edition and Study of Nikulás saga Leikara', pp. 116-17). In the end, these measures are successful, and praises to God follow, marking the epitome of the presence of Christianity in the text.

Social Space

Looking at geography has shown how space is conceptualized on a global scale in *Nítíða saga*, but the text also organizes space on a much smaller scale, in terms of social use within various settings. Space on this smaller scale can be classified primarily in terms of its social function as either public or private, and it is also possible to identify public and private space as predominantly (though not exclusively) masculine and feminine gendered spaces, respectively.[74] Depending on the focus of interpretation, space may also be considered in terms of physical location and natural surroundings – indoor (e.g. halls) versus outdoor (e.g. gardens), or in terms of architectural versus natural space. Perhaps surprisingly, considering the importance given to geography in *Nítíða saga*, dividing space in terms of the familiar versus the foreign (such as domestic France versus exotic India or Constantinople) is not a productive line of enquiry. While descriptions of spaces in different geographical locations are by no means identical, it is evident that the same types of things do happen in different types of places, and distinctions between public and private are also applicable in different locations, as they are all contained within the same courtly romance setting. However, as will be evident especially in my discussion of Serkland and how space functions when characters from Serkland are involved, the distinction between Self and Other is valid, and seems to be a more productive way of thinking about difference. But because this is more a matter of characterization than of geography and spatiality, I only touch on it briefly in the present chapter, reserving more developed discussions of Self and Other in the text for Chapters 4 and 5. In the following cases, I consider how the confusion of basic distinctions between public and private can signal danger, drawing on Foucault's concept of the heterotopia – 'places [...] outside of all places, even though it may be possible to indicate their location in reality',[75] and especially the notion that 'The heterotopia is capable of juxtaposing in a single real place several spaces, several sites that are in themselves incompatible',[76] which will be especially evident in discussing the meaning of space at sea. I will begin by looking at France, before considering Serkland, and ending with the island Visio, on the borders of real and imagined space.

74   Cf. Clunies Ross, 'Land-Taking and Text-Making', pp. 159-84.
75   Foucault, 'Of Other Spaces', p. 24. Foucault contrasts heterotopias with utopias: 'sites with no real place' but which 'present society itself in a perfected form, or else society turned upside down' (p. 24).
76   Foucault, 'Of Other Spaces', p. 25.

Frakkland (France) is an example of a place that *Nítíða saga* presents as real and which is more or less identifiable with its medieval historical equivalent. As to the geography of France itself, the only detail provided in the saga is an incidental reference to 'þær hafner er lægu vt vid Pæris borg' (the harbours which lay outside the city of Paris),[77] perhaps, but not necessarily, suggesting that Paris is here placed on the coast;[78] no mention is made of how far outside of Paris the harbours are but the characters reach Paris from their ships with ease. The first mention of the kingdom of France itself occurs as Nítíða is first introduced: 'Þessi meykongur sat j aunduegi heimsins j Fracklandi jnu goda og hiellt Pæris borg' (This maiden-king sat on the throne of the world in France the Good, and ruled in Paris).[79] Whether deliberately or not, the narrator assigns an implicit value judgement to France by naming (and/or describing) it as *Frackland jd goda*. This name also features in other Icelandic romances such as *Viktors saga ok Blávus*, and it has been thought 'without doubt' originally to have entered Icelandic in the translation of *Karlamagnús saga* from Old French *chansons de geste*, as an approximation of *la dulce France* (sweet France).[80] Still, we cannot be certain that the Icelandic audiences of *Nítíða saga* did not interpret 'Frakkland hið

---

77 'Nitida saga', ed. by Loth, p. 22.
78 Barnes, 'Margin vs. Centre', p. 104.
79 'Nitida saga', ed. by Loth, p. 3.
80 Einar Ólafur Sveinsson, '*Viktors saga ok Blávus*: Sources and Characteristics', p. cix. *Nítíða saga* and *Viktors saga ok Blávus* also both feature *Svíþjóð hin kalda* (lit. Sweden the Cold), which in Loth's summaries is usually translated as 'Scythia?' ('Nitida saga', ed. by Loth, p. 5). Loth does not explain her choice, and it is unclear what exactly she understands 'Scythia' to mean. In the Middle Ages 'Scythia' could refer to a number of different locations, Scandinavia included, and a more common, related, name, *Svíþjóð hin mikla* (lit. Sweden the Great), appears in medieval Icelandic romances and other genres of Old Norse–Icelandic literature (Gahrn, 'Svitjod det stora och Skytien', pp. 5-22; Jackson, 'Scithia er uær köllum miklu Suiþiod'; Simek, 'Elusive Elysia', pp. 267-69; Simek, *Altnordische Kosmographie*, pp. 209-10; and Simek, *Heaven and Earth in the Middle Ages*, pp. 47, 67). The only other place name in *Nítíða saga* taking this format is the homeland of Livorius, *Indíaland hið mikla* (lit. Great[er] India), which also appears in *Gibbons saga* (*Gibbons saga*, ed. by Page, p. 21). Though he does not explain the name itself, Einar Ólafur Sveinsson notes that India first became well known in Iceland through the translation of *Alexanders saga*, and was likely popularized in Iceland through the romance *Rémundar saga keisarasonar*, in which much of the action occurs in India ('*Viktors saga ok Blávus*: Sources and Characteristics', p. cx). It is possible that *Indíaland hið mikla* refers to Greater India (cf. Barnes, *The Bookish Riddarasögur*, pp. 138-41), alluding to the Three Indias described in medieval travel texts like that of Marco Polo, *The Travels*, pp. 260, 294, 303-04. India is also divided into three in *Mandeville's Travels*, ed. by Letts, I, p. 113, although in his note Letts finds them difficult to distinguish (pp. 113-14). A translation of London, British Library, MS Egerton 1982, which Letts used for his edition, has been made by Moseley, *The Travels*. See also Simek, *Heaven and Earth in the Middle Ages*, pp. 56-61 (esp. p. 61). The three Indias are also outlined in Kålund, ed., *Alfræði íslenzk*, III, p. 9.

góða' as literally 'France the Good' (as opposed to *hið illa* [the bad]), instead
of as a name devoid of further meaning once translated. What may be
surprising about the saga's representation of this country is France's location
relative to the rest of the world. As mentioned above in discussing T–O maps
and the saga's geographical shift northwards, Paris is here situated in the
absolute centre, taking the place of Jerusalem.[81] With France as the centre
of the world in *Nítíða saga*, Iceland becomes much closer to that centre in
the saga's cosmography. This also, importantly, gives power and significance
to the 'nordur hælfu veralldarinar' (i.e. Europe) in general, which, while
already closer to the traditional centre than Iceland, is not usually thus
thought of in the Middle Ages. With rather similar diction, the romance
Gibbons saga also locates Paris at the world's centre: '<j> midiv ondvegi
heimsins i Fraklandi j Paris borgg' (in the middle of the centre of the world
in France in the city of Paris).[82] Einar Ólafur Sveinsson interprets this as
indicative of 'the measure of the author's admiration' for France,[83] but there
seems to be more to it than this, certainly in *Nítíða saga*, and perhaps also in
Gibbons saga.[84] Barnes has considered the relationship between centre and
periphery in *Nítíða saga* in detail, arguing that the saga is, 'Geopolitically,
[...] a contest for global primacy, played out in the [bridal-]quest',[85] and that
its 'counter cosmography' realized in the supernatural stones works as 'a
virtual *mappamundi* [... that] positions the northernmost extremity of the
world as its most powerful intelligence gathering source'.[86] France is truly
the hub of international power here, and Nítíða's suitors' intense interest
in gaining her hand further emphasizes the extent of her influence. By
showing in literature how alliances are made and where political power lies,
the narrator demonstrates that Iceland is a real part of the late medieval
international European community. The Europeanization of Scandinavia,

81   Akbari, pp. 19-34; Barnes, 'Margin vs. Centre', p. 104; Heng, *Empire of Magic*, p. 258; Higgins,
'Defining the Earth's Center in a Medieval "Multi-Text"', pp. 34-39. Byzantium (Constantinople)
is also sometimes placed at the centre in Norse texts and other late medieval European romances
(Barnes, *The Bookish Riddarasögur*, pp. 147-81; Heng, *Empire of Magic*, pp. 9-10; Sverrir Jakobsson,
'Centre and Periphery', p. 920).

82   *Gibbons saga*, ed. by Page, p. 43.

83   Einar Ólafur Sveinsson, '*Viktors saga ok Blávus*: Sources and Characteristics', p. cx.

84   There is not room here to discuss the relationship between *Nítíða saga* and *Gibbons saga*
further than I have already in Chapter 2; suffice it to say that *Gibbons saga* is considered one
of the earlier Icelandic romances whose influence is seen in a number of others (Einar Ólafur
Sveinsson, '*Viktors saga ok Blávus*: Sources and Characteristics'; see also Kalinke, 'Scribe, Redactor, Author', pp. 189-93).

85   Barnes, 'Margin vs. Centre', p. 104.

86   Barnes, *The Bookish Riddarasögur*, pp. 35, 37.

begun in Hákon's Norwegian court in the thirteenth century, here reaches its completion in Iceland, through the integration of European knowledge and interest reflected in this popular romance.[87] The Europeanization of Iceland at its zenith is exemplified in the literature of late medieval Iceland, which now incorporates many of the themes, settings, and concerns of European romance in original compositions such as *Nítíða saga*, rather than merely through translations.

If we now consider the basic division of space into public and private in the saga's French locations, Nítíða meets visitors in her hall: Ingi is invited 'heim til hallar med aullum sinum skara' (home to the hall with all his troops).[88] Livorius, too, first visits Nítíða in her hall: he 'gengur nu heim til hallarinnar en drott(ning) stendur vpp j moti honum og setur hann j häsæti hiä sier' (goes now to the hall and the queen stands up to meet him and seats him in the high-seat beside her).[89] By setting him next to her, Nítíða shows she trusts Livorius, a trust he has not yet earned, and one which he betrays. By receiving suitors in the hall's public setting, however, Nítíða keeps herself safer than if she were to receive them in a private space. When Livorius visits later disguised as Eskilvarður, Nítíða likewise 'biooda honum til hallar' (invites him to the hall).[90] That the hall is the appropriate venue to receive guests is reinforced by its repetition in places outside of France: Egidía welcomes Nítíða to Apulia 'giorandi fagra veizlu j sinni hall' (preparing a fair feast in her hall),[91] and in Constantinople Ingi's sister Listalín prepares Nítíða's welcome 'j hallina med miklum heidri og pris' (into the hall with great honour and ceremony).[92] Her reception by her subjects is also associated with her hall. When Nítíða returns from Constantinople, 'kemur m(ey)k(ongur) heim j Franz gangandi hlægiandi j fagra hall' (the maiden-king came home to France, walking laughing into her fair hall).[93] Thus, through its association with the public, the hall in *Nítíða saga* can also to a certain extent be associated with masculinity and acts typically performed by men: as a maiden-*king*, Nítíða carries out the duties of a ruler in appropriate settings, which may traditionally be thought of as masculine-charged spaces. Margaret Clunies Ross has delineated 'male space as the public, nondomestic, social and geographic domain in contrast

87 See also Barnes, 'Travel and *translatio studii*', p. 139.
88 'Nitida saga', ed. by Loth, p. 10.
89 'Nitida saga', ed. by Loth, p. 23.
90 'Nitida saga', ed. by Loth, p. 29.
91 'Nitida saga', ed. by Loth, p. 5.
92 'Nitida saga', ed. by Loth, p. 12.
93 'Nitida saga', ed. by Loth, p. 13.

to female space, which lay within the domestic environment, *innan stokks* ["indoors"]', mainly in considering the *Íslendingasögur* and their depiction of the settlement of Iceland.[94] While this view is arguably also applicable to other types of medieval Icelandic literature, romances like *Nítíða saga* clearly problematize this distinction. I will further consider Nítíða's role as female king and protagonist in Chapters 4 and 5.

Not surprisingly, in contrast to public space, private space – indicated by the *skemma* (bower, private chamber) – is reserved for more personal interactions among characters. Both invited visits to and uninvited intrusions on private space are evident. When Ingi captures Nítíða with the help of Refsteinn, he enters her private room to do so – 'þeir koma til skemmv drott(ningar)' (they come to the queen's chamber)[95] – and this is only possible because he has been made invisible. As strangers, neither Refsteinn nor Ingi would have ever been invited to the *skemma*. Ingi's success in taking Nítíða by force is only guaranteed because he has been able to impinge on her private space – he was not successful in the public hall – and to read this breach in terms of violence and violation, it can also be conceptualized as a sort of rape. Though Ingi does not physically violate Nítíða, it is implied by his violation of her personal chamber, her private space. It also crucially foreshadows Ingi's later actions when a rape is carried out during his second abduction, this time of Nítíða's *ambátt* (bondswoman) Íversa, which I discuss in Chapter 5. When Ingi 'gengur [...] hinn beinasta veg til skemmu drott(ningar)' (goes [...] straight to the queen's chamber) and then 'vt af skemmunni og ofan til skipa' (out from the chamber and down to the ship),[96] his entrance and exit is brief and forceful, and is notably framed by reference to the *skemma*, reinforcing the idea of violation. It is also significant that the physical violation occurs onboard Ingi's ship, neither in France nor Constantinople, but somewhere in between. The ship is at once a private and public space: private as it is small, self-contained, and access is privileged; public as it encloses all sorts of people, from king to retainers to crew. Furthermore, Ingi takes his captive in the open space above deck ('kongur lætur þegar bua sæng i lyptingunni' [The king orders at once to prepare a bed in the raised part of the deck]),[97] to contrast sharply the privacy of the bedroom with this public space on the ship. The ship is, further, a transitional space between one distinct, enclosed, and ostensibly

94   Clunies Ross, 'Land-Taking and Text-Making in Medieval Iceland', pp. 159-60.
95   'Nitida saga', ed. by Loth, p. 12.
96   'Nitida saga', ed. by Loth, pp. 15-16.
97   'Nitida saga', ed. by Loth, p. 16.

'safe', kingdom and another, and can be seen as a heterotopia. Indeed, 'The ship is the heterotopia *par excellence*'.[98] There are many scenes in *Nítíða saga* involving ships, and they can be seen as representing strange, politically and geographically neutral, yet symbolically charged spaces. These ships are heterotopias in the fullest and yet most basic sense as Foucault defines them: 'espaces autres' (other spaces). In this first example, Ingi's ship acts as a private-public space wherein the physical violation of the objectified servant is able to take place. Another instance of ship as heterotopia occurs when Hléskjöldur takes French troops to meet Soldán and fight a sea battle, away from France:

> sigla nu þesser skipa stolar huorir moti audrum. og finnast vnder eÿ einni er Kartagia heiter. [...] taka þeir þegar at beriast er vigliost var. gengur Solldan kongur hetiur hans og blæmenn j gegnum lid Franzeisa suo at ecki stod vit. er þæ ei meira epter en halft þat er Hle(skilldi) fylgdi.[99]

> (These fleets then sailed, each against the other, and met each other close to an island called Kartagia. [...] they immediately took to fighting when it was light enough for war. King Soldán went with his heroes and black men through the French troops so that nothing withstood him; after, it was then not more than half that which Hléskjöldur led.)

The space in which the battle occurs is both very specific (near an island the author has taken the time to name) and also no place at all: the two sides fight not on this island or any other bit of land, but on board each other's ships. The space is representative of a clash of kingdoms, France and Serkland, and so it is nowhere, somewhere, and somewhere else entirely, all at once. Yet because the action never actually takes place in Serkland, as I discuss below, the heterotopic nature of this encounter at sea, near Kartagia, is also the closest that the romance gets to Serkland, the opposition's homeland.

Invited visits and personal conversations within private space also revolve around the *skemma* as much as do the intrusions just mentioned, and in places outside France as well. When Listalín confronts Nítíða's bondswoman Íversa in Constantinople, before speaking to her, 'kuedur fru Lista(lin) burt af skemmvni allar fruʀ og hird konur' (Lady Listalín

98   Foucault, 'Of Other Spaces', p. 27, italics original.
99   'Nitida saga', ed. by Loth, p. 26.

summons away from the chamber all the ladies and court women),[100] in order to construct an illusion of privacy that allows Ingi to listen in hiding. In this case private space is not a reality, but an illusion, that is possible because it involves an unfamiliar setting for the character being spied on. The same type of trick could not as easily be carried out in a setting with which everyone involved was familiar, suggesting that private space might only be truly private if it is one's own space. As guests, or as a hostage in the case of Íversa, the characters are always, to an extent, in a public and not necessarily safe space. In India, Nítíða is brought on arrival 'til skemmu drott(ningar) Syialin' (to the chamber of the princess Sýjalín),[101] a private chamber used as a women's space separate from the men's, but it is not her own private space – Nítíða must share with Sýjalín (who at this point is a stranger). Back in France, it is only once Nítíða has got to know Livorius (disguised as Eskilvarður) better – after he has stayed in her castle for many months – that she welcomes him into her private chamber to look into the magic stones: he 'geingur med þeim j skiemmuna' (goes with them into the chamber),[102] and a second time 'bydur drottning Eskilvard til skiemmunnar' (the queen asks Eskilvarður to the chamber).[103] That he is a guest away from familiar surroundings aids Nítíða's ability to trick and outwit him, in addition to the advantage she has in both the supernatural stones and her inherent cleverness. More significantly, though, when Nítíða explicitly asks Livorius into her private space, it indicates not only that she accepts him but that she may have already chosen him as a suitable partner and husband.

In terms of the construction and presentation of space, the arrival of characters from Serkland to France demonstrates a different consideration of space than we have seen in the preceding examples. When Heiðarlogi is expressly invited to Nítíða's hall, the invitation is only a pretext. He is first told that his brother 'situr nu j haullinni og dreckur' (sits now in the hall and drinks) with Nítíða,[104] in the expected public location for visitors to be received. Upon arrival at the castle, however, Heiðarlogi is, surprisingly, directed 'til skemmu drott(ningar)' (to the queen's chamber),[105] which turns out to be a trap leading to his death. The mixing of public and private space – directing a public guest not previously known to a private area – signals that something is not right, and reinforces the planned deception, as public

100 'Nitida saga', ed. by Loth, p. 17.
101 'Nitida saga', ed. by Loth, p. 24.
102 'Nitida saga', ed. by Loth, p. 30.
103 'Nitida saga', ed. by Loth, p. 30.
104 'Nitida saga', ed. by Loth, p. 20.
105 'Nitida saga', ed. by Loth, p. 21.

and private space is not usually confused in this way. Yet Heiðarlogi misses this clue, and the trick works.[106] We might presume the saga's audience to be attentive to the mixed signals, along with their foreknowledge of the preparation of physical traps. Extant structures, like Nítíða's castle and the rooms it contains, may also be contrasted with the new building projects described in the saga, showing an opposition between fixed stability (the castle) and fluid changeability (new projects). When she learns that armies from Serkland are approaching, Nítíða adds elaborate defences to her castle:

> hvn lætur giora glerhimin med þeirri list at hann liek ä hiolum og mätti fara jnn yfer haufudport borgarinnar og mätti þar mart herfolk ä standa. hon liet og giora diki ferlega diupt framm fyrir skemmunni og leggja ÿfer veyka vidue en þar yfer var breitt skrud og skarlat.[107]

(She commands that a glass roof be made that could move on wheels and could go over the main gate of the castle so that many warriors could stand thereon. She commanded also that a monstrously deep ditch be made before her chamber, and to lay weak wood over it, and over that was to be spread costly stuff and scarlet.)

When the time comes to put these additions to use, France is victorious: the mechanisms work, both to trap the enemy and to set *biki og brennesteini* (pitch and sulphur) and *skotuopnum* (projectiles) showering down on them.[108] These defences not only protect France as a whole by protecting the castle, but the ditch in particular is built directly in front of Nítíða's private chamber (*fyrir skemmunni*), directly and explicitly protecting her private space, which had previously been violated. The newly constructed spaces are thus aligned with private space, and in a reversal of the previous violation of private, indoor space, when the enemy arrives at these 'private', outdoor spaces, it is not they who perform any violation, but they who are 'violated', by annihilation. This type of space is also, then, transitional, akin to the heterotopic ships discussed above, but with the major difference that these inverted spaces here allow for the reversal of roles and for previous violations to be avenged.

---

106 See Chapter 4 for discussion of Heiðarlogi's role, the other characters from Serkland, and why it seems necessary to eliminate them.
107 'Nitida saga', ed. by Loth, p. 18.
108 'Nitida saga', ed. by Loth, p. 20.

Having considered *Frakkland* in detail, I now shift my focus to *Serkland*, a location mentioned by name five times in *Nítíða saga*, and the best example of a place that the saga presents as real, but the location of which does not necessarily readily correspond to one real location, and about which scholars sometimes disagree. Indeed, it seems to have been somewhat problematic even among Icelandic scribes and readers. In post-Reformation versions of *Nítíða saga*, this indeterminate place name is often replaced with more easily identifiable, real-world place names, such as *Miklagarður* (Constantinople) in some eastern Icelandic manuscripts, as I have mentioned in the final case study of Chapter 1, or *Saxland* (Saxony, Germany), in the manuscript Lbs 644 4to, which could possibly be the result of the scribe's inability to understand what was meant by *Serkland*. Various theories have been posited as to the origin of this place name, such as that it came to Scandinavia via Latin *sericum* (the land of silk),[109] or that it is a tribal name – Sariq or Sarik – for one of the Turkic groups that comprised the Khazars residing between the Black and Caspian seas in the Middle Ages.[110] However, the most prominent (and plausible) explanation of *Serkland* is that it is simply a 'land of Saracens', that is, one or all of the predominantly Muslim areas of medieval Europe, Arabia, or Africa,[111] potentially making this place name one of the saga's only implicit references to religion. The identification of Saracens and their localities in other medieval literature is similarly vague, as they appear as Arabs and/or Muslims in Spain, North Africa, the Middle East, or even sometimes places as diverse as Persia, India, Ethiopia, and Armenia in many medieval French *chansons de geste*.[112] Even further, Saracens often denoted simply any non-Christian group of people,[113] and by extension non-Europeans – people outside of Christendom.[114] Ármann Jakobsson takes this approach, calling Serkland 'very primitive and uncivilized and clearly

---

109 Jarring, 'Serkland', pp. 126-28, including his arguments opposing this reading.

110 Jarring, pp. 128-31. See also Jesch, 'Geography and Travel', p. 125.

111 Daniel, *Heroes and Saracens*, pp. 8-9, 66-67, 264; Jesch notes that 'in both runic inscriptions and skaldic verse [Serkland] has emblematic status as the southeastern most destination of the far-travelling Vikings, wherever it was' ('Geography and Travel', p. 125); *An Icelandic-English Dictionary* states that the term is 'used of northern Africa, southern Spain', and that it is 'said to be derived from Arabic *sharkeyn* = *Easterlings*' (Gudbrand Vigfusson, *An Icelandic-English Dictionary*, p. 523). *Serkland* appears in a number of other late medieval Icelandic romances, as well as in the *konungasögur* (kings' sagas) in *Heimskringla*. See also Simek, *Altnordische Kosmographie*, pp. 208-09; Jarring pp. 125-26.

112 Daniel, *Heroes and Saracens*, pp. 8-9, 67.

113 Daniel, *Heroes and Saracens*, p. 264; Tolan, *Saracens*, pp. 127-28.

114 The term was also used, 'in translations of ancient Latin writers, of the Assyrians, Babylonians' (Gudbrand Vigfusson, *An Icelandic-English Dictionary*, p. 523).

pagan',[115] though without commenting further on the religion of Serkland, or offering any evidence of what makes these characters 'pagan', perhaps, though not explicitly, equating them with Saracens.

Whereas both Christianity and Islam are freely referred to and incorporated into many Icelandic romances,[116] *Nítíða saga* does not include any overt references to either religion; not even the word *guð* (God) appears. It might be argued that the presence of Latin in *Nítíða saga* is evidence of the Christian context in which it was conceived and produced. While Latinisms such as those already mentioned in Chapter 2 certainly are evidence of the saga's production in a religious environment within Christendom, none of the Latinisms, nor any other aspect of the saga, suggests that the world in which Nítíða is depicted is a Christian world, whereas other Icelandic romances do. The distinction between the environment in which the saga was conceived and produced and that which the saga characters inhabit is an important one. Without any explicit inclusion of religion, one might be tempted to see *Nítíða saga* as, to a certain extent, ignoring the idea of Europe as Christendom – the geographical region united by religion – or at the very

---

115 'mjög frumstætt og ósiðmenntað og greinilega *heiðið*' (Ármann Jakobsson, *Illa fenginn mjöður*, p. 177, my italics).

116 Just as medieval romances from elsewhere in Europe often display clear evidence of the religious climate in which they were composed and consumed, in Iceland even romances without European sources demonstrate the Christian culture of the scribes and readers who composed and enjoyed them in the late Middle Ages, by the time the religion had taken a real hold in society (van Nahl, *Originale Riddarasögur*, pp. 155-64). One example of this is the explicitly Christian passage of time in many of them. Towards the end of *Sigurðar saga þögla* reference is made to the Christianization of France in order to authenticate the saga's events ('Sigurðar saga þögla', ed. by Loth, pp. 228-29). By including such a reference, the text also asserts that regardless of whether or not it depicts historical events, it is set in a real place and time, that same Christendom to which the saga's Icelandic readers belong, connecting audience with characters and thus making the text more relatable. Other romances refer to Christianity in order to signal that the world the characters inhabit is a romance world, and in turn a part of Christendom, showing not so much the Christian setting, but simply reflecting the Christian social norms of romance. Religious figures (saints, bishops, popes, monks, nuns) and institutions (churches, monasteries) appear regularly in *Saulus saga ok Nikanors* and *Jarlmanns saga ok Hermanns*. Biblical characters, stories, and names are incorporated into *Saulus saga ok Nikanors* and *Adonias saga*. Additionally, many romances including *Adonias saga*, *Ectors saga*, *Sigurðar saga turnara*, and *Jarlmanns saga ok Hermanns* end with prayers or other Christian references, which are also common in Middle English romance (Dalrymple, *Language and Piety*; Thorndike, 'More Copyists' Final Jingles'). *Nikulás saga leikara* in particular has a dense concentration of religious references, with Christianity pervading the story much more readily than in many of the romances already mentioned. Islam also features in many Icelandic romances, even where, given the settings of texts such as *Ectors saga* and *Kirialax saga*, the inclusion of Muslim characters is anachronistic.

least discounting its importance. However, we can still see the saga's Serkland as representative of a non-European (and therefore non-Christian) Other.

On another level, it is even possible to see an element of crusading in the saga, with France representing Christendom and the characters from Serkland as invading Saracens. Barnes favours this type of reading when she argues that *Nítíða saga* is 'a narrative in which the West is threatened by the Saracen East', that Nítíða commits her efforts mainly to defending her kingdom against Saracens, and suggests the sack of Constantinople during the Fourth Crusade in 1204 as a potential influence on the saga's writer.[117] An essential aspect of this argument is not only that *Serkland* should be understood as 'land of Saracens', but also that the word *víkingur* is in *Nítíða saga* 'more or less synonymous with "Saracen"',[118] rather than leaving the characters from Serkland simply as Saracens. In medieval Icelandic literature, *víkingur* usually means either 'Scandinavian seafarer', as in some *Íslendingasögur*,[119] or 'villainous pirate', as in many romances.[120] In *Nítíða saga*, the word appears three times: 1) 'hann [...] drap rænsmenn og vikinga' (He [...] killed robbers and vikings,),[121] 2) 'litur hun j sina næturu steina at siæ [...] ef vikingar kiæmi og villdi strida ǽ hennar ʀiki' (she looks into her supernatural stones to see [...] if vikings were coming to attack her kingdom),[122] and 3) 'eÿ einni er Kartagia heitir. þar var vikinga bæli mikit' (a certain island that is called Kartagia. A great viking camp was there).[123] In the first quotation, the sense is most likely a synonym for 'robbers'. In the second, the sense could be stretched to refer to Saracens, but there is nothing to suggest that this reading is preferable over another. The word could just as easily refer to robbers or more generally to pirates or warriors – these *víkingar* could be anyone, Saracens included, but the information given in the text is not specific enough to draw concrete conclusions as to their precise identity. In the third quotation, the sense of the word is, again, much the same as in the two preceding quotations. Barnes understands *Kartagia* as 'probably the port of Cartagena in southeast Spain, which was known in the Middle Ages for its pirate attacks';[124] certainly the port was part of Muslim al-Andalus until 1245 when it was incorporated into the Castilian kingdom, meaning

117 Barnes, 'Margin vs. Centre', pp. 105-06.
118 Barnes, 'Margin vs. Centre', p. 106.
119 Gudbrand Vigfusson, *An Icelandic-English Dictionary*, p. 716.
120 Gudbrand Vigfusson, *An Icelandic-English Dictionary*, p. 716.
121 'Nitida saga', ed. by Loth, p. 8.
122 'Nitida saga', ed. by Loth, pp. 14-15.
123 'Nitida saga', ed. by Loth, p. 26.
124 Barnes, 'Margin vs. Centre', p. 108.

that this island could easily have been conceived of by medieval scribes and readers as Muslim territory. If Kartagia is to be understood, rather, as Carthage, as suggested above, then associating this place with Saracens would be equally valid. In any case, this indeterminate island location is best understood broadly in connection to Serkland and the characters from that place, rather than in connection specifically with vikings. In none of the instances quoted above does *víkingur* seem to denote anything other than the common senses of the word: a claim that *víkingur* is 'synonymous with "Saracen"' in *Nítíða saga* thus seems questionable. Further, Barnes later states that Nítíða may at one point characterize Eskilvarður of Mundia (i.e. Livorius) as a viking, while never implying that he is a Saracen;[125] he does, in fact, fight against the army of Serkland, identified as Saracens.[126] While this argument stands in opposition to her previous equation of vikings with Saracens, it does, however, echo a medieval European confusion of vikings (and others) with Saracens, particularly in some chansons de geste.[127]

As a final note to conclude my consideration of Serkland, it is interesting to see that at no point in the romance does any of the action occur in Serkland. This, unfortunately, makes it impossible to compare the construction of space in this location to that in others such as France, as discussed above, or Visio, to be considered shortly. However, the absence of Serkland as one of the saga's settings is itself significant. By not describing the place from which the characters from Serkland come, the saga signals their alterity: not only are the other characters' homelands described, allowing them to contribute to the saga's overall chivalric romance setting, but Nítíða travels to, or finds herself in, most of these other places at some point in the saga as well. The closest the reader can come to Serkland is perhaps the encounter near Kartagia, mentioned above as a place between locations, in conjunction with the heterotopic space associated with ships.

Until now I have discussed those places *Nítíða saga* portrays that are understood to exist in the real world. Ármann Jakobsson insists that the places named in *Nítíða saga* bear little if any resemblance to those in the real world, going as far as saying that 'the remote countries where the saga takes place are first and foremost empty names'.[128] On the contrary, it is simple

125 We cannot rule out that the parallel here with *Clári saga*, where Clárus disguises himself as Eskilvarður of *Bláland*, i.e. Ethiopia (rather than Livorius's Eskilvarður of *Mundia*, i.e. the Alps), may still have brought a Saracen association to the minds of *Nítíða saga*'s audience.
126 Barnes, 'Margin vs. Centre', p. 109.
127 Daniel, *Heroes and Saracens*, pp. 66-67.
128 'hinum fjarlægu löndum þar sem sagan gerist en eru fyrst og fremst nöfnin tóm' (Ármann Jakobsson, *Illa fenginn mjöður*, p. 179).

to locate France on a map, and Serkland, while less concretely identifiable, is still conceivable as existing in the physical world, able to be reached by medieval readers as easily as the characters in the story who travel there. But the island of Visio is an imagined, as opposed to a real, location that also merits investigation.[129] Nítíða herself provides the main description of Visio at the beginning of the saga in a conversation with her foster mother Egidía: 'þesse ey liggur vt vndan Suiþiod jnni kaulldu. vt vnder heims skauted. þeirra landa er menn hafa spurn af. j þessari eyjv er vatn eitt stóort. enn j vatninu er holmi sæ er Skoga blomi heiter og suo er mier sagt at huergi j heiminum meigi finnast nátturu steinar epli og læknis graus fleiri en þar.' (This island lies out beyond Sweden the Cold, out past the corner of the world of those lands which people have heard of. In the island is a large lake, and in the lake is that islet which is called The Flower of the Woods, and I have heard that nowhere in the world might one find more supernatural stones, apples, and healing herbs than there).[130] At this point in the story these details are only hearsay, but they prove accurate when an expedition to the island is launched. Once Nítíða and her companions reach Visio, no further details are given, only that they anchor in a hidden cove – *leyni vog* – and upon finding the lake, find also a boat with which to row out to Skóga blómi.[131] The narrator does not comment on the voyage, protesting ignorance of the journey, and cannot state the island's exact whereabouts.[132] It is on Visio that Nítíða sees 'margar eikur med fagri fruckt og ægiætum eplum', and finds, 'j midian holman [...] eitt stein ker med .iiij. hornum. kerit var fullt af vatni. sinn steinn var j huerju horni kersins' (many oaks with fair fruit and fine apples, and finds, in the middle of the islet [...] a stone vessel with four corners. The vessel was full of water, and there was a stone in each corner of the vessel).[133] These stones are Nítíða's *náttúrusteinar*, which, as I have discussed, are integral to her later success. The inclusion of 'oaks with [...] apples', a somewhat strange image, may however comprise a reference to Virgil's *Eclogues*, which are generally thought to have been unknown in Iceland.[134] In *Eclogue 8*, Maenalus sings, 'aurea durae | mala ferant quercus' (let rugged oaks bear golden apples).[135] While it is impossible now to know whether *Nítíða saga*'s author had direct (or indirect) access to the poem, it

---

129 See Hansen, 'Crossing the Borders of Fantastic Space', esp. pp. 65-66.
130 'Nitida saga', ed. by Loth, p. 5.
131 'Nitida saga', ed. by Loth, p. 6.
132 See Chapter 6 for an interpretation of this and other comments made by the narrator.
133 'Nitida saga', ed. by Loth, p. 6.
134 Eldevik, 'Virgil in Medieval Icelandic', p. 616.
135 Virgil, *Eclogue* 8, ll. 52-53 (*Eclogues, Georgics, Aeneid*, I, pp. 78-79).

makes sense as a source for the saga's inclusion of apple-bearing oaks on Visio. Further, *Eclogue 8* also mentions *verbenas pinguis* (rich [medicinal] herbs)[136] – an equivalent to Visio's healing herbs (*lœknis-grös*). Taking these examples of parallel imagery into account, along with the fact that Visio is home to Earl Virgilius (who I discuss further in Chapter 4), it seems reasonable to suggest that the author of *Nítíða saga* may consciously be drawing on the *Eclogues* here.[137]

The description of Visio as mysterious and hidden away beyond the known world and apparently situated in the far reaches of the north also brings to mind the island of Thule, which was known in Iceland.[138] But once Visio is reached, rather than being an obviously northern place, it is lush with fruit trees and by no means a place of snow and ice. Further, Visio is situated to the north east, whereas Thule is always located to the north west, somewhere in the Atlantic Ocean. Schlauch has attempted to equate Visio with Sicily, but does not make a convincing argument of it.[139] Barnes, however, sees Visio as an Earthly Paradise,[140] noting parallels with other medieval Icelandic texts such as *Stjórn* (Guidance), a fourteenth-century Old Norse translation of Old Testament material, and *Konungs Skuggsjá* (King's Mirror), a mid-thirteenth-century Old Norse example of speculum literature, and highlighting the fact that 'Visio is also the source of global knowledge', referring to the power of the stones found there.[141] Rather than simply an Earthly Paradise, however, it seems more useful to see Visio as an example of the topos of the 'locus amoenus' (pleasant place, or 'pleasance'), common throughout medieval literature and originating in antiquity.[142] Paul Piehler's general definition of this topos applies equally well to Visio: an 'enclosed garden, park or paradise, the *locus amoenus*, portrayed as intensely

136   Virgil, *Eclogue* 8, l. 65 (*Eclogues, Georgics, Aeneid*, I, pp. 78-79).

137   There is a portentous apple-bearing oak in *Jómsvíkinga saga* (*The Saga of the Jomsvikings*, ed. and trans. by Blake, pp. 4-5). However, a connection to Virgil, with not only the apples but also the herbs and the earl, seems to be the stronger. Thanks to Shaun Hughes for bringing these parallels to my attention, and for his other apt suggestions regarding the discussion of Visio in this chapter.

138   In the *Alfrœði Íslenzk* Thule (*Tile*) appears next to Iceland (Kålund, *Alfrœði Íslenzk*, III, p. 72), and Saxo Grammaticus identifies it with Iceland (Simek, *Kosmographie*, p. 210). See also Jackson, 'Ultima Thule in Western European and Icelandic Traditions', pp. 12-24; and Rider, 'The Other Worlds of Romance', pp. 115-31.

139   Schlauch, *Romance in Iceland*, pp. 167-68

140   Barnes, *The Bookish Riddarasögur*, pp. 36-37; Barnes, 'Margin vs. Centre', p. 105.

141   Barnes, 'Margin vs. Centre', p. 105.

142   See for example Curtius, *European Literature and the Latin Middle Ages*, pp. 183-202 (esp. pp. 195-202). A study of this topos in medieval literature is in Thoss, *Studien zum Locus Amoenus im Mittelalter*.

desirable, and situated either very remotely or behind inhibiting physical or psychic barriers. [...] in literature the paradisal garden is often the scene of (or even represents) the solution of a problem'.[143] *Nítíða saga*'s remote island of Visio, removed from the rest of the known world, with its lake encircling the islet, its trees, fruits, healing herbs, and supernatural stones that later help her to triumph over negative situations fits this picture perfectly. A possible source for the inclusion of Visio as a pleasance may be found in Johannes de Hauvilla's satirical twelfth-century Latin poem *Architrenius*. At one point in the narrative the eponymous protagonist arrives at the island of 'Tylos', a place of eternal spring presided over by a local deity.[144] While it seems that 'Tylos with its perpetual spring cannot be identified with *Tyle*, the name Johannes employs twice to refer to the place known to ancient poets as Thule',[145] given its very similar name, this island pleasance could easily have been mistaken for Thule by other medieval writers. Indeed, even Curtius features this scene, locating it in Thule, in his discussion of the *locus amoenus*.[146] It is possible that the author of *Nítíða saga*, even without direct access to the poem, could have heard about it and as a result incorporated the idea of setting Visio, as a *locus amoenus*, in the extreme north.

The importance of knowledge and wisdom is also evident in the name of the place itself: it is of course from Visio – from Latin *visus* (vision, the act of seeing, or, apparition),[147] and perhaps intended as a pun – that Nítíða gains not just magical objects, but the powers of supernatural vision. While it is certainly possible for medieval and later audiences of this text to have understood this possibly humorous linguistic connection, it is clear that many post-medieval scribes did not make the connection. In other versions of *Nítíða saga* copied in post-medieval manuscripts, the importance of Visio as the source of knowledge remains, though sometimes in slightly garbled form. The form *Visio* generally remains throughout the transmission of the text in most manuscripts, with occasional differences in spelling like ÍB 132's *Vicio*, AM 568's *Vysia*, and ÍB 116's *Visia*. However, it is in later versions

---

143 Piehler, *The Visionary Landscape*, pp. 77-78.

144 The episode is in Book 6, chap. 2, ll. 20-25 (Johannes de Hauvilla, *Architrenius*, ed. by Wetherbee, pp. 144-45).

145 Johannes de Hauvilla, *Architrenius*, ed. by Wetherbee, p. 262. Wetherbee points instead to another island named Tylos 'so named by Pliny (12.40) and Solinus (52.49). Both report that the trees of this island never lose their leaves, which doubtless suggested to Johannes the perpetual springtime' (p. 262). This other Tylos may have been located in the east, near India, and can possibly be identified as the ancient name for modern Bahrain, placing it in an arguably more traditionally exotic locale than the northern Thule.

146 Curtius, *European Literature and the Latin Middle Ages*, p. 198.

147 As in Macrobius, *Commentary on the Dream of Scipio*, pp. 88-89.

in the nineteenth century when the name's meaning changes but is still significant, as in the eastern Icelandic manuscripts' variations on *Viktoria*, perhaps indicating the ultimate victory that Nítíða gains from the island; or when the name morphs into a form devoid of any further significance, as in the *Vikio* of the nineteenth-century manuscripts SÁM 13 and Reykjavík, Landsbókasafn–Háskólabókasafn Íslands, MSS Lbs 1319 8vo and Lbs 3675 8vo. The name *Virgilius* is generally preserved, with some orthographic variation. The place name may also have originally had connotations of wisdom. In the translated romance *Flóres saga ok Blankiflur*, it says of the protagonist Flóres that 'fœra hann til skóla í þann stað, er á Vísdon heitir' (he went to school in that place, which is called Vísdon).[148] This association with wisdom and learning is significant, and the author of *Nítíða saga* may have been inspired by this name and its context.

That the island is the abode of Earl Virgilius is also suggestive of the learned environment from which *Nítíða saga* was produced, and indeed, as mentioned above, the name could be a direct indication of the author's indebtedness to the poetry of Virgil in these scenes.[149] While casting him as an evil magician might at first seem to clash with the idea that Visio is an Earthly Paradise, within medieval Europe the North was often viewed as a place of 'danger and wildness'.[150] In the saga's description of Visio, which as an isolated island could, as well as a *locus amoenus*, be thought of as a space of wilderness, with its remote wildness intensified through doubling, as it is not merely an island, but an island within an island. The only signs of habitation there are the boat conveniently allowing Nítíða's passage to the central island ('einn bæt fliotandi'), and the box or vessel in which the four *náttúrusteinar* have been placed ('eitt stein ker med .iiij. hornum'). Apart from these crafted objects, Visio and Skóga-blómi are indeed a paradisiacal wilderness. Because of their isolation from the rest of the world, the woods described there are rather different to those experienced by Livorius, who later in the saga encounters a dwarf in the midst of an open space, a space of uncontrolled nature, yet still enclosed by surrounding woods.[151] It has been noted that 'deserts, islands and forests' can exemplify the wilderness, which is 'always perceived as a spatial region fundamentally different from that

---

148 *Flóres saga ok Blankiflur*, ed. by Kölbing, p. 8.

149 For a discussion of the characterization of Virgilius as an antagonist in *Nítíða saga* specifically and of the figure of Virgil's negative reputation in late medieval and early modern Iceland more generally, see Chapter 4.

150 Barnes, *The Bookish Riddarasögur*, pp. 33-34; Barnes, 'Margin vs. Centre', p. 105. See also Shafer, 'Saga Accounts of Norse Far-Travellers', pp. 207-72.

151 'Nitida saga', ed. by Loth, p. 21.

of "normal" space'.[152] Livorius's encounter includes the only other mention of *skógur* (woods) in the romance apart from the place name *Skóga-blómi* (and also the only mention of a *rjóður* [clearing]); Livorius's caution there highlights the potential danger and insecurity of a clearing in the midst of the wild woods, as opposed to cleared, controlled areas more akin to gardens. Though Icelandic texts do not describe cultivated medieval gardens as such, this romance includes nods to the idea, in contrast to the natural clearing just noted. 'Gardens' seem to be associated with private space, but also with fluidity and motion: Nítíða escapes from India out of 'einn lund plantadan er stod vnder skemmunni' (a planted grove that stood below the chamber).[153] The garden's proximity to a private chamber suggests an equivalence of spaces, perhaps as extensions of each other. But whereas the enclosed, indoor spaces suggest security, stability, and predictability, even when a supposed security may be breached, the open, outdoor spaces suggest fluidity, movement, and uncertainty.

Conclusions

In this chapter I have discussed the extent of *Nítíða saga*'s geographical knowledge, and compared it to the presentation of global space and geography in four other romances related to *Nítíða saga* – *Dínus saga drambláta*, *Sigurðar saga þǫgla*, *Clári saga*, and *Nikulás saga leikara*. I have also considered *Nítíða saga*'s presentation of space on a smaller scale, comparing public and private space, particularly as it is presented in the setting of France, and considering how and to what purpose different types of spaces are characterized throughout the text, in anticipation of my discussions of characters and characterization in the following chapters. I have shown that different spaces can hinder or facilitate different characters in combination with their own personal attributes and motivations depending on the circumstances. As has also been mentioned briefly in discussion of the three case studies of different post-Reformation versions of *Nítíða saga* in Chapter 1, it seems that as time passes, some versions show different geographical focuses. Generally speaking, we might say that as time passes there is less of a need for scribes to display their book knowledge, or to portray their degree of learnedness, as can be seen in, for example, the loss of Latinate endings from many place names in later versions. Certainly by the nineteenth century,

152 Harrison, p. 12.
153 'Nitida saga', ed. by Loth, p. 24.

manuscripts of all groups, but especially those that appear for the first time only in the nineteenth century like those from the Icelandic Eastfjords put much less emphasis on place names, and no longer underscore the exoticism of some names: *Miklagarður* becomes *Grikkland*, and *Serkland* becomes *Miklagarður* in the Eastfjords; the composite *Miklagarður í Grikkland* even appears in certain seventeenth-century manuscripts, to clarify with the latter what is meant by the former.

Overall, I have sketched out the literary landscape in which many readers and listeners encountered *Nítíða saga*, while also further reinforcing some of the intertextual relationships I introduced in Chapter 2. I have shown that *Nítíða saga* is innovative in its portrayal of world geography – how on a global scale it divides the world into unprecedented thirds and excludes Africa altogether in order to draw Iceland closer to the world's centre, in contrast to *Dínus saga drambláta*, which divides the world into its traditional thirds but concentrates so closely on Africa that other regions are barely mentioned, and Europe conspicuously ignored. I have also considered the eclecticism of the longer redaction of *Sigurðar saga þǫgla*, whose scribe focuses on Europe overall, but includes so many diverse place names that the text's geography becomes cluttered and disordered, in opposition to *Nítíða saga*'s clearly structured cosmography. Comparisons with *Clári saga* and *Nikulás saga leikara*, both of which include very few place names, have further shown how directed and deliberate *Nítíða saga*'s geographical descriptions are, as a means of demonstrating the proximity of Iceland to the rest of Europe.

Nítíða saga presents a decidedly nordicentric picture of the world. That the text, situating both itself and Iceland within Europe in this way, was copied, read, and heard alongside *Dínus saga drambláta* and *Nikulás saga leikara*, and that thematically it has so much in common with *Clári saga* and *Sigurðar saga þǫgla*, suggests that these texts along with *Nítíða saga* comprise a group of five which, if considered together, act as a complex and relatively complete, yet distinctly Icelandic, picture of late medieval world geography in romance, the realization of geographical desire and cultural appropriation (or even colonization) in a late medieval Icelandic milieu.[154] Through geographical description as well as passing mention of certain places, *Nítíða saga* makes a statement about its place within Europe, and this only becomes more evident when *Nítíða saga* is considered alongside these other sagas: the text's statement is louder and more pronounced when

---

154 Barnes, 'Travel and *translatio studii*', pp. 138-39; McDougall, 'Foreigners and Foreign Languages in Medieval Iceland', p. 233; Tomasch, 'Introduction', p. 2.

it is encountered (in manuscripts) before, after, or between other sagas that, while also possessing their own messages and opinions, also speak of geography and localization in other ways. When *Dínus saga dramblátá* is conventional and centres its action inward on Africa to the exclusion of other settings, *Nítíða saga* disregards tradition completely and is equally self-centred, but in the North, a setting to which Icelanders can relate. Where *Sigurðar saga þǫgla* displays an impressive but somewhat haphazard collection of geographical knowledge, *Nítíða saga* purposefully collects and displays meaningful references with a greater significance in mind. It is not only what *Nítíða saga* says about the relationship between Iceland and Europe, but also the manner in which the saga says it that is meaningful. With its focus clearly set on the peripheral North, and yet with its action mainly centred on France, *Nítíða saga* brings Iceland to the European forefront through its manipulation of traditional medieval geography, and affirms its connection to that major cultural centre of the late medieval world. In doing so, the saga fulfils its author's geographical desire in its inherent depiction of a longing for, and realization of, Europeanization, in the appropriation and adaptation of various aspects of European culture into Icelandic culture.

This chapter's end also marks the end of the first section of this book, in which I have discussed some contextual aspects of *Nítíða saga* – the saga's manuscripts and intertextuality in Chapters 1 and 2, and now in Chapter 3 its setting and atmosphere as seen through its incorporation of geography and negotiation and classification of space. Through geography we have also seen *Nítíða saga* considering its depiction of certain romance norms to produce a text that clearly engages with and challenges its genre and the other texts therein, and also engages with, more broadly, the wider European cultural community from and with which romances, Icelandic and otherwise, emerge and engage. In Part II of this book, I will consider further *Nítíða saga*'s questioning nature by discussing the various characters that populate the text, from the protagonists to the narrator, and how they interact with each other. I first turn, in Chapter 4, to *Nítíða saga*'s hero and the range of characters opposing her.

Part II
Romance Characters

4 The Hero and her Rivals

In this second part of the book, I focus on *Nítíða saga*'s characters and how they interact with each other; I consider in this first chapter the main characters and the hero of the story in particular. I will discuss supporting characters, focusing on the romance's many female characters, in Chapter 5, and I will finish by looking at the role of the narrator in Chapter 6. I will also examine the importance of speech to characterization by comparing dialogue in *Nítíða saga* as represented by both direct and indirect speech. Just as *Nítíða saga* challenges many of the boundaries of the romance genre as we have seen in earlier chapters, so does the saga reconsider traditional or expected norms of romance characterization, most importantly with respect to the hero. In medieval Icelandic romances, heroes are usually identified through features such as a text's introductory and concluding remarks, or its title – these alert the audience to who the story will be about. In almost all Icelandic romances, the saga's eponymous hero is male and the plot focuses on his exploits; in many romances the culmination of the plot is the hero's marriage. Not all romance sagas bear titles as such in manuscript and titles are more common in later post-medieval manuscripts. Of the three medieval (pre-1600) manuscripts of *Nítíða saga*, only one, AM 529, preserves the beginning, and it does not bear any sort of title, nor has a larger opening initial been added, though space has been left in the manuscript. In this manuscript the saga begins immediately after *Gibbons saga*, and without actually reading the words written on the manuscript leaf, it would be difficult to tell simply by glancing at it that a new text has begun. Conversely, most of the sixty post-medieval *Nítíða saga* manuscripts bear a title of some kind, clearly marking off the new text. I will discuss titles further below. However, many romances, whether accompanied by a title or not, begin with a formulaic introduction of their heroes, and end equally formulaically by stating the characters on whom the story has focused. Considering *Nítíða saga*, where the title character is a woman with a prominent role throughout the story,[1] the question of what constitutes this

---

1 Possibly the only other medieval Icelandic romance with a female title character is *Mábel saga sterku*, but unfortunately it is known today only through post-medieval re-tellings in the form of *rímur*; this text is little studied, but see Driscoll, 'In Praise of Strong Women'. *Hervarar saga*, a *fornaldarsaga*, can also be considered a medieval saga named after a woman, but it is also often called *Heiðreks saga* (or *Hervarar saga ok Heiðreks*), featuring the male protagonist. For a discussion of this text see e.g. Hall, 'Changing Style and Changing Meaning'. After the medieval period, many sagas and *rímur* were composed and circulated, which had female protagonists

romance's hero has not yet been satisfactorily addressed. Instead, what little has been written about Nítíða, and mainly only noted in passing, seems to imply that though a powerful maiden-king, she is not a hero, and instead this role must be fulfilled by her suitor Livorius, as the saga resembles a bridal-quest romance.[2]

However, as I argue in this chapter, Nítíða is the hero of a saga that challenges and redefines what it means to be a protagonist and hero in Icelandic romance. I will first offer a definition of the Icelandic romance hero, which I will follow with an exploration of the characterization of Livorius. But Livorius's success alone is not enough to make him the saga's hero. I will show how Nítíða fulfils the criteria for a hero in ways Livorius cannot, and I will explore the support of Nítíða's foster brother Hléskjöldur as an important instrument through which Nítíða's character is reinforced. I will also consider Nítíða's interactions with the saga's major antagonists, Earl Virgilius of Visio and the four characters from Serkland – Soldán, Logi, Vélogi, and Heiðarlogi. Finally, I will look at the three helper characters (Refsteinn, Slægrefur, and the dwarf) who try, but fail, to aid Ingi and Livorius in their bridal-quests. Throughout this chapter, I will show how the text arguably questions and re-evaluates the traditional conceptualization of an Icelandic romance hero in its portrayal of Nítíða in a heroic, central role, which in turn provides an opportunity for audiences to reassess what it means to be a hero, just as in previous chapters I have shown how *Nítíða saga* questions and reinterprets other traditional components of romance, such as the geographical setting its characters inhabit.

Heroes

The categories of hero, helper, and protagonist are unavoidably problematic. I find it unnecessary to distinguish between masculine *hero* and feminine *heroine*, and will use *hero* as a neutral term throughout this chapter, regardless of the character's gender. Further, it is important to be able to call Nítíða a hero, considering the word's connotations in English. One of the meanings of 'hero' in the *Oxford English Dictionary* is 'the man who forms the subject

---

reflected in their titles, e.g. *Amalíu saga drottningar, Flórentínu saga fögru,* and *Helenu saga vænu* (see e.g. Glauser's list in *Isländische Märchensagas,* p. 278), although they have not been edited and published.

2   Ármann Jakobsson, *Illa fenginn mjöður,* pp. 174-77; Driscoll, 'Late Prose Fiction', p. 201; Kalinke, *Bridal-Quest Romance,* pp. 22, 75.

of an epic; the chief male personage in a poem, play, or story; he in whom
the interest of the story or plot is centred'.[3] In this sense, *hero* is essentially
synonymous with *protagonist*, but I favour the former word over the latter
because of its other senses, which highlight 'extraordinary valour' (first in
1586), as well as 'bravery, firmness, fortitude, or greatness of soul' (first in
1661), as key characteristics of a hero.[4] The term *hero* seems thus much more
important, and charged, than *protagonist*, and it fits better the character
and setting of the medieval vernacular tales with which I am concerned, as
notions like the bravery and valour of characters feature strongly in many.

Unfortunately, little scholarship focuses on the question of what
constitutes a romance hero in a specifically medieval Icelandic context,
and what there is does not clearly define its terms. There has also been
surprisingly little work on how Icelandic sagas more generally identify
their protagonists or heroes (the most comprehensive general assessment in
English is from 1970[5]) and there has been even less work on romance sagas in
particular. Some Icelandic scholarship does, however, tackle the issue with
broad strokes. In the second volume of *Íslensk Bókmenntasaga* (Icelandic
Literature), Torfi Tulinius's chapter on Icelandic romance (covering both
riddarasögur and *fornaldarsögur*) discusses the characters of Icelandic
romance. Torfi says that 'Heroes of Icelandic romance can be divided into
two opposite categories',[6] namely, 1) noble, masculine heroes ('of noble
lineage and handsome appearance. He loves noblewomen and his love is
requited')[7] and 2) the *kolbítur* (lit. coal-biter) type ('not handsome, seldom
enjoys success with women [...] usually not of noble lineage').[8] About female
characters, Torfi says that they are 'more often victims than agents and
seldom take a main role',[9] but he names Nítíða specifically as an exception

3   See 'hero, n.' (*OED Online*). This is the fourth of four senses, first attested in 1697, over three
hundred years after the first appearance of *hero* in English in 1387, where the sense is much
more specific, relating directly to the 'men of superhuman strength' in Homeric epic.

4   The sense that a hero is someone of 'superhuman strength', or 'one who does brave or noble
deeds; an illustrious warrior', is not important to me for the idea of a hero, and seems unnecessary
to retain here in the discussion of the hero as protagonist (*OED Online*).

5   Boucher, 'The Hero in Old Icelandic Literature', pp. 41-45. See also Johansen, 'The Hero of
Hrafnkels saga Freysgoða', pp. 265-86.

6   'Hetjum íslenskra rómansa má skipta í tvo andstæða flokka' (Torfi H. Tulinius, 'Íslenska
rómansan', p. 226).

7   'af tignum ættum og fagur ásýndum. Hann ber ástarhug til tiginborinna kvenna og ást hans
er endurgoldin' (Torfi H. Tulinius, 'Íslenska rómansan', p. 226).

8   'ekki fögur, nýtur sjaldan kvenhylli [...] yfirleitt ekki af höfðingjaættum' (Torfi H. Tulinius,
'Íslenska rómansan', p. 226).

9   'oftar þolendur en gerendur og því sjaldan í aðalhlutverki' (Torfi H. Tulinius, 'Íslenska
rómansan', p. 228).

'where the hero is female'.[10] The relationship between *Nítíða saga*'s popularity in manuscript and the tale's female protagonist is also highlighted, and it
is suggested that a woman could have written the saga, but this idea remains
merely speculative, as is not explored in very much detail.[11] Guðbjörg Aðalbergsdóttir, and most recently Jóhanna Katrín Friðriksdóttir, pick up on this
notion and discuss the role of Nítíða as protagonist and the saga as a piece
of feminist writing.[12] However Ármann Jakobsson, while acknowledging
that in *Nítíða saga* 'the point of view of the saga is to a greater extent with
Nítíða than generally with maiden-kings in maiden-king sagas',[13] still insists
on a more traditional stance that 'despite this the man [Livorius] is still the
hero of the saga'.[14] What exactly a hero is, though, remains unexamined,
and this is as far as the discussion of romance heroes and Nítíða's role,
specifically, goes. Outside of Iceland, some important studies of medieval
Icelandic romance skirt the issue and make assumptions about heroes that
are worth interrogating. As noted in the introduction, within the romance
genre, a useful sub-genre into which *Nítíða saga* is often placed is that of
maiden-king romance, itself being a type of bridal-quest romance, another
sub-genre. In *Bridal-Quest Romance in Medieval Iceland*, Kalinke defines
bridal-quest romance as, 'in the strictest sense, [...] a narrative the plot
of which is generated primarily by the hero's efforts to obtain a bride'.[15]
As for maiden-king romances, 'their plot is dominated by a misogamous
female ruler who insists on being called *kongr* ("king") rather than *drottning*
("queen")'.[16] But without indicating precisely what constitutes the hero, its
definition must be inferred: the character who obtains a bride in the end.
But how would a definition like this work for *Nítíða saga* where, I would
argue, the hero is a woman? The solution is not simply to modify it to include
'bride *or groom*', and as is evident in the above quotations, it is often taken
for granted, without questioning, that romance heroes are male. Surely a

10   'sem hetjan er kvenkyns' (Torfi H. Tulinius, 'Íslenska rómansan', p. 228).
11   Torfi H. Tulinius, 'Íslenska rómansan', pp. 228-29, 245.
12   Guðbjörg Aðalbergsdóttir, 'Nítíða og aðrir meykóngar', pp. 49-55; Jóhanna Katrín Friðriksdóttir, *Women in Old Norse Literature*.
13   'sjónarhorn sögunnar er í ríkara mæli hjá Nítíðu en almennt hjá meykóngum í meykón-
gasögum' (Ármann Jakobsson, *Illa fenginn mjöður*, p. 176; the original is italicized apart from
last two words).
14   'þrátt fyrir það er karlinn samt hetja sögunnar' (Ármann Jakobsson, *Illa fenginn mjöður*,
p. 176).
15   Kalinke, *Bridal-Quest Romance*, p. viii. Indeed this view has dominated some scholars'
passing understanding of *Nítíða saga* (as in van Nahl, *Originale Riddarasögur*, p. 28).
16   Kalinke, *Bridal-Quest Romance*, p. 66; Sif Ríkharðsdóttir, 'Meykóngahefðin í riddarasögum',
pp. 410-33.

broader, more inclusive definition can be found for the Icelandic romances, many of which fall under this bridal-quest rubric.

The formalist theory of Vladimir Propp, who analysed folk and fairy tale structure as the combination of a fixed set of narrative variables, holds a certain appeal, as Icelandic romances certainly contain fairy tale elements, such as the bridal-quest itself. Propp notes that 'non-fairy tales may also be constructed according to the scheme' laid out in his *Morphology of the Folktale*, and that 'novels of chivalry', that is, romances, also 'may be traced back to the [fairy] tale'.[17] It is useful to consider Icelandic romances such as *Nítíða saga* in this light, as a mixture of the fairy/folk tale and the European chivalric romance (about which I will say more below). Propp's own definition of a hero is helpful in the context of Icelandic romances:

> The hero of a fairy tale is that character who either directly suffers from the action of the villain [...], or who agrees to liquidate the misfortune or lack of another person. In the course of action the hero is the person who is supplied with a magical agent [...] and who makes use of it or is served by it.[18]

Heroes of Icelandic romance often conform to this definition, even if their quests are motivated by their own need – for example, to find a bride – rather than by someone else's. Whether the bridal-quest dominates the entire plot or is only one of many elements, Propp's hero-type, as the character around whom the plot revolves and who is helped along his or her way when in need, is appealing in its simplicity. Glauser's *Isländische Märchensagas*, an important work on the structure and function of Icelandic romances, is in places influenced by Propp, and as such his interpretations of Icelandic romance heroes are rooted in the formulaic organization of the texts and tend to generalize romance heroes with broad descriptions. He says, for example, that 'beauty, nobility, courtly manners, and strength are among the key features of the *Märchensaga* [lit. fairy-tale-saga] heroes',[19] and that 'the typically ideal hero of the *Märchensagas* is an aristocratic knight among his liegemen'.[20] Such statements are insightful, and will contribute to our

17 Propp, *Morphology of the Folktale*, pp. 99-100.
18 Propp, *Morphology of the Folktale*, p. 50.
19 'Schönheit, Adel, höfische Sitten, Stärke gehören zu den zentralen Merkmalen des Märchensagahelden'; (Glauser, *Isländische Märchensagas*, p. 165).
20 'der idealtypische Held der Märchensagas ist ein aristokratischer Ritter inmitten seiner Lehnsdiener' (Glauser, *Isländische Märchensagas*, p. 181). More recently, Alenka Divjak has also taken a Proppian approach to understanding the structure of the romance *Kirialax saga* and

understanding of Icelandic romance heroes, but must be built upon further as they describe only a broad trend in romance, rather than the nuanced collage of heroes and their traits that might better represent the differences seen among texts.

While a Proppian approach has its place in considering a fantastical romance like *Nítíða saga* that at times verges on the folk-tale, some of Propp's black and white distinctions, between villain and hero, for example, do not adequately deal with the many shades of characters found in most Icelandic romances, including *Nítíða saga*, which as we have already seen is not merely a formulaic tale. Propp's seven character types (villain, donor/ provider, helper, princess/sought-for person and her father [a single type], dispatcher, hero, and false hero) are static, eliminating the possibility of a villain turning into a hero or vice versa,[21] as in *Nítíða saga*, where the previously antagonistic suitors Ingi and Livorius become positive characters in the end. This is not to say that the characters of Icelandic romance are so mutable that they always change from one role into another, but it is fair to say that initially antagonistic characters fulfil a positive role by the story's end. A significant example of this is seen in *Clári saga*'s maiden-king Séréna, who in the end becomes the hero's submissive wife, promoting a moral for its audience, which also conveniently acts to justify the abuse suffered by Séréna at the hands of the saga's male characters, as noted in Chapter 2. As the saga ends, we hear that

> Görðu þeir þetta allt svá sem til prófs hennar staðfestu [...]. En hon þoldi allan þenna tíma angist og armœðu fyrir ekki vætta útan fyrir sína eiginliga dygð og einfaldleik [...]; og þetta allt lagði hon að baki sér og þar með fǫður, frændir og vini og allan heimsins metnað, upp takandi, viljanligt fátœki með þessum hinum herfilega stafkarli, gefandi svá á sér ljós dœmi, hversu ǫðrum góðum konum byrjar að halda dygð við sína eiginbœndr eða unnasta

> (They did all this so as to test her steadfastness [...]. And she endured all the while that anguish and distress only because of her natural virtue and simplicity [...]; and she left everything behind her including her father, family and friends and all worldly ambitions, taking up poverty willingly with that horrible poor beggar, thus making herself a good example, how

---

the function of its characters (*Studies in the Traditions of Kirialax Saga*, esp. pp. 262-85); see also Schäfke, 'The "Wild East" in Late Medieval Icelandic Romances', pp. 845-50.

21   Propp, *Morphology of the Folktale*, pp. 79-80.

it is fitting for other good women to keep faith with their own husbands or sweethearts.)[22]

Whereas Hallberg downplays this ending as no more than 'a rather thin varnish of religious edification',[23] Hughes argues that the saga's end is deliberately moralizing, and that the author 'is using the romance genre as an elaborate exemplum to promote his uncompromising views on the responsible behavio[u]rs of wives towards their husbands'.[24] In demonstrating a character's ability (and willingness) to change from negative to positive, *Clári saga* could also have been used as a didactic tool to teach morals as well as being an entertaining romance, both in the Church or at home amongst families. The shifting of the maiden-king's role from negative to positive is therefore important.

Other scholars of Icelandic romance have found Northrop Frye's conceptions of plot and hero useful. Frye employs a very straightforward definition whereby a 'plot consists of somebody doing something. The somebody, if an individual, is the hero'.[25] This is also easily applied to romance sagas, explaining them really as simply about the exploits of one character. Taking this as a starting point, Hermann Pálsson and Paul Edwards's *Legendary Fiction in Medieval Iceland*, an influential study of a selection of *fornaldarsögur*, puts forward the idea that 'there must be some relationship between the characteristic qualities of the hero, and the kind of action he takes, or for that matter, the tone and even the structure of the tale – the nature of the hero dictates the form of the narrative'.[26] Building on this, Kalinke, too, has argued 'that examination of the hero's quest, as well as motivation for that quest, is necessary if we are to arrive at a more convincing and satisfactory classification and thus at a better understanding of the character and diversity of imaginative Icelandic literature'.[27] This notion of quest as important in the identification of a hero complements Propp's definitions, and fits well with the romances where, as noted, the plot on a basic level does more or less simply follow an individual's adventures ending in marriage, possibly supported by a helper.

---

22   *Clári saga*, ed. by Cederschiöld, pp. 73-74.
23   Hallberg, 'Imagery in Religious Old Norse Prose Literature', p. 166.
24   Hughes, '*Klári saga* as an Indigenous Romance', p. 157.
25   Frye, *Anatomy of Criticism*, p. 33.
26   Hermann Pálsson and Edwards, *Legendary Fiction in Medieval Iceland*, p. 36. For their indebtedness to Frye see pp. 10-12.
27   Kalinke, 'Riddarasögur, Fornaldarsögur, and the Problem of Genre', p. 82. Kalinke elsewhere refers to 'Frye's classification of fiction on the basis of the hero's power of action' in reference to Icelandic romance ('Norse Romance (Riddararsögur)', p. 325).

Considering another perspective on heroes will help to define them in an Icelandic romance context, while situating them within the wider context of medieval European romance, which has also contributed to romance in Iceland. The medieval European romance hero is very different from the specifically Icelandic romance hero, and we must appreciate these differences in order to understand the Icelandic romance hero in general, and in *Nítíða saga* in particular. Tony Hunt describes medieval European romance (by contrast with medieval epic), as 'an inquiring mode, a critical investigation in the course of which more individualistic values are gradually disengaged', and the hero of which is 'a voluntary exile' on a 'discovery of identity' and 'self-realization through "adventure"'.[28] Rather than having internal motives of self-discovery and abstract quests, Icelandic romance heroes generally have concrete, external goals and motivations, such as a bridal-quest. The *Strengleikar* (lit. Stringed Instruments), translated from Marie de France's *lais*, along with the Arthurian stories *Parcevals saga*, *Valvens þáttur*, *Ívens saga*, and *Erex saga* from Chrétien de Troyes' romances, and *Tristrams saga ok Ísöndar* from Thomas of Britain's *Tristan* are the first European romances to be translated into Old Norse.[29] While the introspective heroes and protagonists of the original French texts were not necessarily fully adapted into these translations,[30] these first Old Norse romances did influence, either directly or indirectly, the authors of the later medieval Icelandic romances, and arguably introduced echoes of a different kind of protagonist to Scandinavia, which some authors of Icelandic romance, including that of *Nítíða saga*, may have picked up on and incorporated into their characters and texts. But such heroes of English, French, and other romances are rather different from the decidedly active heroes of Icelandic romance, particularly the action-driven bridal-quest romances. While it may be tempting to think of this also as an issue of courtly or literary versus popular romance regardless of country or language of origin, European popular romance (i.e. later prose romance) was almost certainly not known in medieval Iceland – it was only the earlier literary verse, courtly romances that were translated and reworked in Scandinavia – meaning that it really is a matter of contrasting Icelandic romance with European romance in terms of the active versus the often

---

28   Hunt, 'Chrétien de Troyes' Arthurian Romance, *Yvain*', pp. 128-29.

29   Cook and Tveitane, eds., *Strengleikar*; Kalinke, ed., *Norse Romance I: The Tristan Legend*; Kalinke, ed., *Norse Romance II: Knights of the Round Table*; Kalinke, ed., *Norse Romance III: Hærra Ivan*; Schach, ed., *The Saga of Tristram and Ísönd*.

30   See Sif Rikhardsdottir, *Medieval Translations and Cultural Discourse*, pp. 24-52, 76-112.

more introspective heroes. What comes to be known as popular romance in (especially post-Reformation) Iceland, that is, Icelandic romance plain and simple, developed, directly and indirectly, from the courtly romance of France and Britain. A further integral aspect of European romance heroes is their morality. Josseline Bidard states that 'there is one [quality required of a medieval hero] which sums up and comprehends all the others, i.e. truth'.[31] Very broadly speaking, the heroes of European romances can be thought of as Christian heroes whose abstract quests often include, if they are not exclusively centred on, quests for truth and Christian virtues. These varying constructions of romance heroes involve a moral element and intense focus on the self, and especially the inner self, which is not usually where the focus of Icelandic romances lies. Paul Bibire states the difference quite bluntly: 'The hero of Icelandic Secondary [= non-translated] Romance usually has little or no ethical significance: he does not explore or (usually) significantly exemplify ideals of [...] Christian morality. And since he has no ethical significance, the possibility of tragedy does not exist'.[32] This is of course despite the obviously Christian settings of almost all Icelandic romances, which I have already mentioned briefly in Chapter 3.

As a final contrast, I turn briefly to the hero in a different genre of medieval Icelandic literature, the *Íslendingasögur*. Whereas the romances are in terms of plot very obviously driven by their heroes, this is not often the case in the *Íslendingasögur*, where the driving force is usually the struggles of families spanning several generations, or even a community of many families, rather than the adventures of a single person.[33] To take only two examples, which of course grossly simplifies the genre in question, in *Eyrbyggja saga* and *Vatnsdœla saga* it is difficult with their multiplicity of characters and relationships to pinpoint their heroes in the same way one can for a romance. In both texts, to some extent the only thing the various families of characters have in common is their place of residence, which is in turn reflected in the titles; to consider how romance titles usually contain their heroes' names, the same idea can be transferred to these stories of collective groups and families. The heroes of these *Íslendingasögur* could be thought of as the communities of people living in the locations indicated in their titles, when the sagas' complexity makes naming a single hero complicated. Of course many other *Íslendingasögur* are named after

31 Bidard, 'Reynard the Fox as Anti-Hero', p. 122.
32 Bibire, 'From *riddarasaga* to *lygisaga*', p. 69.
33 O'Donoghue, *Old Norse-Icelandic Literature*, pp. 34-43; Vésteinn Ólason, 'Family Sagas', pp. 101-18.

specific characters who can be thought of as their heroes (such as *Hrafnkels saga* or *Gunnlaugs saga ormstungu*). It is thus reasonable to keep titles in mind when assessing a saga's hero, romance or otherwise, as saga titles are descriptive (although of course a title should not be the main criterion). Kalinke has also argued based on titles in manuscript as to how the focus of *Sigurðar saga fóts* should be considered: 'The full title *Sigurðar saga fóts ok Ásmundar Húnakónungs* suggests that the saga is to be read not as the account of Signý's tragedy, [...] but rather as the tale of two men who start out as rivals for the same bride but who become sworn brothers because of mutual respect'.[34] Of course in this and the cases just mentioned it is true that such sagas' titles vary in their manuscripts as well. Of most importance is the role of characters within the saga, and the degree to which the audience's attention is drawn to one character, making the one who is featured most prominently the protagonist. This brings us back again to the notion of questing, which, while absent or only marginally important in the *Íslendingasögur*, is crucial to both European and Icelandic romance (and fairy tale).

With all of this considered, an Icelandic romance hero might be best defined simply as the protagonist, with two essential criteria: 1) the hero is the character on whom the saga's action focuses and, consequently, 2) the hero is the character with whom the audience is led to sympathize. The hero's action and involvement in the plot therefore function in Icelandic romance to propel the action forward to its end, meaning there is usually some sort of journey or quest to be fulfilled, or some lack or injustice to be righted, as the motivating force behind the hero's decisions and actions. A helper character, then, would best be seen as crucial to success of the hero's quest: not just an incidental acquaintance who offers help in passing, but a character whose help is ongoing.[35] I now turn to the characterizations of Livorius and Nítíða, and the roles of directly supportive characters, to demonstrate the unconventional ways in which *Nítíða saga* portrays the hero, and to consider what this demonstrates about how *Nítíða saga* situates itself, and the Icelandic culture that produced it, in European society and literary culture. In the second part of the chapter I will consider the hero's main antagonists, to see how their depiction works to reinforce her prominence.

---

34   Kalinke, *Bridal-Quest Romance*, p. 196.
35   I thus depart from Propp in his acceptance of almost any cooperative character as a sort of helper (*Morphology of the Folktale*, pp. 80-82).

Livorius and Nítíða

Livorius is the character usually taken for granted as the hero of *Nítíða saga* because by the end of the romance he successfully wins Nítíða's hand. Kalinke, for example, specifically refers to him as the 'hero' and 'male protagonist' of the saga,[36] in keeping with her statement that 'as a rule, bridal-quest narratives have as their protagonist an eligible young bachelor',[37] necessarily making the hero the successful wooer. Undeniably, he is on a bridal-quest to marry Nítíða, a quest that ends in success, after which the saga promptly ends. Further, Livorius is introduced positively, and the manner in which he is described mirrors that in which Nítíða is introduced earlier on in the tale:

> Blebarnius [...] ätti son er Liforinus hiet. hann var vænn at æliti. lios og <Riodur> j anndliti snareygdur sem valur. hrockinn hærdur og fagurt härit. herda breidur enn keikur ä bringuna. kurteis. sterkur og stormannlegur. hann kvnni vel sund og sæfaraʀ skot og skilmingar tafl og runar og bækur at lesa. og allar jþrotter er karlmann mätti pryda. [...] Liforinus lä j hernadi bædi vetur og sumar og afladi sier fjæʀ og frægdar. og þotti hinn mesti garpur og kappi. huar sem hann fram kom. og hafdi sigur j huerri orrustu. hann var suo mikill til kuenna at eingi hafdi næder fyrer honum. en eingua kongs dottur hafdi hann mænadi leingur.[38]

> (Blebarnius [...] had a son called Livorius. He was handsome in appearance, light and rosy in face, sharp-eyed as a falcon, with beautiful curly hair, broad-shouldered, yet upright of chest, and was courteous, strong, and magnificent. He knew well how to swim and sail, how to shoot and fence, play board games and use runes, and to read books, as well as all physical activities that a man should pursue. [...] Livorius engaged in plundering both winter and summer and earned for himself wealth and fame, and was thought the best hero and champion wherever he went, and had victory in each battle. He was so keen on women that none had any peace from him, but he did not stay with any princess longer than a month.)

36 Kalinke, *Bridal-Quest Romance*, pp. 22, 75.
37 Kalinke, *Bridal-Quest Romance*, p. 26.
38 'Nitida saga', ed. by Loth, pp. 8-9.

This lengthy characterization is typical of Icelandic romance heroes, comprising all the courtly expectations of a well-rounded man, and these types of descriptions may have their roots in European romance.[39] Livorius's implied promiscuity, however, seems to be a blind motif,[40] since this is its sole mention, and when the plot turns to him, he is set only on winning Nítíða.[41] Livorius' physical description is even at one point identical to that of Nítíða, also described as *ljós og rjóð í andliti*. This correspondence of outward appearance sets up the possibility that the two will be paired in the end and might be equals in their relationship. In the introduction to her monograph on the depiction of Saracen women in medieval French epic and romance, Jacqueline de Weever notes that when marriages occur in these texts, 'union seems only possible by identification with the other. The Saracen princess who marries the Christian prince must, therefore, resemble him as much as possible'.[42] It is this type of convention that is employed by *Nítíða saga* in the description of Livorius, making him appear as similar as possible to Nítíða in order both to conform to convention and also side-step it, by altering the male character's appearance to match the woman's, rather than the other way around, which would be expected. Furthermore, this imagery, of a man from India having fair and rosy skin comparable to that of a French woman,[43] could also have been potentially unusual and therefore significant for any Icelanders who might have been aware of any physical differences

39 Ármann Jakobsson, *Illa fenginn mjöður*, p. 178 (Ármann also notes Livorius's riding in the woods later in the text as indicative of the influence of the European romance hero on the saga); Kalinke, *Bridal-Quest Romance*, pp. 72-74. See also Curtius, *European Literature and the Latin Middle Ages*, pp. 180-82. However, the topos of a detailed physical description along with a list of accomplishments can be seen in Old Norse literature as early as in *Orkneyinga saga*'s description of Kali Kolsson (*Orkneyinga saga*, ed. by Finnbogi Guðmundsson, pp. 129-30), raising the question of whether the first person verse description of accomplishments there is a poem of boasting alone or whether it could have also been influenced by romance, although there is not the space here to consider this further. The description in *Nítíða saga* adds swimming and fencing to *Orkneyinga saga*'s list.

40 The promiscuous hero motif is also in *Sigrgarðs saga frækna*, where it allows for a reading of the saga in which Sigrgarðr deserves the abuse heaped on him by the maiden-king Ingigerðr. *Bærings saga*, which co-occurs with *Sigrgarðs saga frækna* in manuscripts, also does this (Kalinke, *Bridal-Quest Romance*, pp. 22-23). With this in mind, it then becomes possible, on the one hand, to consider that a contributing factor to Nítíða's restraint towards and acceptance of Livorius may have to do with his pristine character, though, on the other hand, he does attempt abduction by force and magic, which does not make the best impression on Nítíða.

41 Bagerius, *Mandom och mödom*, p. 136.

42 de Weever, *Sheba's Daughters*, p. xx. See also pp. 3-52, which focuses on whitening in particular.

43 Ármann Jakobsson notes Livorius's fair complexion *despite* his Indian origin: '*Þrátt fyrir indverskan uppruna*' (my italics), in *Illa fenginn mjöður*, p. 177 (see also p. 178).

between the inhabitants of Europe and Asia, though in the Middle Ages such knowledge would of course have been very limited. In terms of historical interaction with India and the East, by the early seventeenth century at least one Icelander had travelled to India and returned to Iceland: Jón Ólafsson *Indíafari* (India-traveller) (1593-1679), and while word of his travels may have made India familiar to some early modern Icelanders, there is nothing comparable for the saga's original medieval author and audiences.[44] Even if there was no direct medieval Icelandic knowledge of India in the Middle Ages, something of it was at least known even if only in other romances like *Alexanders saga* and *Rémundar saga keisarasonar*; historiographical and pseudohistoriographical texts based on biblical, classical, and continental medieval texts like *Stjórn*; and encyclopaedic works like those contained in *Alfrœði íslenzk.*[45] Barnes notes that, parallel with the shifting of cartography evident in the saga, and which I discussed in Chapter 3, 'ethnographic norms are upended too',[46] most obviously in Livorius's northern appearance. Livorius is further linked to Nítíða when he is re-introduced relatively late in the saga: 'Nv er at seigia af hinum fræga kongi Liforino' (Now it is said about the famous King Livorius).[47] This phrasing mirrors Nítíða's own character tag, *hin fræga*. Additionally, Nítíða herself twice calls Livorius by name in this way during the seeing-stones scene, perhaps signalling she accepts him as an equal: 'mun Livorius kongr hinn fræge eckj sigla j þesse lond' (will King Livorius the Famous not sail into these lands?) and 'huar mun Liv(orius) hinn fræge vera' (where will Livorius the Famous be?).[48] While these clues are subtle, when considered together they clearly point to the ultimate union of Livorius and Nítíða, and could arguably identify Livorius as the saga's hero. His success in winning Nítíða's hand, as a result of the advice given to him by his aunt Alduria whose brief but important role I discuss in the following chapter, lends Livorius more credibility as the hero, especially if the romance is to be considered a bridal-quest.

---

44 See *The Life of the Icelander Jón Ólafsson Traveller to India*, II.

45 See Würth, 'Historiography and Pseudo-History', pp. 155-72. Other romances also displayed more detailed knowledge of India, as discussed in Barnes, *The Bookish Riddarasögur*, pp. 126-45; and Divjak, *Studies in the Traditions of Kirialax Saga*, pp. 220-39. Of course it is also likely that this aspect of Livorius's characterization is yet another blind motif included according to romance convention but not fully seen through.

46 Barnes, *The Bookish Riddarasögur*, p. 37.

47 'Nitida saga', ed. by Loth, p. 21.

48 'Nitida saga', ed. by Loth, pp. 30-31.

Furthermore, Livorius's similarity to Nítíða also sets him apart from Ingi of Miklagarður,[49] who is also introduced favourably:

> Jngi [...] var allra manna sæmilegastur og best at j þrottum buen. hann lä j hernadi huert sumar og afladi sier suo fiær og frægdar. drap rænsmenn og vikinga. en liet fridmenn fara j nådum.[50]

> (Ingi [...] was the most honourable of all men and the best endowed in athletic arts. He went plundering each summer and in doing so got for himself wealth and fame; he killed robbers and vikings, and let peaceful people move in peace.)

If it were not for the explicit linking of Livorius with Nítíða, Ingi might be considered a viable choice as successful suitor and saga hero, even if his descriptive introduction is significantly shorter than that of Livorius. Ingi is characterized as 'like' the protagonist, whereas the other suitors, Soldán and his sons from Serkland, are decidedly 'other' in their descriptions.[51] Ingi, though neither the hero nor any sort of heroic companion, takes part in the courtly triple wedding that closes the saga despite his previously antagonistic characterization both as a threat to Nítíða (as a forceful suitor willing to resort to abduction) and to Livorius (as rival suitor willing to fight to gain a wife). Ingi's positive, conventional description sets up the possibility, and even expectation, for his positive end, even though he is not the hero.

Ingi's ultimately positive characterization can also be viewed as an example of the foster brother relationship so common in other romances. Once Ingi and Livorius are reconciled after the saga's final battle, they join their families together through marriage, as foster or sworn brothers often do: Ingi falls in love with Livorius's sister Sýjalín, who heals his wounds at Livorius's suggestion, and once their marriage is agreed, Livorius also offers his future foster brother-in-law Hléksjöldur as a husband for Ingi's sister Listalín, fulfilling the traditional role of a foster brother rewarding his foster brother (for his service and help) with not only a bride, but also other family and political connections for his prosperity.[52] This further shows

---

49 Bagerius considers Ingi to be Russian rather than from Constantinople/Byzantium (*Mandom och mödom*, p. 218).

50 'Nitida saga', ed. by Loth, p. 8.

51 Jóhanna Katrín Friðriksdóttir, *Women in Old Norse Literature*, pp. 127-28.

52 This type of behaviour between foster and sworn brothers is evident in other romances including, as only a couple of examples, *Þjalar-Jóns saga* and *Saulus saga ok Nikanors*, and in

how the previously antagonistic Ingi, his kin, and his homeland are in the end elevated to a status comparable to that of Nítíða and Livorius – Constantinople is as courtly and civilized as France and India, and rightly so, considering its favourable depiction throughout Icelandic romance.[53] Ingi's kingdom has at once become doubly strengthened through his connection to Livorius, in his acquisition of a wife with whom to build his own kingdom in Constantinople, in his links to India and France through this wife's family, and in his sister's joining the Apulian kingdom with her own new husband. That this can take place – that a former antagonist can become allied with the protagonists – is possible because of his courtly characterization early on, similar to that of Livorius, and wholly dissimilar to the otherness of the brothers from Serkland, who, because of this, never had a chance to end up as Ingi does. The positive characterization of Ingi thus serves ultimately to strengthen and reinforce the kingdom, and the courtliness, of Livorius, and through him, of Nítíða, who also benefits from these new alliances. With Ingi as Livorius's companion and ally, not only is Nítíða's powerful French kingdom united with and strengthened by India, but it also gains ties with Constantinople. At the saga's end, everyone who has ever been identified as powerful, courtly, or civilized, ends up prosperous.

Even though some of the evidence presented thus far might suggest that Livorius is the saga's hero, there are important problems with his role and characterization, which reveal him to be insufficient as hero. To begin, Livorius is only a major, active character in the second half or even last third of the romance. His exploits only begin in the fourth chapter out of five in the edited version, after nearly all the other characters have enjoyed active roles. When he is re-introduced, the narrator even reminds the audience that the character 'fýrr var nefndur' (was mentioned before), in case he may have been forgotten in the midst of the action up until then.[54] Simply put, his actions do not drive the plot. Further, he is not even introduced or mentioned at all until the second chapter has got under way, again, after all other rival suitors are introduced, and long after Nítíða herself has become known to the audience through her visit to Apulia and expedition to Visio. Livorius's absence from the initial scenes and his absence from much of the tale are uncharacteristic of the introduction of a romance saga

---

fornaldarsögur such as *Hrólfs saga Gautrekssonar*. See also Kalinke, *Bridal-Quest Romance*, pp. 156-202.

53   Barnes, *The Bookish Riddarasögur*, pp. 147-81; Sverrir Jakobsson, 'The Schism that Never Was'.

54   'Nitida saga', ed. by Loth, p. 21.

hero. Conversely, Nítíða's immediate introduction and early expeditions are typical of romance heroes, who often assemble a team of helpers and gain special objects or powers, before embarking on their bridal-quests or other adventures. In Icelandic romance, if the hero is not introduced straight away, then he is usually only preceded by necessary family background information such as a brief family history, as in *Sigrgarðs saga frækna*,[55] or sometimes with the addition of a more or less self-conscious prologue, as in for example *Clári saga*, *Sigurðar saga þögla*, and *Viktors saga ok Blávus*.[56] In *Nítíða saga* there is no prologue, which facilitates Nítíða's immediate introduction.

To demonstrate Nítíða's position as the saga's heroic protagonist, I turn now to evidence that it is she around whom the entire story revolves and that it is she with whom the audience is led to sympathize, two criteria of the hero that Livorius fails to satisfy. To begin, the saga is named after Nítíða, not Livorius. In manuscript, the saga is usually titled *Nítíða (hinni) frægu* and a couple of times as *Meykónginum Nítíða*. It is only a few of the late manuscripts that give the title as *Sagan af Meykónginum Nitedá* (Lbs 1711 8vo [1848]), *Sagann af Meykongýnúm Nýtida* (ÍB 290 8vo [1851]), or simply *Sagann af Nitida* (Lbs 4656 4to [c. 1859-60]). In over sixty other manuscripts from the late fifteenth century onwards, the title, when it exists, is the saga of *Nitida (hinni) frægu*.[57] Livorius is never a part of the title. Some other romances do include the maiden-king and the male hero who marries her in the title of certain later manuscripts, showing that some audiences or scribes interpreted the woman's role as equally important as the man's, but still, significantly, not important enough to change the title fully to that of the woman alone. Examples of this, from a couple of romances with demonstrable connections to *Nítíða saga*, as already discussed above, include *Dínus saga dramblata* titled as *Sagan af Dínus dramblata og Phílómu drottningu* (JS 623 4to [1853], f. 199ʳ), as well as *Clári saga* as *Sagann af Claro Keisarasyne og Serena Drottningu* (AM 395 fol. [1760-66], f. 416ʳ, and similar in Lbs 3021 4to [1877], f. 75ᵛ) or *Saga af Klares og Serena* in the same manuscript as *Nítíða saga* (ÍB 138 4to [1750-99], f. 93ʳ).

Secondly, Nítíða is introduced first and described immediately, which not only positions her as the main character but as one with whom the

---

55 'Sigrgarðs saga frœkna', ed. by Loth, p. 39.

56 See Chapter 6 for a discussion of romance prologues, including these texts.

57 See Chapter 1 for further discussion of *Nítíða saga*'s manuscripts and different versions; for more detailed analyses of the manuscripts see McDonald Werronen, 'Transforming Popular Romance on the Edge of the World', pp. 24-55, and McDonald Werronen, 'Two Major Groups in the Older Manuscript Tradition of *Nítíða saga*', pp. 75-94.

audience can sympathize, rather than with any of her suitors. The saga's first chapter focuses carefully on introducing Nítíða and preparing her for what action is to come throughout the rest of the tale:

> HEYRet vnger menn eitt æfıntyʀ og fagra frasaugn fra hinum frægasta meykongi er verit hefur j nordur hælfu veralldarinar er hiet Nitida hin fræga [...]. Þessi meykongur sat j aunduegi heimsins j Fracklandi jnu goda og hiellt Pàris borg. hun var bædi vitur og væn lios og riod j andliti þuilikast sem en rauda rosa væri samtemprad vid sniohuita lileam. augun suo skiæʀ sem karbunkulus. haurundit suo huitt sem fıls bein. häʀ þuilikt sem gull og fıell nidur à jord vm hana. [...] hun var suo buen at viti sem hinn frodasti klerkur. og hinn sterkasti borgarveggur mætti hun giora med sinu viti yfer annara manna vit og byrgia suo vti annara ræd. og þar kunni hun .x. ʀæd er adrer kunnu eitt.[58]

> (Listen, young people, to an adventure and wonderful account about the most famous maiden-king there has ever been in the northern region of the world. She was called Nítíða the Famous [...]. This maiden-king sat on the throne of the world in France the Good, and ruled in Paris. She was both wise and fair, light and rosy in face just as if the red rose was tempered together with a snow-white lily; her eyes were as bright as a carbuncle, and her skin as white as ivory; her hair was like gold and fell down to the earth around her. [...] She was as endowed with knowledge as the wisest scholar, and, surpassing other people's intelligence, she could make the strongest castle-wall with her own intellect, and thus outmanoeuvre others' plans; and she knew ten answers when others knew one.)

Nítíða's introduction is longer than that of Livorius. As Kalinke notes, Nítíða is physically described in a characteristically European courtly romance manner,[59] from her long golden hair to her *lilia-mixta-rosis* complexion. Compare this to a similar description in the translated romance *Elis saga ok Rósamundu*: 'hennar kinnr voro þvilikaztar, sem þa er ravda rosa væri bland*it* vid hvita lilia*m*' (her cheeks were the most like as though a red rose were blended with a white lily).[60] Some manuscript versions show further similarity to *Elis saga* in their descriptions of Nítíða: in certain manuscripts

58 'Nitida saga', ed. by Loth, pp. 3-4.
59 Kalinke, *Bridal-Quest Romance*, pp. 72-73; Kalinke, *King Arthur*, pp. 94-95.
60 Kölbing, ed., *Elis saga ok Rósamundu*, p. 136.

such as the late eighteenth-century Reykjavík, Landsbókasafn Íslands–
Háskólabókasafn, MS ÍBR 59 4to Nítíða is additionally called 'hin fridasta
frægasta & kurteisasta' (the most beautiful, famous, and courteous),[61] which
is also very similar to Rósamunda's threefold description as 'hin kurtæsia,
hin friða oc hin frægia [...]' (the courteous, the beautiful, and the famous).[62]
Of course these similarities may again be nothing more than evidence
that many formulaic descriptors were adopted into the Icelandic romance
vocabulary from translated romances (as noted in Chapter 2), but it is
intriguing to consider the possibility of a closer relationship between these
two romances, though there is not room to do so here.[63] Focusing again on
the description in *Nítíða saga*, it is also clear that this emphasizes Nítíða's
foreign nature, distancing her from the present reality in Iceland.[64] After
this elaborate introduction, the saga follows Nítíða to Apulia and then to
Visio, before she returns to France having been prepared for what is to
come once her suitors are introduced. Nítíða is equipped in a way similar
to that in which other saga heroes are prepared with the acquisition of
helpful objects and the aid of other characters. It is not simply that *Nítíða
saga* 'presents the heroine in as favourable a light as possible',[65] but that
the audience experiences the saga almost entirely from her point of view,
and thus is better able to sympathize with her.[66] Of course having a female
hero may have been challenging for audiences who might have been more
used to the male heroes of other romances, but *Nítíða saga* could, rather, be
responding to a gap in the market, so to speak.[67] *Nítíða saga*'s extraordinary
popularity clearly attests to its audiences' acceptance of Nítíða as the hero,
and the story's markedly female perspective.

In addition to her lengthy description at the beginning of the romance,
Nítíða is depicted early on as a hero preparing for later adventures. She
equips herself to ensure her safety and gain an advantage over any suitors
who pursue her, by securing the help of her foster brother Hléskjöldur:
'sidan lætur hun bua sina ferd og skipa stol heim til Fracklandz. beidandi
fru Egi(dia) at Hle(skiolldur) hennar son fylgdi henni at styrkia hennar RIKI
fyrir æhlaupum hermanna' (Afterwards she prepares for her journey and
readies her fleets of ships to go home to France, asking lady Egidía that

61   Reykjavík, Landsbókasafn–Háskólabókasafn Íslands, MS ÍBR 59 4to, p. 193.
62   Kölbing, ed., *Elis saga ok Rósamundu*, p. 76.
63   See Chapter 6, which further highlights similarities between the sagas' openings.
64   van Nahl, *Originale Riddarasögur*, pp. 74-75.
65   Bibire, 'From *riddarasaga* to *lygisaga*', p. 67.
66   Cf. Ármann Jakobsson, *Illa fenginn mjöður*, p. 176.
67   Cf. Jóhanna Katrín Friðriksdóttir, *Women in Old Norse Literature*, pp. 107-33.

Hléskjöldur her son accompany her to strengthen her realm against warrior attacks).[68] She then procures magic objects including the *náttúrusteinar*, which later help her: 'drott(ning) gladdist nu vit þessa syn. takandi kerit og alla þessa steina eple og læknis graus. þuiat hun vnder stod af sinni visku hueria nætturu huer bar' (The queen then grows glad at this sight, taking the vessel and all the stones, apples, and healing herbs, because she understood from her wisdom how magical each was).[69] Further, almost immediately after gaining possession of these things, Nítíða must escape from Virgilius with the aid of a magic stone: 'm(ey)kongur tok nu eirn nætturu stein og bra yfer skipit og haufud þeim avllum er jnnan bordz voru. sæ jar(l) þau alldri sidan' (The maiden-king now took a supernatural stone and quickly waved it over the ship and the heads of all who were on board. The earl never saw them again).[70] This first escape foreshadows her later trickery and escapes. Whereas the audience therefore knows how Nítíða will overcome her suitors, in other maiden-king romances it is often a mystery as to how the women will trick the heroes right up until it happens, simply because the action follows the men more closely than the maiden-kings. This is the case in *Clári saga*, when Séréna humiliates Clárus, as well as in *Sigurðar saga þǫgla*, which is in some ways even more misogynistic than *Clári saga*. But if one asks whom *Nítíða saga* is about, clearly the answer is Nítíða herself, and at no time is she characterized as an antagonist. Whereas she resists marriage and aims to defeat her suitors, the romance does not portray the suitors as protagonists but as intruders on Nítíða's peaceful kingdom, which she nonetheless governs proactively, taking precautions against intruders and defending herself when rivals do appear.

Unlike in other maiden-king romances, in *Nítíða saga* the line between the two usually distinct categories of maiden-king and hero is blurred. The saga presents a story in which we find a maiden-king who is never really antagonistic, and is never reduced to submission through humiliation or punishment, but who willingly accepts Livorius after observing his attempt to outwit her as she outwitted her suitors.[71] Ultimately she outwits Livorius again, with both her superior knowledge and her ability to use the magic stones acquired at the outset. Even though Nítíða is willing to marry when the circumstances are right, she does avoid and escape from

68 'Nitida saga', ed. by Loth, p. 7.
69 'Nitida saga', ed. by Loth, p. 6.
70 'Nitida saga', ed. by Loth, p. 7. See below for more on Virgilius.
71 Whereas, as mentioned already, Nítíða does have the suitors from Serkland killed, they are from the beginning typecast as the monstrous Other in order to justify their killing. A more detailed discussion of this follows below.

her suitors, when they attempt to take her by force. Her objection to this negative treatment is something she has in common with maiden-kings from other romances. In her willingness to marry into an equal partnership, Nítíða is unlike other maiden-kings. After allowing his aunt to guide his actions, Livorius's efforts turn from coercive to interpersonal and persuasive, indicating his respect for Nítíða rather than reducing her to an object to possess. Nítíða realizes this difference in Livorius, and that he is uniquely nearly as clever as she. None of her other suitors attempt to outwit her or negotiate on courtly terms to build a relationship before proposing.[72] It is based on these realizations that she agrees to become Livorius's partner. Kalinke, commenting on the 'peculiar character' of Nítíða saga, says that 'the titular heroine appears to be more in charge of her fate than other maiden kings'.[73] This is certainly true and supports Nítíða's comparison and contrast, as hero, not only with cruel maiden-kings, but also with the heroes of romance, in the ultimate reworking of conventional maiden-king romance. In Nítíða saga it is not merely that a woman is the hero, but that the notion of the romance hero itself is challenged, questioning what it means to be the focus of such a saga, and whether this female Icelandic romance hero might also possess some of the introspectivity noted above as a feature of European romance heroes. Nítíða's internal negotiation of the romance world instead of an active quest for a partner is more like some French romance heroes than other heroes of Icelandic romance. In this way the romance genre and its expectations are further challenged through the characterization of a protagonist who, although she abstains from actually engaging in active opposition herself, is intellectually and internally active in her ability to outwit her suitors time and again. Nítíða not only takes 'charge of her fate', so to speak, but does so in a way that highlights her nature as an individual rather than as just a particular romance 'type'. In this way, the saga further questions traditional Icelandic romance norms, giving this female hero more psychological depth than might be expected.[74]

An important aspect of romance heroes touched on only briefly above is their usual accompaniment by a helper, like a foster brother. The heroes often do not function well without someone to support them. Such characters

---

72   The consent of women became an important aspect of marriage in medieval Iceland, and especially by the late medieval period from which Nítíða saga survives. See Agnes S. Arnórsdóttir, Property and Virginity, and Jochens, 'Consent in Marriage', pp. 142-76. See also Jóhanna Katrín Friðriksdóttir, Women in Old Norse Literature, pp. 128-30.

73   Kalinke, Bridal-Quest Romance, p. 102; see also Driscoll, 'Nitida saga', p. 432.

74   See also Jóhanna Katrín Friðriksdóttir, Women in Old Norse Literature, pp. 129-30.

are found in a great number of maiden-king and other Icelandic romances,[75] such as Viktor and Blávus, Jarlmann and Hermann, and Sigurður fótur and Ásmundur; even in *Clári saga*, Clárus has his teacher Pérus to help him, although his part is far more sinister than that of most foster brother figures in his role in Séréna's humiliation and abuse. To reward their efforts, helpers usually find or are given a bride of their own, which accounts for the high occurrence of double and triple wedding scenes that conclude most late medieval Icelandic romances, noted above: the triple wedding in *Nítíða saga* sees Nítíða marry Livorius, Hléskjöldur (Nítíða's foster brother) marry Listalín (Ingi's sister), and Ingi (Nítíða's first suitor) marry Sýjalín (Livorius's sister). In *Nítíða saga*, Livorius does not have a personal helper who accompanies him throughout his quest. Whereas he stumbles upon a benevolent dwarf who unsuccessfully attempts to get Nítíða into Livorius's power, and takes advice from his aunt, these characters are only introduced when necessary and are not the sort of companions who provide ongoing support. Considering this, it is therefore especially significant that Nítíða's foster family is introduced before her adventure to the island of Visio, and it is significant also that her foster brother Hléskjöldur accompanies her, setting his presence with her throughout the rest of the saga, carrying out her commands.

In one sense, Nítíða cannot properly function as a ruler without Hléskjöldur's assistance. Boberg, in her *Motif-Index of Early Icelandic Literature*, strangely considers this foster sibling relationship romantic.[76] It is also conceivable that in this romance, the main character, the hero, could be split into two parts – one female (Nítíða), one male (Hléskjöldur), in order to make a complete, fully-functioning whole. This idea has also recently been put forth by Jóhanna Katrín Friðriksdóttir, who suggests that 'The control that Nitida exerts over Hleskiolldur suggests that the pair could be seen as split aspects of the same character where the female aspect takes care of decision making while the male element executes her orders in the male sphere'.[77] The rationale for this would be that whereas for a woman to perform all the duties and tasks that in this saga are carried out by Hléskjöldur (e.g. engaging in battle with her suitors) might cast her character as 'unfeminine', and therefore more like a traditional maiden-king;[78] if her male

---

75   Kalinke, *Bridal-Quest Romance*, pp. 156-202.

76   Boberg, *Motif-Index of Early Icelandic Literature*, motif P274.1, 'Love between foster-sister and foster-brother' (p. 213).

77   *Women in Old Norse Literature*, p. 128.

78   Nítíða is not like 'traditional' maiden-kings like Þórnbjörg in *Hrólfs saga Gautrekssonar*, or Sedentiana in *Sigurðar saga þǫgla*, whose excessive violence towards her suitors even sometimes results in their death.

counterpart enacts her commands, she therefore continues to be a powerful figure while distancing herself from the violence and deception that her role as king sometimes calls for. Because Nítíða is portrayed throughout as successful, wise, and quintessentially feminine, it might follow that in her reluctance or inability to adopt male traits she cannot alone be considered a good ruler. Thus Hléskjöldur would not merely be a conventional helpful foster brother, but an inextricable part of Nítíða's ruling maiden-king hero character. A reading this extreme, however, is not necessary, and I propose instead reading Hléskjöldur as an ordinary helper to Nítíða's hero. As the hero in her own right, supported by her foster brother, Nítíða is thus even more like other heroes. Hléskjöldur lacks the motivations of his own needed to make him any more than a stock companion character, as his only aims are to serve Nítíða. For example, when Nítíða instructs him to gather her army and fight Soldán at sea, she addresses her foster brother in direct speech, and he assents only indirectly: 'Hl(eskiolldur) giorer suo' (Hléskjöldur does so).[79] In this way, the focus remains on the active female character who instigates the action, even though it is carried out by the male character. Further, when Nítíða asks her foster mother Egidía to send Hléskjöldur back to France with her, he is not consulted about the matter:

> sidan lætur hun bua sina ferd og skipa stol heim til Fracklandz. beidandi fru Egi(dia) at Hle(skiolldur) hennar son fylgdi henni at styrkia hennar ʀiki fyrir æahlaupum hermanna. hennar fostur modur veiter henni þetta sæmilega[80]

> (Afterwards she makes preparations for her journey and readies her fleets of ships to go home to France, asking lady Egidía that Hléskjöldur her son accompany her to strengthen her realm against attacks by raiders. Her foster mother grants her this graciously)

It is the women who are the decision-makers in this early episode, again foreshadowing Nítíða's independence and sovereignty throughout the romance. Hléskjöldur is not even given direct speech until he lures the brothers from Serkland to Nítíða's deadly trap,[81] and only asserts himself at the saga's end when he tells Nítíða that he will no longer serve her unless she marries Livorius. Nítíða's complexity of character, from her

79 'Nitida saga', ed. by Loth, p. 26.
80 'Nitida saga', ed. by Loth, p. 7.
81 'Nitida saga', ed. by Loth, p. 19.

resourcefulness and wisdom to her relationship with her foster brother, shows she is a worthy and able hero, regardless of her gender. This further allows for sharper contrast between this romance and others, and to see how *Nítíða saga* questions and re-evaluates their conventions.

Though I have argued that Nítíða is the saga's hero, one could, however, raise issues against this.[82] A major factor is of course her gender. It upsets the conventions of Icelandic romance to have a female hero, considering the well-established bridal-quest paradigms of many Icelandic romances, but considering everything else about Nítíða's characterization as hero, this is by all means a deliberate upset meant to provoke the interrogation of assumptions about heroes. With Nítíða as one of the only female heroes in medieval Icelandic romance, this makes the saga unique and unconventional in its negotiation of the genre's themes, plots, and motifs. In the sense that all romances (and indeed other texts) that are aware of their genre question it, it is tempting to say that few romances do so in the way that *Nítíða saga* does. Furthermore, rather than attempting to act as a man, Nítíða's passive affirmation of her own femininity reinforces her gender, meaning that at no point do characters have the opportunity to forget that she is a powerful woman, if also a powerful king. Nítíða is 'presented as the epitome of femininity, the ideal woman',[83] and never actively engages in battle or directly challenges her suitors, except verbally, and even then her words are firm, but not abusive. When she speaks up for herself directly, it is in reference to her kingdom, with her own power only indirectly implied, for example, when rejecting Ingi's offer of marriage. Their exchange begins with the narrator indicating Nítíða's initial question: 'drott(ning) spurdi Jn(ga) kong huert erendi hans væri' (The queen asked King Ingi what his errand might be).[84] This is followed by Ingi's response in direct speech: 'þat er mitt erendi j þetta land at bidia ydar mier til eigin konu. gefandi þar j moti gull og gersemar. land og þegna' (I have come to this land to ask you to me to be my wife; giving you in return gold and treasures, land and servants).[85] Nítíða's response is likewise direct, and is a rather dramatic speech:

þat viti þier. Jn(gi) kongur. at þier hafıt eingvan rikdom til motz vit mig. hafa og litit lond ydar <ad> þyda vit Frackland jd goda og .xx. konga ʀiki er þar til liggia. nenni eg og ecki at fella mig fyrer neinum kongi nu

82   Kalinke, *Bridal-Quest Romance*, pp. 68, 90, 102.
83   Kalinke, 'The Misogamous Maiden Kings of Icelandic Romance', pp. 56-57.
84   'Nitida saga', ed. by Loth, p. 10.
85   'Nitida saga', ed. by Loth, p. 10.

rikianda. en fullbodit er mier fyrir manna saker. en þo þurfi þier ecki
þessa mæla at leita optar.[86]

(You know, King Ingi, that you have no riches to match with mine. Your
lands have also little to compare with France the Good and the twenty
kings' realms that lie therein. I am also not inclined to give myself over
to any king now ruling, and I am well enough off regarding marriage
proposals already; and moreover, it will be no use for you to bring up
this suit again.)

Not only does she definitively answer Ingi, leaving no doubt that it is she rather
than he who will call the shots, but she also justifies her answer, reiterating
some of the expository information presented at the beginning of the text,
regarding her realm. This in turn is made complete with further elaboration
detailing the maiden-king's point of view on the subject of partnership and
marriage, foreshadowing failure in Ingi's further attempts to win Nítíða,
and also the other suitors' failures. Because all this is relayed through direct
speech from a major protagonist, the audience is meant to take note, perhaps
more so than if the information were conveyed indirectly. We know the
speech reflects Nítíða's true feelings because she is allowed to speak directly:
had the narrator said it, its importance would not be stressed as much. Additionally, the exchange here is formal. Nítíða uses the second person plural
þér and *yðar* when addressing Ingi, which not only mirrors his formal address
to her (*að biðja yðar mér til eigin konu*), but also indicates her diplomacy and
respect towards him, even while harshly rejecting him. Nítíða's speech here
is as aggressive as she becomes with her suitors in person. In contrast, some
other maiden-kings arrogantly refer to themselves as kings and demand
that others do so too, the best example being Þórnbjörg in the *fornaldarsaga
Hrólfs saga Gautrekssonar*,[87] who, ruling a third of Sweden, goes by the name
King Þórbergur and not only confronts her suitors personally, with words,
but in battle as well. In *Nítíða saga*, only the narrator and other characters
call Nítíða *meykóngur*, and it is her foster brother who carries out her plans
to trick Vélogi and Heiðarlogi to their deaths. No matter how questionable
this may seem, an important part of Nítíða's character is her intelligence and
ability to plan defences, as highlighted in her initial description.

86 'Nitida saga', ed. by Loth, pp. 10-11.
87 On this maiden-king see Jóhanna Katrín Friðriksdóttir, *Women in Old Norse Literature*, pp.
112-16.

Another reason initially to question Nítíða's role as hero is her lack of an obvious, externally motivated quest that dominates a large portion of the plot. While she does travel to Visio in search of supernatural stones and is successful on that quest, it only occurs in the beginning of the story as a means of introducing the fact that she will be protected later on by the magic she can wield through these stones. This mini-quest is not her ultimate aim, and the saga's plot does not revolve around her success in the way that other romances' bridal-quests form the basis of much of their plots. This quest is very important nonetheless, resulting in the source of her power over her suitors. If Nítíða had not acquired the magical stones, apples, and herbs, she would not have been able to evade her suitors and prepare defences against them. Ultimately, the outcome of the quest allows her the ability to choose for herself the man she will marry. Whereas Livorius is specifically looking for a wife, Nítíða does not fulfil what might be called a traditional heroic role because she is not on a quest for a husband. Nítíða's quest is much more internal and introspective. She negotiates the romance world in which she finds herself, rather than actually seeking anything. As such, Nítíða is more like the introspective heroes of early European romance, like the original romances of Chrétien de Troyes and Marie de France, while at the same time lacking the strongly self-reflective character of such heroes – she remains true to Icelandic romance style in that respect. *Nítíða saga* thus also resembles the literary, courtly romances of France, while remaining close enough to the Icelandic style to call it and its values deliberately into question. By working with the norms of Icelandic romance to stretch them and question their value, *Nítíða saga* is still bound by certain expectations of the genre, and even in fulfilling them the saga does so unconventionally. Nítíða must employ the most effective strategy to outwit her suitors when they attempt to take her by force, so that she may keep an advantage over them. In choosing Livorius, she has already made up her mind when she calls together her under-kings for counsel:

> So er sagt ad m(ey)k(ongur) hafe sendt j allar halfur landsins til 20 konga, er aller þionudu under hennar Ryke. byrjar Liv(orius) kongr nu bönord sitt vid m(ey)k(ong) med fagurlegum frammburde og mikille Rögsemd, stirkia hans mäl aller kongar og hoffdingar ad þesse Raadahagr takest.[88]

> (So it is said that the maiden-king had sent word to all the regions of the land, to twenty kings, who all served under her power. King Livorius then

88 'Nitida saga', ed. by Loth, p. 32.

begins his marriage proposal to the maiden-king with fair words and great reason; all the kings and nobles at this counsel support his speech, agreeing that this proposal should be taken.)

While Nítíða evidently has advisors when needed, the choice is still her own, and she still has the last word concerning the arrangements with Hléskjöldur, who, being her foster brother, is her closest advisor. Furthermore, Livorius's proposal is restricted to being reported indirectly, instead of through direct speech, once more reinforcing Nítíða's central role. This is the culmination of a scene that highlights Nítíða's superior intelligence and ability to outwit her suitor: leading up to it, Nítíða reveals her knowledge of Livorius's disguise: '"Liv(orius) kongur" seiger hun, "legg aff þier dular kufl þinn, hinn fyrsta dag er þu komst kienda eg þig, fær þu afftur gulled Aldvia, þui ydur stendur þad lyted leingur med þad ad fara". Liv(orius) kongr lætur nu ad ordum drottningar' ('King Livorius', she says, 'remove your cloak of disguise. The first day when you came I knew you. Take off Alduria's gold, because it will do you no good to continue in this way any longer'. King Livorius now obeys the queen's words).[89] Of course, Nítíða speaks directly, and again Livorius does not – instead he is humbled, and subordinate to Nítíða. His subsequent proposal, indicated almost as hearsay (beginning with *svo er sagt*), doubly reinforces his position in relation to the maiden-king, again reflecting her prominence. With all of this considered, it seems difficult to consider Nítíða as anything but the hero of her saga.

Rivals

I now turn to antagonistic characters, who could be called the villains of the romance. They are the only characters portrayed exclusively as negative threats to Nítíða and her kingdom – unredeemable characters to be outwitted and escaped from (in the case of Virgilius), or eliminated outright (in the case of the four characters from Serkland). On her expedition to Visio, Nítíða deliberately sets out to steal magical objects from Virgilius, and she states her intentions to her foster mother. A benevolent helper does not give her these objects, nor does she simply find them, as occurs in other romances like *Nikulás saga leikara*, whose corresponding and related scenes I discussed in Chapter 2. Nítíða knows who seems to own the stones, apples, and herbs that she finds, and takes them nevertheless. But while (apparently in subtle

89   'Nitida saga', ed. by Loth, p. 31.

judgement of Nítíða's actions) the narrator states that 'jarlinn verdur vis hueriu hann er rœntur' (the earl discovers by whom he is robbed),[90] Virgilius is specifically characterized as an antagonist, an obstacle in the way of the hero's goal. *Nítíða saga* here draws on a medieval literary tradition that sees Virgil as a negative character rather than a positive Classical author.[91] The epitome of such characterization in Iceland might best be represented by *Virgilíus rímur*, which carries on the tradition of Virgil as a negative character, and in particular, as a pagan sorcerer.[92] Nítíða calls Virgilius 'vitur og fiolkunnigur' (wise and skilled in magic: specifically witchcraft or sorcery – 'bad' magic) when she mentions him and her intention to find Visio early in the saga.[93] The only other characters who are associated with the word *fjölkunningur* are Ingi's helpers Refsteinn and Slægrefur, who are likewise obstacles or hindrances to Nítíða, who I discuss below. Virgilius functions only as an initial challenge for Nítíða to overcome in order to reinforce her position as hero and foreshadow her ability to outwit everyone else. Consequently, despite being characterized as a sorcerer, Virgilius is powerless against Nítíða once she has gained possession of his magic objects, and she returns to Apulia unscathed. Nítíða's quest is a success, and the fact that the magical objects were previously associated with an evil sorcerer is of no importance. When they enter Nítíða's possession, the objects become associated with her alone, and she converts their previous association with negative magic to positive magic intended to help her throughout the rest of the romance.

While the use of magical objects seems, in *Nítíða saga*, to be associated with good, productive magic in the interests of protecting the protagonists and securing their success (as in Nítíða's use of the *náttúrusteinar* and Alduria's use of a magic charm to see Livorius's success in wooing the maiden-king), a figure's natural ability to practise magic is, rather, associated with bad magic or sorcery. We see this not only in Virgilius's inherent magical powers, but also in those of Refsteinn, Slægrefur, and the dwarf,

90 'Nitida saga', ed. by Loth, p. 6.

91 See Kallendorf, *The Other Virgil*; Spargo, *Virgil the Necromancer*. Ziolkowski and Putnam, eds., *The Virgilian Tradition*, pp. 825-1024, contains the relevant texts tracing the development of the legend of Virgil as magician.

92 Mitchell and Gísli Sigurðsson, 'Virgilessrímur', pp. 881-88. The history of this story of Virgil's revenge on a woman who tricked him is given in Ziolkowski and Putnam, eds., *The Virgilian Tradition*, pp. 874-90, from which it appears that the *rímur* is not directly indebted to any of these earlier versions.

93 'Nitida saga', ed. by Loth, p. 5. On Virgil as magician, see Baswell, *Virgil in Medieval England*; Comparetti, *Virgil in the Middle Ages*; Petzoldt, 'Virgilius Magus', pp. 549-68; Wood, 'Virgil and Taliesin', pp. 91-104.

who also use magical objects like charms and a cloak, but who, significantly, can cause magical occurrences with nothing more than their own abilities.[94] I will touch on this again shortly. Virgilius is forgotten once he serves his function as the maiden-king's first challenger. In some of Finnur Jónsson's only remarks about *Nítíða saga*, he describes Virgilius's role as 'somewhat subordinate and pathetic',[95] and takes this to mean that 'this character is poorly utilized by the author'.[96] Such a simplistic view misses the point that the character's main function is to draw the saga's focus back to Nítíða. Once she escapes and 'sæ jar(l) þau alldri sidan' (the earl never saw them again),[97] the story returns to its positive portrayal of Nítíða, reinforcing her position as hero. There is no need to develop Virgilius's character – it is enough that Nítíða has outwitted him, a character with a name full of significance and suggestion. As noted in Chapter 3, in all versions of the saga, including in later centuries, Virgilius is present and known by this name, and he serves this same important function.

I now turn to Nítíða's destruction of Serkland's armies and the brutal deaths of the four named characters from there, which has come up in a number of discussions in previous chapters. First Vélogi and Heiðarlogi are killed in France through deception, followed by Soldán and Logi in a separate battle outside France. This act of elimination is in some ways comparable to the abuse and even killing of unwelcome suitors found in other maiden-king romances, such as Séréna arranging the flogging of Clárus in *Clári saga*, Fulgida covering in tar and flogging Viktor after cutting his hair in *Viktors saga ok Blávus*, and Sedentiana shaving and tarring Sigurður's brothers Hálfdan and Vilhjálmur in *Sigurðar saga þǫgla*. However, whereas the maiden-king's violence in these romances generally serves to further the misogynistic portrayal of women as negative figures, in *Nítíða saga*, the violence Nítíða authorizes characterizes her positively. The number of named, active characters from Serkland is greater than those from elsewhere because the threat they form is recognized not only

94 Jóhanna Katrín Friðriksdóttir discusses the use of magical objects for good and the differ-ence between various types of magic used by women in Icelandic sagas across genres (*Women in Old Norse Literature*, esp. pp. 31, 110). Wick also distinguishes between 'black, grey, and white wizardry' when discussing magic in *Nikulás saga leikara* ('An Edition and Study of Nikulás saga Leikara', p. 199).

95 'noget underordnet og ynkelig' (Finnur Jónsson, *Den oldnorske og oldislandske litteraturs historie*, III, p. 113).

96 'denne person er dårlig udnyttet af forf[atteren]' (Finnur Jónsson, *Den oldnorske og oldis-landske litteraturs historie*, III, p. 113).

97 'Nitida saga', ed. by Loth, p. 7.

by Nítíða and her French subjects and advisors, but also by Livorius, who likewise joins forces to protect Nítíða and her kingdom. Furthermore, the four characters are all from the same family and the three brothers share similar names. The father's name, Soldán, comes from French 'sultan', and was imported along with medieval French romances designating someone from the East, or a Saracen.[98] It is a suitable name for the family's father as it indicates the characters' 'type', and other Icelandic romances also give this name to similar Saracen characters. The sons' names, however, all contain the element *logi* 'flame', or 'wildfire'.[99] *Cleasby-Vigfússon* also gives a second meaning under the entry *logi* as 'a pr[oper] name; of a mythical king', alone and in compounds, thus also providing Logi, Vélogi and Heiðarlogi with connotations of power as well as the danger associated with fire.[100] The combined force of all three names, as well as the frightening description of one of them (discussed below) solidifies these characters as formidable pairs of threats.

The characters work in pairs as doubles,[101] enhancing the danger that Serkland poses by making Nítíða defend her kingdom in two battles on one occasion and against two major antagonists on another, which comes about as revenge for the first defeat. Additionally, the doublings and parallels allow Nítíða multiple opportunities to prove herself and reinforce her positive role, along with those who help her, namely Hléskjöldur in the first instance and Livorius in the second. The negative Serkland characters, then, exist exclusively to strengthen Nítíða's character, and are indispensable to the plot. They feature consistently in other versions of the saga as well. While the fathers of Ingi and Livorius, for example, are sometimes omitted, as they

98 Gudbrand Vigfusson, *An Icelandic-English Dictionary*, p. 578. As noted also in Chapter 3, the name could have had associations with crusading (cf. *Sverris saga*, p. 150).

99 Interpreting *logi* as not merely 'flame' (as in Gudbrand Vigfusson, *An Icelandic-English Dictionary*, p. 397) but the more destructive 'wildfire' has a precedent in the prose *Edda*, where Útgarðaloki explains the name of his retainer Logi, a voracious eater, as *villieldr* (wildfire) (Snorri Sturluson, *Edda: Prologue and Gylfaginning*, ed. by Faulkes, p. 43). Thanks to Shaun Hughes for this reference.

100 Gudbrand Vigfusson, *An Icelandic-English Dictionary*, p. 397. Separating the two compound names into their respective parts, *vé-logi* can be understood as 'heathen wildfire', as as *vé* can mean not only 'house, mansion', but also '(heathen/pagan) temple' (p. 687). Additionally, *heiðar-logi* can be understood as 'heath wildfire' (p. 247). It seems clear that all of these names were intended to be lexically meaningful, and chosen to evoke consistent negative imagery – in particular the uncontrollable natural force of wildfire, but also the negative spaces of heath and pagan temple. See also Barnes, *The Bookish Riddarasögur*, pp. 114-15, who favours 'Flame of the heath' for Heiðarlogi.

101 See Propp, *Morphology of the Folktale*, pp. 74-75, in which trebling of various story elements is discussed; the same can be said of doubling.

are really no more than names to introduce those characters,[102] Soldán, the father of Logi, Vélogi, and Heiðarlogi, is a fuller character with a specific function in the plot, although he does not actively move against Nítíða until the end. When the saga turns to Vélogi and Heiðarlogi travelling to France to try to force Nítíða to marry one of them, it seems as though their introduction earlier and their role now is conventional only, in that their father is mentioned as background information before focusing on the real antagonists, the sons. But when Soldán appears later with Logi to avenge their deaths, the dual antagonist structure is revealed.

In the first instance, as soon as Nítíða discovers that the brothers are on their way to France with 'ovigan her af Serklandi' (an invincible army from Serkland),[103] she begins to plan her defence and eliminate the threat they pose. Communication between Hléskjöldur (on Nítíða's behalf) and the brothers also demonstrates the significance of direct speech as compared to indirect speech. Whereas it is Nítíða who plans to trick Vélogi and Heiðar-logi, her plan is only evident indirectly, as the audience is not privileged to hear her conversation with Hléskjöldur, only that 'kallar m(ey)k(ongur) Hleskiolld ä sinn fund. og bad hann ganga til herskipa og seiger honum fyrir alla hlute hueriu hann skal fram fara' (the maiden-king calls Hléskjöldur to a meeting with her, and asked him to go to the warships and tells him all things about how he should proceed).[104] These words are incredibly vague, and the indirect nature of the communication indicates that Hléskjöldur is the focus of this scene, which is also shown by the significant amount of direct speech he enjoys in the subsequent conversations with the brothers. The first conversation begins with reported speech, which quickly becomes direct:

> Hle(skiolldur) gengur nu til skipa og fretter huort kongar fara med fridi. Heidarlogi s(eger) 'ef drott(ning) vill giptast audrum huorum ockrum brædra. þä er þetta land og ʀiki friælst fyrir ockrum hernadi. ella munu vit eÿda landit. brenna og bæla og þyrma aungu'. Hle(skiolldur) svarar 'eigi kenner m(ey)k(ongur) sig mann til at hallda strid vit Serkia her. og suo ægiæta kongs sonu sem þit erud. vil eg seigia þier Velogi trunad

---

102 Ingi's father Hugon (called Februarius in the manuscripts from eastern Iceland) is absent from some eighteenth-century manuscripts with versions similar to the edited version (e.g. ÍB 132, ÍB 138, ÍB 312, Lbs 1172), and Livorius's father Blebarnius (in most other manuscripts called Februarius or Fabrutius) appears in neither the nineteenth- and twentieth-century eastern Icelandic manuscripts, nor those same manuscripts, just listed, in which Ingi's father is absent.
103 'Nitida saga', ed. by Loth, p. 18.
104 'Nitida saga', ed. by Loth, pp. 18-19.

m(ey)k(ongs). hun vill tala vit sier huorn ẏckaʀn og profa visku ẏckra og mäl snilld. vill hon at þu ganger snemma ä̈ hennar fund ä̈dur en broder þinn stendur vpp. þuiat eg veit at hon kys þig til bonda'. binda þeir þetta nu med sier.[105]

(Hléskjöldur now goes to the ships and learns whether or not the kings come in peace. Heiðarlogi says, 'If the queen wants to marry either of us brothers, then this land and kingdom is free from our plundering, or else we shall destroy the land, burn and consume it, and spare nothing'. Hléskjöldur answers, 'The maiden-king does not think herself equipped to wage war against Serkland's army and such excellent princes as you are. I will tell you, Vélogi, the maiden-king's promise: she wants each of you to speak with her, and to test your wisdom and eloquence. She wants you to go early to meet her before your brother gets up, because I know that she chooses you as husband'. They now bind this pledge with each other.)

This conversation is detailed and contains important information. It is also the first in the text among more than two interlocutors. Hléskjöldur begins by addressing both brothers (*kóngar*), and Heiðarlogi replies on behalf of them both, using the dual pronouns *okkrum* (us two) and *við* (we two). Hléskjöldur's answer begins directed at both brothers with the second person dual *þið* (you two), but the rest of his reply appears directed to Vélogi only (*Vil ég segja þér, Véloga*), using informal, second person singular pronouns. The familiarity now projected shows that no extra care is taken to show these strangers – foreign princes – the respect they might rightly deserve (despite their threatening greeting), hinting at the treachery behind the words. While the audience can reasonably expect to interpret Hléskjöldur's words to Vélogi ironically, considering foreknowledge of the defences Nítíða has constructed in preparation for this encounter, neither brother suspects foul play, and in his initial reply Heiðarlogi appears confident, relying on the force of his threats and strength of his army. Interestingly, Vélogi never speaks, and after this agreement, he meets his death. This may have been anticipated in the fact that Heiðarlogi acts as the mouthpiece for the both of them. However, later, when Hléskjöldur speaks privately with Heiðarlogi, he is not given direct speech himself, perhaps demonstrating that his end is also near: the narrator only relates (after Hléskjöldur's direct speech) that 'Heidarlogi þackar honum sinn trunad og fyrir gongu'

105 'Nitida saga', ed. by Loth, p. 19.

(Heiðarlogi thanks him for his good faith and visit).[106] That the brothers from Serkland are essentially silenced once Hléskjöldur speaks to them individually to relate Nítíða's so-called *trúnað* (promise) only reinforces their doom, Nítíða's power, and the power of speech itself and its strong association with living.

The romance continues by describing Nítíða's preparations for battle, which include the construction of a retractable glass roof and a hidden ditch. With these devices in place, the brothers are lured there one by one with Hléskjöldur's help. The outcome of the two battles sees few from Serkland survive; their downfall is described in detail:

> lætur Hleskiolldur vinda framm yfer þä glerhimininn. og hella yfer þä biki og brennesteini. Enn Hleskiolldur gengur at þeim af borginni med skotuopnum og storum havggum. [...] og sem þeir ganga fram ä klædin brestur nidur vidurinn. Enn þeir steyptust j dikit. j þessu þeyser Hles(kiolldur) ovigan her vʀ borginni og bera griot j haufud þeim og skot vopn og drepa huern mann[107]

> (Hléskjöldur commands [his men] to winch the glass roof forward over them, and to pour pitch and sulphur over them. And Hléskjöldur attacks them from the castle with projectiles and great blows. [...] and as they walk forward on the cloth, the wood collapses, and they plunge into the ditch. At this Hléskjöldur rushes an invincible army out of the castle and they throw stones onto their heads, and projectiles, and kill every man)

If this were not brutal enough, it is perhaps most disturbing that the narrator passes over these scenes without any question or comment, in order to praise Nítíða and her ability to outwit her enemies: 'fer og flygur ä huert land frægd og megt su er m(ey)k(ongur) fieck' (The maiden-king's new fame and might hastens and flies to every land).[108] The text focuses again on Nítíða to reinforce her position as hero without question, and the slaughter of the brothers from Serkland functions to characterize her as a tactically superior opponent. Significantly, Nítíða succeeds here without the magical aid of her *náttúrusteinar*. Rather, this episode underlines her initial characterization as the woman who is smart as 'hinn frodasti klerkur' (the wisest scholar), naturally able to outwit others 'med sinu viti' (with her

---

106 'Nitida saga', ed. by Loth, p. 20.
107 'Nitida saga', ed. by Loth, pp. 20-21.
108 'Nitida saga', ed. by Loth, p. 21.

own intellect), and knew '.x. ʀæd er adrer kunnu eitt' (ten answers when others knew one).[109] Some late manuscripts emphasize her linguistic abilities in addition to her intelligence, appearing either to confuse the mention of ten solutions to any problem, or deliberately to substitute 'languages' for 'answers'.[110] This suggests that her superior intelligence need not be reinforced through further example and instead the opportunity is taken to enhance her characterization even further. Her abilities to outwit are confirmed in these scenes, dispelling any question that she may be helpless without her magical objects. The destruction of most of Serkland's army thus specifically functions as reinforcement of an important part of Nítíða's characterization, which explains why it is taken in stride by the narrator and does not sully Nítíða's character, just as her 'robbing' Virgilius – an action that could elsewhere be considered negative – also reinforces her position as the hero of the text.

The characters from Serkland are destined to be killed from their very introduction at the beginning of the romance because they are character-ized as dangerous Others. This is the function of the extended physical description of Heiðarlogi, which also 'typifies the sexually aggressive Saracen predator' intent on marriage to a European woman:[111]

> hann hafdi svart hæʀ og skegg. hann var hokulængur og vanga suangur. skack tentur og skiopul myntur. og vt skeifur. annad auga hans horfdi æ bast en annad ä kuist. hann var hermadur allmikill. og fullur vpp af golldrum og giorningum og rammur at afli. og fieck sigur j huerri orrostu.[112]

> (He had black hair and beard. He was long-chinned and thin-cheeked, crooked-toothed and crooked-mouthed, and splayfooted. One of his eyes looked inwards and the other outwards. He was a very great warrior, and knew much sorcery and witchcraft. He was physically strong and got victory in every battle.)

By focusing on how unlike this character is from those described already and by using negative terms to do so, the saga places Heiðarlogi, and by extension the others from Serkland, outside of the courtly romance world

---

109 'Nitida saga', ed. by Loth, p. 4.
110 See e.g. Reykjavík, Landsbókasafn–Háskólabókasafn Íslands, MS Lbs 3165 4to (1870-71), p. 48.
111 Barnes, *The Bookish Riddarasögur*, p. 114.
112 'Nitida saga', ed. by Loth, p. 8.

to which everyone else belongs.[113] As Jóhanna Katrín Friðriksdóttir has written, 'this depiction codes them as racially Other, malevolent threats who deserve their fate, like many of the giants, giantesses, and other nonhuman creatures in the fornaldarsögur'.[114] Not only are the four characters from Serkland uncivilized and different, they are inhuman, and as such necessary to eliminate. In addition to this, Jacqueline de Weever, whose interpretive framework I also mentioned in the previous chapter, discusses the portrayal of black Saracen women in medieval French literature, and many of her conclusions are applicable also to the representation of these characters in *Nítíða saga*, despite it being a different type of text produced in a very different world than the French texts she considers, which come out of a culture actively engaged with Saracens in the Crusades. Speaking of the 'vituperative' portraits French poets paint of such characters, de Weever states that 'the aim is not only to withhold [audience] admiration but also to control all that [the black Saracen] represents and to annihilate that representation when [he or] she dies on the battlefield'.[115] The destruction of Serkland in *Nítíða saga* thus not only proves Nítíða's own prowess and the strength of her kingdom, but also denies any memory of this Other opponent to live on once it has been eliminated. The outcomes of the battles are absolute, unlike those between Nítíða's army and that of Ingi, who, because he is characterized as like Nítíða (even though she refuses to marry him), is allowed to return to the story as an ally after his rejection and last defeat. Finally, it is also notable that Nítíða deceives Vélogi and Heiðarlogi to their deaths without first giving them the chance to speak to her, as she allowed Ingi to do. The saga only shows them telling Hléskjöldur their intentions to marry or ravage the land, and he answers definitively for Nítíða.[116] This act of silencing also shows them to be the Other, further confirming the fate that had been sealed when their characterization arguably drew on both a native Icelandic folk tradition of non-humans (such as trolls or other supernatural figures) being categorized as Other alongside a foreign French tradition of categorizing Saracens as Other.

In the latter half of the romance, the deaths of Logi and Soldán are also described in a detailed battle scene. Instead of constructing elaborate traps,

---

113 Ármann Jakobsson, *Illa fenginn mjöður*, p. 178.
114 Jóhanna Katrín Friðriksdóttir, *Women in Old Norse Literature*, p. 128.
115 de Weever, *Sheba's Daughters*, p. 54.
116 After Hléskjöldur speaks with Vélogi and Heiðarlogi there is perhaps a day that passes before they are lured into Nítíða's traps: the saga briefly introduces the betrayal scene after the conversation with Hléskjöldur, with 'at næstu natt lidinni' (At the end of the next night) ('Nitida saga', ed. by Loth, p. 19).

this time Nítíða organizes an army of her own to fight that of Soldán, but again, it is her foster brother who is left to put her plans into action. She tells him, 'hallt þessum <her> ä moti Solldani kongi, þuiat eg vil ecki hann komi j mitt ʀiki' (Lead this army to meet King Soldán, because I do not want him to come into my kingdom).[117] As far as Nítíða is concerned, she really does only make the plans this time, and does not further influence the course of the battle, which occurs outside of France. She remains in Paris, and we might imagine her watching at a safe distance in a magic stone. Thus in contrast to the previous battles against the first pair where Nítíða's own intelligence and abilities to orchestrate defences are proven, here it is the skill of her armies and the loyalty of her subjects that are tested to show Nítíða not only as a great ruler but also surrounded by a worthy kingdom eager to serve her. It is therefore an interesting develop-ment when on the second day of battle, Livorius arrives and fights on France's side. Since at this point Livorius has not yet succeeded in winning Nítíða, he might view this opponent as a rival suitor. His ability to defeat Soldán in single combat may contribute to Nítíða's acceptance of him; Hléskjöldur would surely have related the details of the battle to Nítíða afterwards. These two men whose relationships with Nítíða are different but both significant, are named as those who defeat these last two faces of Serkland: 'at sidustu þeirra vidrskipti lagdi hann einum brynþuara fyrer briost Solldani kongi suo at vt gieck vm herdarnar. fiell hann þæ daudur nidur. Lif(orinus) leitar nv at Hles(killdi) en hann lä þæ j einum dal sær nær til olifis. en Logi lä daudur hia honum' (At the end of their exchange he [Livorius] laid a halberd into King Soldán's breast so that it came out through the shoulders. He then fell down dead. Livorius now searches for Hléskjöldur, who then lay in a dale, wounded near to death, and Logi lay dead next to him).[118] This shared experience of fighting to defend Nítíða and her kingdom also allows the men to form a bond before it is certain that Livorius will marry Nítíða, as further foreshadowing of their union and the future friendly relations between France and India. Significantly, though France initiated the battle against Serkland, India enjoys the victory and for a brief moment becomes the focal point in its power: 'tekur Lif(orinus) þar nu mikit herfang og verdur frægur af þessi orrustu vida vm lond. sigla nu heim til Jnndialandz med faugrum sigri' (Livorius now takes great booty there and becomes famous far and wide throughout the lands on account

117 'Nitida saga', ed. by Loth, pp. 25-26.
118 'Nitida saga', ed. by Loth, p. 27.

of this battle. Then they sail home to India with fair victory).[119] The plural verb *sigla* here indicates that Livorius brings Hléskjöldur back to India with him in order to heal his injuries, instead of letting him return to France directly. When Hléskjöldur is ready to leave India, Livorius makes a point of saying that it would be better for Nítíða to have him back, and gives him ten ships so he will not return to France empty handed.[120] These demonstrations of hospitality and consideration shine a favourable light on Livorius. We can infer that through this he impresses Nítíða even further, though it is not stated directly, apart from the simple declaration upon Hléskjöldur's return: 'verdur m(ey)k(ongur) all glod vit hans heimkomv' (the maiden-king becomes very joyful at his homecoming).[121] Thus, again, the ultimate purpose behind the defeat of Serkland is to develop the major characters, and always to direct the story back to Nítíða before moving it forward by turning to another scene.

In the remainder of this chapter I discuss Refsteinn and Slægrefur, the two mysterious characters who on separate occasions act as helpers to Ingi in his quest to take Nítíða by force after she refuses his initial offer. I treat them here together for much the same reason that the four characters from Serkland were discussed together above. In addition to these figures, I will also discuss here the nameless dwarf who helps Livorius, because each of these three characters is associated with the failure of Nítíða's suitors to win her. As will be clear shortly, the suitors' failures are connected to their understanding of Nítíða as subordinate to them, rather than seeing her as an equal in the way that Livorius eventually does. Beginning with Refsteinn and Slægrefur, they are two sides of the same coin, a doubled antagonistic helper character, in the same way that the two pairs from Serkland are doubled antagonists. This is reinforced not only by their helping the same character, but also through their similar names, which both share the element *refur* (fox), indicating their wiliness and deceit.[122] The manner of their introduction also reinforces these characters' connection with each other. When Ingi meets Refsteinn, their exchange begins with indirect speech, but the conversation that follows uses direct speech, lending a sense of immediacy to their dialogue:

---

119 'Nitida saga', ed. by Loth, p. 27.
120 'Nitida saga', ed. by Loth, pp. 27-28.
121 'Nitida saga', ed. by Loth, p. 28.
122 In addition to its literal sense, *refr* (fox) in Old Icelandic could be understood metaphorically as 'a tricky person, sly fox' and was used 'mostly in sayings' (Gudbrand Vigfusson, *An Icelandic-English Dictionary*, p. 488).

kongur spurdi þenna mann at nafni. hann kuedzt Refsteinn heita. kongur
spyʀ ef hann væri suo sem hann hiet til. hann s(eger) 'þat ætla eg at mig
skorti vit einguan mann kukl og galldur og fiolkingi huad sem giora skal'.
kongur m(ælti) 'Eg vil giora þig fullsælan at fie og baurn þin ef þu kemur
mier j hendur Nitida bardaga laust'. Ref(steinn) s(eger) 'fyrer þessu er mier
ecki'. kongur m(ælti) 'gack vt æ skip min med mier og fullgior þat er þu
hefer heitit. er hier gullhringur stor er eg vil giefa þier og .xx. ælner rautt
skarlat er þu skalt færa konu þinni'. Ref(steinn) þackar nu kongi mikilega.
byʀ sig og ganga æ skip.[123]

(The king asked this person his name. He said he was called Refsteinn.
The king asks if he might be such as he was called. He said, 'I suppose that
my knowledge is inferior to no person in terms of sorcery and spell-craft
and wizardry, whatever one might do'. The king said, 'I will make you and
your children wealthy in riches if you get Nítíða into my hands, without
battle'. Refsteinn says, 'This is nothing to me'. The king said, 'Go out to my
ships with me and fulfil that which you have promised; here is a great gold
ring which I want to give to you, and twenty ells of red scarlet which you
must bring to your wife'. Refsteinn now thanks the king greatly, prepares
himself, and they go onto the ship.)

This direct speech is framed by indirect narration, which nevertheless
propels the action forward with a quick, sharp exchange in brief sentences.
Once the conversation turns into direct speech, it continues on at a steady
pace, but each character's statements become progressively longer and
more drawn out as the conversation proceeds, conveying more information,
and essentially drawing up a contract between them. Further, Refsteinn's
subordinate position to Ingi (at least in Ingi's view) is demonstrated by the
informal, second person singular pronouns Ingi employs. The conversation ends as a contract between the two. This exchange is so similar to
that between Ingi and Slægrefur, the former's second helper, that the first
conversation can be viewed as a template for the second: it begins indirectly,
reported by the narrator, and amounts to the same type of back-and-forth
banter. Ingi again addresses his helper informally.[124]
　　Their deceitful nature may also indicate in advance their inability to
succeed in helping Ingi. Further, they are agents of sorcery – magic intended
to harm rather than for good – similar to Virgilius, noted above. Refsteinn

123 'Nitida saga', ed. by Loth, pp. 11-12.
124 'Nitida saga', ed. by Loth, p. 14.

says he can do 'kukl og galldur og fiolkingi' (sorcery and spell-craft and wizardry),[125] and Slægrefur says 'ei kann eg minni fiolkÿnki en Re(f)st(einn)' (I am not able to do less wizardry than Refsteinn).[126] Refsteinn's talents in magic are only evident in the good wind he magically provides for Ingi to sail to France and his ability to produce an invisibility cloak,[127] which while allowing Ingi to abduct Nítíða, cannot guarantee success. Slægrefur, though he promises to do better, helps Ingi even less, and this second mission is doomed to fail because of Nítíða's foresight – they abduct the bondswoman Íversa instead. Whereas there is evidence to confirm Refsteinn's claims, Slægrefur does nothing, according to the text, to prove he really can accomplish any 'wizardry'. Once in France, all he does is enter Nítíða's hall with Ingi, without providing any magical objects or casting any spells. The saga only says that 'kongur hleÿpur at og steÿper ÿfer hana suartre sueipu. og fer þegar vt af skemmunni' (the king runs in and casts a black hood over her, and immediately goes out of the chamber).[128] It does not explicitly say that Slægrefur provides the hood, although it is the same colour (*svart*) as the cloak that made Ingi invisible and the same verb (*steypa*) is used to lay the items on their objects. This seems to imply a deliberate connection of the two objects and, accordingly, magical properties, though nothing more is said of the hood. The similar diction links the two figures and reinforces their relationship as two faces of the same double character. In his surprising ineffectiveness, Slægrefur also reinforces Refsteinn's failure, and any action taken by the first is cancelled out by the total inactivity of the second.[129] In other ways too, Slægrefur is more an incomplete shadow of Refsteinn than a functional independent character: when Ingi encounters Refsteinn, the saga says that 'þeir sia mann einn ganga ofan af eyiunni. helldur mikinn og alldradan' (they see a person walking down from the island who looked rather large and old), whereas meeting Slægrefur, the saga only states that 'þeir siä mann ganga ofan af nesinu' (they see a person walking down from the headland).[130] The mystery surrounding both figures (including the shadowy evening settings in which they appear), and their inability to help

125 'Nitida saga', ed. by Loth, p. 11.
126 'Nitida saga', ed. by Loth, p. 14.
127 The journey to France takes 'en beinasta byr' (the straightest course), '*þuiat* Ref(steinn) gaf þeim nogan byʀ og hagstædan' (*because* Refsteinn gave them enough of a favourable wind), and then 'steyper R(efsteinn) yfer kong kufli suortum' (Refsteinn cast a black cloak over the king) ('Nitida saga', ed. by Loth, p. 12, my italics).
128 'Nitida saga', ed. by Loth, p. 16.
129 Ármann Jakobsson, *Illa fenginn mjöður*, p. 179.
130 'Nitida saga', ed. by Loth, pp. 11, 14.

Ingi succeed both shows Nítíða to be a more powerful character and more skilled in the use of magic attributes than those characterized as wizards or sorcerers, and also foreshadows the failure of the third mysterious figure, the dwarf, to help Livorius when his approach to fulfil his aims is still the same as Ingi's – coercive and uncourtly, viewing Nítíða as an object to be won rather than a partner with whom to share his life.

This dwarf, who tries to help Livorius after they appear to meet by chance one day in the woods, is a character whose role not only mirrors Ingi's helpers, but also reinforces the saga's aims in challenging certain romance norms. The anonymous dwarf is perhaps one of the only benevolent dwarves in any medieval Icelandic romance whose assistance does not produce the desired result and lead to the character's success.[131] Significantly, the reasons for this failure seem to have to do with Nítíða, not Livorius, being the saga's hero. Dwarves in other romances allow heroes to succeed, whether by helping them do something, giving them magical objects, or acting as intermediaries. Thus, the dwarf's ultimate ineffectiveness in *Nítíða saga* upturns this expectation, especially when, initially, the help provided appears to work (Nítíða is in fact brought to India). Unlike the unexplained nature of Refsteinn and Slægrefur, where it is uncertain whether they are human or some sort of supernatural figures, Livorius, and consequently the audience, seems to be familiar with the dwarf as a type of being from which he might get help but of which he must be wary, and with the setting of their meeting being the brightness of day rather than the evening when Ingi meets his helpers, Livorius's certainty of what the dwarf is, is further reinforced. His reaction upon seeing the dwarf is telling: 'kongss(on) renner nu sinu ersi æ milli steinsins og duergsins og viger hann vtan steins' (The prince then runs his horse between the stone and the dwarf, and separates him from the stone).[132] There is an element of fear in Livorius's reaction, and an uncertainty as to whether interacting with the dwarf will prove helpful or harmful; it is up to the dwarf to reveal his willingness to help before Livorius will ask for it.

The differences between Ingi's dialogues with his helpers and that between Livorius and the dwarf are apparent from the beginning of the exchange when it is the dwarf who initiates the conversation, in contrast to Ingi's initiation of dialogue both times before, and, so, confounding any expectation that their conversation will be carried out as were those

131 Ármann Jakobsson, 'Enabling Love', pp. 183-206; Ármann Jakobsson, *Illa fenginn mjöður*, p. 179; Schäfke, 'Was ist eigentlich ein Zwerg?', pp. 197-299.
132 'Nitida saga', ed. by Loth, p. 21-22.

between Ingi and his helpers. The dwarf's words are not brief either: 'meiri frægd væri þier j at leika vt me(y)k(ong) j Franz enn banna mier mitt jnni eda heyrer þu ei þæ frægd er fer og flygur vm allan heimen af hennar megt at hvn vt leikur alla konga med sinni spekt og vizku' (You would gain greater fame to out-play the maiden-king in France than to ban my entry, or have you not heard of the fame which hastens and flies throughout all the world concerning her strength, that she out-plays all kings with her foresight and wisdom?).[133] Unlike in the cases seen above, here the helper assesses the situation better than the king and offers advice accordingly, before Livorius can ask for it. Further, the dwarf (perhaps surprisingly) addresses Livorius informally, essentially turning the tables on the preceding exchanges. Having the dwarf take control of the situation in the first instance also reinforces Livorius's uncertainty as to whether the dwarf might be helpful or harmful. The dwarf not only initiates conversation and takes control, but in doing so sets the tone of their exchange, which is initially slightly confrontational. The conversation continues, and Livorius reciprocates the dwarf's informal address without challenging it:

> kongur s(eger) 'mart hef eg heÿrt þar af sagt og ef þu villt fylgia mier til Fracklandz og vera mier hollur so at med þinu kynstri og kuckli mætti eg fæ m(ey)k(onginn) mier til eiginnar pusu þä skylldi eg giora þig fullsælan og born þin'. duer(gur) mælti 'þat mun eg vpp taka at fylgia þier. helldur en missa steininn. þuiat eg veit at þu ert ägiætur kongur'.[134]

> (The king says, 'I have heard much said of this, and if you want to ac-company me to France and be loyal to me so that with your magical arts and sorcery I might get the maiden-king as my wife, then I shall make you and your children very wealthy'. The dwarf said, 'I will agree to accompany you, rather than lose the stone, because I know that you are an excellent king'.)

The entire conversation between these characters suggests that unlike Ingi's pair of helpers, simply the *idea* of the dwarf endows this character with real power, and that power turns out to be real when help is provided. Once they have reached their agreement, the conversation continues in France in order to carry out their plan, and it is again the dwarf who speaks further, giving Livorius detailed instructions about how to use a magic ring to bring

133 'Nitida saga', ed. by Loth, p. 22.
134 'Nitida saga', ed. by Loth, p. 22.

Nítíða back to the ship: 'legg þina hond med gullinv vpp ä berann hæls m(ey)k(ong)s. þæ mun gullit fast vit hennar liosa likam. fanga hana sidan. en eg skal giora ʀæd fyrir at eingi epterfauʀ sie veitt' (Put your hand with the gold up on the bare neck of the maiden-king, and then the gold will be stuck to her radiant body. Seize her then, and I shall make sure that no chase will be made).[135] These instructions are very precise, and the use of informal address likewise continues in this extension of their previously agreed verbal contract, in contrast with Ingi's conversations with Refsteinn and Slægrefur, which ceased before their pursuit of Nítíða. The dwarf's plan is successful and he even helps further, causing Nítíða's courtiers to be stuck to their seats, ensuring Livorius's escape.[136] To top it all off, 'duer(gurinn) gefur þeim fagran býʀ heim til Jnndia landz' (the dwarf gives them a fair wind home to India),[137] confirming that this helper means to see the task through to completion, unlike Refsteinn and Slægrefur, who are not mentioned again after Ingi's abductions take place. In a different romance, this may have been sufficient help to secure the suitor's success, but it is because Nítíða, characterized as the hero, can use her náttúrusteinar first to anticipate their arrival and second to escape back to France, that the dwarf's efforts do not pay off. Thus, even the dwarf, a seemingly insignificant, anonymous character, draws more attention to Livorius's efforts and characterization, reinforcing his central role in the saga, and the fact that he, unlike Ingi, will be successful in his quest for Nítíða (despite the failure of the dwarf's efforts to help him in the long run). The dwarf also highlights Nítíða's role as hero and reinforces the interrogation of romance conventions that makes up such a significant part of the text.

Conclusions

Over the course of this chapter I have discussed the ways in which the portrayal of the saga's hero – its protagonist – is different and unconventional in *Nítíða saga*. In the following chapter I will look at relationships among other characters who also reinforce Nítíða's characterization as hero, particularly the other female characters. As I have demonstrated,

135 'Nitida saga', ed. by Loth, p. 23.
136 This motif also occurs in *Nikulás saga leikara* (Wick, 'An Edition and Study of Nikulás saga Leikara', p. 152, and noted by Wick as parallel with *Nítíða saga*, pp. 225-26), among other Icelandic texts (see Boberg, *Motif-Index of Early Icelandic Literature*).
137 'Nitida saga', ed. by Loth, p. 24.

Nítíða saga's plot is centred not on a male protagonist's bridal-quest for Nítíða, but on Nítíða's negotiations and manoeuvres through the world of bridal-quest to emerge in marriage as an equal with her husband, and the saga ends placing them on a par with each other: 'lykur so þessu æfentyre af hinne frægu Nitida og Livorio konge' (so ends this adventure of the famous Nítíða and King Livorius).[138] Significantly, Nítíða, though no longer called the 'maiden-king', is still named before Livorius (who is now 'king') even though the saga began with her alone and she is now married, in keeping with the consistent favouring of Nítíða and highlighting women's resourcefulness over that of men. Jóhanna Katrín Friðriksdóttir, classifying *Nítíða saga* as proto-feminist, notes that it is centred more on female friendships than on romantic relationships, which are not normally seen in bridal-quest or maiden-king romances, which instead favour male friendships, with romantic relationships featuring merely as the saga's end goal to be fulfilled.[139] This theme will be considered further in the following chapter.

However, when later versions of the romance are considered, the overall focus sometimes shifts. Different manuscript versions show different priorities in terms of the presentation of Nítíða and Livorius. While all versions maintain the essential prominence of Nítíða in a way that she can be recognized as the hero, in some versions Livorius's role is increased, sometimes diminishing the impact that Nítíða's character has on the saga and its overall message. For example, in the closely related seventeenth- and eighteenth-century manuscripts JS 27 and Add. 4860, discussed above in Chapter 1, the focus is much more on Livorius as a leader and king at the end, once he has married and allied with Nítíða, whose role more or less ends when she marries. While many post-medieval manuscripts preserve Nítíða's powerful, central role to the very end, and some – notably those from Iceland's Dales and Westfjords regions (e.g. JS 166) – enhance her image even further when closing the saga, that priority seen in the medieval version discussed in this chapter evidently diminished in importance for some scribes and audiences in later centuries. This would suggest shifting cultural values and perhaps even a deliberate disconnect from the medieval world that produced a saga that showcases a female hero so strongly with the purpose of questioning the idea of the medieval romance in literature and culture. Perhaps once this had been questioned, some versions of the texts developed that unselfconsciously aimed merely to entertain or hearken

---

138 'Nitida saga', ed. by Loth, p. 37.
139 Jóhanna Katrín Friðriksdóttir, *Women in Old Norse Literature*, p. 130.

back to an imagined Middle Ages that differed from that in which *Nítíða saga* really was composed.

As I have shown, *Nítíða saga* is not just another bridal-quest maiden-king romance like all others apart from its female protagonist. Nítíða does not simply take on the attributes of a bridal-quest hero. Rather, by unsettling audience expectations relating to questions of the characterization of heroes and antagonists, the saga presents a story with a female protagonist, and it is from her point of view that the story unfolds. The story contains elements of bridal-quest without being a fully bridal-quest romance. It seems better to think of *Nítíða saga* not exclusively as a bridal-quest or maiden-king romance, but as a deliberate response to other bridal-quest and maiden-king romances.[140] It is, furthermore, even an inverted bridal-quest romance in which the quest is portrayed from the point of view of the sought-after woman, and an inverted maiden-king romance in which the woman is not only portrayed positively but is the saga's hero. The characterizations of Livorius and Nítíða support such readings. In *Nítíða saga* the idea of the hero is turned upside down through its characterization, facilitating an opportunity for audiences to reassess what it means to be a hero in this type of literature, insofar as it can be agreed that the saga fits into a homogenous single genre at all. Although, arguably, any individual romance, like much of medieval literature, can be and is self-reflective, and depends on the texts that shape its genre, metatextual discourse is at the forefront of *Nítíða saga*, and indeed, is one of its defining characteristics, more so than in many other Icelandic romances. This helps to explain why it seems to be a bridal-quest romance, yet focuses so keenly on Nítíða, her feelings and concerns, and her relationships. The text's internal inquiry could also be seen as more in line with other European vernacular romance, and the idea of Europeanization discussed in Chapter 3 could be said to extend to the conceptualization of *Nítíða saga*'s protagonist and the representation of the protagonist's quest. In extending the idea of the late medieval Icelandic romance hero to include Nítíða, then, I have discussed not simply how *Nítíða saga* is different from other bridal-quest and maiden-king sagas, but also certain ideas about what a so-called 'traditional romance hero' is in late medieval Iceland. I will develop these themes in the following chapter, in which I discuss characterization and the further portrayal of the hero by means of the other female characters and relationships featured in the text.

140 Bibire, 'From *riddarasaga* to *lygisaga*', pp. 67, 70.

5   Women Helping Women, and Other Minor Characters

In this chapter I continue and develop some of the issues raised in the previous chapter, in which I dealt with the question of *Nítíða saga*'s hero and the characterization of Livorius, Nítíða, and her main rivals. While the relationships between Nítíða and the characters already discussed serve to reinforce Nítíða's powerful role as the saga's hero, the same can be demonstrated of the characterization of the remaining figures in the saga, particularly the other female characters. In this chapter I will show how audience sympathy for Nítíða is encouraged through all of her relationships and interactions with other women (and with her smith Ypolitus), and how these minor characters all function to draw attention back to Nítíða, regardless of whether or not Nítíða herself plays a part in some of the episodes. I begin by analysing the characterization of two important female figures, Sýjalín of India and Listalín of Constantinople – the sisters of Nítíða's suitors Livorius and Ingi, respectively – and their relationships with both their brothers and with Nítíða. Particular attention will be given to the intimate relationship between Nítíða and Sýjalín for the unique light it may shed on female homoeroticism in medieval Icelandic literature. I will then consider the characterization of the two servant figures at Nítíða's court, the bondwoman Íversa and the smith Ypolitus. I will conclude by discussing the brief but important roles played by Egidía of Apulia (Nítíða's foster mother) and Alduria of Småland (Livorius's aunt). I will also bring into consideration specific differences in the presentation of these characters in some post-Reformation versions of *Nítíða saga*, including the general trends and overall differences in characterization evident in these paper manuscripts.

Sýjalín of India, the sister of Livorius, and Nítíða's eventual sister-in-law, is an important source of support for Nítíða, even if her presence in the romance is small. Because of her inability to see through her brother's disguise as Prince Eskilvarður when he visits her and Nítíða in Paris, and because she does not have a readily identifiable influence over the actions of other characters, unlike Listalín of Constantinople (as I discuss below), Sýjalín may at first seem unimportant in the grand scheme of the romance. She does not even have any direct speech. Sýjalín's most important role, however, is as Nítíða's companion. When Nítíða escapes from India, she abducts Sýjalín in retaliation against her abductor Livorius, and brings

her back to France. The two women develop a close relationship, despite
the less than ideal circumstances that drew them together; there is no
indication that their care for each other is not mutual, and the two women
also get along well with one another before leaving India. Nítíða is brought
to Sýjalín's quarters upon arrival, and her escape is not immediate, but
some time later. The escape scene begins, 'þat var einn dag at drott(ning)
var gengin fram vnder einn lund plantadan er stod vnder skemmunni' (It
happened one day that the princess had gone down to a planted grove that
stood below the chamber).[1] Nítíða seems to have stayed in India for at least
a few days, getting to know both Sýjalín and the location of her captivity,
and waiting for an opportunity to return to Paris.

Of the women's relationship in France the saga says: 'tok huor at vnna
annari sem sinni modur' (each loved the other as she would her own
mother).[2] That the friendship between the young women develops and is
described in this way is significant because Nítíða seems to have essentially
kidnapped Sýjalín by bringing her back to France. The audience is not told
whether or not she went willingly, but it is clear that either way, the women
subsequently grow very close. These scenes are important because they
function as an example of the type of romance themes and motifs evident
in the saga as a whole. On a micro-level Nítíða's abduction of her own suitor's
sister exemplifies the degree of control Nítíða wields in the romance world
she inhabits. The abduction, as well as the women's relationship, mirrors the
bridal-quest motif within the wider romance genre: the author here plays
with this convention and presents it to the audience for scrutiny, comment,
and question in a prime example of the challenging of one of the genre's
norms. Further, the norm of a man taking and marrying a wife is here
inverted to portray a woman taking a friend (or, possibly, a lover – see below)
in the same way. Nítíða's relationship with Sýjalín serves the additional
purpose of foreshadowing her relationship with Livorius, complete with
Nítíða's scheme that again turns the tables to outwit her future spouse in
the seeing-stones scenes. On a grand scale the saga shows France 'abducting'
India and the two becoming close partners, first between the women, and
ultimately in political terms through the marriage of the two rulers – the
two 'kings'.

---

1   'Nitida saga', ed. by Loth, p. 24. I wish here to thank Shaun Huges for his careful reading of
an earlier version of this chapter and for the many references and suggestions he offered, which
I found very helpful to improve my discussion of the women of *Nítíða saga*.
2   'Nitida saga', ed. by Loth, p. 25.

On another level, it is significant that the relationship between Sýjalín and Nítíða is described in mother-daughter terms, even though, as I will discuss shortly, it may as such be purely metaphorical. Neither woman's mother is mentioned at all in the saga. In fact, the only female character whose mother is mentioned is Ingi's sister Listalín, of whose parents the saga says, 'Hvgon er kongur nefndur. hann ried fyrer Miklagardi. hann ætti drott(ning) og .ij. bavrn. son hans hiet Jngi. [...] Listalin hiet dotter hans' (A king is named Hugon; he ruled over Constantinople. He had a queen and two children. His son was called Ingi; [...] his daughter was named Listalín).[3] The only other mother in the saga is Hléskjöldur's – Egidía, who, as I discuss later in this chapter, also acts as a maternal figure for Nítíða. This is consistent with the general paucity of mothers depicted in Old Norse literature. According to Jenny Jochens, mother-daughter relationships in particular are extremely rare,[4] and 'even less evidence has surfaced of daughters' love for mothers'.[5] In a therefore somewhat rare case among the extant literature, Nítíða enjoys the benefits of an important and positive maternal figure in her foster mother Egidía, with other female bonds also being important and necessary in her life. It is significant that while Nítíða has a foster mother, no foster father or other paternal figure is mentioned, and this lack of a male role model does not impact her negatively; indeed, it perhaps allows her to inhabit the male role of maiden-*king* more easily. Once more, her fosterage is a further example of Nítíða's characterization as the saga hero, taking on the conventionally male characteristics of other heroes. That Nítíða is fostered by a woman only further reinforces this inversion of expected gender norms.[6]

The importance of Sýjalín and Nítíða's close relationship is also hinted at early in the saga, when Sýjalín is first introduced as 'suo væn og listug at hun mundi forpris þott hafa allra kuenna j veraulldvnni. ef ei hefdi þvilikur

---

3   'Nitida saga', ed. by Loth, pp. 7-8.

4   Jochens, 'Old Norse Motherhood', pp. 201-22. Jochens notes the relatively few mother-daughter relationships depicted in Old Norse sagas (p. 213), with positive relationships in the minority – 'When mothers are included in the narratives, they are more likely to be callous or indifferent' (p. 202) – and explores infanticide, fostering, and illegitimacy as factors which might have caused mothers in the Old Norse world to have been emotionally reserved towards their children.

5   Jochens, 'Old Norse Motherhood', p. 213. It seems that 'at best texts occasionally mention grown women's fondness for their old foster mothers' (p. 213).

6   Jochens, 'Old Norse Motherhood', p. 208: 'The pervasive male focus of saga authors is undoubtedly the reason that more boys than girls are reported as being fostered away from home. A few cases indicate, however, that it also happened to girls. [... and] foster mothers are also in evidence'.

gimsteinn hiæ̈ verit sem Nitida hin fræga' (so fair and skilled that she would have been thought to be most prized of all the women in the world, if nearby there had not been such a jewel as Nítíða the Famous).[7] This description places the two women on a par with each other and suggests the possibility that they could be compatible equals in friendship, in a similar manner to Nítíða and Livorius's parity in terms of physical description, discussed in the previous chapter. Werner Schäfke has recently argued that the relationship between Nítíða and Sýjalín is strictly homosexual, and that this ultimately works as a further example of inversion in the saga.[8] The key passage suggesting this reading occurs after Nítíða escapes from India, bringing Sýjalín with her. I have considered part of it already, but it is worth quoting the passage now in full:

> Nu er þar af at seigia at drottn(ingar) koma heim j Páris tekur m(ey)k(ongur) Syialin kongs dottur og setur hana j hæsæti hiæ̈ sier dreckandi af einv keri bædar og skilur huorki suefn ne mat vit hana. tok huor at vnna annari sem sinni modur[9]

> (Now it is said that the queens come home to Paris. The maiden-king takes Princess Sýjalín and sets her in the high seat next to her, both drinking from one cup, and separates from her neither in sleeping nor eating. Each loved the other as her own mother.)

In Schäfke's view, these few lines are indicative not only of a 'close social bond' between the women, but of 'camouflaged' female homosexuality:

> There is no question that in this scene, a partnership between the maiden-king Nítíða and Prince Livorius's sister Sýjalín is implied. The verb *unna* means a close social bond between two figures [...] While same-sex love in this scene is recognizable because of the vocabulary used, sexualization is only camouflaged here as a deducible subtext. The wording that they do not sleep or eat separate from each other implies sharing a bed, which in turn implies sexual intercourse.[10]

---

7   'Nitida saga', ed. by Loth, p. 9. See Chapter 2 for further discussion of the imagery this quotation employs.
8   Schäfke, *Wertesysteme*, pp. 220–22. See also Barnes, *The Bookish Riddarasögur*, pp. 39–40 (n. 22).
9   'Nitida saga', ed. by Loth, p. 25.
10   'Es steht außer Frage, dass in dieser Szene ein partnerschaftliches Verhältnis zwischen der Jungfrauenköningen Nítíða und Prinz Liforinús' Schwester Sýjalín impliziert wird. Das Verb

In particular, Schäfke interprets the drinking cup shared by the two women as the vagina and takes this to mean, specifically, that 'it would therefore be homosexual cunnilingus which is camouflaged here'.[11] This reading is certainly possible, and would reveal perhaps the only description of female homosexual behaviour in Old Norse literature: in her overview of Old Norse sexuality, Jenny Jochens only mentions female homosexuality very briefly, with the conclusion that 'no evidence has surfaced in the narratives [...] of women kissing and embracing each other'.[12] I am, however, hesitant to agree fully with Schäfke concerning the precise nature of the behaviour that is only hinted at in the text. Although it does not seem to be attested elsewhere in the literature, homoeroticism between women must have existed in Old Norse society. The 1178 Penitential (*skriftaboð*) of Bishop Þorlákur, primarily concerned with regulating sexual behaviour, prescribes the same penance for homosexual acts between women as between men: 'ef konor eignaz uith þangath thil er þeim leysir girnd. skal bioda þuilikt skrift sem korlum þeim er enn liotazsta hordom fremia sijn amillum' (if women have relations with each other to the point that the lust is discharged between them [i.e. reach orgasm], [each] must undergo the same penance as those men who perform the most hideous whoredom between each other).[13] While same-sex female relations are unambiguously condemned in the Penitential, the nature of the acts themselves is not specified, or even hinted at. Þorlákur's silence here echoes the relatively widespread tendency of medieval penitential literature to condemn homoerotic relations between women, but also to conceive of them as unspeakable.[14] The refusal of such literature to acknowledge female sexuality distinct from male, particularly with their intended use as guides for confessors, can thereby be said, in the words of Edith Benkov, to

unna bezeichnet eine enge soziale Bindung zwischen beiden Figuren [...] Während gleichge-schlechtliche Liebe in dieser Szene aufgrund des verwendeten Vokabulars erkennbar wird, ist Sexualisierung hier nur camoufliert als Subtext erschließbar. Die Formulierung, dass sie sich weder zum Schlafen noch zum Essen voneinander trennen, impliziert das Teilen eines Bettes, das wiederum Geschlechtsverkehr implizier' (Schäfke, *Wertesysteme*, p. 221).

11   'es würde sich also zum homosexuellen Cunnilingus handeln, der hier camoufliert wird' (Schäfke, *Wertesysteme*, p. 221).

12   Jochens, 'Old Norse Sexuality', p. 390.

13   *Diplomatarium Islandicum*, ed. by Jón Sigurðsson and others, I, p. 243.

14   Benkov, 'The Erased Lesbian', pp. 103-09. Benkov also discusses how secular legal writing generally parallels the silence of religious writing regarding female homoeroticism (pp. 109-11). The twelfth-century *Livre des manières* of the bishop Étienne de Fougères provides a rare contrast to this silence surrounding sex between women, though, significantly, female homoeroticism is there 'evok[ed] but not represent[ed]' through phallic metaphors presented as examples of what homoerotic women are *not* doing (see Clark, 'Jousting without a Lance', p. 160 (see also esp. pp. 154-66).

'perpetuate a phallic model of sexuality that denies agency to women'.[15] It has also been argued that same-sex female desire and relations were difficult (if not nearly impossible) for the phallocentric, heteronormative society of the Christian European Middle Ages to comprehend, and that it is for that reason that female homoeroticism is often portrayed as unspeakable, and actively silenced by male writers.[16] Because Þorlákur's Old Norse Penitential does not specify how women might 'discharge [their] lust' together, we can also see the suppression of female homoeroticism there, as it is assimilated to an existing understanding of male behaviours rather than considered in separate terms. Since writers in Old Norse are unwilling (or unable) to discuss same-sex love between women,[17] we might then also proceed with caution when defining the nature of the potential homoeroticism in *Nítíða saga*. Ultimately, the nature itself may not matter – that there are here any hints of female homoeroticism at all, and the possible reasons for it, is what is most remarkable. The shared drinking cup, therefore, need not necessarily be a specific representation of female anatomy,[18] but may rather be a shorthand that represents the physical intimacy (whether or not it is also sexual) that is clearly shared by Nítíða and Sýjalín in this scene.

Significantly, however, later manuscripts omit the reference to the drinking cup. In the seventeenth-century JS 166, the scene between Nítíða and Sýjalín reads, 'Enn frä jungfrünum*m* er þad ad seigia, ad þær koma heim i Frackland, tekur meyko*ng*urin*n* Suÿalÿn til sÿn med suo m*i*klum*m* kiærleika, skiliande huørke vid hana sess, suefn nie samneyte. Tök til ad vn*n*a huør an*n*are sem sin*n*e möd*i*r' (And about the young women it is said that they come home to France. The maiden-king takes Svíalín to

---

15   Benkov, 'The Erased Lesbian', p. 104.

16   Schibanoff, 'Hildegard of Bingen and Richardis of Stade', esp. pp. 56-60; Benkov, 'The Erased Lesbian'; and Brooten, *Love between Women*.

17   Jochens, 'Old Norse Sexuality', p. 390.

18   In her monograph on female homoeroticism as it was understood in the early Christian era, Bernadette Brooten discusses a passage from Tertullian's *De Resurrectione Carnis* (first quarter of the third century), which refers to *frictrices*, that is, 'women who have sexual relations with other women' (Brooten, *Love Between Women*, p. 318), and which makes for an interesting parallel to the image in *Nítíða saga*. In order to prove that bodies (and not just souls) can be judged and held responsible for sinful actions, Tertullian gives the example of a drinking cup. He says that 'we would not want to take a sip from a drinking cup from which a *frictrix* [...] has drunk, thereby infecting it with their breath, any more than we would want their kisses' (p. 319). While Brooten does not discuss the meaning of this image, focusing instead on the portrayal of the *frictrix*, it seems clear that the cup, tarnished by the mouth of a lesbian, is then itself directly associated with homosexual acts. While it is uncertain whether the author of *Nítíða saga* could have had something along these lines this in mind, it casts an interesting light on the meaning of the shared cup in the text.

herself with such great love, separating from her neither sitting, sleeping, nor in company. Each took to loving the other as her own mother).[19] The same is recorded in the late eighteenth-century manuscripts JS 632 (f. 108ʳ) and Rask 32 (f. 32ᵛ), keeping the mother-daughter reference, which may be equally suggestive of same-sex desire (as I will discuss shortly), but not the cup. In one of the youngest manuscripts preserving the romance – the early twentieth-century Lbs 3941 – the scene is omitted completely, and the chapter instead ends after the women disappear from the garden.[20] The elision of the drinking cup in early modern manuscripts, along with the more striking total absence of the women's relationship in the even younger manuscript, suggests that whether it was a shorthand for same-sex intimacy or a more direct sexual reference, the drinking cup (and therefore the portrayal of intimacy between the women) was not necessarily something that post-medieval scribes were comfortable transmitting. The late medieval version of the romance copied in the manuscript AM 529 (the edited text), therefore, is the more radical in its willingness to discuss openly the relationships and desires of the women it portrays, however subtly.

The question of subtlety in these portrayals is important, particularly when the narrator both acknowledges the relationship and also keeps it at a distance, drawing attention away from the description of women loving each other, while also not denying its existence. It is in this way not unlike the paraliptic language that could be used by confessors – 'diction that simultaneously named but did not name, invoked but contained the sexual sin in question' in an effort 'to fulfil these somewhat contradictory goals of discretion and thoroughness' in hearing confessions.[21] Further, pseudo-Cicero speaks of paralipsis as 'a [rhetorical] device [...] for creating suspicion without running the risk of direct reference that is tedious or "undignified"'.[22] This could be said of the treatment of the women's relationship, not only in terms of the drinking cup imagery, but also the mother-daughter bond. In using the sexualized female referent ('mother') almost certainly deliberately, rather than the asexual, chaste referent of 'sister' to describe the relationship between Nítíða and Sýjalín, the narrator

---

19   JS 166 fol., f. 186ᵛ.

20   'liðu þær svo í loft upp, en menn hlupu í höllina og sögðu kóngi þau tíðindi sem höfðu gerst, og ógladdi það hann mjög' (they thus glided up into the air, and people ran into the hall and told them and the king the news which had happened, and he was very unhappy) (Lbs 3941 8vo, f. 13ʳ).

21   Schibanoff, 'Hildegard of Bingen and Richardis of Stade', p. 58.

22   Schibanoff, 'Hildegard of Bingen and Richardis of Stade', p. 75 (n. 37). The quotation is from pseudo-Cicero's *Rhetorica ad Herennium* (c. 86-82 BC), which was known in the Middle Ages.

raises the issue while refusing to spell it out in detail. The closeness of a
mother and daughter at first glance could seem an innocent and normal
description of love between friends, not necessarily homoerotic. Read
against the grain, however, describing the relationship in this way can
be seen as a means of disguising female homoerotic discourse, 'merg[ing]
the mother-daughter affectional expectations and responses with same-
sex love between two women',[23] following Susan Schibanoff's reading
of Hildegard of Bingen's relationship with the younger nun Richardis of
Stade, which was represented in similar terms.[24] Schibanoff argues that in
Hildegard's letters her 'presentation of Richardis as her spiritual daughter
is both conventional and accurate, yet in creating even this traditional
metaphorical filiation, Hildegard introduced the possibility of entertaining more intimate relationships between herself and Richardis'.[25] There is
arguably something similar happening in *Nítíða saga*. If instead we took
this apparent mother-daughter bond at face value, it would not necessarily
have been suggestive of a positive, or expected, type of relationship among
medieval and early modern Icelandic readers, as the lack of positive mothers
in Icelandic literature demonstrates, as noted above. As a final point, the
relationship between these two women is somewhat different than the
female homoerotic relationships discussed and analysed in most of the
literature I have referred to so far. Particularly, the relationship is presented
as out in the open – Nítíða 'setur hana j hæsæti hiä sier' (sets [Sýjalín] in
the high seat next to her), and they are apart 'huorki suefn ne mat' (neither
in sleeping nor eating) – neither woman cross dresses at any point (although
Nítíða's role as *meykóngur* does at times suggest a masculine persona, if
not in actions, at least in mentality),[26] and their bond, though significant

---

23   Schibanoff, 'Hildegard of Bingen and Richardis of Stade', p. 61.
24   Schibanoff, 'Hildegard of Bingen and Richardis of Stade', pp. 60-63.
25   Schibanoff, 'Hildegard of Bingen and Richardis of Stade', p. 61. Schibanoff identifies this
most strongly in a letter to Richardis in which Hildegard expresses her grief at their separation.
Here, 'Hildegard moves out of her maternal role', which she has constructed for herself in the
letter's poetic language, 'and momentarily merges herself into Richardis, crossing the boundary
between them into Richardis's role as daughter' (p. 62).
26   As Francesca Canadé Sautman notes in an essay discussing female same-sex relationships in two fourteenth-century *chansons de geste* where cross-dressing and male identity are
significant features, 'It is important to distinguish between [...] adopting male identity every
day [...] and appearing to change temporarily into a man by donning armour [...] which implies
"manly behavio[u]r" but no change in the construction of identity' ('What Can They Possibly Do
Together?', p. 202). In *Nítíða saga* neither of these cases fully applies, with Nítíða's masculine
identity being more of a literary device of the author to symbolize the character's importance
and privilege in the text, than it is a developed feature of the character herself in physical terms.

and meaningful, is not permanent. For Nítíða, her masculine traits are not about physically passing as male, but about being treated and respected as a woman, in ways that are conventionally reserved in the sagas for men. Therefore, while her arguably homoerotic relationship with Sýjalín is only momentary, Nítíða's masculine identity is not – the end of their (physical) relationship does not mark a return to a 'female, strictly gendered identity',[27] because this was not normatively constructed in the first place, as I have detailed in Chapter 4. While the relationship therefore is certainly a type of 'pair bond', and might even be seen as a type of 'unmarriage' such as those discussed by Ruth Mazo Karras,[28] their relationship and homoerotic interactions are not presented as a marriage, sustained lifestyle, or identity. Rather, it is a type of behaviour that does not preclude the return, by the end of the romance, to the heteronormative ideals of late medieval Icelandic society. The saga privileges marriage over other bonds, while still, uniquely, raising the possibility of other types of (homo)social bonds.

Jóhanna Katrín Friðriksdóttir sees the women's relationship – that of close friendship only – as important evidence of the deeper workings of the text: 'the friendship between Nitida and the sister of her suitor whom she abducts, [conveys] an interest in women's psychological existence outside marriage, whereas in the other [Icelandic romance] sagas, if the woman is seen interacting with anyone other than suitors, it is usually her father'.[29] In this way, Sýjalín, though a less obviously active character than some, without even speaking, plays a very important role, whether or not her interactions with Nítíða are homoerotic. She provides moral support and companionship for Nítíða in the latter part of the saga, including during the winter months when Livorius, disguised, is visiting. Significantly, Sýjalín is also present each time Nítíða shows Livorius the regions of the world in the supernatural stones – these are not privileged, or intimate, scenes between Nítíða and her future husband. But in addition to companionship and support, the relationship between these two women foreshadows what is to follow it – Nítíða's marriage to Sýjalín's brother. Overall, her role reinforces the saga's

---

27 Canadé Sautman, 'What Can They Possibly Do Together?', p. 200.

28 Karras, *Unmarriages*. While Karras focuses on heterosexual pair bonds other than marriage, the idea of an 'unmarriage' may also be useful in thinking about pair bonds between members of the same sex. Karras notes that 'There are plenty of cases we can point to of two men or two women sharing living quarters. We do not know what their physical relationship was, but we do not demand proof of sexual relations to assume that two people of opposite sex were, in fact, a couple, so why should we demand it for two people of the same sex?' (*Unmarriages*, p. 9). The passage in *Nítíða saga* is of course more direct than the women simply sharing living quarters.

29 Jóhanna Katrín Friðriksdóttir, *Women in Old Norse Literature*, p. 130.

interest in women and their relationships, and in challenging the norms of the genre with respect to gender. We can also note that Ingi, once he has fallen in love with Sýjalín, does not discuss possibility of marriage with her, and instead raises the issue with Nítíða, as maiden-*king*, and Livorius. In treating the subject in this way, the saga preserves the patriarchal privilege of males to determine the futures of women, and reinforces heteronormative gender roles. Nítíða's characterization in the male role of *meykóngur* does not threaten this privilege, but rather reinforces it, while also reinforcing her own privileged role in the text. The homoerotic interlude, as an inversion of the marriage contracted later, therefore serves primarily as a further example of Nítíða in the romance's principal, active role, showcasing her power and influence, itself an inversion of the gender norms of the maiden-king saga, while also, importantly, drawing rare attention to the lives of women apart from their relationships with men.

A further important aspect of Sýjalín is her direct contrast with Nítíða again at the end of the text, when her skill as a doctor is highlighted. Livorius calls his sister to heal the wounded after the final battle because 'hun uar hinn agiætaste lækner og enn kunne hun framar j þessu enn m(ey)k(ongur)' (she was the most excellent physician and she knew more about this than the maiden-king).[30] This calls to mind the saga's first comparison between the two women, as well as their friendship, while also showing that Nítíða does not excel in everything, even with the help of her magical stones; this, further, does not detract from her skill and power as the ruler of her own kingdom and all the powers of negotiation and abilities to outwit she enjoys, for it is these, more internal, intellectual skills and wisdom, rather than such practical skills as medicine, that make Nítíða the maiden-king hero that she is. This is maintained even in some of the youngest versions of the romance, although with updated vocabulary. In the manuscript SÁM 13 (1851), for example, Nítíða is described as being wise 'sem eirn vel Lærður doktor' (as a very learned doctor)[31] – consequently, Sýjalín is not described as a better physician than Nítíða: Livorius simply 'bád sistur sina leggja sinar hendur yfir Ingja og so gjörir hún' (asked his sister to lay her hands over Ingi and she did so).[32] Nítíða is described with the modern loan *doktor*, more or less a modern synonym for the Old Norse *klerkur* (scholar), as a teacher or person with a doctoral degree, rather than *læknir* (physician). As a final note, it is interesting that Sýjalín, as an Indian princess, is

---

30   'Nitida saga', ed. by Loth, p. 35.
31   SÁM 13, f. 164^r.
32   SÁM 13, f. 176^v.

characterized in the medieval text as an excellent physician. It may have been more conventional to cast Listalín of Constantinople in that role. In her chapter on the depiction of Constantinople in medieval Icelandic romances, Geraldine Barnes discusses the characterization of Byzantine princesses in Icelandic romances as great scholars and physicians skilled in healing, attributing this to the possibility of knowledge in medieval Iceland of female physicians in Constantinople and the Byzantine Empire.[33] In *Nítíða saga*, the role is given instead to the Indian Sýjalín, who not only heals the Byzantine Ingi, but eventually marries him, sealing a political alliance between their eastern lands, and also ultimately between both these lands and France, as kin of Nítíða's Indian husband. The arguably less important union between Listalín and Hléskjöldur of Apulia, still politically advantageous to Nítíða with her connection to Apulia through fostering, may account for the stronger characterization of Nítíða's close companion and future sister-in-law Sýjalín as the best physician in the saga's worldview.

Listalín of Constantinople, who like Nítíða is skilled intellectually, occupies a different type of role than that of Sýjalín. Listalín is given direct speech in the saga, and it is obvious that she possesses the ability to influence those around her. When compared with her brother Ingi, Listalín is presented as the more perceptive and intuitive of the two. The best example of this occurs when Listalín raises doubts after Ingi believes he has succeeded in abducting Nítíða. Listalín asks him,

'er þier eingi grunur ä̈ hueria konu þu hefur heim flutt j landit. synist mier tiltæki hennar ei likt og m(ey)k(ongsins) og fleiri greinir adraʀ eʀ mier sagt ä̈ at vier sieum[34] vit braugdum at siä̈. vil eg nu foruitnast vm j dag at giora nockra til raun. enn þu statt j nockru leyni og heÿʀ ä̈'. kongur giorer nu svo.[35]

('Do you not have any suspicion as to what woman you have brought home into the land? Her behaviour, and many other things, seems to me not like the maiden-king's. It is said to me that we ought to beware of seeing tricks. I will inquire today about doing some kind of test, and you should stay in a certain hiding-place and listen'. The king now does so.)

---

33 Barnes, *The Bookish Riddarasögur*, pp. 166-67.
34 This has been emended from Loth's reading 'sem' ('Nitida saga', ed. by Loth, p. 17). See n. 5 to the Appendix for the other manuscript readings on which the emendation is based.
35 'Nitida saga', ed. by Loth, pp. 16-17.

Listalín addresses her brother familiarly, as would be expected, but this also highlights her as the scene's primary agent, which is only further reinforced when Ingi is quickly passed over in order to, again, showcase Listalín's words when she speaks directly to the disguised bondswoman Íversa. It is significant both that Listalín questions the identity of the supposed maiden-king, and that Ingi agrees, without a word, to follow her advice. He does not even respond verbally to defend his perception of the woman he believes he has abducted and married, but instead immediately does as his sister suggests. Ingi's intense anger at the revelation that Nítíða has fooled him for a second time thus seems unjustified; he appears to have given the situation no previous thought. Listalín thus acts as Ingi's counsellor, and although she does realize that he has not successfully taken Nítíða, Listalín does not offer further counsel as to how to win his bride. In this her counsel differs from that of Alduria, as counsellor for Livorius, discussed below. Listalín's importance is seen further in her discussions with Íversa, who has taken on Nítíða's appearance through the magic stones. In the only conversation between two women represented, apart from Nítíða's conversation with Egidía at the beginning of the saga, Listalín says, 'drott(ning) min. huad velldur þui er þier vilet eda meigit vit aungvan mann tala. e(dr) þann beiska grat er alldri gengur af ýdrum augum. þuiat kongur og allur landz lydur bidia suo sitia og standa huern mann sem ydur best liki' (My queen, what causes it, that you do not want to – or cannot – speak with any person? And what causes that bitter weeping which never leaves your eyes? Because the king and all the courtiers of the land ask how to sit and stand, so that everyone might please you best).[36] Listalín addresses Íversa formally, using the pronouns *þér, yðrum*, and *yður*, which show her respect and concern for the woman who appears (physically) to be Nítíða, but whom she suspects may be someone else. Also significantly, their conversation is allowed to continue, even though the direct speech is then limited to Íversa's immediate reply, which I discuss separately, below. This bit of dialogue showcases the importance and influence of female characters and their crucial roles in driving the saga's action forward, even when Nítíða is not directly involved in the scene. However, apart from her introduction as a courtly lady *hladin kuenlegum listum* (skilled in feminine arts),[37] and her interactions with Íversa, Listalín only appears again at the end of the saga when her marriage to Hléskjöldur is arranged by Livorius and Ingi. She has no further speaking parts and obediently arrives to be married when bidden. What power, influence, and independence she

36   'Nitida saga', ed. by Loth, p. 17.
37   'Nitida saga', ed. by Loth, p. 8.

displays earlier seems to be forgotten as the saga ends, and traditional gender roles are once again reinforced. Listalín is not consulted about her marriage, and significantly, even Ingi does not suggest it himself but passively agrees to Livorius's suggestion, which reinforces the latter's role as the successful suitor, and, accordingly, the most powerful character alongside Nítíða. The marriage of Listalín to Hléskjöldur works to further Livorius's alliance with Constantinople, through his future wife Nítíða's foster brother.

That the saga must fall back on traditional gender roles and models of behaviour at the end of the story can at first glance seem puzzling, considering that the text has, up until this point, actively challenged these traditional elements of romance. But while it is able to transgress political and sexual norms in order to confirm Nítíða's role as a hero in her own right, worthy of the respect of not only the other male and female characters in the story, but also of the story's audience, the romance is at the same time uninterested in fully upturning the social systems that perpetuate the patriarchal privilege of men to negotiate and sanction the marriages of women under their protection or control. What is brought to question here through the primacy of Nítíða and the women of the romance is undoubtedly not the male-centred social system itself, but individual abuses of such a system that facilitates the systemic maltreatment of women, and which maltreatment is then played out, often in vivid detail, by other bridal-quest and maiden-king romances. If late medieval Icelandic romances are acting to reinforce social norms that suppress the voices and privileges of women, then the author of *Nítíða saga* is using this romance to interrogate and even reinterpret these norms, while remaining aware that they cannot easily be overthrown. On a purely superficial level, too, the traditional conclusion satisfies certain romance norms, while at the same time invests new meaning into a conventional happy ending. The stronger, more influential role played by Listalín, for example, is not undermined by her more traditional role at the end, as the saga re-focuses on Nítíða, as it should, and as the audience will have come to expect.

While it is clear from these analyses that women are important and positive figures in *Nítíða saga*, we must not forget a minor female character who appears in the middle of the saga, and who could be said to have a slightly more worrying role than some of the other female characters: Íversa, the *þýgju* (bondwoman) and *ambátt* (servant, slave woman), whom Nítíða uses to save herself from marrying Ingi.[38] In a scene where at first Nítíða appears to be uncaring and emotionless, we see a more conventional picture

---

38   See Bagerius, *Mandom och mödom*, p. 264 (n. 493), as well as Glauser, *Isländische Märchensagas*, pp. 182-85.

of class relations that is somewhat jarring when juxtaposed with the saga's subversive depictions of women and female relationships – it is here that we see clearly that sharp distinctions between the upper and lower members of society are maintained as the status quo in the text. What makes the episode problematic is not what could be called Nítíða's objectification of the woman, but that she is not a flat stock character, but has a sympathetic voice of her own. Íversa's brief appearance characterizes her as a kind woman with her own feelings and concerns, who by the end of the episode may have garnered sympathy from the audience for having suffered injustice at Nítíða's hands. Íversa is introduced as follows: Nítíða 'kallar til sin eina arma þygiu er þionadi j gardinum. hun ätti bonda og .iij. born. þau geymdu suina j gardinum. drott(ning) tekur nu ambattina. hun hiet Jversa' (summons a poor bondwoman who serves in the yard. She had a husband and three children; they kept swine in the yard. The queen now takes the slave woman; she was called Íversa).[39] After 'taking' Íversa, Nítíða transforms her into a mirror image of herself with her magic stones and herbs, and causes her to become mute by giving her apples to eat, which 'bäru þau nätturu lif at hun mätti ecki mæla ä næsta mänudi' (held the supernatural property that she could not speak for the next month).[40] Once all of this is complete, Nítíða renders herself invisible, again with a supernatural stone, to complete her plan to trick Ingi into abducting and marrying the woman, acting against her will as decoy. This plan succeeds and Nítíða remains safe in France, but Íversa is left Ingi's captive and it is clear from what follows that she is miserable because of it. When asked by Ingi's sister Listalín, Íversa replies, 'þat velldur minum grati og þungum harmi at m(ey)kong(ur) hefur skilit mig vit bonda minn og bauRn og mun eg huorcki siæ sidan' (What causes my tears and heavy grief is that the maiden-king has separated me from my husband and children, and I will never see them again).[41] It is not enough for the narrator or another character to state that this woman has been traumatized but leave her silent, which would make her a less significant and perhaps easily forgettable character. Instead, she is given her own voice, making it much easier for the audience to sympathize with her and even to question Nítíða's integrity. Further, the romance does not even say whether Íversa can return to her family in France; as soon as Ingi hears she is not the real maiden-king, the story shifts its focus to his anger and ultimately back to Nítíða again. The scene ends by saying that 'fer nu og flÿgur ä huert land

39   'Nitida saga', ed. by Loth, p. 15.
40   'Nitida saga', ed. by Loth, p. 15.
41   'Nitida saga', ed. by Loth, p. 17.

þetta gabb og suivirding' (this mockery and disgrace now hastens and flies to every land).[42] So this episode, though somewhat disturbing, also furthers Nítíða's characterization as a woman of superior intelligence than her suitors and who can use magic effectively to outwit them. In doing so, the episode also reinforces a traditional, courtly medieval social hierarchy where the upper echelons of society have power over the members of the lower levels of society. While class relations are essentially maintained, the name and voice given to Íversa may make a subtle nod towards reconsidering them, even if the author was not interested in actively challenging or subverting this aspect of social order itself.

While, as an echo of the chivalry introduced through medieval European romances, this may be something that was not necessarily fully understood within Icelandic society and culture, of course the Icelandic romances are still very much the sagas of the high society of late medieval Iceland, 'assimilating newly imported courtly values and behavio[u]r for Icelandic audiences, and in the process defining and upholding appropriate behavio[u]r for men and women of the dominant class'.[43] These romances are essentially 'aristocrats' literature', as Glauser calls them, where 'the lower strata [...] enjoy little sympathy' and 'slaves are [...] depicted as fearful'.[44] Íversa and the poor treatment she endures, therefore, is the exception that proves the rule when it comes to female characters and the powerful and influential roles we see them enjoying in *Nítíða saga*. As a romance for the educated, literate, higher class in medieval Iceland, the characterization of the bondswoman Íversa cannot run parallel with that of the other noblewomen depicted, and thus elite relationships must be valued over common ones. Íversa's different social class reflects the different rules associated with it. As a final note that brings this character's lower status into even sharper focus, it is also significant that Livorius does not face this trick; instead, it reflects badly only on Ingi, and essentially confirms that he will never win the independent maiden-king Nítíða – he can only ever attain a poor reflection of her. At the same time, then, the way is subtly paved for Livorius to become Nítíða's chosen suitor. These scenes might be easier to accept as such if Íversa were not a dynamic, named, character, or if the narrator, who is conspicuously silent here, had provided some comment on her treatment.

---

42 'Nitida saga', ed. by Loth, p. 18.

43 Jóhanna Katrín Friðriksdóttir, *Women in Old Norse Literature*, p. 108. See also Barnes, *The Bookish Riddarasögur*, pp. 183 ff.

44 'Aristokratenliteratur', where 'Die niedrigen Schichten [...] genießen wenig Sympathie' and 'Sklaven werden [...] als ängstlich gezeichnet' (Glauser, *Isländische Märchensagas*, p. 184).

That Íversa is provided with a name in this version is nevertheless significant. In nearly all of the other versions of the romance, the woman has no name at all, and is called instead simply an *ambátt* (servant). The only manuscripts in which she is named are AM 529 (the version quoted above); AM 537, also associated with this version; and Reykjavík, Landsbókasafn–Háskólabókasafn Íslands, MS Lbs 3128 4to, which is merely a summary written in 1885 and which states after its title that it is based on both AM 529 and 537. As an example of how the woman is described in other versions, that in JS 166, discussed in Chapter 1, states simply that Nítíða 'kallar til sÿn a<mb>att eina er j Gardinum*m var*' (called to herself a certain servant woman who was in the yard).[45] No mention is made of her husband and children until the end of the episode when Listalín speaks with her. In this version, the impact of the servant woman revealing that she has a family is not as strong as it would be if she had been introduced as having a family, occupation, and name, as occurs in the edited version, on which my discussion above has focused. Instead, this character, when left anonymous, remains far less sympathetic, and so, less problematic. This suggests that it is possible, and even likely, that this character really should not be named, and that the few instances where she is mark a scribal innovation. This may explain the name's absence from the rest of the manuscript tradition, indeed even from the other manuscripts with texts most similar to the edited version. Clearly, other scribes and audiences did not find it convenient to name the *ambátt*, as such a personal characterization also, to a certain extent, problematizes the characterization of Nítíða.

The other servant figure in *Nítíða saga* is the smith Ypolitus, who is introduced after Nítíða's description at the beginning of the saga as someone who 'kunni allt at smida af gulli og silfri gleri og gimsteinum. þat sem giorast mætti af manna hondum' (knew how to craft all things – from gold and silver, glass and jewels – that could be made with one's hands).[46] Like Íversa, Ypolitus's primary function is to highlight Nítíða's character, to show her as industrious, able to defend herself, and to facilitate her escape from dangerous and undesirable situations. Unlike Íversa, however, Ypolitus does not have a speaking role, and his characterization does not extend past his mastery of craftsmanship described in the passage just quoted. After this brief introduction, Ypolitus does not reappear in the text until his services are needed, towards the middle of the romance when Nítíða prepares defences against an attack on France by Serkland. At that point, it

45   JS 166 fol., f. 184ʳ.
46   'Nitida saga', ed. by Loth, p. 4.

is clear that Nítíða herself has planned two defensive construction projects, which she then passes on to Ypolitus to carry out:

> Nu er at seigia af m(ey)k(ongi) at hun helldur ei kÿrru fyrir. þuiat hun lætur saman lesa smidu og meistara. fyrir þeim var Ypolitus. hvn lætur giora glerhimin med þeirri list at hann liek ä hiolum og mätti fara jnn yfer haufudport borgarinnar og mätti þar mart herfolk ä standa. hon liet og giora diki ferlega diupt framm fyrir skemmunni og leggia ÿfer veyka vidu. en þar yfer var breitt skrud og skarlat.[47]

> (Now it is said of the maiden-king that she does not sit still nor idle, because she summons together her smiths and masters; Ypolitus oversaw them. She commands that a glass roof be made that could move on wheels and could go over the main gate of the castle so that many warriors could stand thereon. She commanded also that a monstrously deep ditch be made before her chamber, and to lay weak wood over it, and over that was to be spread costly stuff and scarlet.)

This is Ypolitus's only other mention. From what follows, his involvement in the projects is beneficial, as the newly constructed mechanisms provide the means by which Hléskjöldur and the French army win the battle for Nítíða. Ypolitus's skill as a smith and his competence in overseeing these projects reflect back on Nítíða as a competent ruler whose subjects and servants have been chosen well for their skill and loyalty. As a smith, Ypolitus might also be compared to dwarfs in other Icelandic romances, who are sometimes skilled as smiths in addition to being characterized as the helpers of heroes.[48]

In other versions of *Nítíða saga*, however, Ypolitus is not always viewed as an essential character. Only eight manuscripts name Ypolitus (or some variation on that name, like *Ipolitus* or *Hippolitus*) at the beginning of the saga, and they are all relatively early manuscripts, which can be grouped together with those edited and similar to Add. 4860, discussed in Chapter 1. The name was most likely taken from the figure Hippolytus of Classical mythology, although it seems that the author or scribes merely liked the name, as there are not any obvious connections between *Nítíða saga*'s Ypolitus and the mythological figure. At most, the name further reinforces the medieval author or scribes' high level of education in a clerical setting, as I have discussed in the first part of this book. There are, moreover, three

---

47 'Nitida saga', ed. by Loth, p. 18.
48 See Ármann Jakobsson, 'Enabling Love'; and Schäfke, 'Was ist eigentlich ein Zwerg?'.

other versions of the smith's name, all significantly different from the form Ypolitus. In the nineteenth-century eastern Icelandic manuscripts, as well as in ÍBR 47, the smith is introduced at the beginning and named Bonius (or Bomus). In the nineteenth- and twentieth-century manuscripts SÁM 13, Lbs 1319 8vo, Lbs 1305 4to, and Lbs 3675 8vo this character is also introduced at the beginning and called Vibuls (or Vipilius), which very interestingly seems most likely to have derived from the alternative, Latin, name of the Classical Greek Hippolytus – that is, Virbius.[49] A late group of manuscripts with versions of *Nítíða saga* containing reference to *Nikulás saga leikara* (ÍB 233 4to, Lbs 644 4to, Lbs 3966 4to, Lbs 1137 8vo, and Lbs 3165 4to) does not introduce the smith until he is needed later, in the midst of the saga, and he is then called Produs; all but one of these manuscripts (Lbs 644, from 1730-31) are from the nineteenth century. Additionally, in whole groups of other manuscript versions, which I have generally not discussed in this book, a smith character is not present in any form. Overall, it appears that for some post-medieval scribes and audiences the smith best known as Ypolitus was not important enough to retain as a named character, or perhaps also likely, it was simply a name not widely known among the average Icelanders copying the text in the centuries after the Middle Ages (reinforcing the saga's authorship by an educated cleric), and further was not an enduring enough character to retain the same identification across different versions of the romance. When the smith does appear, as seen in the quoted examples above, his purpose is to remind the audience of Nítíða's primacy as a resourceful ruler, enhancing her fame in the same way that the negative treatment of the servant woman Íversa is ostensibly justified because it highlights Nítíða's superior intellect and heroic character.

Before bringing this chapter to a close I will discuss two final examples of female solidarity that appear in *Nítíða saga* – Egidía of Apulia and Alduria of Småland, the female relatives whose roles might initially seem small, but who have important influences on both Nítíða and Livorius. While Egidía appears in the saga only briefly, she is integral to Nítíða's characterization. In naming Egidía, the author may have borrowed from the translated romance *Elis saga ok Rósamundu*'s own Egidius,[50] which is that saga's translation of the French name Giles: the saga begins in 'lande hins helga Egidij' (the land of Saint Giles).[51] If this is the name's source in *Nítíða saga*, it is interesting that the originally masculine name is here feminized for a female character, who

49   Grimal, *A Concise Dictionary of Classical Mythology*, pp. 204, 450-51.
50   van Nahl, *Originale Riddarasögur*, p. 139.
51   Kölbing, ed., *Elis saga ok Rósamundu*, p. 1.

occupies an important role in the text. First and foremost, Egidía establishes Nítíða's characterization by reinforcing her foster daughter's reputation as a powerful sovereign, by welcoming her with feasts and later sending her off with lavish gifts and the support of her son: 'hennar fostur modur [...] vt leidandi <hana> med fogrum fegiofum og ægiætum dyrgripum j gulli og gimsteinum og dyrum vefium' (her foster mother [...] leading her out with fair gifts of money, fine jewels of gold and jewels, and precious woven cloth).[52] Additionally, as foster mother of a young woman whose own mother the saga never mentions, Egidía's relationship with her foster daughter is even more meaningful as a mother-daughter relationship, and it can be inferred that Egidía may actually have raised Nítíða due to her own mother's absence. Thus an even deeper bond arguably exists between the two women than at first might be suggested by their fosterage relationship on which the text does not elaborate. Nítíða trusts and relies on her foster mother, which is why she travels to Apulia to meet with her: she knows Egidía will help and support her. Egidía does not, however, provide much in the way of counsel for Nítíða, and what concerns she does raise, Nítíða discounts rather than accepts: 'drott(ning) Egidia taldi tormerki ä ferdinni. og þotti häskaleg. meyk(ongur) vard þo at räda' (Queen Egidía raised difficulties about the journey, and thought it dangerous; the maiden-king nevertheless decided to go).[53] Egidía's very brief reply (after Nítíða states her intentions to go to Visio) is only relayed by the narrator indirectly, in sharp contrast to Nítíða's words immediately preceding, which constitute the first example of direct speech in the saga. That Egidía's response is indirect reflects the lesser degree of importance the saga imparts on it, compared to Nítíða's speech and the desires expressed there. Further, the lack of importance given to the reply anticipates Nítíða's disregard of it when she decides to go ahead with her plan despite Egidía's warning. Egidía's indirect concerns work to highlight Nítíða's direct speech:

mier er sagt at fyrer eyiu þeirri er Visio heiter rædi jarl sä er Virgilius heiter [...] og suo er mier sagt at huergi j heiminum meigi finnast næturu steinar epli og læknis graus fleiri en þar. Nu vil eg hallda þangad einnskipa og son þinn Hleskiolldr med mier.[54]

52 'Nitida saga', ed. by Loth, p. 7.
53 'Nitida saga', ed. by Loth, p. 5.
54 'Nitida saga', ed. by Loth, p. 5.

(I am told that beyond that island which is called Visio rules that earl who is called Virgilius [...] and so I am told, that nowhere in the world might one find more supernatural stones, apples, and healing herbs than there. Now I wish to travel there in a ship and to take your son Hléskjöldur with me.)

It is a lengthy and rather detailed speech, but Nítíða's own, active, intentions (*nú vil ég*) emerge only after she relays indirect, reported knowledge about the place she means to visit. While her desire to travel to Visio indicates her belief in the reports about it, the passive manner in which the information is presented (*mér er sagt*) indicates that she has no way of verifying such reports until she goes herself. When Nítíða speaks to Egidía directly, she does so familiarly, with the informal second person singular pronoun *þinn*, which is not surprising, considering their close relationship. The conversation between Livorius and his aunt Alduria, below, also uses informal address. Alongside her practical, motherly concerns, Egidía continues to support Nítíða in her determination to carry out the quest, recognizing her independence and capabilities, as is evident when she consents to equip Nítíða with her son's aid as she travels back to France upon her successful return to Apulia from Visio. In this way, Egidía plays the part of a benevolent helper to Nítíða in her preliminary preparatory adventures, which are integral to her later success.

Livorius's aunt Alduria provides him with crucial aid in her important, though brief, role. Livorius seeks her out specifically because of her reputation: 'þu ert kaullud vitur kona og klok. legg til ʀæd at eg mætti m(ey)k(ong) vt leika og aast hennar nä' (you are considered a wise and cunning woman. Give me counsel that I might out-play the maiden-king and gain her love).[55] Significantly, Livorius wants to be able to *útleika* (out-play, outwit) Nítíða; throughout the saga, this word describes the maiden-king's victories. Livorius has, after his failure to win her by force, realized that he must take a different approach, and that his only chance might rest on being able to beat Nítíða at her own game. Alduria understands this well. Not only is she *vitur* (wise) – an adjective used elsewhere only of Nítíða and in Nítíða's evaluation of Virigilius and Livorius[56] – she is also *klókur* (cunning). This

---

55 'Nitida saga', ed. by Loth, p. 28.

56 The narrator says of Nítíða: 'hun var bædi vitur og væn' (she was both wise and beautiful) ('Nitida saga', ed. by Loth, p. 3). Nítíða says of Virigilius: 'hann er vitur og fiolkunnigur' (he is wise and skilled in magic) ('Nitida saga', ed. by Loth, p. 5). The narrator also reveals Nítíða's first impression of Livorius (disguised as Eskilvarður): 'virdist henne hann vitur madur' (she judged him a wise man) ('Nitida saga', ed. by Loth, p. 29).

is the saga's only instance of the adjective (as noted briefly in Chapter 2, borrowed into Old Norse from Low German), which may have had negative connotations to do with magic or sorcery, but not necessarily so. Some texts use the word *klókur* to describe dwarves, who often have magical powers;[57] medieval Icelandic religious literature also sometimes uses *klókur* to characterize the devil.[58] It may not, then, be coincidental that Alduria resides in Småland in Sweden, which with its far north eastern location is sometimes is a favourite saga setting for strange happenings and the scene of the otherworldly (or even evil) North[59] – an often 'problematic direction for Icelanders',[60] which, advantageously in *Nítíða saga*, is reoriented away from the periphery and closer to the centre, as discussed in Chapter 3. Alduria's advice to Livorius demonstrates her knowledge of magic, highlighting her as *klókur* perhaps more concretely than as *vitur*: 'nu er þad mitt Rad, ad þu sigler þetta sumar til Fracklands og nefnest Eskilvardur, sonur kongs af Mundia, og haff þar vetursetu, eg skal gefa þier gull þad er þig skal eingenn madur kienna, hvorki meÿkongur nie þyn systir' (Now, it is my counsel that you sail this summer to France and call yourself Eskilvarður, son of the king of the Alps, and stay there over the winter. I will give you gold, so that nobody will know you, neither the maiden-king nor your sister).[61] Alduria's use of magic is not negative here, but shown as a practical means to an end, not dissimilar to Nítíða's own uses of the *náttúrusteinar* or to Livorius's use of the dwarf's ring. And it is because Alduria is *vitur* (wise) that she advises Livorius to win Nítíða's favour by building a relationship with her: 'eff þu situr þar allann þann vetur, þa er undur, eff þu fær eckj fang a henne' (if you remain there for the whole winter, it will be a wonder if you do not get a hold on her).[62] Ármann Jakobsson reads Alduria's help here as the single instance in the romance where someone manages to outwit Nítíða,[63] but it

---

57   For example, *Viktors saga ok Blávus*, ed. by Jónas Kristjánsson, p. 14, and *Samsons saga fagra*, ed. by Wilson, p. 21.

58   For example, Unger, ed., *Stjórn*, p. 34: 'Hǫggorminn uar klokaztr og slægaztr af ollum kuikendum' (The viper was cleverest and most cunning of all creatures), and then proceeding to the story of Eve's betrayal by the devil in the form of such a creature, and Unger, ed., *Mariu saga*, p. 523: 'fiandinn er klokr' (the devil is clever).

59   Strange things happen in Sweden in sagas such as *Hrólfs saga Gautrekssonar* (the hard and quick-tempered woman Þórbergur rules, in the guise of a man, part of Sweden). See also Shafer, 'Saga Accounts of Norse Far-Travellers', pp. 207-72, on the mysterious and dangerous North in the *fornaldarsögur*.

60   Barnes, *The Bookish Riddarasögur*, pp. 34-35.

61   'Nitida saga', ed. by Loth, pp. 28-29.

62   'Nitida saga', ed. by Loth, p. 29.

63   Ármann Jakobsson, *Illa fenginn mjöður*, pp. 176-77.

seems clear that Nítíða knows all along that it is Livorius, disguised, who wins her over, and that she is not outwitted – why should the audience not believe Nítíða when she tells him so? Indeed, it may also be a way for Nítíða to test Livorius, not letting on that she knows his identity, to see whether his behaviour towards women has improved from their previous encounter. Alduria's role is crucial to Livorius's success in winning Nítíða over, as she understands not only the best courtly way to go about it, but also how important an actual relationship is for building a marriage, at least from a female point of view.[64] Nítíða's change of heart has been read as 'unmotivated and carried out suddenly',[65] but her reasons for agreeing to Livorius's proposal instead of continuing to scorn him are obvious: Alduria's courtly advice does not fail Livorius as the different approach to marriage that he now takes is something Nítíða clearly also values.

Conclusions

This analysis of *Nítíða saga*'s characters – whether major, like the princesses Listalín and Sýjalín, or the minor figures Íversa and Ypolitus – has revealed much about the inner workings of the saga, its hero, and some of the socio-cultural attitudes reflected in the text. Other, more cursory discussions of *Nítíða saga*'s plot and the functions of its characters have concluded that it is merely derivative, and even a 'strained' narrative relying on the reduplication of a single theme – for example, in showing how *Nítíða saga* is different from other romances in its use of the maiden-king motif, Astrid van Nahl concludes that 'in *Nítíða saga* the basic theme of the deceptive princess is tripled [...]. The narrative element appears strained and thereby ultimately loses its appeal'.[66] I have, however, shown in this chapter that, far from laboriously and blindly repeating the motif of the maiden-king avoiding marriage, the repetitions and doublings of scenes and characters serve, rather, to enhance Nítíða's character in terms of power, influence, and audience sympathy. More recent considerations of the saga, while much more generous in their assessments of the story's value and meaning – such as Jóhanna Katrín Friðriksdóttir's feminist readings and Geraldine Barnes's

---

64   Cf. Jóhanna Katrín Friðriksdóttir, *Women in Old Norse Literature*, pp. 129-30.

65   '[U]nmotiviert und plötzlich vollzog' (van Nahl, *Originale Riddarasögur*, p. 41).

66   'In der *Nitida saga* ist das Grundmotiv der betrügerischen Prinzessin verdreifacht [...]. Das Erzählelement erscheint dadurch strapaziert und verliert letzten Endes seinen Reiz' (van Nahl, *Originale Riddarasögur*, pp. 37-38).

focus on the significance of geography – still also overlook the significance of, especially, the romance's minor characters and the role each figure plays in demonstrating Nítíða's primacy. In *Nítíða saga*, the characterization of what might normally be considered simple minor characters works alongside the depiction of Nítíða to reconfigure the traditional ideas of what it means to be a hero in Icelandic romance, demonstrating how Icelanders (authors, scribes, and audiences) were able and seemingly happy to question, re-evaluate, and re-invent the idea of the hero and to a certain extent other typical character roles in romance. Further, it is not only the idea of the hero that is interrogated and inverted when compared to the norm, but also ideas about women's relationships with each other, which we have seen particularly in the depiction of Nítíða's intimate, if brief, relationship with Sýjalín that challenges ideas about gender and sexuality in the Middle Ages. Once again, seeing the saga as a reaction to and revaluation of traditional bridal-quest and maiden-king romance (as likewise discussed in Chapter 2) also further clarifies and puts into perspective the romance's reflexivity and innovation in other areas, such as its image of travel and geography, as discussed in Chapter 3. I have shown how *Nítíða saga* problematizes all of these notions through the means of Nítíða's characterization, through the characterization of other major figures like Livorius, Ingi, and Hléskjöldur, and through the characterization of the minor supporting characters, helpers, and, just as importantly, its antagonists. I have also demonstrated some of the variation in depicting these characters, as we can see in some of the early modern and later manuscript versions of the romace. Overall, the findings of this and the chapter preceding it are the foundation for the final chapter of this book, in which I consider the figure and function of *Nítíða saga*'s narrator.

6 Romance through the Eyes of the Narrator

This chapter will complete my consideration of characterization and relationships among characters in this second part of the book, by looking at the voice of *Nítíða saga*'s anonymous narrator, seen through his (or her) comments in the first person voice.[1] I will focus especially on the narrator's interventions in the saga's opening and closing, which I will also compare with those of other Icelandic romances. The narrator is important in *Nítíða saga* as the teller of the tale, and as such is portrayed as a character with a personality and opinions, which are sometimes revealed freely. In the discussions that follow, I have chosen in general not to distinguish between author, scribe, and narrator when discussing late medieval Icelandic romances. Of course, I recognize that each is usually a very different person, and that the medieval texts we study today are often amalgamations of at least two versions – that of author and that of scribe, as I have pointed out in Chapter 1. Whether the narrator in *Nítíða saga* or any other Icelandic romance can be identified with either or both an author or a specific scribe is difficult to discern in the early versions. While I acknowledge that author, scribe, and narrator are separate, I will in this chapter refer to the narrator as a character, for it is the narrator who is most readily visible in the texts with which I am concerned. The author's views or intentions are virtually impossible to determine unless through (nearly) blind conjecture because of the impossibility to match a name or precise location to *Nítíða saga*'s author. However, the narrator and his or her views as they exist in the version of the text under consideration could be interpreted as a complex mixture of the original author, his (or her) sources and influences, and the anonymous scribes through which the story has been preserved up until this version. In speaking of scribes instead of narrator characters, Marianne Kalinke has said that 'Icelandic scribes were an individualistic lot' with varying 'attitudes to the texts they were transmitting'.[2] Such diversity of

---

1   While in this chapter I will not argue either way for an explicitly gendered narrator, the narrators of Icelandic sagas generally seem to be referred to as male; in the case of *Nítíða saga*, however, I see no reason why the narrator could not be understood as female, given the text's arguably female focus and the issues it raises, which I have already discussed, particularly in Chapters 4 and 5.

2   Kalinke, 'Scribes, Editors, and the *Riddarasögur*', p. 39. See also Kalinke, 'Scribe, Redactor, Author'.

style, attitude, and opinion will be evident in the romances discussed in this chapter, as each scribe (Kalinke's choice in the quotation above), or narrator (an alternative perspective, which I generally employ here), relates to the story told in a slightly different manner.

A saga's beginning and ending, related by the narrator, are integral elements of the text. They frame the story, and may situate it within a wider literary context: in the case of *Nítíða saga*, the endings in some manuscript versions, as we know from Chapters 1 and 2, link this text with *Nikulás saga leikara*. With all of this in mind, my discussion of the narrator here is also influenced by Suzanne Fleischman's suggested model for analysing medieval narrators, as a part of her consideration of the differences between history and fiction as modes of composition in medieval narratives, seeing distinct trends in romance approaches to narration. In her study, romance is contrasted with epic, but other forms of narrative (such as the chronicle) are also assessed. The discussion of narrators is particularly helpful for Icelandic romance, as its narrators are often such prominent and vocal figures. In considering 'the apparent presence or absence in the account of a narrative *ego*', Fleischman asks questions such as:

> What sort of distance does the narrator set up between himself and the events he relates? Does he intervene in the narrative, or is he effaced? Does he display self-consciousness? To what extent does he function as an interpreter, mediating between his text and its consumers?[3]

Along with narrator involvement she also considers questions of narrative authenticity, authorial intent, and the social function of the romance, which also come into play in the following discussions. I will use this approach in conjunction with a specifically Old Norse model of interpretation in Paul Schach's analysis of narrators in the *Íslendingasögur*. The five forms Schach identifies are 'use of the first person', authorial 'value judgements', 'enlightening observations on life in the "saga age"', 'source references', and 'cross references'.[4] Most of these are also present in Icelandic romances, making this study another useful model. I will begin by considering romance prologues and the figure of the narrator as is evident at the beginning of the

---

3   Fleischman, 'On the Representation of History and Fiction in the Middle Ages', p. 295, italics original.

4   Schach, 'Some Forms of Writer Intrusion', pp. 154-55. Also useful for an understanding of narrators and authorial voices in medieval Icelandic literature are Einar Ólafur Sveinsson, 'Fact and Fiction in the Sagas', pp. 293-306; Harris, 'Saga as Historical Novel', pp. 227-60; and Scott, 'The Icelandic Family Saga as Precursor to the Novel', pp. 3-13.

saga, comparing and contrasting *Nítíða saga*'s opening with those of other medieval Icelandic romances. I will then turn to the end of the saga and the narrator's role there, again in comparison with other romances. In the final part of this chapter, I will discuss the role and function of the narrator as seen throughout the main text, including brief comparisons of the narrator's role among some of *Nítíða saga*'s many other manuscript versions.

It is very common for Icelandic romances to begin with a prologue, through which we can sometimes see the first glimpse of the narrator. These prologues are often defensive and self-conscious, and while not entirely formulaic, they do often follow a pattern of either attributing the romance in question to a real or imagined ancient authority, or to the authority of the written word more generally. Romances that include the first type of prologue have come to be known as 'graffiti sagas', since some claim to have been found inscribed on walls,[5] and Geraldine Barnes has recently discussed them and the implications of the prologues in her study of 'bookish' Icelandic romances.[6] While such claims about origins are easily dismissed today, these narrators appeal to both the authority of the written word in the Middle Ages, and also to the authority of ancient authors like Homer and Virgil – 'a process of *translatio studii*' from the ancient world'.[7] However unlikely it is that any one author actually found these stories written on walls is, naturally, beside the point; what matters is that in the Middle Ages the idea appealed to Icelanders (and of course others), who thus justified their enjoyment of romances by linking them to known authors, and to the written word more generally.[8] While this does not necessarily mean that audiences absolutely believed these attributions and thought of these sagas as accounts of true events, such details are clearly included

5   Barnes, 'Romance in Iceland', p. 271; O'Connor, 'History or Fiction?', p. 129. In *Vilhjálms saga sjóðs* the narrator attributes the saga to Homer, assuming this will make the text more credible: 'þessi saga var tekin af steinuegginum j Babbilon hjnni miklu. og meistari Humerus hefer samsett hana' (This saga was taken from stone walls in Babylon the Great, and master Homer had composed it) ('Vilhjálms saga sjóðs', ed. by Loth, p. 3). *Jarlmanns saga ok Hermanns* similarly opens by appealing to the classical authority of Virgil: '<M>Eistari Uirgilius hefer samansett marga fræde til skemtanar maunnum j bok þeirre er Saxfræde heiter, en sögu þæ sem nu munu uær byria fann hann skrifada æ steinuegginum borgar þeirrar er Licibon heiter i Franz' (Master Virgilius has composed many tales of entertainment for people in the book which is called *Saxfrædi*, and the saga which now we must begin he found written on a stone wall of the city in France which is called Lisbon) ('Jarlmanns saga ok Hermanns', ed. by Loth, p. 3).

6   Barnes, *The Bookish Riddarasögur*, pp. 77-81.

7   Barnes, *The Bookish Riddarasögur*, p. 79.

8   See Hall and others, ed., '*Sigurðar saga fóts*', pp. 67-70. For these views in medieval literature generally and discussions about the idea of medieval authorship and authority, see Dragonetti, *Le mirage des sources*.

for a purpose, playing on the very notion of authorization and the value, or truth, inherent in the texts. These types of prologues represent their romances not as indigenous to Iceland (which they in reality are), but as inherited and translated from wise masters of the past, introducing a great distance between the story's source and the narrator who tells it,[9] along with, contrastingly, the power of continuity for the written as this very distance is essentially negated by the manuscript page.

Clári saga begins with a brief prologue in which its narrator not only appeals to the authority of a bishop, but to the authority of Latin, and a European romance tradition: 'Þar byrjum vér upp þessa frásögn, sem sagði virðuligr herra Jón byskup Halldórson, ágætrar áminningar, – en hann fann hana skrifaða með látínu í Frannz, í þat form, er þeir kalla "rithmos", en vér köllum hendingum, – ok byrjar svá' (There we begin this account, as told by the venerable lord Bishop Jón Halldórsson, of excellent memory, – and he found it written in Latin in France, in that form, which they call 'rithmos', but we call *hendingum*, – and it begins thus).[10] The narrator (whose voice, however conventional this may be, we see here directly in the first person plural *vér*) is compelled to provide background information about not only the saga's origin, but also about its presumed composer or translator, and its form. The temporal proximity of Jón Halldórsson 'ágætrar áminningar' (of excellent memory) to the narrator further reinforces the credibility of the tale and its claim to truth and plausibility. This prologue has prompted some to regard *Clári saga* as a translated romance rather than an Icelandic composition. Shaun Hughes, however, has argued the opposite, and explains the prologue's function as an authorizing and authenticating technique: 'Latin is the prestige language, and France is the home of the romance'.[11] This appeal to French literary authority is also echoed in the beginning of *Nikulás saga leikara*, but instead of attributing the romance to any identifiable source, the prologue simply provides a named figure, alongside other anonymous wise men: 'suo seÿgia sannfröder menn *og* meÿstarar ad sä ko*ngur* hafe rädid f*irer* v*ng*ar*i*a er Faustus hiet. enn søgn þessa fan*n* he*r*ra biarne j pärÿs ä Fraclande. sÿdann skrifadi huer sem mätti j sÿnu lÿki j þann tÿma' (Well informed people and scholars say this, that the king who ruled over Hungary was called Fástus. And Sir Bjarni found this saga in Paris in

---

9   Fleischman, 'On the Representation of History and Fiction', pp. 295-97.

10   *Clári saga*, ed. by Cederschiöld, p. 1. On the literary terminology – *rithmos* and *hendingum* – see Hughes, '*Klári saga* as an Indigenous Romance', p. 137, nn. 6-7).

11   Hughes, '*Klári saga* as an Indigenous Romance', p. 158; see also pp. 146-48 for a more detailed argument.

France. After that everyone wrote it in their own way at that time).[12] What matters is here that a name is given as a source – it does not matter who this Bjarni is, or whether he really existed.[13] The saga is further legitimized in reinforcing its facts by sages and scholars, and its status as a romance by its ostensible origin in Paris, in the saga's only mention of that city. This not only connects *Nikulás saga leikara* by its brief prologue to *Clári saga*, but also to *Nítíða saga*, whose action centres on Paris.

Moving away from 'graffiti sagas' and romances naming particular authors and translators, *Sigurðar saga þǫgla* opens simply with an appeal to book learning: '<M>Argir fyrri men hafa saman sett til scemtanar monnum margar frasagner. sumar eptir fornkuædum e(dur) frædimonnum enn sumar eptir fornum bokum er j fyrstu hafa samann settar verit med skiotu male. enn sidan med hagligum ordum fylldar' (Many people in former times have composed many fair tales for people's entertainment. Some come from old tales or learned men, and some from old books which at first were composed with a brief narrative, and later filled out with skilful words).[14] In this, the narrator seems accurately to explain just what this saga's redactor has done, that is, to fashion a story based on an existing narrative by fleshing it out and embellishing it at will.[15] An appeal to old books, especially, is an appeal to the authority of the written word; an appeal to old tales, whether written or oral, is an appeal to the authority and implied gravity of antiquity in and of itself. Schach notes that 'Quite frequently [...] saga writers [...] tend strongly to accept the written word rather than oral tradition' to support their stories.[16] There is no interest in presenting new, original work; rather it is more credible and even usual to report or rework what someone else wrote long ago.[17] Either ironically or fittingly, the same prologue in this redaction of *Sigurðar saga þǫgla* appears in two manuscripts of the *fornaldarsaga Göngu-Hrólfs saga* (Reykjavík, Stofnun Árna Magnússonar í íslenskum fræðum, MSS AM 589 f 4to and AM 567 XI β 4to),[18] demonstrating the fluidity of such textual elements and their ability to be incorporated into various works. This also confirms the degree of borrowing done by

---

12   Wick, 'An Edition and Study of Nikulás saga Leikara', pp. 62, 162.
13   Schach, 'Some Forms of Writer Intrusion', p. 145.
14   'Sigurðar saga þǫgla', ed. by Loth, p. 95.
15   *Dínus saga drambl, áta* begins similarly, appealing to previously written narratives: 'Suo finst j fornumm fræde bökumm skriffad' [Thus it is found written in old wise books] (*Dínus saga drambl, áta*, ed. by Jónas Kristjánsson, p. 3).
16   Schach, 'Some Forms of Writer Intrusion', p. 140.
17   See e.g. Barnes, 'Travel and *translatio studii*', pp. 123-39.
18   'Sigurðar saga þǫgla', ed. by Loth, p. 96n; See also O'Connor, 'Truth and Lies', pp. 361-78.

Sigurðar saga þǫgla's eclectic redactor, as I have discussed in relation to geography in Chapter 3. Nevertheless, the frequency of these prologues among the Icelandic romances demonstrates a general concern with the truth value of these texts, which often contain blatantly non-realistic elements, but still ring true for Icelanders in the later Middle Ages and beyond. While not imploring readers to believe that everything related is *true* in the modern sense of being *factual* or *historical*, these narrators at least desire the stories they tell to be taken seriously and enjoyed as 'truthful stories', if not necessarily 'true' stories.[19] Modern readers might call this fiction, but to apply this to the medieval saga is arguably anachronistic, especially considering that a *saga* means not only a 'story', but alternatively, a 'history'. It is interesting to note that it was not until the nineteenth century that fiction was recognized as a literary genre in Iceland, and a new word was coined to refer to the novel: *skáldsaga* (lit. poetic or composed history). In the 1878 preface of *Sagan af Hèðni og Hlöðvi*, the editors directly link the idea of medieval Icelandic romance to that of fiction, in describing the saga as 'Að líkendum er saga þessi eigi annað en skáldsaga (Roman), eins og flestar riddarasögur vorar' (Most likely this saga is nothing other than a *skáldsaga* [novel], like most of our *riddarasögur*).[20] In earlier centuries, distinguishing the 'fiction' from the 'history' was not as much of a concern. Ralph O'Connor has discussed the use of the term *lygi* (lie),[21] with reference to its medieval attestations, and argued for interpreting romance prologues' truth claims as genuine arguments in support of the stories' veracity, and not necessarily as fiction.[22] While this is certainly a valid argument, I would like to think that such defensive narrators and prologues are not necessarily the by-product of overly credulous audiences but of a society that has come to associate the written word with truth, although it is notable that in the eighteenth century, when Icelandic sagas were often mined for information about the early histories of other Scandinavian countries, even the most outlandish *fornaldarsögur* were used as such sources.[23] Similarly, Eggert

---

19   Driscoll, 'What's Truth Got to Do with It?', p. 18.

20   *Sagan af Hèðni og Hlöðvi*, ed. by Jónas Jónsson and Stefán Egilsson, p. 2. Thanks to Shaun Hughes for this reference, as well as those below in nn. 23-24.

21   Barnes, 'Authors, Dead and Alive, in Old Norse Fiction', pp. 5-22; Jakob Benediktsson, 'Lygisögur'; Driscoll, 'Late Prose Fiction'; Glauser, 'Lygisaga', p. 398; Kalinke, 'The Genesis of Fiction in the North', pp. 464-78.

22   O'Connor, 'History or Fiction?', pp. 133-41.

23   For example the *Historia rerum Norvegicarum* of Danish Royal Historiographer Þormóður Torfason (perhaps better known by his Latinized name Tormod Torfæus), which draws on *fornaldarsögur* as a source for early Scandinavian history.

Ólafsson described the credulity of *rímur* poets and their audiences at the fishing camps on Snæfellsnes in the eighteenth century: 'Oft hittast hér skáld, sem hafa það at atvinnu að yrkja rímur út af sögum. Það, sem verst er í því efni, er það, að rímnaskáld þessi taka sér jafnt hinar lélegustu lygisögur að yrkisefni og hinar, sem sannar eru, enda eru þeir fáir, sem kunna að greina þar á milli' (Often one meets here poets, who have that for an occupation to compose *rímur* out of sagas. That, which is worst in this respect, is that these *rímur*-poets take on equally the worst *lygisögur* for their inspiration, as those that are true, and they are few who know how to distinguish between them).[24] This could be understood in two ways. Either these people were unable to distinguish between stories that Eggert saw to be *sannur* (true) and those that are not (those that can be said to *ljúga* [lie]); or, they simply saw no need to make such a distinction. It also seems reasonable to apply this later type of audience understanding of Icelandic romances to the times of their composition and earlier consumption. The medieval romances of Iceland can, generally, be thought of as taken at face value, and certainly enjoyed as such. The presence of a prologue, in whatever form it takes, indicates a perceived need by the author or scribe to defend and authenticate the text further, perhaps in the face of critics. *Nítíða saga*, by contrast, has no prologue, but presents the story, simply on its own terms, potentially because of the narrator's (or author's) confidence, rather than in spite of it.

Nítíða saga's lack of a prologue can be seen as demonstrative of its narrator's lack of anxiety about whether the story will be taken seriously, and the aparant willingness to believe readers will enjoy it, without needing to defend it.[25] Rather than starting with a substantial prologue, the narrator begins *Nítíða saga* by saying 'HEYRet vnger menn eitt æfintyR og fagra frasaugn fra hinum frægasta meykongi er verit hefur j nordur hælfu veralldarinar er hiet Nitida hin fræga' (Listen, young people, to an adventure and wonderful account about the most famous maiden-king there has been in the northern region of the world, who is called Nítíða the Famous).[26] This opening echoes that of the thirteenth-century translated romance *Elis saga ok Rosamundu*, which also starts by bidding its audience listen:[27] 'HÆyrit,

---

24 Eggert Ólafsson and Bjarni Pálsson, *Ferðabók Eggerts Ólafssonar og Bjarni Pálssonar*, trans. by Steindór Steindórsson frá Hlöðum, § 519, I, p. 204.

25 O'Connor, 'History or Fiction?', pp. 101-69. van Nahl states that this saga's brief address to the audience is not typical of introductions in the genre, and as such is not really the same kind of prologue (*Originale Riddarasögur*, p. 13).

26 'Nitida saga', ed. by Loth, p. 3.

27 van Nahl, *Originale Riddarasögur*, pp. 138-39.

horskir men*n*, æina fagra saugu' (Listen, wise people, to a fair story).[28] Some other manuscript versions of *Nítíða saga* are even more similar to this phrasing, as in the version found in the single-leaf fragment ÍB 201 (1650-99): 'Heÿred hǫsker men*n* <á>gi<æ>t æfen*n*ty<r> og fagrar fraso*gur*' (Listen, wise people, to an excellent adventure and fair tale).[29] With these words, the narrator shows what could be seen as one part of the saga's intended audience: 'ungir menn', young people and perhaps children, although it is of course also likely that this opening consists of no more than a simple formula for beginning a written, or performed, text. With this in mind, Sverrir Tómasson, notes that 'the text stat[es] that it was meant for "youngsters"'.[30] Significantly, the tale is specified as being listened to rather than read, highlighting the role of an active communal audience rather than a possibly more passive individualistic readership. Taking this opening at face value, we might also by extension see another intended audience, that is, those who read or tell this story to the 'ungir menn', such as parents, extended family, or other members of a reading (or story-telling) community. These first few words, in suggesting an audience of children being read to by adults, also suggest the setting in which such readings may have taken place, the *kvöldvaka* (evening-wake), during the *sagnaskemmtun* (saga-diversion) – it was then that texts including romances like *Nítíða saga* were read aloud or copied in Icelandic farmhouses during long winter nights,[31] as I first noted in Chapter 1. Direct evidence of the *kvöldvaka* has been recorded in Icelandic farmsteads of the eighteenth and nineteenth centuries, but there seems to be a consensus that the practice has its roots in traditions stretching back to the Middle Ages.[32] With the written saga setting the scene in this way, private readers can also experience something of the romance's performative aspects. In only the first three words then, the narrator paints a picture of the environment in which *Nítíða saga* may have been consumed, and the types of people who may have taken it in there. The narrator presents the saga as one to be enjoyed by both young (who are named specifically), and old (whose appreciation may be inferred).

In contrast to *Nítíða saga*'s lack of any prologue longer than the sentence just discussed, and in contrast to those prologues noted above, appealing to

---

28   Kölbing, ed., *Elis saga ok Rosamundu*, p. 1.

29   ÍB 201 8vo, f. 6ᵛ.

30   Sverrir Tómasson, 'Old Icelandic Prose', p. 145.

31   Magnús Gíslason, *Kvällsvaka*, 'Läsning', pp. 95-100; Davíð Ólafsson, 'Wordmongers', pp. 118-22, 154-58; Driscoll, *The Unwashed Children of Eve*, pp. 38-46.

32   Barnes, *The Bookish Riddarasögur*, pp. 183-85; Driscoll, *The Unwashed Children of Eve*, p. 38; Mitchell, *Heroic Sagas and Ballads*, pp. 92-114.

written authority, the medieval Icelandic romance *Viktors saga ok Blávus* begins by mixing the oral and written. On the one hand, the narrator appeals to King Hákon himself and the translations he commissioned:

> <M>arga merkiliga hlute heyrdum wer sagda heidarligum herra Hakoni Magnus syni Norigs kongi. einkannliga ad hann hiellt mikit gaman at fogrum fra sogum. ok hann liet venda morgum riddara sogum jnoræenu ur girzsku ok franzeisku mali.[33]

> (Many remarkable things we hear told about the venerable lord Hákon Magnusson the king of Norway, especially that he considered fair tales very amusing, and he ordered many knights' sagas translated into Norwegian from Greek and French.)

The written word and the authority of a respected king are invoked, and in doing so, royal approval is conceived as being granted to these kinds of stories, romances. On the other hand, the narrator continues the prologue by framing the story as one for young and even 'simple' people, contrasting them with older, and perhaps wiser, people:[34]

> ok þui weit ek ad goder gamler menn uilia likia sig ok sina skemtan epter hans fogrum haatum enn af leggia hlaatur ok hopp danzs ok dáraskap ok hégomligt herianskit. Enn til þess at eigi þegi huer at audrum byrium wer eina boguliga fra sogn bornum ok ofrodum monnum til skemtanar[35]

> (and so I know that good old people desire to liken themselves and their entertainment to his fair custom and leave off laughter and leaping dance and dumbfoolishness, and puffed up pernicious behaviour. And so that each after the other is not silent we begin an unpretentious tale for the entertainment of children and unlearned people)

Here the word *barn* (child) is employed, rather than the less explicit phrase *ungir menn* (young people) used by *Nítíða saga*'s narrator. The pairing of children with *ófróðum mönnum* (unlearned, illiterate, simple people) is also noteworthy, as this connection reinforces the intended audience as people not developed to their potential, either intellectually or physically.

---

33 *Viktors saga ok Blávus*, ed. by Jónas Kristjánsson, p. 3.
34 Cf. Barnes, *The Bookish Riddarasögur*, pp. 41-42.
35 *Viktors saga ok Blávus*, ed. by Jónas Kristjánsson, p. 3.

That children are the intended audience of *Viktors saga ok Blávus* suggests that similar Icelandic romances, with their adventure and action, may have been thought appropriate as children's entertainment. Einar Ólafur Sveinsson notes that 'some of the [romance] authors yield to the temptation to set forth the history of the translation, and in doing so sometimes lay it on rather thick' (as seen above with the 'graffiti sagas'), but that here, the author 'follows this custom, but without departing excessively from the way of the truth'.[36] By referring to the king and his customs regarding entertainment, the opening of *Viktors saga ok Blávus* is almost immediately more realistic, or believable, but I do not think that 'departing excessively from [...] the truth' need equal implausibility or tackiness, as seems to be the implication here. Many approaches to authenticating a saga are valid, and while the former may seem excessive or desperate to some, it serves the same purpose as the latter, arguably, more toned-down, approach employed in defence of *Viktors saga ok Blávus*. O'Connor's scepticism of interpreting prologues as ironic or necessarily indicative of fiction in the sense of that which is blatantly unrealistic and untrue is helpful here.[37] Overall, though, a prologue seems to indicate an anxiety to defend and authenticate the text, which *Nítíða saga* does not share.

Alternatively, *ungir menn* need not refer specifically to children, though they could still be included within a larger audience comprising a certain level or cross-section of society rather than one based strictly on age. The young people could be young adults, the next generation of medieval Icelanders, possibly more progressive than their elders in their literary tastes. *Nítíða saga* might be declaring itself a new text for a new generation, or at least for those people receptive to a new aesthetic in literature – the blossoming genre of romance composed in Iceland by Icelanders for Iceland-ers – as opposed to the older, established, 'classic' family sagas, or indeed imported European romances (arguably self-consciously prestigious in their somewhat exotic origin). Significantly, rather than appeal to old authorities, written or oral, the narrator lets the text speak for itself, in contrast both to many other native Icelandic romances and to medieval Icelandic writers of history, such as the late eleventh- to early twelfth-century author of *Íslendingabók*, Ari Þorgilsson *inn fróði* (the wise), who looks to oral sources to authenticate his work.[38]

---

36 Einar Ólafur Sveinsson, '*Viktors saga ok Blávus*: Sources and Characteristics', p. clxxix.

37 O'Connor, 'History or Fiction?', pp. 129-30.

38 *Íslendingabók* contains many references to oral sources, from the anonymous 'It is said with accuracy that' and 'Wise men have also said that', to the specific 'Hallr Órœkjuson said so' and

In the next few opening words, the narrator further holds the audience's attention by building on what has already been said. What *ungir menn* are being asked to listen to is *eitt ævintýr og fagra frásögn*: an adventure (or perhaps even an exemplum, an edifying story) and a wonderful account. The narrator builds the audience's interest by hinting that what follows will be exciting, good or useful, and also a pleasure to read or hear. Finally, the narrator piques the audience's interest once more, by at last revealing what the story is about: 'fra hinum frægasta meykongi er verit hefur j nordur häälfu veralldarinar'. The narrator has now presented in the opening a number of ingredients for a romance adventure story about the most famous maiden-king in the north, seeking to draw in the audience, young and old alike. In introducing the saga, the narrator subtly tries to persuade the intended Icelandic audience of its worth. While this may have been a winning strategy in the late Middle Ages and early modern period, these same words have alternatively convinced nineteenth- and early twentieth-century critics (such as Finnur Jónsson) of this saga's worthlessness along with the other so-called frivolous and non-realistic romances, reinforcing the notion that cultural assumptions and values are reflected in both the literature and its audiences, however receptive they might or might not be. In opening, the narrator also, importantly, hints at the story's relevance to its Icelandic audience: the saga is not about just any maiden-king, but about one who rules *í norður hálfu veraldarinar*. An Icelandic audience is of course geographically situated in precisely that part of the world. It is only after Nítíða has been introduced in the remainder of this first sentence that the audience learns exactly where she reigns – 'j aunduegi heimsins j Fracklandi jnu goda' (on the throne of the world in France the Good).[39] Now, the narrator has set the scene in France, far away from the Iceland in which the audience sits and listens or reads; but the narrator has also made Nítíða's realm relevant and familiar to Iceland by situating it in such a way that the centre of the world could seem just around the corner, or at least in the same region. The narrator has played with the audience's preconceived geographical perceptions in such a way that a location readers may have understood to be a place far away from marginal Iceland now becomes comparable to it. As I discussed in Chapter 3, the reorganization of global

'in accordance with what Bjarni the Wise, their paternal grandfather, had said, who remembered Þórarinn the lawspeaker and six of his successors' (Grønlie, trans., *Íslendingabók; Kristini saga*, pp. 4, 5, 11). Despite this, Ari also concedes that 'whatever is incorrectly stated in these records, it is one's duty to prefer what proves to be more accurate' (p. 3).

39 'Nitida saga', ed. by Loth, p. 3.

geography and the juxtaposition of the northern hemisphere and the world's centre makes Iceland part of that centre, and a part of Europe.[40] Looking back at the opening as a whole, the narrator, in only a couple of sentences, centralizes Europe, and Europeanizes Iceland.[41]

Different versions of *Nítíða saga*, and particularly later, post-medieval versions, have different openings, which, as with other variants discussed earlier, convey different messages and priorities. A relatively early manuscript witness from the Icelandic Westfjords, Lbs 715 (1670-80) begins: 'Hier mega unger menn heÿra hÿstoriú og fagra fræsógú af einre kongs ᴅottúr fagre og frÿdre er hiet Nɪᴛɪᴅᴀ hin fræga' (Here can young people hear a story and beautiful tale of a lovely and fair princess who is called Nitida the Famous).[42] The narrator in this version likewise introduces the story and mentions a possible intended audience – again, 'young people' – but does so in a more matter-of-fact way. Instead of summoning listeners to a recital of the story, as in the version discussed above, the narrator here rather refers to the possibility of hearing the story, with the inclusion of the modal verb *mega* (can). Alternatively, the version preserved in the much later Reykjavík, Landsbókasafn Íslands–Háskólabókasafn, MS Lbs 2786 8vo (1869) focuses at once on the story and the hero: 'Sá meikóngr ʀiedi fyrir nordr løndum, edr nordr álfu heimsins, er Nitida hiet. hún var hin fridasta frægasta og kurteisasta mær j þann tima' (That maiden-king rules over northern lands, or the northern region of the world, who is called Nitida. She was the prettiest, most famous, and most courteous maiden in that time).[43] Other manuscripts containing this opening also include Reykjavík, Landsbókasafn Íslands–Háskólabókasafn, MSS JS 56 (1760), ÍBR 59 (1798/99), Lbs 4492 4to (1892), Lbs 4493 4to (1902), and Lbs 2918 4to (1900s). There is no mention of an audience, and the storyteller's voice is left to the individual reader, whether reading aloud to a group or alone silently.

It is at the end of the romance that we find probably its most significant comment on the situation of Iceland within Europe, and at the same time one of the most self-conscious of the narrator's many asides. Furthermore, it is one of the most often quoted passages from *Nítíða saga*, and indeed that with which I opened this book: 'er og ei audsagt med öfrodre tungu i utlegdumm veralldarinnar, so mönnum verde skemtelegt, hvor fögnudur vera munde i midiumm heimenum af sliku hoffolke samannkomnu' (It is

---

40   Barnes, 'Margin vs. Centre'; Barnes, 'Travel and *translatio studii*', pp. 123-39.
41   Sverrir Jakobsson, 'Centre and Periphery'.
42   Lbs 715 4to, p. 85.
43   Lbs 2786 8vo, p. 14.

also not easily said with an unlearned tongue in the outer regions of the world, so that it might be entertaining for people, what joy might be in the middle of the world when such courtiers come together).[44] The deliberate references to periphery and centre – *í útlegðum veraldarinnar* and *í miðjum heiminum*, respectively – reflect the narrator's own view of his or her place in the world. This statement near the end appears to contradict the saga's earlier view at the opening, portraying Iceland and the Icelanders as not far from Europe and the world's centre in this text's geography. The idea that the Icelandic language is an 'unlearned tongue', seems also to reinforce the notion that Iceland is a marginal backwater while Europe is a central and learned place. But again, the narrator's recognition of Iceland's peripheral geographical location compared to France and the rest of Europe indicates an understanding of European ideas.[45] Were the narrator really as ignorant as this claim suggests, and especially were the Icelandic language as inadequate as implied, the saga itself might not have been written. Such a modesty topos could also be further invitation for audience participation, encouraging the audience to imagine the scene for themselves, while the description is already being made through the narrator's language of denial as a sort of *occultatio* – in describing the weddings by refusing to describe them fully. The narrator proves invalid this 'rhetorical gesture of modesty', by already having crafted the saga using the same language claimed to be inappropriate for such a purpose.[46] Barnes adds that 'The two indices of Icelandic marginality delineated by *Nítíða saga* – distance and language – were matters of topical concern in fourteenth- and fifteenth-century Iceland':[47] the island's increasingly different form of language developing in the late Middle Ages in arguably relative isolation from other Scandinavian languages reinforces Iceland's physical distance from Norway.[48] Anxieties about language were likely in the mind of the saga author and/or its later scribes, and these concerns are here placed in the mouth of the narrator. Perhaps such a narrator would be more comfortable using Icelandic to write about Iceland itself. This demonstration of self-consciousness about writing in the Icelandic language is one of the best examples of the narrator's voice within the saga and the influence he or she may have thus had on the audience.[49]

44 'Nitida saga', ed. by Loth, p. 36.
45 Sverrir Jakobsson, 'Centre and Periphery', p. 918.
46 Barnes, 'Romance in Iceland', p. 272; Barnes, 'Travel and *translatio studii*', pp. 138-39.
47 Barnes, 'Margin vs. Centre', p. 111.
48 Braunmüller, 'Language Contacts in the Late Middle Ages and in Early Modern Times'.
49 Fleischman, 'On the Representation of History and Fiction', pp. 295-96.

The descriptions of the triple wedding ceremony's splendour immediately preceding the narrator's aside are especially telling, and prove the usefulness of Icelandic for the purposes of storytelling, and of stories set in particular *í miðjum heiminum* (in the centre of the world; here, France). Immediately preceding this statement, the saga says that 'þar var allskins skemtun framinn i burtreidumm og hliodfæraslætte, enn þar sem kongarner geingu var nidurbreidt pell og purpure og heidurleg klæde' (There were all kinds of entertainment consisting of bohourt and musical concerts, and wherever the kings walked were spread down costly fabric, and cloth of purple, and valuable raiment).[50] Not only is this a rich depiction of the wedding festivities, but it contains foreign words and courtly activities like tournaments among knights that a truly simple language on the edge of the world may not necessarily be expected to contain, but which are all part of an Icelandic romance vocabulary. The word *burtreið* (bohourt, or team tourney, distinct from and not to be confused with 'joust')[51] entered Icelandic through medieval French, possibly via German, and is first attested in the thirteenth century; the word and concept almost certainly entered Old Norse through the French romances translated at that time,[52] although the form of the word, containing the element *reið* (ride) also suggests a degree of folk etymologization: the population must have been actively using and contemplating the word and its meanings for it eventually to have taken such a form,[53] considering that tournaments were not something taken up in Iceland, but existed solely in literature. The word *pell* (costly raiment) comes from Latin *pallium* (blanket, bed cover), via either Old English or Middle Low German,[54] and *purpuri* (cloth of purple) also comes from Latin.[55] The pair 'pell og purpuri' appears in other Icelandic romances including *Sigurðar saga þögla*,[56] and so may also be a formulaic way of denoting expensive, beautiful, foreign cloth; in each case, 'pell og purpuri' is said to be found, geographically, nowhere near Iceland. The denotations of these words thus show that the narrator has in the Icelandic language the raw materials with which to describe in adequate terms the events of the story;

50 'Nitida saga', ed. by Loth, p. 36.

51 See also n. 39 in Chapter 1, which explains the translation of *burtreið* in this way.

52 de Vries, *Altnordisches etymologisches Wörterbuch*, p. 65.

53 In arguing for a reconsideration of the dates of early Norse romance translations, Suzanne Marti discussed this and other loan words in her presentation at the 2012 International Saga Conference: 'Hvenær var Tristrams saga snúið?'.

54 de Vries, *Altnordisches etymologisches Wörterbuch*, p. 424.

55 de Vries, *Altnordisches etymologisches Wörterbuch*, p. 429.

56 'Sigurðar saga þögla', ed. by Loth, pp. 156, 183.

even if loans, they had become a part of Icelandic vocabulary. Furthermore, other loaned words, as well as many Latinate-looking names appear regularly throughout the saga.[57] Additionally, the narrator's protestation itself juxtaposes not only Icelandic and foreign languages like French or Latin, but also native and imported words to refer to 'the world' on the edge of which Iceland is supposed to be and of which France is supposed to be the centre: *veröld* and *heimur* both, in this context, mean 'world'. Only the latter, however, is a native Icelandic word; *veröld* possibly entered Icelandic in the late Middle Ages, perhaps through Old English *weorold*.[58]

A very similar assertion to *Nítíða saga*'s narrator's false modesty also appears in *Adonias saga*, when the narrator speaks of one of that romance's many battles: 'Nu er yfer farit med ofrodligum ordum at s(egia) fra orrostum og efni þess ofridar er gerdizt j milli Palestini og Galicie med Spanis' (Now an account has been given, with unlearned words, to tell about battles and the materials of this warfare which is carried out between Palestine and Galicia against Spain).[59] It is especially the use of the phrases *ofrodligum ordum* and *j milli Palestini*, compared with *Nítíða saga*'s *ófróðri tungu* and *í miðjum heiminum* that suggests this passage may echo that in *Nítíða saga* (or vice versa). These two texts do seem to be unique in using the adjectives *ófróðr* and *ófróðligr* in this way.[60] In both cases, the primary concern rests on the adequacy of the words with which the stories have been crafted, and not necessarily the abilities of the author or narrator to work with those words themselves. In these romances, both narrators simultaneously display confidence – in their own narrating abilities – and doubt – about the

57 Latinate personal names include *Alduria, Blebarnius* (*Februarius* in most other manuscripts), *Egidia, Livorius, Nítíða, Virgilius*, and *Ypolitus*. Two of these, *Livorius* and *Egidia*, occasionally inflect according to Latin grammar: *Livorius* becomes *Li[v]orino* in the dative ('Nitida saga', ed. by Loth, p. 21), and *Livorini* in the genitive ('Nitida saga', ed. by Loth, p. 28). *Egidia* becomes *Egidiam* in the accusative ('Nitida saga', ed. by Loth, p. 35). The name *Nítíða*, however, never inflects according to Latin grammar, possibly because it is only actually mentioned four times ('Nitida saga', ed. by Loth, pp. 3, 9, 11, 37). Many place names take Latinate forms as well, as discussed in Chapter 3.

58 de Vries, *Altnordisches etymologisches Wörterbuch*, p 657. Interestingly, this word is used in modern Icelandic most often in ecclesiastical writings (Gudbrand Vigfusson, *An Icelandic-English Dictionary*, p. 699), as I noted in discussing the saga's relationship with *Nikulás saga leikara* in Chapter 2. The Old Norse universal history compiled largely from ecclesiastical Latin sources is called *Veraldar saga* (Saga, or, History of the World).

59 'Adonias saga', ed. by Agnete Loth, p. 223. On *Adonias saga* and its learned elements see Barnes, *The Bookish Riddarasögur*, pp. 96-110.

60 *Ordbog over det norrøne prosasprog* <http://dataonp.hum.ku.dk> shows that across twenty-seven entries *ófróðr* usually modifies *maðr* (man), and there is no apparent pattern for *ófróðligr*. The ten entries for the related adverb *ófróðliga* see it most commonly paired with *spyrja* (to ask).

words available to them in Icelandic. And just as in *Nítíða saga*, the narrator of *Adonias saga* appeals to the idea that the happenings *í milli*, at the centre of the world,[61] are that much less accessible when related in Icelandic.

Following the narrator's complaint about the difficulty of describing the wedding scene, we see further evidence of the narrator's voice in a brief reference to the transitory nature of mundane treasures and even, by extension, of life itself. After carefully taking the time to describe the provisions, entertainment, and general festivities, the narrator ends the scene by declaring that 'og nu med því ad oll þessa heims dyrd kann skiott ad lida, þa voru brudkaupinn utdruckinn, og höfdingiarner utleidder med fögrum fiegiðfumm' (And now because all of this world's splendour can quickly pass away, the wedding then was over, and the nobles are led out with wonderful gifts).[62] This seemingly casual statement is concise but telling. It momentarily draws the audience's attention away from the wedding, and even away from the saga itself, to dwell briefly on the transience of life. The key phrase is *öll þessa heims dýrð kann skjótt að líða*, and this is stated as unquestionable fact. It draws almost the entire story preceding it into question, as the text itself is merely fleeting worldly entertainment; yet by presenting the text now in this light, its potential to edify its readers through reflection on the nature of the world and its treasures and entertainments is laid out before the audience. But the message is so brief that, fittingly, before the audience has time to dwell on it and fully understand its significance, the story is back in full swing, with worldly gifts 'i gulle og gimsteinum og gödumm vefiumm' (in gold and jewels and good woven cloth),[63] but the moment has passed – the wedding is over and the guests are parting. The fleeting nature of the message – its brevity – strongly reinforces the message it seeks to convey, that life is transitory. The form of the statement mirrors its function. Through this quotation we see, through the voice of the narrator, an awareness of Christian moralizing diction, and a willingness to employ it, but without actually making any Christian references; this somewhat ironically highlights the saga's lack of religious material, suggesting this to be a conscious and significant choice.

Moving now to the very end of the text, the narrator closes the story in a similar way to its beginning: 'og lykur so þessu æfentyre af hinne frægu Nitida og Livorio konge' (And so ends this adventure of the famous

---

61   While Palestine is not explicitly said to be near the centre of the world, it could have been seen as such by a medieval audience due to its proximity to Jerusalem.

62   'Nitida saga', ed. by Loth, p. 36.

63   'Nitida saga', ed. by Loth, p. 36.

Nítíða and King Livorius).[64] While the ending is formulaic, the narrator uses convention to bring the story full-circle and reminds the audience of the saga's protagonist and the type of story that has been presented. The narrator points back at 'hinne frægu Nitida', repeating the character tag first applied at the beginning – her fame. But the saga does not end exactly as it began: Livorius has the last word, as he has now joined with Nítíða, not only in marriage, but also politically. Furthermore, the narrator notes again that *Nítíða saga* is an *ævintýr*. In adventure story and fairy-tale fashion, the closing is also conventional and formulaic, just as is the opening, in this way fulfilling the expectations of the genre.[65] The romance is thus symmetrical, and the audience is here reminded that it was called an *ævintýr* at its opening (the word is, significantly, not used elsewhere in the text), and prompted to consider whether the story has fulfilled the narrator's promises in opening and reflect on just the type of story it has been.

Back at the beginning of *Nítíða saga*, the narrator's voice emerges as characteristically self-conscious. The first interjection is a remark on Nítíða's journey: 'hef eg ei heyrt sagt fra þeirra ferd ne farleingd fyrr en þau taka eyna Visio' (I have not heard it said about their journey, nor their journey's length, before they reached the island of Visio).[66] This forceful aside brings the saga's action to an abrupt halt and draws attention to the narrator,[67] although it could also be seen as the narrator deliberately glossing over the action and fast-forwarding to the destination. The narrator claims complete ignorance of this sea journey, which though inessential, might have been expected by the audience either to have been included, or else skipped over completely, without any comment. Rather, we have a first person admission that the narrator knows nothing about its circumstances, and specifically, that nobody has told him or her about it.[68] These words suggest three important things. First, that the saga's plot has been *told* to the narrator by some source, that is, the narrator has not *read* it anywhere. This may be a useful fiction created to sustain the idea of audience participation and transmission suggested by the text's opening words in the same way that the written sources of other romances are fictive, but these are still important, purposeful fictions. Second, the words suggest that the narrator is setting up

64 'Nitida saga', ed. by Loth, p. 37.

65 van Nahl, *Originale Riddarasögur*, pp. 22-23.

66 'Nitida saga', ed. by Loth, p. 6.

67 van Nahl, *Originale Riddarasögur*, p. 191.

68 See Schach, 'Some Forms of Writer Intrusion', pp. 138-40: 'Occasionally saga writers state that they have or have not heard reports of certain information, or that they can or cannot truthfully make certain assertions' (p. 138).

a fiction of meticulous adherence to the available facts, refusing to fabricate details that cannot be confirmed. The third, and possibly most important, point is that the narrator is concerned with reliability and perhaps hopes to gain credibility and the audience's confidence. The emphasis on the aural rather than the written here connects this remark to the saga's prologue-less opening, while also complementing another method of validation, through the mention that young people 'have heard'. That there should be any eagerness to convey a source for the saga independent of the narrator is further significant. Despite not participating in the tradition of authentication through a prologue, here it nevertheless seems unacceptable simply to have made up the story: it is still assumed, and important, that the narrator has a source.[69] *Nítíða saga*'s narrator may feel uneasy about the saga's truth value thus far, especially after having related the magical objects expected to be found on Visio, along with its location 'vt vnder heims skautid. þeirra landa er menn hafa spurn af' (out past the corner of the world of these lands which people have report of), even if this description could reasonably be taken at face value. The 'corner' or the edge of the physically flat *mappa mundi* would be just the place for a marginal, unknown island such as Visio.[70] Further, the narrator (or author) may have had in mind concerns about wanting to appear truthful, even if everything in the story is not necessarily true. While not imploring readers to believe that everything related so far as well as what lies ahead is *true* in the sense of its being *real* or *historical*, the narrator here at least desires that the story be taken seriously, and enjoyed, moving away from a black and white distinction between fact and fiction, truth and falsehood, that some readers might wish to employ.[71] The *saga* is asking to be embraced as the 'history', or the account of events whether or not they are true, that it is. Towards the end of the prologue of *Sigurðar saga þǫgla*, the issue of truth in opposition to fiction is drawn together: 'Nu uerdr huerki þat ne annat gert eptir allra hugþocka. þuiat einngi þarf trunad æ slict ath leggia nema vile enn þat er bezt og frodligazt at hlyda medann fra er sagt' (Now neither that nor anything else will be done in accordance with the understanding of everyone, because no one needs to believe in such matters except those who wish to, yet it is best and wisest to listen while the matter is being related).[72] This rather sensibly leaves the question of whether or not to believe the story that follows up to each

69   Fleischman, 'On the Representation of History and Fiction', pp. 295-96.
70   Cf. e.g. Mittman, *Maps and Monsters in Medieval England*, pp. 18-21.
71   Fleischman, 'On the Representation of History and Fiction', pp. 305-06.
72   'Sigurðar saga þǫgla', ed. by Loth, p. 96.

individual member of the audience, while encouraging people to devote their attention to it regardless of their credulity. While this prologue is not by any means an assertion of the fictivity of romance, it acknowledges that not everyone might appreciate it, or believe the account to be true. Although in *Nítíða saga* this is not stated explicitly, a similar attitude to the truth value of romance seems to be favoured, where the story ought principally to be enjoyed for the enjoyment it might give.

However, for most of the romance the narrator is relatively quiet, and only punctuates the story with the set phrase 'Nu er at seigia' (Now it is said) every now and then. This interjection directs the plot and marks its phases, reminding the audience of the narrator's presence. The phrase works primarily as a means of transition from one scene to another, no matter how unrelated the scenes may be, thus minimizing narrative disruption. That the interjection is an impersonal construction simultaneously draws attention to the narrator and also distances the narrator from the act of personally telling the story. However, the phrase also highlights the narrator's control. While audiences can only very minimally shape the story they read or hear – for example (if reading) by choosing to skip over a sentence, paragraph, or section, or (if listening) by leaving or not paying attention – the story still exists in full, in the form decided on by the narrator (and scribe). Further, that this transitional phrase is in the present tense and begins with *nú* (now) rather than *þá* (then) also demonstrates the narrator's voice surfacing in the text, for even though the saga switches rather freely from past to present tenses throughout the text, as is normal in medieval Icelandic prose, the immediacy of *nú* and present tense *er* (is) suggests a narrative urgency. The phrase *nú er að segja* appears ten times over the course of the romance, and at each instance, the narrator's presence comes crisply back into focus. When used, the phrase also reminds silent readers that the saga might be performed or read aloud in a lively manner, and it reminds reader and listening audience alike of the narrative form of the tale. The text is alive, revived and renewed at each reading, yet it has also been crafted by an author, whose hand becomes present here in the voice of the narrator.[73] The romance could be told or written without such transitional phrases, for they are not a *part* of the story, but of the narrative art used to *compose* the story, signalling the involvement of an outside force – author, scribe, or narrator – on the tale. O'Connor notes that in these types of brief asides a 'typical saga-narrator speaks as if carrying the authority of a tradition from the past, and he usually expresses himself in passive or impersonal

---

73   Schach, 'Some Forms of Writer Intrusion', pp. 132-36, 150-51.

constructions [...] or, less frequently, in the first person plural'.[74] In such asides the first person plural is, notably, much more common than the first person singular, and the former is sometimes also used for the latter in *Nítíða saga*. In roughly the middle of the romance, the narrator addresses the reader in order to make the transition from the present scene to the next: 'lætum Jn(ga) kong nu huilast vm tima. Enn vendum sogunni j annan stad og seigium af sonum Solldans kongs' (let us now leave King Ingi for a while, and let us turn the saga to another place and let us tell of King Soldán's sons).[75] Here, instead of the singular, ostensibly referring to him- or herself only, the narrator now includes the audience by using the first person plural *látum* (let us leave) and *vendum* (let us turn). Such use of the first person plural provides not only a sense of immediacy for the audience and the feeling that the saga is directed at each individual reader or listener, but also allows the narrator to involve the audience in the crafting of the saga. By including readers and listeners in this way, emphasis is also placed on the idea that the reading and hearing of the saga is a communal experience involving interaction with others. Simultaneously individual and collective, saga reading is an active experience by which individual appreciation is validated, as well as collective enjoyment. It is not the narrator alone who turns from one scene to the next, but also each reader, whose active involvement – in reading or listening, that is, engaging – allows the story to unfold. Without having to prove anything to the audience anymore (considering the earlier arguable unease regarding reliability), the narrator can now, in one sense, express appreciation towards the audience by including them in the saga's unfolding.[76]

Conclusions

In this chapter I have considered the characterization of *Nítíða saga*'s anonymous narrator by looking at the asides and comments made in the first person voice throughout the text. These discussions also complete my consideration of the romance's various characters in this second part of the book, which began with my analyses of the hero, her rivals, and other supporting characters in Chapters 4 and 5. Having seen the narrator's interventions in the opening and closing of the text, and having compared

74   O'Connor, 'History or Fiction?', p. 120.
75   'Nitida saga', ed. by Loth, p. 18.
76   Schach, 'Some Forms of Writer Intrusion', pp. 132-33.

these with the prologues and endings of other Icelandic romances, I have shown how *Nítíða saga*'s narrator is characterized as the teller of this version of the tale, with a recognizable personality, opinions, and doubts, through comments on the truth value and usefulness of the story. The narrator reinforces the romance's focus on the maiden-king Nítíða, and while the narrator's confidence in the tale seems, overall, greater than that of many other narrators of Icelandic romance as seen in their prologues, we have seen that there is still a desire to portray the text as a real and worthy story, if not necessarily a true, historical one. The use of the first person plural, especially, both includes the saga's audience in its creation, and also reminds the reader that the saga-telling or -writing process is active and living. No matter what the plot, at a deeper level, the romance shows, by even just its process of composition, the mindset of the Icelandic individual who chose to record either what he or she envisioned in his or her own mind as an interesting and entertaining story, or what had already been read or heard told by another. The saga only comes into being through the actions of individuals; it is brought to life and lives at each reading and retelling, and so it also requires the participation of audiences, as first discussed in my consideration of different manuscript versions of the romance in Chapter 1. Further, not only do the many transitional phrases ease the shift from one scene to the next, but they are deliberate statements that characterize the narrator, from thanks to the audience and their inclusion in the creative process of shaping the journey through the saga, to comments on the nature of this romance itself. Whether coercive or not, proud or humble, the narrator's words display confidence, and maintain credibility with the audience. The narrator's confidence in the story that is told, along with the absence of a prologue, is a demonstration of one further aspect of *Nítíða saga*'s rather unconventional nature as a late medieval Icelandic romance.

Conclusion

This book has considered the late medieval Icelandic romance *Nítíða saga* from a variety of perspectives. My overall aim has been to demonstrate how this text explores and challenges some of the norms of the Icelandic romance genre in which it finds itself. From its unconventional portrayal of geography to its strong female hero and other important female characters, *Nítíða saga* approaches romance from a unique point of view and asks its audiences to reconsider not only what it means to be a romance in Iceland but also what it means to be an Icelander in Scandinavia and Europe in the later Middle Ages, and even into the post-Reformation era. The first two chapters of Part I discussed *Nítíða saga* in terms of both its physical manuscript witnesses, which have preserved the saga over hundreds of years, and the intertextual connections demonstrating some of the relationships the saga has with other Icelandic romances. In Chapter 1, the value of textual variation among *Nítíða saga* manuscripts from different times and different parts of Iceland was highlighted. The textual variation was notable in the case of two groups of manuscripts, an earlier one originating in Iceland's Westfjords and Dales, and a later one originating in the Eastfjords. Also discussed was the diversity of scribal attitudes towards and interpretations of the medieval saga through the case studies of three post-medieval manuscript versions. Chapter 2 considered some of the intertextual relationships evident in *Nítíða saga* through case studies of *Clári saga*, which was an important influence on *Nítíða saga*'s author; and *Nikulás saga leikara*, which was in turn almost certainly influenced by *Nítíða saga*. I demonstrated how *Nítíða saga* relates to these and other texts – both romance and religious – in the Christian literary-cultural milieu in which it was produced and from which its author drew inspiration. The romance's setting and the worldviews it exhibits were considered in Chapter 3 – different contextual aspects from within the romance – and it is here that *Nítíða saga*'s challenging of some of the norms of romance comes to the forefront. I discussed how the text's portrayal of geography shifts the medieval world's centre closer to Iceland, along with its presentation of public and private space on a smaller scale. I also considered examples of *Nítíða saga* challenging certain romance norms in order to reconsider the genre it belongs to, and more broadly to engage with the wider medieval European cultural community from and with which this and other Icelandic romances emerge and engage. In the first section of the book, the focus was thus centred on the different contexts that could enrich our understanding of the text as it is discussed in the subsequent primarily literary-analytical chapters.

Part II therefore took *Nítíða saga*'s characters and their various relationships with one another as its focus. In Chapter 4, the portrayal of the saga's female hero was discussed. Her negotiations and manoeuvres through the world of bridal-quest were seen to allow her to emerge at the end of the romance as an equal in marriage alongside her husband. In addition to this, the characterizations of the suitors Livorius and Ingi – and how they fall short of heroic status – were considered, as well as the form and function of the romance's various antagonists. In Chapter 5, I showed how the characterization of minor figures, and particularly the romance's strong supporting female characters, works alongside the depiction of Nítíða as protagonist in order further to overturn the conventional understanding of an Icelandic romance hero. In particular, the close, and potentially homoerotic, relationship that the text depicts between Nítíða and Sýjalín was shown to interrogate the norms of gender at work in so many other medieval Icelandic romances, while also reinforcing the maiden-king's role as hero. In the sixth and final chapter of this book, discussion of the narrator's characterization was featured, and his or her confidence, as well as the saga's lack of a prologue, demonstrated two further aspects of *Nítíða saga*'s challenging attitudes towards some of the conventions often adhered to in late medieval Icelandic romances. In this second section of the book the saga was thus considered from a literary perspective in order to focus on the way the characters propel the story forward and to see how their place in the text is significant, both in their own right and also as a means of reinforcing the position of Nítíða in the romance's principle role. In considering also some of the most notable textual variations preserved in other, later manuscripts, the characters were also shown to have been purposefully developed by the saga's author in the first instance, and by its many diverse scribes subsequently.

In both parts of this book I have in turn uncovered aspects of the text, its composition, reception, and reconfiguration across time and space in medieval and early modern Iceland, and even into the early twentieth century. It is *Nítíða saga*'s deliberate problematization of romance norms and, specifically, the conventions of medieval Icelandic maiden-king and bridal-quest romance that arguably have allowed this medieval tale to endure generation after generation among a society whose place in the world was often questioned and lacked stability under the rule of others during the later Middle Ages, the Reformation, and afterwards. The appropriation of a European identity through what could be called the cultural colonization of European romance can be said to have reached its apex in *Nítíða saga*, which reinvents both Icelandic romance in its early feminist outlook and also European romance in its uniquely nordic attitudes. The value of Nítíða's story continued to speak to Icelanders long after its composition, and with each reworking of the text – from the shifts in perspective and focus seen in many of the different versions instigated by largely anonymous early modern scribes, to its radical rewriting in some of the youngest surviving manuscripts – appreciation of this saga arguably grew and inspired further reworkings, many of which (particularly the poetic *rímur*) I have not been able to consider in this book. *Nítíða saga* is evidently a timeless story that crosses traditional boundaries of time, place, and genre, speaking to new audiences despite, or perhaps sometimes because of, its medieval Icelandic composition. This popular story's unique representations of female rela-tionships and the hero Nítíða, as well as its continual challenging of other romance conventions and its adaptability in terms of the details through which it was told, ensured its survival, as well as its popularity in Iceland from the late Middle Ages right up to the present day.

Appendix   *Nítíða saga* Text and Translation[1]

Normalized Icelandic Text

1

Heyrið ungir menn eitt ævintýr og fagra frásögn frá hinum frægasta mey-kóngi er verið hefur í norður hálfu veraldarinnar er hét Nítíða hin fræga er stýrði sínu ríki með heiður og sóma eftir sinn föður Ríkon keisara andaðan. Þessi meykóngur sat í öndvegi heimsins í Frakklandi hinu góða og hélt Párisborg. Hún var bæði vitur og væn, ljós og rjóð í andliti þvílíkast sem hin rauða rósa væri samtemprað við snjóhvíta lileam, augun svo skær sem karbunkulus, hörundið svo hvítt sem fíls bein, hár þvílíkt sem gull, og féll niður á jörð um hana. Hún átti eitt höfuðgull með fjórum stöplum, en upp af stöplunum var einn ari markaður, en upp af aranum stóð einn haukur gjör af rauða gulli, breiðandi sína vængi fram yfir hennar skæra ásjónu jungfrúinnar að ei brenndi hana sól. Hún var svo búin að viti sem hinn fróðasti klerkur, og hinn sterkasta borgarvegg[2] mátti hún gjöra með sínu viti yfir annara manna vit og byrgja svo úti annarra ráð, og þar kunni hún tíu ráð er aðrir kunnu eitt. Hún hafði svo fagra raust að hún svæfði fugla og fiska, dýr og öll jarðlig kvikindi, svo að unað þótti á að heyra. Hennar ríki stóð með friði og farsæld.

Ypolitus hét einn smiður í Frakklandi með meykónginum. Hann kunni allt að smíða af gulli og silfri, gleri og gimsteinum, það sem gjörast mátti af manna höndum.

Nú er að segja af meykónginum, hún býr nú ferð sína heiman út á Púl. Þar stýrði ríki sú drottning er Egidía hét; hún hafði fóstrað meykóng í barn-æsku. Hún átti son er Hléskjöldur hét. Siglir drottning nú með sínu dýru fólki fagurt byrleiði, þar til er hún kemur út á Púl. Gengur frú Egidía móti meykóng, og hennar son, og öll þeirra slekt og veraldar mekt og heiður, gjörandi fagra veislu í sinni höll, um allan næstan hálfan mánuð.

1   The text and translation in this appendix are updated versions of those previously published in *Leeds Studies in English*. A number of errors and inconsistencies have been corrected, and the translation, in particular, has been altered to reflect the original language more closely (e.g. in terms of verb tense). The text and translation are printed here with the journal's kind permission.
2   Emended from MS *hinn sterkasti borgarveggur* ('Nitida saga', ed. by Loth, p. 4).

Einn dag veislunnar gengur meykóngur á dagþingan við sína fóstur-
móður svo talandi: 'Mér er sagt að fyrir eyju þeirri er Visio heitir ráði jarl sá
er Virgilius heitir; hann er vitur og fjölkunnigur. Þessi ey liggur út undan
Svíþjóð hinni köldu, út undir heimsskautið, þeirra landa er menn hafa spurn
af. Í þessari eyju er vatn eitt stórt, en í vatninu er hólmi sá er Skóga-blómi
heitir og svo er mér sagt að hvergi í heiminum megi finnast náttúrusteinar,
epli, og læknis-grös fleiri en þar. Nú vil ég halda þangað einskipa og son
þinn Hléskjöldur með mér'.

Drottning Egidía talaði tormerki á ferðinni, og þótti háskaleg. Meykóngur
varð þó að ráða, býst Hléskjöldur nú í ferð þeirra og sigla með heiður út af
Púl fagurt byrleiði. Hef ég ei heyrt sagt frá þeirra ferð né farlengd fyrr en
þau taka eyna Visio.

Einn dag, leggjandi skipið í einn leynivog, ganga síðan upp um eyna
þar til er þau finna vatnið. Þau sjá einn bát fljótandi, taka hann og róa út í
hólminn. Þar voru margar eikur með fagri fruckt og ágætum eplum. Sem
þau fram koma í miðjan hólmann sjá þau eitt steinker með fjórum hornum.
Kerið var fullt af vatni; sinn steinn var í hverju horni kersins. Meykóngur
leit í steinana; hún sá þá um allar hálfar veraldarinnar, þar með kónga og
kónga sonu og hvað hver hafðist að, og allar þjóðir hvers lands og margar
ýmislegar skepnur og óþjóðir. Drottning gladdist nú við þessa sýn, takandi
kerið og alla þessa steina, epli, og læknis-grös, því að hún undirstóð af sinni
visku hverja náttúru hver bar. Skundar nú sínum veg aftur til skips síns,
siglandi burt af Visio hvað þau máttu.

Nú er að segja að jarlinn verður vís hverju hann er ræntur. Má þar sjá
mart skip siglandi og róandi eftir þeim. Sjá nú hvorir aðra. Meykóngur tók
nú einn náttúrustein og brá yfir skipið og höfuð þeim öllum er innan borðs
voru. Sá jarl þau aldri síðan, en þau meykóngur og Hléskjöldur halda fram
ferðinni, léttandi ei fyrr en þau koma heim á Púl.

Gengur frú Egidía móti þeim með miklum prís og fagnaði. Situr nú
meykóngur þar um hríð. Síðan lætur hún búa sína ferð og skipastól heim
til Frakklands, beiðandi frú Egidía að Hléskjöldur hennar son fylgdi henni
að styrkja hennar ríki fyrir áhlaupum hermanna. Hennar fóstur-móður
veitir henni þetta sæmilega, sem allt annað það er hún beiði, út leiðandi
hana með fögrum fégjöfum og ágætum dýrgripum í gulli og gimsteinum og
dýrum vefjum. Skilst þessi hoflýður með miklum kærleik. Siglir meykóngur
í sitt ríki með miklum heiður og veraldlegri mekt. Verður allur landslýður
henni feginn stýrandi sínu ríki með friði og náðum.

2

Hugon er kóngur nefndur; hann réð fyrir Miklagarði. Hann átti drottning og tvö börn. Son hans hét Ingi; hann var allra manna sæmilegastur og best að íþróttum búinn. Hann lá í hernaði hvert sumar og aflaði sér svo fjár og frægðar; drap ránsmenn og víkinga, en lét friðmenn fara í náðum. Listalín hét dóttir hans; hún var fríð sýnum og vinsæl, og hlaðin kvenlegum listum.

Soldán hét kóngur; hann réð fyrir Serklandi. Hann átti þrjá sonu: hét einn Logi, annar Vélogi, þriðji Heiðarlogi – hann var þeirra elstur. Hann hafði svart hár og skegg. Hann var hökulangur og vangasvangur, skakktentur og skjöpulmyntur, og út-skeifur. Annað auga hans horfði á bast en annað á kvist. Hann var hermaður allmikill, og fullur upp af göldrum og gjörningum og rammur að afli, og fékk sigur í hverri orrostu. Bræður hans, Logi og Vélogi, voru vænir og gildir menn og herjuðu öllum sumrum.

Februarius[3] er kóngur nefndur; hann réð fyrir Indíalandi hinu mikla. Hann átti son er Livorius[4] hét; hann var vænn að áliti, ljós og rjóður í andliti snareygður sem valur, hrokkinnhærður og fagurt hárið, herðabreiður en keikur á bringuna, kurteis, sterkur og stórmannlegur. Hann kunni vel sund og sæfarar, skot og skylmingar, tafl og rúnar og bækur að lesa, og allar íþróttir er karlmann mátti prýða. Hann átti dóttur er Sýjalín hét; hún var svo væn og listug að hún mundi forprís þótt hafa allra kvenna í veröldunni, ef ei hefði þvílíkur gimsteinn hjá verið sem Nítíða hin fræga.

Livorius lá í hernaði bæði vetur og sumar og aflaði sér fjár og frægðar, og þótti hinn mesti garpur og kappi, hvar sem hann fram kom, og hafði sigur í hverri orrustu. Hann var svo mikill til kvenna að engi hafði náðir fyrir honum, en enga kóngs dóttur hafði hann mánaði lengur.

Nú er að segja af Inga kóngi að hann býr sinn skrautlega skipastól, siglandi með fagran byr út af Miklagarði, léttandi ei fyrr sinni ferð en hann hlóð sínum seglum framan fyrir Párisborg. Nú sem meykóngur sá þeirra sigling og gullskotin segl, þá sendir hún Hléskjöld ofan til skipa að bjóða þessum kóngi til ágætrar veislu, ef hann fer með friði. Hléskjöldur fullgjörir frúinnar erindi, gengur til skipana, heilsandi Inga kóngi, bjóðandi honum heim til hallar með öllum sínum skara. Mátti þar sjá margan stoltan riddara í hvorum tveggja flokkinum.

3 Emended from MS *Blebarnius*, which I have determined is a scribal error (McDonald, 'Variance Uncovered', p. 314).

4 In the manuscript (AM 529), the form of the name is *Livorinus* or *Liforinus* (with an extra <n>). I have normalized the form of the name to *Livorius* throughout the text, for the sake of consistency. See also n. 15 to the Introduction to this book.

Meykóngur fagnar vel Inga kóngi, heiðrandi hann í orðum. Drottning spurði Inga kóng hvert erindi hans væri utan allt af Miklagarði og í svo fjarlæg lönd. Hann segir 'það er mitt erindi í þetta land að biðja yðar mér til eiginkonu, gefandi þar í móti gull og gersemar, land og þegna'.

Drottning segir 'það viti þér, Ingi kóngur, að þér hafið engan ríkdóm til móts við mig. Hafa og lítið lönd yðar að þýða við Frakkland hið góða og tuttugu kónga ríki er þar til liggja. Nenni ég og ekki að fella mig fyrir neinum kóngi nú ríkjandi, en fullboðið er mér fyrir manna sakir, en þó þurfi þér ekki þessa mála að leita oftar'.

Kóngur verður nú reiður við orð hennar, og hugsar það að þau skulu ei skiljast við svo búið. Heldur hann burt af Frakklandi þegar byr gaf og herjar víða um sumarið.

Það var eitt kveld að þeir lágu undir ey einni, þeir sjá mann einn ganga ofan af eyjunni, heldur mikinn og aldraðan. Kóngur spurði þenna mann að nafni. Hann kveðst Refsteinn heita. Kóngur spyr ef hann væri svo sem hann hét til. Hann segir 'það ætla ég að mig skorti við engan mann kukl og galdur og fjölkyngi hvað sem gjöra skal'.

Kóngur mælti 'ég vil gjöra þig fullsælan að fé og börn þín ef þú kemur mér í hendur Nítíða bardaga-laust'. Refsteinn segir 'fyrir þessu er mér ekki'.

Kóngur mælti 'gakk út á skip mín með mér og fullgjör það er þú hefir heitið, er hér gullhringur stór er ég vil gefa þér og tuttugu álnir rautt skarlat er þú skalt færa konu þinni'.

Refsteinn þakkar nú kóngi mikillega, býr sig og ganga á skip. Sigla nú hinn beinasta byr til Frakklands því að Refsteinn gaf þeim nógan byr og hagstæðan, svo að stóð á hverju reipi. Þeir koma að landi og leggja í einn leynivog.

Refsteinn gengur nú á land og kóngur með honum. Þá steypir Refsteinn yfir kóng kufli svörtum. Þeir ganga nú, þar til er þeir koma til skemmu drottningar. Hún var þá á leiki með sínum leikmeyjum. Kóngur undirstendur að engi maður sér hann, og gengur að meykóngi og steypir yfir hana kuflinum, gengur með hana til herskipa. Vinda síðan segl og sigla í burt og leggja sín segl ei fyrr en í Miklagarði.

Listalín gengur í móti bróður sínum og meykónginum kærlega og öll ríkisins ráð. Er drottning nú leidd í höllina með miklum heiðri og prís. Verður nú skjótt búist við ágætri veislu og brúðlaupi og þangað boðið öllu ríkisins ráði, er dýrast var í landinu. Nú er meykóngur settur í hásæti hjá Listalín og allur kvenna-skari, sem frúna skyldi til sængur leiða, og þær voru út undir beran himin komnar. Þá nemur meykóngur staðar og mælti 'litum í loftið; gætum að stjörnugangi; má þar af marka mikla visku um örlög manna'.

Ok eftir svo talað, bregður hún einum steini yfir höfuð sér, þann hafði hún haft úr eynni Visio. Í þessu líður drottning upp úr höndum þeirra. Hverfur hún burt úr höndum þeirra og augsýn. Hlaupa menn nú í höllina og segja kóngi þessi tíðindi. Kóngur og öll hirðin verður mjög hrygg við þenna atburð.

En næsta dag eftir kemur meykóngur heim í Frans gangandi hlæjandi í fagra höll. Verður nú allur Frakklands her henni feginn. Fer þetta nú á hvert land hversu drottning hafði Inga kóng útleikið. Unir Ingi kóngur allilla við og hyggst aftur skulu rétta á frúinni sína smán og svívirðing.

Líður nú af veturinn og þegar er vorar, leggur hann í hernað allt þetta sumar, og eitthvert sinn síð um kveld leggur hann undir eitt nes, takandi stórt strandhögg. Þeir sjá mann ganga ofan af nesinu. Kóngur spyr þenna mann að nafni. Hann segist Slægrefur heita. Kóngur mælti 'ég vildi að þú værir sem þú heitir til, eða kanntu nokkuð kukl?'

Slægrefur segir 'ei kann ég minni fjölkyngi en Refsteinn og ei mundi meykóngur hafa hlaupið burt úr höndum þér ef ég hefði svo nær verið sem hann var'. Kóngur segir 'ef þú kemur drottningu svo í mitt vald sem hann, þá skal ég gefa þér þrjá kastala og gjöra þig jarl'. Slægrefur segir 'ég er albúinn að fylgja þér'. Þeir ganga á skip og sigla blásanda byr hinn beinasta til Frakklands.

3

Nú er að segja af meykóngi að daglega lítur hún í sína náttúrusteina að sjá um veröldina ef víkingar kæmi og vildi stríða á hennar ríki. Sér nú hvar Ingi kóngur siglir og er kominn að Frakklandi síðla eins dags. Drottning hugsar sitt ráð og kallar til sín eina arma þýju er þjónaði í garðinum. Hún átti bónda og þrjú börn. Þau geymdu svina í garðinum. Drottning tekur nú ambáttina, hún hét Íversa. Færir hana nú úr hverju klæði takandi einn stein og lætur þýjuna sjá sig í, laugandi áður steininn í vatni einhverju, er þar var. Hún þvo og allan hennar búk, og þar með gefur hún henni mörg náttúruepli að éta, þau er hún hafði sótt í eyna. Eftir svo gjört færir hún hana í skínanda drottningarbúnað setjandi hana upp á einn gullstól. Ambáttin bar þá svo skæra ásjónu sem meykóngur að hvoruga mátti kenna frá annari. Eplin báru þau náttúrulíf að hún mátti ekki mæla á næsta mánuði. Drottning leit þá í annan náttúrustein og mátti þá engi sjá hana hvort er hún sat eða stóð.

Nú er að segja að þeir Ingi kóngur eru landfastir vorðnir. Gengur hann á land upp, og Slægrefur með honum, hinn beinasta veg til skemmu drottningar og sem þeir inn ganga sjá þeir hvar meykóngur situr með skínandi ásjónu á gullstóli. Kóngur hleypur að og steypir yfir hana svartri sveipu, og fer þegar út af skemmunni og ofan til skipa. Kóngur lætur þegar búa sæng í lyftingunni, án allri dvöl, því að þeir vildu nú flýta brúðlaupinu svo að meykóngur mátti eingin undanbrögð hafa. Þau liggja nú bæði saman alla þessa nótt með fögrum faðmlögum. Ingi kóngur unir nú vel sínu ráði; þykist nú hefnt hafa sinnar sneypu. Vinda nú seglin og létta ei sinni ferð fyrr en þeir koma til Miklagarðs.

Frú Listalín og allur lýður gengur í móti kóngi og drottningu með allri mekt, heiður, og veraldar prís. Er nú mikill fagnaður í Miklagarði í mey-kóngsins tilkomu. En að næsta mánuði liðnum var það einn dag að frú Listalín talar við kóng bróður sinn. 'Er þér engi grunur á hverja konu þú hefur heim flutt í landið. Sýnist mér tiltæki hennar ei líkt og meykóngsins og fleiri greinir aðrar. Er mér sagt á að vér séum við brögðum að sjá.[5] Vil ég nú forvitnast um í dag að gjöra nokkra tilraun, en þú statt í nokkru leyni og heyr á'. Kóngur gjörir nú svo.

Þenna sama dag kveður frú Listalín burt af skemmunni allar frúr og hirðkönur, svo talandi: 'Drottning mín, hvað veldur því er þér vilið eða megið við öngvan mann tala, eður þann beiska grát er aldrei gengur af yðrum augum, því að kóngur og allur landslýður biðja svo sitja og standa hvern mann sem yður best líki'.

Hún svarar 'það veldur mínum gráti og þungum harmi að meykóngur hefur skilið mig við bónda minn og börn og mun ég hvorki sjá síðan'. Listalín spurði hvar bóndi hennar eða börn væri. Hún svarar og segir þá allt hið sanna og hversu farið hafði.

Ingi kóngur sprettur þá fram undan tjaldinu mjög reiðuri og lét fletta hana hverju klæði og drottningarskrúða og fylgir þar þá öll fegurð og blómi. Kóngur unir nú stórilla við. Fer nú og flýgur á hvert land þetta gabb og svívirðing.

Látum Inga kóng nú hvílast um tíma, en vendum sögunni í annan stað og segjum af sonum Soldáns kóngs, Heiðarloga og Véloga, að þeir spyrja hversu Ingi kóngur er útleikinn af meykóngi. Búa þeir óvígan her af Serklandi. Skipa þeir sínum skipastól til Frakklands.

5   This has been emended from Loth's reading 'sem' ('Nitida saga', ed. by Loth, p. 17). Loth lists only two conflicting variants in the edition, from AM 537, 'kannskie hier haffe uerid vid brogdum ad sia' (f. 4ʳ), and Papp. 4to nr. 31, 'higg eg ad vier sieum vmm brogd' (f. 14ᵛ). The manuscript itself simply has *se* with a nasal stroke over the <e>. Comparison with readings from other manuscripts, however, suggests that *sieum*, the present subjunctive of *sjá* (see), was probably intended, in the phrase *sjá við* (to beware of) (Gudbrand Vigfusson, *An Icelandic Dictionary*, p. 533). These other readings include nearly identical phrasing in e.g. JS 166, 'er mer grunur a ad vier sieamm med brogdumm' (f. 184ᵛ), JS 632 (f. 105ᵛ), and Rask 32 (f. 31ᵛ).

Nú er að segja af meykóngi að hún heldur ei kyrru fyrir, því að hún lætur saman lesa smiðu[6] og meistara; fyrir þeim var Ypolitus. Hún lætur gjöra glerhimin með þeirri list að hann lék á hjólum og mátti fara inn yfir höfuðport borgarinnar og mátti þar mart herfólk á standa. Hún lét og gjöra díki ferlega djúpt fram fyrir skemmunni og leggja yfir veika viðu, en þar yfir var breitt skrúð og skarlat.

Nú sem kóngssynir koma í land kallar meykóngur Hléskjöld á sinn fund, og bað hann ganga til herskipa og segir honum fyrir alla hluti hverju hann skal fram fara. Hléskjöldur gengur nú til skipa og fréttir hvort kóngar fara með friði. Heiðarlogi segir, 'ef drottning vill giftast öðrum hvorum okkrum bræðra, þá er þetta land og ríki frjálst fyrir okkrum hernaði, ella munum[7] við eyða landið, brenna og bæla og þyrma öngu'.

Hléskjöldur svarar 'eigi kennir meykóngur sig mann til að halda stríð við Serkja her, og svo ágæta kóngssonu sem þið eruð. Vil ég segja þér, Vélogi, trúnað meykóngs. Hún vill tala við sér hvorn ykkar og prófa visku ykkar og málsnilld. Vill hún að þú gangir snemma á hennar fund áður en bróðir þinn stendur upp, því að ég veit að hún kýs þig til bónda'. Binda þeir þetta nú með sér.

Að næstu nóttliðinni gengur Vélogi heim til borgarinnar með tíu hundruð manna, og er þeir koma undir höfuðport borgarinnar lætur Hléskjöldur vinda fram yfir þá glerhimininn, og hella yfir þá biki og brennisteini. En Hléskjöldur gengur að þeim af borginni með skotvopnum og stórum höggum. Fellur þar Vélogi og hver maður er með honum var. Er nú rudd borgin og hreinsuð af dauðum mönnum.

Nú gengur Hléskjöldur ofan til herskipa og talar svo fallið til Heiðarloga: 'Meykóngur biður þig koma á sinn fund, því að hún vill tala við ykkur báða bræðurna og prófa beggja ykkra visku og er Vélogi fyrir löngu upp kominn og situr nú í höllinni og drekkur. Vildi ég ei að hann talaði við hana; veit ég að hún kýs þig en ekki hann, fyrir sakir afls og hreysti, að verja ríki sitt. Þætti oss mál að hún giftist svo að menn stæði ei lengur í stríði og ónáðum'.

Heiðarlogi þakkar honum sinn trúnað og fyrirgöngu. Býr sig nú með tuttugu hundruð manna og ganga til borgarinnar í stað. En Hléskjöldur talar þá: 'Nú skulu þeir ganga til skemmu drottningar, en ég skal vitja Véloga bróður þíns og tálma fyrir honum því að ég vil að þú talir fyrri við drottningu'.

---

6 I have kept this unexpected accusative plural form from the MS ('Nitida saga', ed. by Loth, p. 18).
7 Emended from MS *munu* (Loth, p. 19).

Heiðarlogi snýr fram að skemmunni, og sem þeir ganga fram á klæðin brestur niður viðurinn, en þeir steyptust í díkið. Í þessu þeysir Hléskjöldur óvígan her úr borginni og bera grjót í höfuð þeim og skotvopn og drepa hvern mann er Heiðarloga fylgdi. Nú býr Hléskjöldur út óvígan her Frakka af Párisborg og býður þeim til bardaga, en þeir sjá ei sinn kost til varnar, höfuðingjalausir við allan Frakkaher. Halda nú heim í Serkland. Fer og flýgur á hvert land frægð og mekt sú er meykóngur fékk.

4

Nú er að segja af hinum fræga kóngi Livorius er fyrr var nefndur að hann reið út á skóg einn dag að skemmta sér. Lítur hann í einu rjóðri einn stein standandi og þar nær einn dverg. Kóngssonur[8] rennir nú sínu essi á milli steinsins og dvergsins og vígir hann utan steins. Dvergur mælti: 'Meiri frægð væri þér í að leika út meykóng í Frans en banna mér mitt inni, eða heyrir þú ei þá frægð er fer og flýgur um allan heiminn af hennar mekt að hún útleikur alla kónga með sinni spekt og visku'.

Kóngur segir: 'Mart hef ég heyrt þar af sagt og ef þú vilt fylgja mér til Frakklands og vera mér hollur svo að með þínu kynstri og kukli mætti ég fá meykónginn mér til eiginnar púsu þá skyldi ég gjöra þig fullsælan og börn þín'. Dvergur mælti: 'Þat mun ég upp taka að fylgja þér, heldur en missa steininn, því að ég veit að þú ert ágætur kóngur'. Livorius gaf honum gull-hring stóran, 'ok tak af hjörð minni naut og sauði, svín og geitur, sem þeir þarfast'.

Kóngur lætur nú búa úr landi skrautlegan skipastól með dýru hoffólki, leggjandi sín segl ei fyrr en þeir komu í þær hafnir er lágu út við Párisborg. Meykóngur vissi fyrir komu Livorius kóng, berandi á sig alla sína nát-túrusteina. Gengur Hléskjöldur ofan til skipa, bjóðandi heim kóninum til virðulegrar veislu, eftir meykóngsins boði. Kóngur gengur nú á land með öllum sínum hoflýð.

Dvergurinn talar þá til hans: 'Hér er eitt gull er ég vil gefa þér; drag það á þinn fingur. Legg þína hönd með gullinu upp á beran háls meykóngs. Þá mun gullið fast við hennar ljósa líkam. Fanga hana síðan, en ég skal gjöra ráð fyrir að engi eftirför sé veitt'.

Kóngur gengur nú heim til hallarinnar en drottning stendur upp í móti honum og setur hann í hásæti hjá sér með góðum orðum og kærlegu viðbragði. Livorius tekur nú sinni hægri hendi með gullinu upp á háls

8   Emended from Loth's expansion of MS *kongss* to 'kongss(on)' ('Nitida saga', ed. by Loth, p. 21).

drottningu; var þá föst höndin með gullinu. Kóngur grípur sinni vinstri hendi undir hennar knésbætur, springandi með frúna fram yfir borðið. Meykóngur kallar á sína menn sér til hjálpar. Hléskjöldur og allur Frakklands lýður býst til upphlaups, en hann og allir meykóngsins menn voru fastir í sínum sætum. Livorius gengur nú til sinna manna án allri dvöl, og allur hans lýður dragandi upp sín segl flýtandi sinni ferð. Dvergurinn gefur þeim fagran byr heim til Indíalands.

Nú er að segja að kóngs dóttir, Sýjalín, gengur í móti sínum bróður og meykóngi, og allur Indíalands her með allri mekt. Þá voru hörpur og gígjur og allra handa strengfæri. Öll stræti eru þar þökt með skarlat og dýra vefi, en kórónaðir kóngar leiddu meykóng til skemmu drottningar Sýjalín. Er nú búist við virðulegri veislu og boðið til öllum Indíalands höfuðingjum.

Og það var einn dag að drottning var gengin fram undir einn lund plantaðan er stóð undir skemmunni. Þá var meykóngur allkát; hún hafði þá í hendi þann náttúrustein er hún hafði úr eynni Visio. Hún brá þá steininum upp yfir höfuð þeim báðum. Því næst líða þær báðar í loft upp svo að þær voru skjótt ur augsýn. Fara nú jungfrúr, og allt fólk það er við var á völlunum hjá lundinum hlaupa inn og sögðu kónginum þenna atburð og varð hann mjög óglaður við.

Nú er þar af að segja að drottningar koma heim í Páris; tekur meykóngur Sýjalín kóngsdóttur, og setur hana í hásæti hjá sér drekkandi af einu keri báðar og skilur hvorki svefn né mat við hana. Tók hvor að unna annari sem sinni móður.

5

Nú er að segja af Soldáni kóngi að hann fréttir lát sona sinna; hann fyllist upp ferlegri reiði. Lætur ganga herör um öll sín ríki og safnar að sér blámönnum og bannsettum hetjum og alls kyns óþjóð og illþýði. Ætlar nú að halda þessum her til Frakklands brenna og bæla landið nema meykóngur vili giftast honum.

Það var einn dag að þær frúrnar líta í sína náttúrusteina og þær sjá hvað Soldán kóngur hefst að. Lætur meykóngur kalla Hléskjöld, svo talandi til hans, 'Þú skalt láta ganga herör um allt landið og öll mín kónga ríki og stefna hverjum manni til þeim er skildi gæti valdið. Hald þessum her á móti Soldáni kóngi, því að ég vil ekki hann komi í mitt ríki'.

Hléskjöldur gjörir svo, og þegar herlið hans var búið, heldur hann burt af ríkinu. Sigla nú þessir skipastólar hvorir móti öðrum, og finnast undir ey einni er Kartagia heitir. Þar var víkinga bæli mikið. Þar þurfti ekki að sökum að spyrja. Taka þeir þegar að berjast er vígljóst var. Gengur Soldán kóngur hetjur hans og blámenn í gegnum lið Franseisa svo að ekki stóð við, er þá ei meira eftir en hálft það er Hléskildi fylgdi.

Annan dag árla hefst annar bardagi af nýju, og að kveldi annars dags þá stóð ei fleira upp af hans liði en fimmtán hundruð manna. Halda menn upp friðskildi, og bindur hver sár sinna manna. Nú gjöra menn að líta hvar mikill dreki siglir og skrautlegur og ógrynni annara skipa. Sigla nú af hafi og halda sínum seglum öðru megin undir eyna. Fer maður af drekanum og allur herlýður gengur á land upp með fylktu liði. Hann var digur og hár svo að hans höfuð bar upp yfir allan herinn. Hann lét geisa sitt merki gullofið fram móti Soldáni kóngi, en Hléskjöldur móti Loga. Tekst nú hið þriðja sinn orrosta hin harðasta.

Hefja kóngar nú sitt einvígi, Livorius og Soldán, með stórum höggum og sterku stríði. Gengur þessi atgangur allt til nætur. Að síðustu þeirra viðskipti lagði hann einum brynþvara fyrir brjóst Soldáni kóngi svo að út gékk um herðarnar. Féll hann þá dauður niður. Livorius leitar nú að Hléskildi en hann lá þá í einum dal sár nær til ólífis, en Logi lá dauður hjá honum. Livorius tekur upp Hléskjöld og ber ofan til skipa. Kóngur lætur nú kanna valinn. Voru þar gefin grið þeim er beiddi, en allir aðrir voru drepnir.

Tekur Livorius þar nú mikið herfang og verður frægur af þessi orrustu víða um lönd. Sigla nú heim til Indíalands með fögrum sigri. Svo er sagt að kóngur sjálfur sat yfir og græddi Hléskjöld þar til er hann var heill. En þegar vor kom var það einn dag að kóngur gekk til sjófar og Hléskjöldur með honum. Hann mælti þá: 'Annað mun meykóngi hentilegra og hennar ríki en ég haldi þér hér lengur. Hér eru í höfn minni tíu skip er ég vil gefa þér með mönnum og herförum; skaltu ekki héðan fara sem förumaður'.

Hléskjöldur tekur nú orðlof, þakkaði kóngi sína veislu og stórar gjafir. Siglir Hléskjöldur heim til Frakklands. Verður meykóngur allglöð við hans heimkomu.

Þetta sumar heldur Livorius kóngur í hernað og kemur sínum skipum við Smáland. Þar ríkti sú drottning er Alduria hét; hún var móðir systir Livorius kóngs. Drottning tók við honum báðum höndum og situr hann þar í ágætri veislu.

Einn dag talar drottning við sinn frænda 'hvað veldur ógleði þinni, hvort þreyr þú á meykónginn er nú er frægust í heiminum'. Livorius mælti 'þú ert kölluð vitur kona og klók. Legg til ráð að ég mætti meykóng útleika og[9] ást hennar ná'.

---

9   The text in AM 529 ends here. As noted by Loth, 'after this word there is a lacuna (the rest of the saga = 2 ½ folios) in the MS; the [rest of the base] text is taken from [AM] 537, 6r-8v' ('Nitida saga', ed. by Loth, p. 28).

Drottning mælti 'þar vilda ég allt til gefa þú næðir þínu yndi eftir þínum vilja. Nú er það mitt ráð, að þú siglir þetta sumar til Frakklands og nefnist Eskilvarður, sonur kóngs af Mundia, og haf þar vetursetu. Ég skal gefa þér gull það er þig skal einginn maður kenna, hvorki meykóngur né þín systir, ef þú situr þar allan þann vetur, þá er undur ef þú fær ekki fang á henni'.

Nú tekur Livorius við þessu ráði, og býr sín fimmtán skip, siglir af stað og kemur til Frakklands um haustið. Meykóngur lætur nú bjóða honum til hallar og á tal við sig; virðist henni hann vitur maður. Drottning býður Eskilvarð að bíða þar um veturinn með sitt fólk. Það þiggur Eskilvarður kóngur og kemur jafnan til drottningar því hann var listamaður á hörpuslátt og öll hljóðfæri. Hann kunni af hvoru landi að segja nokkuð. Drottning þótti að honum hin mesta gleði.

Leið nú veturinn af, að vori býst hann til ferðar. Nokkurn dag áður en hann var albúinn, talar meykóngur við hann, 'þú Eskilvarður hefur jafnan skemmt okkur frú Sýjalín í vetur, með þínum hljóðfærum, og fögrum frásögum; nú vil ég að þú gangir í dag með okkur: skulum við nú skemmta þér'.

Eskilvarður þiggur það gjarnan, og gengur með þeim í skemmuna. Meykóngur tók upp stein og bað hann í líta. Hann sá þá yfir allt Frakkland, Provintiam, Ravenam, Spaniam, Galiciam,[10] Frísland, Flandren, Norðmandiam, Skottland, Grikkland, og allar þær þjóðir þar byggja. Meykóngur mælti, 'ekki siglir Livorius kóngur í þessar hálfur heimsins, eða mun hann heima vera'.

Annan dag býður drottning Eskilvarð til skemmunnar: 'þú hefur jafnan skemmt oss í vetur'. Drottning bað Eskilvarð enn líta í steininn. Þá sáu þau norður hálfuna alla, Noreg, Ísland, Færeyjar, Suðureyjar, Orkneyjar, Svíþjóð, Danmörk, England, Írland, og mörg lönd önnur, þau er hann vissi ei skil á. Drottning mælti 'mun Livorius kóngur hinn frægi ekki sigla í þessi lönd'. Eskilvarður sagði 'hann er fjarlægur þessum löndum'.

Meykóngur vindur upp enn einn stein, sjáandi þá nú austur hálfuna heimsins, Indíaland, Palestinam, Asiam, Serkland, og öll önnur lönd heimsins, og jafnvel um brúnabeltið, það sem ei er byggt. Drottning mælti, 'bardagar miklir eru nú í Serklandi, og Ingi kóngur situr nú heima í Miklagarði og herjar hvorgi, en hvar mun Livorius hinn frægi vera? Ég sé hann ekki heima í Indíalöndum, og ei er hann í Smálöndum hjá frændkonu sinni. Nú sjáist öll úthöfin um lá og leynivoga, hvorgi er hann þar, og hvorgi er hann í öllum heiminum utan hann standi hér hjá mér'. Meykóngur talar þá, 'Livorius

---

10   Emended from MS *Hallitiam*, which I have determined is a scribal error (see above, Chapter 1, n. 53).

kóngur', segir hún, 'legg af þér dularkufl þinn. Hinn fyrsta dag er þú komst kennda ég þig. Fær þú aftur gullið Alduria,[11] því yður stendur það lítið lengur með það að fara'.

Livorius kóngur lætur nú að orðum drottningar, leggjandi af sér gullið og nafnið, takandi upp sín tignar klæði. Frú Sýjalín[12] gengur nú að sínum bróður, og verður þeirra á milli mesti fagnaðarfundur. Meykóngur setur Livorius kóng í hásæti hjá sér. Er þar ágæta veisla.

Svo er sagt að meykóngur hafi sent í allar hálfur landsins til tuttugu kónga, er allir þjónuðu undir hennar ríki. Byrjar Livorius kóngur nú bónorð sitt við meykóng með fagurlegum framburði og mikilli röksemd. Styrkja hans mál allir kóngar og höfðingjar að þessi ráðahagur takist. Meykóngur svarar orðum þeirra: 'Ég hefi heyrt að höfðingjum landsins leiðist stríð og ónáðir í ríkinu. Er nú og líkast að það muni fyrir liggja að fá þann kóng er yður þikir mikils háttar vera'.

Hléskjöldur mælti 'ef þér viljið mér nokkra þjónustu lengur gefa, þá vil ég að þér takið Livorius kóng yður til herra, skal ég og ekki önnur laun þiggja, og lengur í yðar ríki vera'. Meykóngur segir 'mikinn heiður á ég yður að launa, fyrir margan mannháska og raunir, er þér hafið minna vegna. Er það líkast ég taki þetta upp síðan og sé það allra höfðingja ráð og vilji; veit og ei æðri kóng ríkjandi en Livorius kóng'.

Livorius kóngur verður við þetta allglaður. Var þetta nú staðfest og ályktað með öllu ríkis ráði; skyldi brúðkaupið vera um haustið. Meykóngur talar nú til Livorius og annara manna: 'Ég vil ekki yðar burtferð að sinni úr minni náveru, því ég meina við munum ekki lengi við kyrrt sitja mega'.

Nú er að segja af Inga kóngi, að hann spyr þessi tíðindi; verður hann reiður og kveðst öngva konu skyldi eiga utan meykóng ella liggja dauður. Lætur nú ganga herör um allt sitt ríki, og safnar saman múga og margmenni, skyldi þar koma hvor sá er skildi gæti valdið. Verður þetta ótal lið, svo að sjór þótti svartur fyrir herskipum. Heldur Ingi kóngur öllum þessum skipastól í Frakkland með ákefð og reiði, því hann vildi koma áður brullaupið væri drukkið.

Nú sem Ingi kóngur var landfastur orðinn lætur hann tjalda herbúðir á landi. Livorius kóngur ríður þegar ofan til skipa, bjóðandi Inga kóngi alla sætt og sæmd meykóngs vegna, hvað er Ingi kóngur vill ei: hann vill ei annað en berjast. Síga nú saman fylkingar. Lætur Livorius kóngur bera sitt merki mót Inga kóngi. Tókst nú hörð orusta með geysilegum gný og mannfalli. Gengur Ingi kóngur í gegnum Frakkaher höggvandi tvó menn í hvorju

11 From here until the end, the name is *Aldvia* in the MS (i.e. AM 537).
12 Here until the end, the name is *Suyialyn* in the MS (i.e. AM 537).

höggi. Slíkt hið sama gjörir Livorius kóngur, þar sem hann fer verður meiri mannföll í liði stólkóngs. Verður mikið mannfall af hvoru tveggju hernum, og allir vellir voru þaktir af dauðra manna líkum.

Í þrjá daga gengur þessi aðgangur, og árla hinn fjórða daginn kallar Livorius kóngur hárri röddu til Ingja kóngs: 'Þetta er óviturlegt bragð að berjast svo, því við látum hér þá vildustu frændur, vini, og höfðingja. Er það betra ráð að við berjumst tveir, eigi sá meykóng er hærra hlut ber af okkar viðskiptum'.

Ingi kóngur játar þessu blíðlega, og hefja þeir sitt einvígi með stórum höggum og sterkum aðgangir, bresta hlífar hvorutveggja, berast og sár á báða, en þó fleiri á Ingja kóng. Luktist svo þeirra einvígi að Ingi kóngur féll til jarðar af mæði og blóðrás, því hann flakti allur sundur af sárum. Livorius kóngur lætur leggja Inga kóng í veglega sæng, en hann leggst í aðra og taka þeir nú að smyrja þeirra sár með dýrum smyrslum.

Livorius býður systur sinni, að leggja góða hönd á Inga kóng sem sín sár. Hún gjörir síns bróður boð, því hún var hinn ágætasti læknir og enn kunni hún framar í þessu en meykóngur. Færðist nú gróður í sár kónga; sér Ingi kóngur að Sýjalín er afbragð annarra kvenna um öll norðurlönd að fráteknum meykóngi. Lítur hann skjótt ástaraugum til hennar. Hefur nú skjótt sitt bónorð við kóngsdóttur. Meykóngur og allur landslýður er fylgjandi að sá ráðahagur takist að öll ríkin fengu frið og náðir og Ingi kóngur sættist við Livorius kóng.

Kóngurinn talar þá til Ingja kóngs: 'viljir þú gifta Hléskildi mínum góða vin og fóstbróður Listalín, þá skulu þessi ráð takast: stendur hann einn til arfs og ríkis út á Púli eftir móður sína Egidíam; þar til vil ég gefa þeim þriðjung Indíalands, og er hann þó betra verður'.

Nú gengur meykóngur og allir ríkjanna höfðingjar með þessum erindum, og með þeirra bæn og fagurlega framburði; fullgjörðust þessi kaup hvorutveggju. Eru nú orð send eftir frú Listalín; kemur hún þar eftir liðinn tíma til Frakklands með dýrlegu föruneyti. Hefjast nú þessi þrjú brúðkaup í upphafi Augusti mánaðar og yfir stendur allan þann mánuð með miklum veraldar prís og blóma. Þar var fallega étið og fagurlega drukkið með allskyns matbúnaði og dýrustu drykkjum. Þar var allskyns skemmtun framinn í burtreiðum og hljóðfæraslætti, en þar sem kóngarnir gengu var niðurbreidt pell og purpuri og heiðurleg klæði. Er og ei auðsagt með ófróðri tungu í útlegðum veraldarinnar, svo mönnum verði skemmtilegt, hver fögnuður vera mundi í miðjum heiminum af slíku hoffólki samankomnu. Stendur nú svo hófið í mikilli þessa heimsgleið með dýrlegum tilföngum. Og nú með því að öll þessa heims dýrð kann skjótt að líða, þá voru brúðkaupinn útdrukkinn, og höfðingjarnir útleiddir með fögrum fégjöfum í gulli og gimsteinum og góðum vefjum. Skildist þar hoflýðar með fögrum friði og kærleika hvor við annan.

Siglir nú Ingi kóngur og hans frú til Miklagarðs, en Hléskjöldur og Listalín út á Púl, stýrandi þar ríki til dauðadags. Livorius og meykóngur stýrðu Frakklandi. Áttu þau ágæt börn, son er Ríkon hét eftir sínum móður föður er síðan stýrði Frakklandi með heiður og sóma eftir þeirra dag. Og lýkur svo þessu ævintýri af hinni frægu Nítíða og Livorius kóngi.

English Translation

1

Listen, young people, to an adventure and wonderful account about the most famous maiden-king there has ever been in the northern region of the world. She was called Nítíða the Famous and ruled her kingdom honourably and gloriously, after her father, the Emperor Ríkon, died. This maiden-king sat on the throne of the world in France the Good, and ruled in Paris. She was both wise and fair, light and rosy in face just as if the red rose was tempered together with a snow-white lily; her eyes were as bright as a carbuncle, and her skin as white as ivory; her hair was like gold and fell down to the earth around her. She had a gold headdress with four pillars, and up on top of the pillars, an eagle was depicted. On top of the eagle stood a hawk made of red gold, spreading its wings forward over the bright face of the young woman so that the sun did not burn her. She was as endowed with knowledge as the wisest scholar, and, surpassing other people's intelligence, she could make the strongest castle-wall with her own intellect, and thus outmanoeuvre others' plans; and she knew ten answers when others knew one. She had such a beautiful voice that it made birds, fish, wild animals, and all worldly creatures sleep, so delightful was it to hear. Her kingdom stood in peace and prosperity.

There was a smith named Ypolitus in France with the maiden-king. He knew how to craft all things – from gold and silver, glass and jewels – that could be made with one's hands.

Now it is said of the maiden-king that she prepares for a journey from her home out to Apulia. A queen named Egidía ruled the realm there; she had fostered the maiden-king in her childhood. She had a son who was called Hléskjöldur. Queen Nítíða sails with her nobles on a fine, favourable wind, until she arrives in Apulia. Lady Egidía meets the maiden-king with her son and all of their kind with honour and ceremony, holding an excellent feast in the hall for the whole next fortnight.

One day during the feast, the maiden-king goes to a meeting with her foster mother, saying, 'I am told that beyond that island which is called Visio rules that earl who is called Virgilius; he is wise and skilled in magic. This island lies out beyond Sweden the Cold, out past the corner of the world of those lands which people have heard of. In the island is a large lake, and in the lake is that islet which is called The Flower of the Woods, and so I am told, that nowhere in the world might one find more supernatural stones, apples, and healing herbs than there. Now I wish to travel there in a single ship and take your son Hléskjöldur with me'.

Queen Egidía raised difficulties about the journey, and thought it dangerous; the maiden-king nevertheless decided to go, and arranges with Hléskjöldur for their journey, and they sail with ceremony out from Apulia on a beautiful, favourable wind. I have not heard it said about their journey, nor their journey's length, before they reached the island of Visio.

One day, mooring the ship in a hidden cove, they walk up across the island until they find the lake. They see a boat floating there, take it, and row out to the islet, where there are many oaks with fair fruit and fine apples. When they come to the middle of the islet they see a stone vessel with four corners. The vessel was full of water, and there was a stone in each corner of the vessel. The maiden-king looked into the stones; then she saw all the regions of the world, including kings and princes and what each did, and all peoples, of every land, and many diverse creatures and monsters. The queen then grows glad at this sight, taking the vessel and all the stones, apples, and healing herbs, because she understood from her wisdom how magical each was. Now they hurriedly make their way back to their ship, sailing away from Visio as best they could.

Now it is said that the earl discovers by whom he is robbed. They can see there many ships sailing and rowing after them, and now they see each other. The maiden-king now took a supernatural stone and quickly waved it over the ship and the heads of all who were on board. The earl never saw them again, and the maiden-king and Hléskjöldur hold fast on their course, not stopping before they come home to Apulia.

Lady Egidía goes to meet them joyfully and with great ceremony, and the maiden-king remains there for a while. Afterwards she makes preparations for her journey and readies her fleets of ships to go home to France, asking lady Egidía that Hléskjöldur her son accompany her to strengthen her realm against attacks by raiders. Her foster mother grants her this graciously, as with everything else that she asked for, leading her out with fair gifts of money, fine jewels of gold and jewels, and precious woven cloth. The retinues part with great friendship. The maiden-king sails to her kingdom with great honour and worldly power. All the people of the land become pleased at her ruling her kingdom peacfully and gracefully.

2

There is a king named Hugon; he ruled over Constantinople. He had a queen and two children. His son was called Ingi, and was the most honourable of all men and the best endowed in athletic arts. He went plundering each summer and in doing so got for himself wealth and fame; he killed robbers and vikings, and let peaceful people move in peace. King Hugon's daughter was named Listalín; she was beautiful and popular, and skilled in feminine arts.

There was a king called Soldán; he ruled over Serkland. He had three sons: one was called Logi, the second Vélogi, and the third Heiðarlogi – he was the oldest of them. He had black hair and beard. He was long-chinned and thin-cheeked, crooked-toothed and crooked-mouthed, and splayfooted. One of his eyes looked inwards and the other outwards. He was a very great warrior, and knew much sorcery and witchcraft. He was physically strong and got victory in every battle. His brothers Logi and Vélogi were promising and respected men and plundered all summer.

There is a king named Februarius. He ruled over Greater India. He had a son who was called Livorius. He was handsome in appearance, light and rosy in face, sharp-eyed as a falcon, with beautiful curly hair, broad-shouldered, yet upright of chest, and was courteous, strong, and magnificent. He knew well how to swim and sail, how to shoot and fence, play board games and use runes, and to read books, as well as all physical activities that a man should pursue. King Februarius also had a daughter called Sýjalín; she was so fair and skilled that she would have been thought to be the most prized of all the women in the world, if nearby there had not been such a jewel as Nítíða the Famous.

Livorius engaged in plundering both winter and summer and earned for himself wealth and fame, and was thought the best hero and champion wherever he went, and had victory in each battle. He was so keen on women that none had any peace from him, but he did not stay with any princess longer than a month.

Now it is said about King Ingi that he prepares his splendid fleets, sailing with a fair wind out from Constantinople, not stopping his journey before he furled his sails at the city of Paris. Now when the maiden-king saw Ingi's fleets, with their sails woven with gold, she sends Hléskjöldur down to the ships to ask this king to an excellent feast, if he comes in peace. Hléskjöldur carries out this task, goes to the ships, greeting King Ingi, and inviting him home to the hall with all his troops. One could see there many proud knights in each of the two retinues.

The maiden-king welcomes King Ingi warmly, praising him with her words. The queen asked King Ingi what his errand might be all the way out from Constantinople and in such a distant land. He says, 'I have come to this land to ask you to me to be my wife; giving you in return gold and treasures, land and servants'.

The queen says, 'You know, King Ingi, that you have no riches to match with mine. Your lands have also little to compare with France the Good and the twenty kings' realms that lie therein. I am also not inclined to give myself over to any king now ruling, and I am well enough off regarding marriage proposals already; and moreover, it will be no use for you to bring up this suit again'.

The king now becomes angry at her words, and thinks that they must not part in this way. He heads out from France as soon as the wind permitted and plunders far and wide throughout the summer.

It was on one evening that Ingi's ships were lying near an island. They saw a person walking down from the island who looked rather large and old. The king asked this person his name. He said he was called Refsteinn. The king asks if he might be such as he was called. He said, 'I suppose that my knowledge is inferior to no person in terms of sorcery and spell-craft and wizardry, whatever one might do'.

The king said, 'I will make you and your children wealthy in riches if you get Nítíða into my hands, without battle'. Refsteinn says, 'That's no problem for me'.

The king said, 'Go out to my ship with me and fulfil that which you have promised; here is a large gold ring which I want to give to you, and twenty ells of red scarlet which you must bring to your wife'.

Refsteinn now thanks the king greatly, prepars himself, and they go onto the ship. Now they sail the straightest course to France because Refsteinn gave them enough of a favourable wind so that it filled all the sails. They come to land and moor in a hidden cove.

Refsteinn now goes onto land and the king with him. Then Refsteinn casts a black cloak over the king. They walk now until they come to the queen's chamber. She was then at leisure with her maidens. The king realises that no person can see him, and goes to the maiden-king and casts over her the cloak, and walks with her to the warships. Then they hoist the sails and sail away, and do not furl their sails before reaching Constantinople.

Listalín, along with all of the kingdom's council, goes lovingly to meet her brother and the maiden-king. The queen is now led into the hall with great honour and ceremony. A handsome feast and a wedding are now prepared, and all those of the kingdom's counselors who were noblest in the land were invited to it. Now the maiden-king is placed in the high-seat next to Listalín, and all the company of women who must lead the wife to the marriage-bed; and they had come out under the open sky. Then the maiden-king stops and said, 'Let us look at the sky and keep watch over the course of the stars; there we can gain great insights about people's fates'.

And after saying this, she quickly waves a stone over her head, the one she had gotten from the island of Visio. At this, the queen glides up out of their grasp; she vanishes out of both their grasp and their sight. People now run into the hall and tell the king this news. The king and all the court become very sad after this incident.

The next day, the maiden-king comes home to France, walking and laughing, in her fair hall. All of France's people become joyful for her. The news now travels to every land, how the queen had outwitted King Ingi. King Ingi is very badly satisfied and plans again how he should set right the disgrace and shame he got from the lady.

Now winter passes, and when it is spring he heads out plundering, and continues all summer. And one time late in the evening, he puts into a headland, raiding the coast extensively. They saw a person walking down from the headland. The king asks this person his name. He says he is called Slægrefur. The king said, 'I would like it if you lived up to your name – or do you know how to do any sorcery?' Slægrefur says, 'I am not able to do less wizardry than Refsteinn, and the maiden-king would not have run away out of your hands if I had been as near as he was'. The king says, 'If you get the queen into my power, as he did, then I will give you three castles and make you an earl'. Slægrefur says, 'I am ready to follow you'. They go onto the ship and sail with a strong wind the straightest way to France.

3

Now it is said of the maiden-king that daily she looks into her supernatural stones to see throughout the world if vikings were coming and would attack her kingdom. Now she sees where King Ingi sails, and has come to France late one day. The queen thinks the matter over and summons a poor bondwoman who serves in the yard. She had a husband and three children; they kept swine in the yard. The queen now takes the slave woman; she was called Íversa. Now she undresses her, taking a stone, and lets the bondwoman see herself in it, bathing the stone beforehand in some of the water. She also washed her whole body, and gives her many supernatural apples to eat – those which she had gotten from the island. After this was done, she dresses her in shining, queenly clothes, placing her up on a golden seat. Then the slave-woman had just as a bright a face as the maiden-king, so that no one could tell one from the other. The apples held the supernatural property that she could not speak for the next month. The queen Nítíða then looked into another supernatural stone so that nobody could see her, whether she sat or stood.

Now it is said that King Ingi and his men have landed. He goes up onto land, and Slægrefur with him, the straightest way to the queen's chamber, and as they walk in they see where the maiden-king sits with a shining face on a golden chair. The king runs in and casts a black hood over her, then immediately goes out of the chamber and down to the ship. The king orders at once to prepare a bed in the raised part of the deck, without any delay, because they now wanted to hurry the wedding so that the maiden-king could not arrange any tricks. They now both lie together the whole night, with fair embraces. King Ingi is now well satisfied with his plan, he now considers his disgrace to have been avenged. The sails are then unfurled and they do not stop their journey before they come to Constantinople.

Lady Listalín and all the courtiers go to meet the king and queen with all strength, honour, and worldly ceremony; there is now great rejoicing in Constantinople at the maiden-king's coming. But when the next month had passed, it happened one day that Lady Listalín speaks with the king her brother: 'Do you not have any suspicion as to what woman you have brought home into the land? Her behaviour, and many other things, seems to me not like the maiden-king's. It is said to me that we ought to beware of seeing tricks. I will inquire today about doing some kind of test, and you should stay in a certain hiding-place and listen'. The king then does so.

That same day, Lady Listalín summons away from the chamber all the ladies and court women and says, 'My queen, what causes it, that you do not want to – or cannot – speak with any person? And what causes that bitter weeping which never leaves your eyes? Because the king and all the courtiers of the land ask how to sit and stand, so that everyone might please you best'.

She answers, 'What causes my tears and heavy grief is that the maiden-king has separated me from my husband and children, and I will never see them again'. Listalín asked where her husband or children might be. She then answers and speaks the truth about everything, and how it had happened.

King Ingi then jumps out from under the tapestry, very angry, and ordered that all her clothes and queen's apparel should be stripped off, and all her beauty and radiance comes off with them. The king is now very discontented. This mockery and disgrace then hastens and flies to every land.

We now leave King Ingi for a while, and we turn the story to another place and tell of King Soldán's sons, Heiðarlogi and Vélogi, that they hear about how King Ingi was outwitted by the maiden-king. They prepare an invincible army from Serkland, and they ready their fleets of ships for France.

Now it is said of the maiden-king that she does not sit still nor idle, because she summons together her smiths and masters; Ypolitus oversaw them. She commands that a glass roof be made that could move on wheels and could go over the main gate of the castle so that many warriors could stand thereon. She commanded also that a monstrously deep ditch be made before her chamber, and to lay weak wood over it, and over that was to be spread costly stuff and scarlet.

Now as the princes come to the land, the maiden-king calls Hléskjöldur to a meeting with her, and asked him to go to the warships and tells him all things about how he should proceed. Hléskjöldur now goes to the ships and learns whether or not the kings come in peace. Heiðarlogi says, 'If the queen wants to marry either of us brothers, then this land and kingdom will be free from our plundering, or else we shall destroy the land, burn and consume it, and spare nothing'.

Hléskjöldur answers, 'The maiden-king does not think herself equipped to wage war against Serkland's army and such excellent princes as you are. I will tell you, Vélogi, the maiden-king's promise: she wants each of you to speak with her, and to test your wisdom and eloquence. She wants you to go early to meet her before your brother gets up, because I know that she chooses you as husband'. They now bind this pledge with each other.

At the end of the next night Vélogi goes up to the castle with ten hundreds of men, and when they come under the main castle gate Hléskjöldur commands his men to winch the glass roof forward over them, and to pour pitch and sulphur over them. And Hléskjöldur attacks them from the castle with projectiles and great blows. Vélogi falls there, and every man who was with him. The castle is now cleared and cleansed of the dead.

Now Hléskjöldur goes down to the warships and speaks to Heiðarlogi: 'The maiden-king asks you to come meet with her, because she wants to speak with both of you brothers and test the wisdom of you both. Vélogi came up a good while ago, and is now sitting in the hall drinking. I did not want him to speak with her; I know that she chooses you and not him to defend her kingdom, because of your physical strength and prowess. It seemed to us that she should marry so that people would no longer remain in conflict and unrest'.

Heiðarlogi thanks him for his good faith and visit. He now prepares himself with twenty hundreds of men and goes to the castle straight away. But then Hléskjöldur says, 'Now they must go to the queen's chamber, and

I shall visit your brother Vélogi and delay him because I want you to speak with the queen first'.

Heiðarlogi turns towards the chamber, and as they walk forward on the cloth, the wood collapses, and they plunge into the ditch. At this Hléskjöldur rushes an invincible army out of the castle and they throw stones onto their heads, and projectiles, and kill every man who accompanied Heiðarlogi. Now Hléskjöldur leads out the invincible French army from Paris and orders them into battle, and they saw they had no chance of defending themselves, leaderless, against the whole French army – now they head home to Serkland. The maiden-king's new fame and might hastens and flies to every land.

4

Now it is said about the famous King Livorius, who was mentioned before, that he rode out into the woods one day to amuse himself. He sees in a forest-clearing a standing stone, and near it a dwarf. The prince then runs his horse between the stone and the dwarf, and separates him from the stone. The dwarf said, 'You would gain greater fame to out-play the maiden-king in France than to ban my entry, or have you not heard of the fame which hastens and flies throughout all the world concerning her strength, that she out-plays all kings with her foresight and wisdom?'

The king says, 'I have heard much said of this, and if you want to accompany me to France and be loyal to me so that with your magical arts and sorcery I might get the maiden-king as my wife, then I shall make you and your children very wealthy'. The dwarf said, 'I will agree to accompany you, rather than lose the stone, because I know that you are an excellent king'. Livorius gave him a large gold ring – 'And take from my herds cattle, sheep, pigs and goats as you need them'.

The king now has a fleet of ornamented ships readied to leave his land, manned with noble courtiers, and he does not lower his sail before they come into the harbour which lay outside Paris. The maiden-king foresaw the arrival of King Livorius, carrying with her all of her supernatural stones. Hléskjöldur walks down to the ship, inviting the king home to a magnificent feast according to the maiden-king's instructions. The king now goes on land with all his courtiers.

Then the dwarf says to him, 'Here is a gold ring which I want to give to you; draw it onto your finger. Put your hand with the gold up on the bare neck of the maiden-king, and then the gold will be stuck to her radiant body. Seize her then, and I shall make sure that no chase will be made'.

The now king goes home to the hall and the queen stands up to meet him and seats him in the high-seat beside her, with good words and a loving countenance. Livorius now takes his right hand with the gold up onto the queen's neck; the hand was then stuck by the gold. The king grips under the backs of her knees with his left hand, springing off over the table with the lady. The maiden-king calls to her men for help. Hléskjöldur and all the French courtiers prepare themselves for a riot, but he and all the maiden-king's men were stuck fast in their seats. Livorius now goes to his men without any delay, and all his army are now hoisting his sails, now speeding his voyage. The dwarf gives them a fair wind home to India.

Now it is said that Princess Sýjalín goes to meet her brother and the maiden-king with India's whole army and all ceremony. There were harps and fiddles and every kind of stringed instrument. All the streets there are thatched with scarlet and precious woven cloths, and crowned kings led the maiden-king to the chamber of princess Sýjalín. Now a magnificent feast is prepared and all of India's nobles sent for.

It happened one day that the princess had gone down to a planted grove that stood below the chamber. The maiden-king was very happy then: she had then in her hand that supernatural stone that she had from the island of Visio. She then quickly waved the stone up over both their heads. Next, they both glide up into the sky so that they were quickly out of sight. The young ladies now go, and all the people who were in the fields near the grove run in and tell the king this news, and he became very downcast.

Now it is said that the queens come home to Paris; the maiden-king takes Princess Sýjalín and sets her in the high seat next to her, both drinking from one cup, and separates from her neither in sleeping nor eating. Each loved the other as her own mother.

5

Now it is said about King Soldán that he hears about the death of his sons; he is filled with terrible rage. He sent out a summons to war throughout his kingdom, and gathered to himself black men and outlaws and all kinds of wild people and rabble. He now intends to bring this army to France to burn and ravage the land unless the maiden-king wanted to marry him.

It was one day that the women look into Nítíða's supernatural stones and they see what King Soldán was beginning to do. The maiden-king calls to Hléskjöldur, saying thus to him, 'You must let a summons to war go throughout all the land and all my kings' kingdoms, and call together every man who can bear arms. Lead this army to meet King Soldán, because I do not want him to come into my kingdom'.

Hléskjöldur does so, and when his troop was ready, he travels away from the kingdom. These fleets now sail, each against the other, and met each other close to a certain island that is called Kartagia. A great viking camp was there. There was no need to discuss anything; they immediately took to fighting when it was light enough for war. King Soldán went with his heroes and black men through the French troops so that nothing withstood him; after, it was then not more than half that which Hléskjöldur led.

Early the second day another battle begins, and by the evening of the second day no more from his army than fifteen hundreds of men still stood. People hold up a peace-shield, and each binds the wounds of their men. Then people notice a great and ornamented dragon-ship sailing with an enormous number of other ships, which now sail from the sea and steer with their sails along one side of the island. A man leaves the dragon-ship, and all the troops go up on land with an assembled force. He was stout, and so tall that his head was above the whole army. He let his gold-woven standard rage against King Soldán, and Hléskjöldur against Logi. Now they start on the third and hardest of their battles.

The kings Livorius and Soldán begin their single combat, with great blows and violent combat. This battle goes on until night. At the end of their exchange he laid a halberd into King Soldán's breast so that it came out through the shoulders. He then fell down dead. Livorius now searches for Hléskjöldur, who then lay in a dale, wounded near to death, and Logi lay dead next to him. Livorius picks up Hléskjöldur and carries him down to the ships. The king now orders to search for the slain. A truce was given to those who asked for it, and all the others were killed.

Livorius now takes great booty there and becomes famous far and wide throughout the lands on account of this battle. Then they sail home to India with fair victory. It is said that the king himself sat over and healed Hléskjöldur until he was well. And one day, when spring came, the king went on a sea-voyage with Hléskjöldur. He said then, 'It would be more befitting to the maiden-king and her kingdom for me to do otherwise than to keep you here any longer. Here in my harbour are ten ships, which I want give to you with men and war-gear; you shall not journey from here as a vagrant'.

Hléskjöldur now praises him, thanking the king for his hospitality and great gifts. He sails home to France, and the maiden-king becomes very joyful at his homecoming.

That summer King Livorius goes plundering and arrives with his ships at Småland. The queen who ruled there was called Alduria; she was King

Livorius's aunt. The queen took him by both hands and he sits there at a handsome feast.

One day the queen says to her kinsman, 'What causes your unhappiness? Do you long for the maiden-king who now is the most famous in the world?' Livorius said, 'you are considered a wise and cunning woman. Give me counsel that I might out-play the maiden-king and obtain her love'.

The queen said, 'I want to give you everything so that you might obtain your joy in accordance with your wish. Now, it is my counsel that you sail this summer to France and call yourself Eskilvarður, son of the king of the Alps, and stay there over the winter. I will give you gold, so that nobody will know you, neither the maiden-king nor your sister. If you remain there for the whole winter, it will be a wonder if you do not get a hold on her'.

Now Livorius accepts this counsel and prepares his fifteen ships, sails from that place, and comes to France in the autumn. The maiden-king now has him invited into the hall to speak with her – she judges him a wise man. The queen asks Eskilvarður to remain there throughout the winter with his retinue. King Eskilvarður accepts, and always comes to the queen because he was skilled at striking the harp and all musical instruments, and he could say something about every land. The queen took the greatest delight in his company.

Now winter passes, and in spring he prepares himself for a journey. A certain day before he was ready, the maiden-king says to him, 'You, Eskil-varður, have always entertained Lady Sýjalín and me during the winter with your music-making and wonderful stories. Now I want you to come with us today: we shall now entertain you'.

Eskilvarður accepts the invitation readily, and goes with them into the chamber. The maiden-king took up a stone and asked him to look in it. Then he saw over all France, Provence, Ravenna, Spain, Galicia, Frisia, Flanders, Normandy, Scotland, Greece, and all the peoples who live there. The maiden-king said, 'King Liforinus is not sailing in these parts of the world; might he be at home instead?'

Another day the queen invites Eskilvarður to the chamber: 'You have always entertained us in the winter'. The queen asked Eskilvarður to look into the stone. Then they saw all the northern region, Norway, Iceland, the Faeroes, the Hebrides, the Orkneys, Sweden, Denmark, England, Ireland, and many other lands, which he did not know of. The queen said, 'Will King Livorius the Famous not sail into these lands?' Eskilvarður said, 'He is far from these lands'.

The maiden-king lifts up a stone, seeing then the eastern region of the world, India, Palestine, Asia, *Serkland*, and all other lands in the world, and also the burning-belt, which is uninhabited. The queen said, 'There are now great battles in Serkland, and King Ingi is sitting at home in Constantinople and is not out raiding, but where must Livorius the Famous be? I do not see him at home in India, and he is not in Småland with his kinswoman. Now we are seeing all the oceans lying around hidden coves; neither is he there nor is he anywhere in the whole world, unless he might be standing here beside me'. Then the maiden-king speaks, 'King Livorius', she says, 'remove your cloak of disguise. The first day when you came I knew you. Take off Alduria's gold, because it will do you no good to continue in this way any longer'.

King Livorius now obeys the queen's words, removing from himself both gold ring and name, and taking up his noble clothing. Lady Sýjalín goes now to her brother, and there is the most joyful reunion between them. The maiden-king sets King Livorius in the highseat beside her, and there is an excellent feast.

So it is said that the maiden-king had sent word to all the regions of the land, to twenty kings, who all served under her power. King Livorius then begins his marriage proposal to the maiden-king with fair words and great reason; all the kings and nobles at this counsel support his speech, agreeing that this proposal should be taken. The maiden-king answers their words: 'I have heard that the nobles of the land are growing tired of war and unrest in the kingdom. The most likely way to forestall that is to accept the king who seems to you to be of great promise'.

Hléskjöldur said, 'If you want me to offer my service any longer, then I want you to take King Livorius as your lord; indeed I shall not accept any other repayment, or remain any longer in your kingdom'. The maiden-king says, 'I have great honour to repay you, for the many dangers and trials which you have undertaken for my sake. It is most fitting that I should take this up, especially since it is the counsel and desire of all the nobles, for I do not know a more exalted king ruling than King Livorius'.

King Livorius is delighted at this. This was now firmly arranged, and agreed with all the kingdom's councillors; the wedding should be in the autumn. The maiden-king then says to Livorius and other people: 'I do not want you to journey away at once from my presence, because I believe that we will not be able to remain at peace for very long'.

Now it is said of King Ingi, that he learns of these tidings; he becomes angry and says that he would have no woman except the maiden-king, and would otherwise lie dead. He now summons all his kingdom to war, and collects together a crowd and mob; everyone had to come there who could bear arms. Countless troops arrive, so that the sea seemed black with warships. King Ingi eagerly and angrily directs all these fleets to France, because he wanted to arrive before the wedding might be over.

Now when King Ingi had reached land, he commands that tents be pitched. King Livorius rides at once down to the ships, offering King Ingi all honour and a settlement on behalf of the maiden-king, which, however, King Ingi does not desire: he wants nothing other than to fight. Now the armies descend on one another. King Livorius raises his banner against King Ingi. Now a hard battle began, with great din and slaughter. King Ingi goes through the army of the French, hewing two men with each blow. King Livorius does the same, but wherever he goes more slaughter appears in the army of the Byzantine king. There is great slaughter to each of the two armies, and all the fields were thatched with dead people's bodies.

This assault goes on for three days, and early on the fourth day King Livorius calls with a loud voice to King Ingi, 'It is an unwise move to fight like this, because we are losing our dearest kinsmen, friends, and nobles here. It is better counsel that the two of us fight each other: let the one who gains the upper hand in our exchange win the maiden-king'.

King Ingi agrees to this gladly, and they begin their single combat with great blows and strong assaults. They break each other's shields; both also were wounded, though King Ingi was more so. Their single combat thus ended as King Ingi fell to the ground from exhaustion and bleeding, for he was coming to pieces from his wounds. King Livorius makes King Ingi lie in a splendid bed, and he lies in another, and they now begin to anoint their wounds with precious salves.

Livorius asks his sister to lay her gentle hands on King Ingi's wounds. She does her brother's bidding, because she was the most excellent physician and she knew more about this than the maiden-king. The king's wounds then begin to heal, and King Ingi sees that Sýjalín surpassed other women throughout all the northern lands, excepting the maiden-king. He soon cast loving eyes on her and he brought up his proposal of marriage with the princess. The maiden-king and all of the land's courtiers agreed that this proposal should be accepted, so that all the kingdoms should receive peace and harmony, and King Ingi and King Livorius were reconciled.

The king said then to King Ingi, 'Should you want to marry Listalín to Hléskjöldur, my good friend and foster brother, then this proposal would be accepted: he is the sole heir with respect to the inheritance and the kingdom out in Apulia after his mother Egidía; and in addition I will give them a third of India – though he is worthy of more'.

Now the maiden-king and all the kingdoms' nobles go with these messages, and with their request and fine proposal; they succeeded fully in both these things. Word is now sent to Lady Listalín; after a little while she comes to France with a splendid entourage. Now they hold these three weddings at the beginning of the month of August and they last the whole month, with great worldly ceremony and glory. There was excellent dining and exquisite drinking, with all kinds of dishes, and the most expensive drinks. There were all kinds of entertainment, consisting of bohourt and musical concerts, and wherever the kings walked were spread down costly fabric, and cloth of purple, and valuable raiment. And it is also not easily said with an unlearned tongue in the outer regions of the world, so that it might be entertaining for people, what joy might be in the middle of the world when such courtiers come together. So the celebration now continues in this great worldly gladness, with costly provisions. And now because all of this world's splendour can quickly pass away, the wedding then was over, and the nobles are led out with wonderful gifts in gold and jewels and good woven cloth. There each of the courtiers parted peacefully and lovingly.

King Ingi and his lady sail to Constantinople, and Hléskjöldur and Listalín out to Apulia, ruling the kingdom there until death. Livorius and the maiden-king ruled France. They had handsome children, including a son who is called Ríkon after his mother's father, who later ruled France with honour and glory. And so ends the adventure of Nítíða the Famous and King Livorius.

Bibliography

I have alphabetized the names of Icelanders by first name and following the alphabets of Icelandic and other Scandinavian languages, according to the conventions of Old Norse–Icelandic scholarship. Names beginning with Å or Þ, for example, appear after Z, and accented vowels follow unaccented vowels.

Manuscripts

Baltimore, MD, The Johns Hopkins University Library
    Nikulás Ottenson Collection of Icelandic Manuscripts MS 100, Nr. 17
Copenhagen, Den Arnamagnæanske Samling
    MS Rask 32
Copenhagen, Det Kongelige Bibliotek
    MS Nks 331 8vo
    MS Nks 1804 4to
Ithaca, NY, Cornell University Library,
    Fiske Icelandic Collection MS Ic F75 A125
London, The British Library
    MS Add. 4860 fol.
Reykjavík, Landsbókasafn Íslands–Háskólabókasafn
    MS ÍB 116 4to
    MS ÍB 138 4to
    MS ÍB 277 4to
    MS ÍB 312 4to
    MS ÍB 132 8vo
    MS ÍB 201 8vo
    MS ÍB 233 8vo
    MS ÍB 290 8vo
    MS ÍBR 47 4to
    MS ÍBR 59 4to
    MS JS 27 fol.
    MS JS 166 fol.
    MS JS 56 4to
    MS JS 625 4to
    MS JS 628 4to
    MS JS 632 4to
    MS Lbs 644 4to
    MS Lbs 998 4to
    MS Lbs 1172 4to
    MS Lbs 1510 4to
    MS Lbs 2148 4to
    MS Lbs 2152 4to
    MS Lbs 2918 4to

MS Lbs 2929 4to
MS Lbs 3128 4to
MS Lbs 3165 4to
MS Lbs 3966 4to
MS Lbs 4492 4to
MS Lbs 4493 4to
MS Lbs 4656 4to
MS Lbs 1137 8vo
MS Lbs 1305 8vo
MS Lbs 1319 8vo
MS Lbs 1711 8vo
MS Lbs 2405 8vo
MS Lbs 2406 8vo
MS Lbs 2780 8vo
MS Lbs 2786 8vo
MS Lbs 3510 8vo
MS Lbs 3675 8vo
MS Lbs 3941 8vo

Reykjavík, Stofnun Árna Magnússonar í íslenskum fræðum
MS AM 529 4to
MS AM 537 4to
MS AM 567 XI β 4to
MS AM 568 4to
MS AM 576 c 4to
MS AM 582 4to
MS AM 589 f 4to
MS SÁM 13
MS SÁM 66

Stockholm, Kungliga biblioteket–Sveriges nationalbiblioteket
MS Pergaments-Handskrifter, 8vo nr. 10 VII
MS Pappers-Handskrifter, fol. nr. 1
MS Pappers-Handskrifter, 4to nr. 31

Uppsala, Universitetsbiblioteket
MS De La Gardie 4-7 fol.

Printed Works: Primary

'Adonias saga', in *Late Medieval Icelandic Romances*, ed. by Agnete Loth, 5 vols., Editiones Arnamagnæanæ, B20-24 (Copenhagen: Munksgaard, 1962-65), III (1963), 66-230

Árni Magnússon and Páll Vídalín, *Jarðabók Árna Magnússonar og Páls Vídalíns*, 2nd ed., 13 vols. (Reykjavík: Hið íslenska fræðafélag í Kaupmannahöfn, 1980-1990), VII: *Ísafjarðar- og Strandasýsla* (1984)

Clári saga, ed. by Gustaf Cederschiöld, Altnordische Saga-Bibliothek, 12 (Halle a.S.: Niemeyer, 1907)

Cook, Robert and Matthias Tveitane, eds., *Strengleikar: An Old Norse Translation of Twenty-One Old French lais*, Norrøne tekster, 3 (Oslo: Norsk historisk kjeldeskrift-institutt, 1979)

Diplomatarium Islandicum: Íslenzkt fornbréfasafn, ed. by Jón Sigurðsson and others, 16 vols.
    (Copenhagen and Reykjavík: Hið Íslenzka Bókmenntafélag, 1857-1972)
Dínus saga dramblása, ed. by Jónas Kristjánsson, Riddarasögur, 1 (Reykjavík: Háskóli Íslands, 1960)
Flóres saga ok Blankiflur, ed. by Eugen Kölbing, Altnordische Saga-Bibliothek, 5 (Halle a.S.:
    Niemeyer, 1896)
Gering, Hugo, ed., *Íslendzk ævintýri: Isländische Legenden, Novellen und Märchen,* 2 vols. (Halle
    a.S.: Buchhandlungen des Waisenhauses, 1882-83)
Gibbons saga, ed. by R.I. Page, Editiones Arnamagnæanæ, B2 (Copenhagen: Munksgaard, 1960)
Grønlie, Siân, trans., *Íslendingabók; Kristni saga: The Book of the Icelanders; The Story of the
    Conversion* (London: Viking Society for Northern Research, 2006)
'Guðmundar biskups saga', in *Biskupa sögur,* ed. by Jón Sigurðsson, Gubrandur Vigfússon and
    others, 2 vols. (Copenhagen: Hið íslenzka bókmenntafélag, 1858-78), II (1878), 3-187
Hall, Alaric, Steven D.P. Richardson, and Haukur Þorgeirsson, '*Sigrgarðs saga frækna:* A Normal-
    ised Text, Translation, and Introduction', *Scandinavian-Canadian Studies,* 21 (2012-13), 80-155
Hall, Alaric and others, '*Sigurðar saga fóts* (The Saga of Sigurðr Foot): A Translation', *Mirator,*
    11 (2010), 56-91
Hermann Pálsson and Paul Edwards, trans., *Seven Viking Romances* (London: Penguin, 1985)
'Hungrvaka', in *Byskupa sǫgur,* ed. by Jón Helgason, Part 1 (Copenhagen: Munksgaard for Det
    Kongelige Nordiske Oldskriftselskab, 1938), 25-115
Isidore of Seville, *The Etymologies of Isidore of Seville,* trans. by Stephen A. Barney and others
    (Cambridge: Cambridge University Press, 2006)
—, *Isidori Hispalensis episcopi etymologiarum sive originum libri XX,* ed. by W.M. Lindsay, 2 vols.
    (Oxford: Clarendon Press, 1911)
—, *Traité de la nature [De natura rerum],* ed. by Jacques Fontaine, Bibliothèque de l'École des
    hautes études hispaniques, 28 (Bordeaux: Féret, 1960)
'Jarlmanns saga ok Hermanns', in *Late Medieval Icelandic Romances,* ed. by Agnete Loth, 5 vols.,
    Editiones Arnamagnæanæ, B20-24 (Copenhagen: Munksgaard, 1962-65), III (1963), 1-66
Jarlmanns saga ok Hermanns i yngre handskrifters redaction, ed. by Hugo Rydberg (Copenhagen:
    Møller, 1917)
Johannes de Hauvilla, *Architrenius,* ed. and trans. by Winthrop Wetherbee, Cambridge Medieval
    Classics, 3 (Cambridge: Cambridge University Press, 1994)
Jón Ólafsson, *The Life of the Icelander Jón Ólafsson Traveller to India,* trans. by Bertha Phillpotts,
    Hakluyt Society, 2.53, 2.68, 2 vols. (London: Cambridge University Press, 1923-31)
Kalinke, Marianne E., ed., *Norse Romance I: The Tristan Legend* (Cambridge: Brewer, 1999)
—, *Norse Romance II: Knights of the Round Table* (Cambridge: Brewer, 1999)
—, *Norse Romance III: Hærra Ivan* (Cambridge: Brewer, 1999)
'Katerine saga', in *Heilagra Manna Søgur: Fortællinger og Legender om hellige Mænd og Kvinder,*
    ed. by C.R. Unger, 2 vols. (Christiania [Oslo]: Bentzen, 1877), I, 400-21
Kölbing, Eugen, ed., *Elis saga ok Rosamundu: mit Einleitung, deutscher Übersetzung und An-
    merkungen* (Heilbronn: Henninger, 1881; Rpt. Niederwalluf bei Wiesbaden: Sändig, 1971)
Kålund, Kristian, ed., *Alfræði íslenzk: Islandsk encyklopædisk litteratur,* 3 vols., Samfund til
    udgivelse af gammel nordisk litteratur, 37, 41, 45 (Copenhagen: Møller, 1908-18)
Macrobius, Ambrosius Aurelius Theodosius, *Commentary on the Dream of Scipio,* trans. by
    William Harris Stahl, Records of Civilization, Sources and Studies, 48 (New York: Columbia
    University Press, 1990)
Mandeville's Travels: Texts and Translations, ed. by Malcolm Letts, 2 vols., Hakluyt Society,
    Second Series 101-102 (London: Hakluyt Society, 1953), 1: 1-223

'Marthe saga ok Marie Magdalene', in *Heilagra Manna Søgur: Fortællinger og Legender om hellige Mænd og Kvinder*, ed. by C.R. Unger, 2 vols. (Christiania [Oslo]: Bentzen, 1877), I, 513-53

'Martinus saga Byskups III', in *Heilagra Manna Søgur: Fortællinger og Legender om hellige Mænd og Kvinder*, ed. by C.R. Unger, 2 vols. (Christiania [Oslo]: Bentzen, 1877), I, 607-642

McDonald, Sheryl, '*Nítíða saga*: A Normalised Icelandic Text and Translation', *Leeds Studies in English*, 40 (2009), 119-44

'Michaels saga', in *Heilagra Manna Søgur: Fortællinger og Legender om hellige Mænd og Kvinder*, ed. by C.R. Unger, 2 vols. (Christiania [Oslo]: Bentzen, 1877), I, 676-713

Moseley, C.W.R.D., trans., *The Travels of Sir John Mandeville*, Rev. ed. (London: Penguin, 2005)

'Nikolaus saga II', in *Heilagra Manna Søgur: Fortællinger og Legender om hellige Mænd og Kvinder*, ed. by C.R. Unger, 2 vols. (Christiania [Oslo]: Bentzen, 1877), II, 49-158

Nikulás saga leikara (Winnipeg: Prentfjelag Heimskringlu, 1889)

'Nitida saga', in *Late Medieval Icelandic Romances*, ed. by Agnete Loth, 5 vols., Editiones Arnamagnæanæ, B20-24 (Copenhagen: Munksgaard, 1962-65), V (1965), 1-37

O'Connor, Ralph, trans., *Icelandic Histories and Romances* (Stroud: Tempus, 2002)

Orkneyinga saga, ed. by Finnbogi Guðmundsson, Íslenzk fornrit, 34 (Reykjavík: Hið Íslenzka Fornritaféla, 1965)

'Ólafs saga Tryggvasonar', in *Flateyjarbok: En samling af norske konge-sagaer med indskudte mindre fortællinger om begivenheder i og uden for Norge samt annaler*, ed. by Guðbrandur Vigfusson and C.R. Unger, 3 vols. (Christiania [Oslo]: Malling, 1860-68), I (1860), 39-583

Partalopa saga, ed. by Lise Præstgaard Andersen, Editiones Arnamagnæanæ, B28 (Copenhagen: Reitzel, 1983)

Polo, Marco, *The Travels*, trans. by R.E. Latham (London: Penguin, 1958)

Rémundar saga keisarasonar, ed. by Sven Grén Broberg, Samfund til udgivelse af gammel nordisk litteratur, 38 (Copenhagen: Møller, 1909-12)

The Saga of the Jomsvikings, ed. and trans. by N.F. Blake, Nelsons Icelandic Texts, (Edinburgh: Nelson, 1962)

The Saga of Tristram and Ísönd, ed. by Paul Schach (Lincoln: University of Nebraska Press, 1973)

Sagan af Hèðni og Hlöðvi, ed. by Jónas Jónsson and Stefán Egilsson (Reykjavík: Einar Þórðarson, 1878)

Sagan af Nikulási konungi leikara (Reykjavík: Helgi Árnason, 1912)

Samsons saga fagra, ed. by John Wilson, Samfund til udgivelse af gammel nordisk litteratur 65.1 (Copenhagen: Møller, 1953)

Sanders, Christopher, ed., *Tales of Knights: Perg. fol. nr 7 in The Royal Library, Stockholm (AM 167 VI β 4to, NKS 1265 IIc fol.)*, Manuscripta Nordica: Early Nordic Manuscripts in Digital Facsimile, 1 (Copenhagen: Reitzel, 2000)

'Sigrgarðs saga frœkna', in *Late Medieval Icelandic Romances*, ed. by Agnete Loth, 5 vols., Editiones Arnamagnæanæ, B20-24 (Copenhagen: Munksgaard, 1962-65), V (1965), 39-107

Sigurðar saga þögla: The Shorter Redaction, ed. by Matthew Driscoll, Rit, 34 (Reykjavík: Stofnun Árna Magnússonar á Íslandi, 1992)

'Sigurðar saga þǫgla', in *Late Medieval Icelandic Romances*, ed. by Agnete Loth, 5 vols., Editiones Arnamagnæanæ, B20-24 (Copenhagen: Munksgaard, 1962-65), II (1963), 93-259

Snorri Sturluson, *Edda: Prologue and Gylfaginning*, ed. by Anthony Faulkes (London: Viking Society for Northern Research, 2005)

Spaulding, Janet Ardis, '*Sigurðar saga turnara*: A Literary Edition' (unpublished PhD dissertation: University of Michigan, 1982)

Sverris saga, ed. by Þorleifur Hauksson, Íslenzk fornrit, 30 (Reykjavík: Hið Íslenzka Fornritafélag, 2007)

Unger, C.R., ed., *Mariu saga: Legender om jomfru Maria og hendes jertegn* (Christiania [Oslo]: Brögger & Christie, 1871)
—, ed., *Stjórn: Gammelnorsk bibelhistorie fra verdens skabelse til det babyloniske fangenskab* (Christiania [Oslo]: Feilberg & Landmark, 1862)
Viktors saga ok Blávus, ed. by Jónas Kristjánsson, Riddarasögur, 2 (Reykjavík: Handritastofnun Íslands, 1964)
'Vilhjálms saga sjóðs', in *Late Medieval Icelandic Romances*, ed. by Agnete Loth, 5 vols., Editiones Arnamagnæanæ, B20-24 (Copenhagen: Munksgaard, 1962-65), IV (1964), 1-136
Virgil, *Eclogues, Georgics, Aeneid*, trans. by H.R. Fairclough, revd. by G.P. Goold, 2 vols., Loeb Classical Library, 63-64 (Cambridge, MA: Harvard University Press, 1999)
Wick, Keren H., 'An Edition and Study of Nikulás saga Leikara' (unpublished PhD thesis, University of Leeds, 1996)

Printed Works: Secondary

Agnes S. Arnórsdóttir, *Property and Virginity: The Christianization of Marriage in Medieval Icelandic 1200-1600* (Aarhus: Aarhus University Press, 2010)
Akbari, Suzanne Conklin, 'From Due East to True North: Orientalism and Orientation', in *The Postcolonial Middle Ages*, ed. by Jeffrey Jerome Cohen (New York: Palgrave, 2001), pp. 19-34
Amory, Frederic, 'Things Greek and the *riddararsögur*', *Speculum: A Journal of Medieval Studies*, 59 (1984), 509-23
Andersson, Theodore M., *The Icelandic Family Saga: An Analytic Reading* (Cambridge, MA: Harvard University Press, 1967)
Andrews, A. Le Roy, 'The Lygisögur', *Scandinavian Studies*, 2 (1914-16), 255-63
Ármann Jakobsson, 'Enabling Love: Dwarfs in Old Norse-Icelandic Romances', in *Romance and Love in Late Medieval and Early Modern Iceland: Essays in Honor of Marianne Kalinke*, ed. by Kirsten Wolf and Johanna Denzin, Islandica, 54 (London: Cornell University Press, 2009), pp. 183-206
—, *Illa fenginn mjöður: lesið í miðaldatexta* (Reykjavík: Háskólaútgáfan, 2009)

Bagerius, Henric, *Mandom och mödom: Sexualitet, homosocialitet och aristokratisk identitet på det senmedeltida Island*, Avhandling frå Institutionen för historiska studier (Göteborg: Göteborgs Universitet, 2009)
Bandlien, Bjørn, 'Muslims in *Karlamagnúss saga* and *Elíss saga ok Rósamundar*', in *'Á austrvega': Saga and East Scandinavia*, Preprint Papers of the Fourteenth International Saga Conference, Uppsala, 9-15 August 2009, ed. by Agnete Ney, Henrik Williams, and Fredrik Charpentier Ljungqvist, 2 vols. (Gävle: Gävle University Press, 2009), I, 85-91
Barnes, Geraldine, *The Bookish Riddarasögur: Writing Romance in Late Mediaeval Iceland*, The Viking Collection, 21 (Odense: Syddansk Universitetsforlag, 2014)
—, 'Cognitive Dysfunction in *Dínus saga dramblata* and *Le Roman de Perceval*', *Arthuriana*, 22 (2012), 53-63
—, 'Byzantium in the Riddarasögur', in *'Á austrvega': Saga and East Scandinavia*, Preprint Papers of the Fourteenth International Saga Conference, Uppsala, 9-15 August 2009, ed. by Agnete Ney, Henrik Williams, and Fredrik Charpentier Ljungqvist, 2 vols. (Gävle: Gävle University Press, 2009), I, 92-98

—, 'Travel and *translatio studii* in the Icelandic riddarasögur', in *Übersetzen im skandinavischen Mittelalter*, ed. by Vera Johanterwage and Stephanie Würth, Studia Medievalia Septentrionalia, 14 (Vienna: Fassbaender, 2007), pp. 123-39

—, 'Margin vs. Centre: Geopolitics in Nitida saga (A Cosmographical Comedy?)', in *The Fantastic in Old Norse/Icelandic Literature: Sagas and the British Isles*, Preprint Papers of the Thirteenth International Saga Conference, Durham and York, 6-12 August 2006, ed. by John McKinnell, David Ashurst, and Donata Kick, 2 vols. (Durham: Centre for Medieval and Renaissance Studies, 2006), I, 104-12

—, 'Romance in Iceland', in *Old Icelandic Literature and Society*, ed. by Margaret Clunies Ross (Cambridge: Cambridge University Press, 2000), pp. 266-86

—, 'Authors, Dead and Alive, in Old Norse Fiction', *Parergon: Bulletin of the Australian and New Zealand Association for Medieval and Renaissance Studies*, 8 (1990), 5-22

—, 'Some Current Issues in Riddararsögur-Research', *Arkiv för nordisk Filologi*, 104 (1989), 73-88

—, 'The *riddarasögur* and Mediæval European Literature', *Mediaeval Scandinavia: A Journal Devoted to the Study of Mediaeval Civilization in Scandinavia and Iceland*, 8 (1975), 140-58

—, 'The *Riddarasögur*: A Medieval Exercise in Translation', *Saga-Book of the Viking Society for Northern Research*, 19 (1977), 403-41

Benkov, Edith, 'The Erased Lesbian: Sodomy and the Legal Tradition in Medieval Europe', in *Same Sex Love and Desire among Women in the Middle Ages*, ed. by Francesca Canadé Sautman and Pamela Sheingorn, The New Middle Ages (New York: Palgrave Macmillan, 2001), pp. 101-22

Baswell, Christopher, *Virgil in Medieval England: Figuring the 'Aeneid' from the Twelfth Century to Chaucer* (Cambridge: Cambridge University Press, 1995)

Bettelheim, Bruno, *The Uses of Enchantment: The Meaning and Importance of Fairy Tales* (New York: Knopf, 1976)

Bibire, Paul, 'From *riddarasaga* to *lygisaga*: The Norse Response to Romance', in *Les Sagas des Chevaliers (Riddarasögur): Actes de la 5ième Conférence Internationale sur les Sagas (Toulon, Juillet 1982)*, ed. by Régis Boyer (Paris: Presses de l'Université de Paris-Sorbonne, 1985), pp. 55-74

Bidard, Josseline, 'Reynard the Fox as Anti-Hero', in *Heroes and Heroines in Medieval English Literature: A Festschrift Presented to André Crépin on the Occasion of his Sixty-Fifth Birthday*, ed. by Leo Carruthers (Cambridge: Brewer, 1994), pp. 119-23

Björn Lárusson, *The Old Icelandic Land Registers*, trans. by W.F. Salisbury, Ekonomisk-Historiska Föreningen i Lund, 7 (Lund: Gleerup, 1967)

Blaisdell, Foster W., Jr., 'The Value of the Valueless: A Problem in Editing Medieval Texts', *Scandinavian Studies*, 39 (1967), 40-46

—, 'Some Observations on Style in the *riddarasögur*', in *Scandinavian Studies: Essays Presented to Dr. Henry Goddard Leach on the Occasion of His Eighty-Fifth Birthday*, ed by Carl F. Bayerschmidt and Erik J. Friis (Seattle: University of Washington Press, 1965), pp. 87-94

Boberg, Inger M., *Motif-Index of Early Icelandic Literature*, Bibliotheca Arnamagnæana, 27 (Copenhagen: Munksgaard, 1966)

Bornholdt, Claudia, *Engaging Moments: The Origins of Medieval Bridal-Quest Narrative* (Berlin: de Gruyter, 2005)

Boucher, Alan, 'The Hero in Old Icelandic Literature', *Atlantica and Iceland Review*, 8 (1970), 41-45

Braunmüller, Kurt, 'Language Contacts in the Late Middle Ages and in Early Modern Times', in *The Nordic Languages: An International Handbook of the History of the North Germanic Languages*, ed. by Oskar Bandle, and others, 2 vols., Handbücher zur Sprach- und Kommunikationswissenschaft, 22 (Berlin: de Gruyter, 2002-05), II (2005), 1222-33

Brewer, Derek, *Symbolic Stories: Traditional Narratives of the Family Drama in English Literature* (Woodbridge: Brewer, 1980)

The British Library, *Catalogue of Additions to the Manuscripts, 1756-1782: Additional Manuscripts 4101-5017* (London: Trustees of the British Museum, 1977)

—, *Catalogue of Additions to the Manuscripts in the British Museum in the Years MDCCCLIV-MDCCCLXXV: Additional Manuscripts 24,027-29,909*, 2 vols. (London: Trustees of the British Museum, 1877)

Brooten, Bernadette J., *Love Between Women: Early Christian Responses to Female Homoeroticism* (Chicago: University of Chicago Press, 1996)

Canadé Sautman, Francesca, 'What can they Possibly do Together?: Queer Epic Performance in *Tristan de Nanteuil*', in *Same Sex Love and Desire among Women in the Middle Ages*, ed. by Francesca Canadé Sautman and Pamela Sheingorn, The New Middle Ages (New York: Palgrave Macmillan, 2001), pp. 199-232

Cerquiglini, Bernard, *In Praise of the Variant: A Critical History of Philology*, trans. by Betsy Wing (Baltimore: Johns Hopkins University Press, 1999)

Cisne, John Luther, 'How Science Survived: Medieval Manuscrips' "Demography" and Classic Texts' Extinction', *Science*, 307 (2005), 1305-07

Clark, Robert L.A., 'Jousting without a Lance: The Condemnation of Female Homoeroticism in the *Livre des manières*', in *Same Sex Love and Desire among Women in the Middle Ages*, ed. by Francesca Canadé Sautman and Pamela Sheingorn, The New Middle Ages (New York: Palgrave Macmillan, 2001), pp. 143-77

Clunies Ross, Margaret, 'Land-Taking and Text-Making in Medieval Iceland', in *Text and Territory: Geographical Imagination in the European Middle Ages*, ed. by Sylvia Tomasch and Sealy Gilles (Philadelphia: University of Pennsylvania Press, 1998), pp. 159-84

Comparetti, Domenico, *Virgil in the Middle Ages*, trans. by E.F.M. Benecke (London: Swan Sonneschein, 1895)

Curtius, Ernst Robert, *European Literature and the Latin Middle Ages,* trans. by Willard R. Trask, Bollinger Series, 36 (Princeton: Princeton University Press, 2013)

Dalrymple, Roger, *Language and Piety in Middle English Romance* (Cambridge: Brewer, 2000)

Daniel, Norman, *Heroes and Saracens: An Interpretation of the Chansons de geste* (Edinburgh: Edinburgh University Press, 1984)

Davíð Ólafsson, 'Wordmongers: Post-Medieval Scribal Culture and the Case of Sighvatur Grímsson' (unpublished PhD thesis: University of St Andrews, 2009) <http://hdl.handle.net/10023/770>

de Weever, Jacqueline, *Sheba's Daughters: Whitening and Demonizing the Saracen Woman in Medieval French Epic* (London: Garland, 1998)

Divjak, Alenka, *Studies in the Traditions of Kirialax Saga* (Ljubljana: Inštitut Nove revije, zavod za humanistiko, 2009)

Dragonetti, Roger, *Le mirage des sources: l'art du faux dans le roman médiéval* (Paris: Seuil, 1987)

Driscoll, Matthew, '"Um gildi gamalla bóka": Magnús Jónsson í Tjaldanesi und das Ende der isländischen Handschriftenkultur', in *Text – Reihe – Transmission: Unfestigkeit als Phänomen skandinavischer Erzählprosa 1500-1800*, Beiträge zur Nordischen Philologie, 42 (Tübingen: Francke, 2012), pp. 255-82

—, 'What's Truth Got to Do with It: Views on the Historicity of the Sagas', in *Skemmtiligastar lygisögur: Studies in Honour of Galina Glazyrina*, ed. by Tatjana N. Jackson and Elena A. Melnikova (Moscow: Dimitriy Pozharskiy University, 2012), pp. 15-27

—, 'The Words on the Page: Thoughts on Philology, Old and New', in *Creating the Medieval saga: Versions, Variability, and Editorial Interpretations of Old Norse Saga Literature*, ed. by Judy

Quinn and Emily Lethbridge, The Viking Collection, 18 (Odense: Syddansk Universitetsforlag, 2010), pp. 85-102

—, 'Editing the *Fornaldarsögur Norðurlanda*', in *'Á austrvega': Saga and East Scandinavia*, Preprint Papers of the Fourteenth International Saga Conference, Uppsala, 9-15 August 2009, ed. by Agnete Ney, Henrik Williams, and Fredrik Charpentier Ljungqvist, 2 vols. (Gävle: Gävle University Press, 2009), I, 207-12

—, 'Late Prose Fiction (*lygisögur*)', in *A Companion to Old Norse–Icelandic Literature and Culture*, ed. by Rory McTurk, 2nd edn. (Oxford: Blackwell, 2007), pp. 190-204

—, 'In Praise of Strong Women', in *Frejas Psalter: En psalter i 40 afdelinger til brug for Jonna Louis-Jensen*, ed. by Bergljót S. Kristjánsdóttir and Peter Springborg (Copenhagen: Det arnamagnæanke Institut, 1997), pp. 29-33

—, 'The Oral, the Written, and the In-Between: Textual Instability in the Post-Reformation *Lygisaga*', in *Medieval Insular Literature Between the Oral and the Written, II: Continuity of Transmission*, ed. by Hildegard L.C. Tristram, ScriptOralia, 97 (Tübingen: Narr, 1997), pp. 193-220

—, *The Unwashed Children of Eve: The Production, Dissemination and Reception of Popular Literature in Post-Reformation Iceland* (Enfield Lock: Hisarlik Press, 1997)

—, 'Traditionality and Antiquarianism in the Post-Reformation *Lygisaga*', in *Northern Antiquity: The Post-Medieval Reception of Edda and Saga*, ed. by Andrew Wawn (Enfield Lock: Hisarlik Press, 1994), pp. 84-99

—, '*Nitida saga*', in *Medieval Scandinavia: An Encyclopedia*, ed. by Phillip Pulsiano and others (New York: Garland, 1993), p. 432

—, 'Þögnin mikla: Hugleiðingar um riddarasögur og stöðu þeirra í íslenskum bókmenntum', *Skáldskaparmál*, 1 (1990), 157-68

Eggert Ólafsson and Bjarni Pálsson, *Ferðabók Eggerts Ólafssonar og Bjarni Pálssonar um ferðið þeirra á Íslandi árin 1752-1757*, trans. by Steindór Steindórsson frá Hlöðum, 2nd edn. (Reykjavík: Örn og Örlygur, 1975)

'Einar Guðmundsson Skáleyjum á Breiðafirði úr', on *Handrit.is*, National and University Library of Iceland, 2009-15, <http://handrit.is/en/biography/view/EinGud005> [accessed 30 May 2011]

Einar Ólafur Sveinsson, 'Fact and Fiction in the Sagas', in *Dichtung, Sprache, Gesellschaft: Akten des IV Internationalen Germanisten-Kongress 1970 in Princeton*, ed. by Victor Lang and Hans-Gert Roloff (Frankfurt am Main: Athenäum, 1971), pp. 293-306

—, '*Viktors saga ok Blávus*: Sources and Characteristics', in *Viktors saga ok Blávus*, ed. by Jónas Kristjánsson, Riddarasögur, 2 (Reykjavík: Handritastofnun Íslands, 1964), pp. cix-ccix

Eldevik, Randi, 'Virgil in Medieval Icelandic', in *The Virgilian Tradition: The First Fifteen Hundred Years*, ed. by Jan M. Ziolkowski and Michael C.J. Putnam (New Haven: Yale University Press, 2007), pp. 616-22

Engel, Pál, *The Realm of St Stephen: A History of Medieval Hungary, 895-1526*, trans. by Tamás Pálosfalvi (London: Tauris, 2001)

Finnur Jónsson, *Den oldnorske og oldislandske litteraturs historie*, 2nd edn., 3 vols. (Copenhagen: Gad, 1920-24)

Finnur Sigmundsson, *Rímnatal*, 2 vols. (Reykjavík: Rímnafélagið, 1966)

Fleischman, Suzanne, 'Philology, Linguistics, and the Discourse of the Medieval Text', *Speculum: A Journal of Medieval Studies*, 65 (1990), 19-37

—, 'On the Representation of History and Fiction in the Middle Ages', *History and Theory*, 22 (1983), 278-310

Foote, Peter G., 'Sagnaskemtan: Reykjahólar 1119', in *Aurvandilstá: Norse Studies*, The Viking Collection, 2 (Odense: Syddansk Universitetsforlag, 1984), pp. 65-83

Foucault, Michel, 'Of Other Spaces', trans. by Jay Miskowiec, *Diacritics*, 16 (1986), 22-27

Frederiksen, Britta Olrik, 'Dansksprogede bøger fra middelalderen – i tørre og mindre tørre tal', in *Levende or dog lysende billeder: Den middelalderlige bogkultur i Danmark. Essays*, ed. by Erik Petersen (Copenhagen: Det Kongelige Bibliotek, 1999), pp. 154-62

Frye, Northrop, *Anatomy of Criticism: Four Essays* (Princeton: Princeton University Press, 1957)

Gahrn, Lars, '*Svitjod det stora* och Skytien – ett exempel på norrön tolkning av latinske områdesnamn', *Scandia: Tidskrift för historisk forskning*, 68 (2002), 5-22

Ginzburg, Carlo, 'Microhistory: Two or Three Things I Know About It', trans. by John Tedeschi and Anne C. Tedeschi, *Critical Inquiry*, 20 (1993), 10-35

Gísli Sigurðsson, 'Melsted's Edda: The Last Manuscript Sent Home?', in *The Manuscripts of Iceland*, ed. by Gísli Sigurðsson and Vésteinn Ólason (Rekjavík: Árni Magnússon Institute in Iceland, 2004), pp. 179-84

Glauser, Jürg, 'Romance (Translated *riddarasögur*)', in *A Companion to Old Norse–Icelandic Literature and Culture*, ed. by Rory McTurk, 2nd edn. (Oxford: Blackwell, 2007), pp. 372-87

—, 'The End of the Saga: Text, Tradition and Transmission in Nineteenth- and Early Twentieth-Century Iceland', in *Northern Antiquity: The Post-Medieval Reception of Edda and Saga*, ed. by Andrew Wawn (Enfield Lock: Hisarlik Press, 1994), pp. 101-41

—, 'Lygisaga', in *Medieval Scandinavia: An Encyclopedia*, ed. by Phillip Pulsiano and others (New York: Garland, 1993), p. 398

—, *Isländische Märchensagas: Studien zur Prosaliteratur im spätmitterlalterlichen Island*, Beiträge zur nordischen Philologie, 12 (Basel: Helbing und Lichtenhahn, 1983)

Gödel, Vilhelm, *Katalog öfver Kongl. Bibliotekets fornisländska och fornnorska handskrifter* (Stockholm: Nordstet & Söner, 1897-1900)

Grimal, Pierre, *A Concise Dictionary of Classical Mythology*, ed. by Stephen Kershaw, trans. by A.R. Maxwell-Hyslop (Oxford: Blackwell, 1990)

Gunnar Karlsson, *Iceland's 1100 Years: The History of a Marginal Society* (Reykjavík: Mál og Menning, 2000)

Guðbjörg Aðalbergsdóttir, 'Nítíða og aðrir meykóngar', *Mímir*, 32-33 (1993-94), 49-55

—, 'Nítíða saga: Meykóngur í aðalhlutverki' (unpublished BA thesis: Reykjavík, 1993)

Hall, Alaric, 'Translating the Medieval Icelandic Romance-Sagas', *RMN Newsletter*, 8 (2014), 65-67

—, 'Changing Style and Changing Meaning: Icelandic Historiography and the Medieval Redactions of *Heiðreks saga*', *Scandinavian Studies*, 77 (2005), 1-30

Hall, Alaric and Katelin Parsons, 'Making Stemmas with Small Samples: Testing the Stemma of *Konráðs saga keisarasonar*, and New Media Approaches to Publishing Stemmas', *Digital Medievalist*, 9 (2013) <http://www.digitalmedievalist.org/journal/9/hall/> [accessed 10 February 2014]

Hallberg, Peter, 'Imagery in Religious Old Norse Prose Literature', *Arkiv för nordisk Filologi*, 102 (1987), 120-70

—, 'A Group of Icelandic "Riddarasögur" from the Middle of the Fourteenth Century', in *Les Sagas des Chevaliers (Riddarasögur): Actes de la 5ième Conférence Internationale sur les Sagas (Toulon, Juillet 1982)*, ed. by Régis Boyer (Paris: Presses de l'Université de Paris-Sorbonne, 1985), pp. 8-53

Halldór Hermannsson, *Sir Joseph Banks and Iceland*, Islandica, 18 (London: Cornell University Library, 1928)

Halvorsen, E.F., *The Norse Version of the Chanson de Roland*, Bibliotheca Arnamagnæana, 19 (Copenhagen: Munksgaard, 1959)

Hamilton, Bernard, 'The Lands of Prester John: Western Knowledge of Asia and Africa at the Time of the Crusades', *The Haskins Society Journal: Studies in Medieval History*, 15 (2004), 126-41

Hansen, Anna, 'Crossing the Borders of Fantastic Space: The Relationship Between the Fantastic and the Non-Fantastic in *Valdimars saga*', *Parergon: Bulletin of the Australian and New Zealand Association for Medieval and Renaissance Studies*, 26 (2009), 57-74

Hansen, Anne Mette, 'The Icelandic *Lucidarius*, Traditional and New Philology', in *Old Norse Myths, Literature and Society*, Proceedings of the 11th International Saga Conference 2-7 July 2000, University of Sydney, ed. by Geraldine Barnes and Margaret Clunies Ross (Sydney: Centre for Medieval Studies, 2000), pp. 118-25

Harris, Joseph, 'Saga as Historical Novel', in *"Speak Useful Words or Say Nothing": Old Norse Studies by Joseph Harris*, ed. by Susan E. Deskis and Thomas D. Hill, Islandica, 53 (Ithaca: Cornell University Press, 2008), pp. 227-60

Harrison, Dick, *Medieval Space: The Extent of Microspatial Knowledge in Western Europe During the Middle Ages* (Lund: Lund University Press, 1996)

Hast, Sture, *Pappershandskrifterna till* Harðar saga, Bibliotheca Arnamagnæana, 23 (Copenhagen: Munksgaard, 1960)

Haugen, Odd Einar, 'On the Birth and Death of Medieval Manuscripts', paper presented at the Fifteenth International Saga Conference, Aarhus, Denmark, 10 August 2012

—, 'The Spirit of Lachmann, the Spirit of Bédier: Old Norse Textual Editing in the Electronic Age', Paper Presented at the Annual Meeting of The Viking Society, University College London, 8 November 2002 <http://www.ub.uib.no/elpub/2003/a/522001> [Accessed 18 May 2011]

Helgi Þorláksson, 'Historical Background: Iceland 800-1400', in *A Companion to Old Norse–Icelandic Literature and Culture*, ed. by Rory McTurk, 2nd edn. (Oxford: Blackwell, 2007), pp. 136-54

Heng, Geraldine, *Empire of Magic: Medieval Romance and the Politics of Cultural Fantasy* (New York: Columbia University Press, 2003)

Hermann Pálsson and Paul Edwards, *Legendary Fiction in Medieval Iceland*, Studia Islandica, 30 (Reykjavík: Heimspekideild Háskóla, 1971)

Higgins, Iain Macleod, 'Defining the Earth's Center in a Medieval "Multi-Text": Jerusalem in *The Book of John Mandeville*', in *Text and Territory: Geographical Imagination in the European Middle Ages*, ed. by Sylvia Tomasch and Sealy Gilles (Philadelphia: University of Pennsylvania Press, 1998), pp. 29-53

Hufnagel, Silvia, '*Sörla saga sterka* – Studies in the Transmission of a Fornaldarsaga' (unpublished PhD thesis: University of Copenhagen, 2012)

Hughes, Shaun F.D., '*Klári saga* as an Indigenous Romance', in *Romance and Love in Late Medieval and Early Modern Iceland: Essays in Honor of Marianne Kalinke*, ed. by Kirsten Wolf and Johanna Denzin, Islandica, 54 (London: Cornell University Press, 2009), pp. 135-63

—, 'Late Secular Poetry', in *A Companion to Old Norse–Icelandic Literature and Culture*, ed. by Rory McTurk, 2nd edn. (Oxford: Blackwell, 2007), pp. 205-22

—, 'The Re-emergence of Women's Voices in Icelandic Literature, 1500-1800', in *Cold Counsel: Women in Old Norse Literature and Mythology*, ed. by Sarah M. Anderson (New York: Routledge, 2002), pp. 93-128

—, 'Aspects of Courtly Literature in the Riddarasögur', [*Ball State University*] *Forum*, 29 (1988), 5-20

Hunt, Tony, 'Chrétien de Troyes' Arthurian Romance, *Yvain*', in *The New Pelican Guide to English Literature, Vol. I: Medieval Literature, Part II: The European Inheritance*, ed. by Boris Ford (Harmondsworth: Penguin, 1983), pp. 126-41

Jackson, Tatjana N., '"Scithia er uær köllum miklu Suiþiod": Memory, Fiction, or Something Else?', paper presented at the Fifteenth International Saga Conference, Aarhus, Denmark, 6 August 2012

—, 'Ultima Thule in Western European and Icelandic Traditions', *Northern Studies: The Journal of the Scottish Society for Northern Studies*, 39 (2005), 12-24

Jakob Benediktsson, 'Lygisögur', in *Kulturhistorisk leksikon för nordisk middelalder fra vikingetid til reformationstid*, 11 (1966), col. 18

Jakobsen, Alfred, *Studier i Clarus saga: Til spørsmålet om sagaens norske proveniens* (Bergen: Universitetsforlaget, 1964)

Jakobson, Alfred, 'Geographical Literature', in *Medieval Scandinavia: An Encyclopedia*, ed. by Phillip Pulsiano and others (New York: Garland, 1993), p. 225

Jarring, Gunnar, 'Serkland', *Namn och Bygd: Tidskrift för Nordisk Ortnamnsforskning*, 71 (1983), 125-32

Jesch, Judith, 'Geography and Travel', in *A Companion to Old Norse–Icelandic Literature and Culture*, ed. by Rory McTurk, 2nd edn. (Oxford: Blackwell, 2007), pp. 119-35

Jenny Jochens, 'Old Norse Sexuality: Men, Women, and Beasts', in *Handbook of Medieval Sexuality*, ed. by Vern L. Bullough and James A. Brundage (New York: Routledge, 2010), pp. 369-400

—, 'Before the Male Gaze: The Absence of the Female Body in Old Norse', in *Sex in the Middle Ages: A Book of Essays*, ed. by Joyce E. Salisbury, Garland Medieval Case Books, 3 (New York: Garland, 1991), pp. 3-29

—, 'Old Norse Motherhood', in *Medieval Mothering*, ed. by John Carmi Parsons and Bonnie Wheeler, The New Middle Ages, 3 (New York: Garland, 1996), pp. 201-22

—, 'Consent in Marriage: Old Norse Law, Life, and Literature', *Scandinavian Studies*, 58 (1986), 142-76

Johansen, Jan Geir, 'The Hero of Hrafnkels saga Freysgoða', *Scandinavian Studies*, 67 (1995), 265-86

Johansson, Karl G., 'Bergr Sokkason och Arngrímur Brandsson – översättare och författare i samma miljö', in *Old Norse Myths, Literature and Society*, Proceedings of the 11th International Saga Conference 2-7 July 2000, University of Sydney, ed. by Geraldine Barnes and Margaret Clunies Ross (Sydney: Centre for Medieval Studies, 2000), pp. 181-97

Johanterwage, Vera, 'The Use of Magic Spells and Objects in the Icelandic Riddarasögur: *Rémundar saga keisarasonar* and *Viktors saga ok Blávus*', in *The Fantastic in Old Norse/Icelandic Literature: Sagas and the British Isles*, Preprint Papers of the Thirteenth International Saga Conference, Durham and York, 6-12 August 2006, ed. by John McKinnell, David Ashurst, and Donata Kick, 2 vols. (Durham: Centre for Medieval and Renaissance Studies, 2006), I, 446-53

Jones, Gwyn, 'History and Fiction in the Sagas of Icelanders', *Saga-Book of the Viking Society for Northern Research*, 13 (1946-53), 285-306

Jorgensen, Peter A., 'Rímur', in *Medieval Scandinavia: An Encyclopedia*, ed. by Phillip Pulsiano and others (New York: Garland, 1993), pp. 536-37

—, 'The Neglected Genre of Rímur-Derived Prose and Post-Reformation Jónatas Saga', *Gripla*, 7 (1990), 187-201

Jóhanna Katrín Friðriksdóttir, *Women in Old Norse Literature: Bodies, Words, and Power*, The New Middle Ages (New York: Palgrave Macmillan, 2013)

Jón Johnsen, *Jarðatal á Íslandi, með brauðalýsingum, fólkstölu í hreppum og prestaköllum, ágripi úr búnaðartölflum 1835-1845, og skýrslum um sölu þjóðjarða á landinu* (Copenhagen: Trier, 1847)

Jón Karl Helgason, 'Continuity? The Icelandic Sagas in Post-Medieval Times', in *A Companion to Old Norse–Icelandic Literature and Culture*, ed. by Rory McTurk, 2nd edn. (Oxford: Blackwell, 2007), pp. 64-81

Jónas Kristjánsson, 'The Court Style', in *Les Sagas des Chevaliers (Riddarasögur): Actes de la 5ième Conférence Internationale sur les Sagas (Toulon, Juillet 1982)*, ed. by Régis Boyer (Paris: Presses de l'Université de Paris-Sorbonne, 1985), pp. 431-40

—, 'Hannes Gunnlaugsson braut stafina', in *Afmælisrit til dr. phil. Steingríms J. Þorsteinssonar prófessors 2. júlí 1971 frá nemendum hans*, ed. by Aðalgeir Kristjánsson and others (Reykjavík: Leiftur, 1971), pp. 89-96

Kalinke, Marianne, 'Scribe, Redactor, Author: The Emergence and Evolution of Icelandic Romance', *Viking and Medieval Scandinavia*, 8 (2012), 171-98

—, '*Clári saga*: A Case of Low German Infiltration', *Scripta Islandica*, 59 (2008), 5-25

—, 'Table Decorum and the Quest for a Bride in *Clári saga*', in *At the Table: Metaphorical and Material Cultures of Food in Medieval and Early Modern Europe*, ed. by Timothy J. Tomasik and Juliann M. Vitello, Arizona Studies in the Middle Ages and Renaissance, 18 (Turnhout: Brepols, 2007), pp. 51-72

—, 'The Genesis of Fiction in the North', in *The Fantastic in Old Norse/Icelandic Literature: Sagas and the British Isles*, Preprint Papers of the Thirteenth International Saga Conference, Durham and York, 6-12 August 2006, ed. by John McKinnell, David Ashurst, and Donata Kick, 2 vols. (Durham: Centre for Medieval and Renaissance Studies, 2006), I, 464-78

—, *The Book of Reykjahólar: The Last of the Great Medieval Legendaries* (Toronto: University of Toronto Press, 1996)

—, 'Old Norse-Icelandic Literature, Foreign Influence On', in *Medieval Scandinavia: An Encyclopedia*, ed. by Phillip Pulsiano and others (New York: Garland, 1993), pp. 451-54

—, *Bridal-Quest Romance in Medieval Iceland*, Islandica, 46 (London: Cornell University Press, 1990)

—, 'The Misogamous Maiden Kings of Icelandic Romance', *Scripta Islandica: Isländska sällskapets årsbok*, 37 (1986), 47-71

—, 'Norse Romance (Riddarasögur)', in *Old Norse-Icelandic Literature: A Critical Guide*, ed. by Carol Clover and John Lindow (London: Cornell University Press, 1985), pp. 316-63

—, 'Riddarasögur, Fornaldarsögur, and the Problem of Genre', in *Les Sagas des Chevaliers (Riddarasögur): Actes de la 5ième Conférence Internationale sur les Sagas (Toulon, Juillet 1982)*, ed. by Régis Boyer (Paris: Presses de l'Université de Paris-Sorbonne, 1985), pp. 77-91

—, 'The Foreign Language Requirement in Medieval Icelandic Romance', *The Modern Language Review*, 88 (1983), 850-61

—, 'Scribes, Editors, and the *Riddarasögur*', *Arkiv för nordisk Filologi*, 97 (1982), 36-51

—, *King Arthur North-By-North-West: The Matière de Bretagne in Old Norse-Icelandic Romances*, Bibliotheca Arnamagnæana, 37 (Copenhagen: Reitzel, 1981)

—, and Geraldine Barnes, 'Riddarasögur', in *Medieval Scandinavia: An Encyclopedia*, ed. by Phillip Pulsiano and others (New York: Garland, 1993), pp. 528-33

—, and P.M. Mitchell, *Bibliography of Old Norse-Icelandic Romances*, Islandica, 44 (London: Cornell University Press, 1985)

Kallendorf, Craig, *The Other Virgil: Pessimistic Readings of the Aeneid in Early Modern Culture* (Oxford: Oxford University Press, 2007)

Karras, Ruth Mazo, *Unmarriages: Women, Men, and Sexual Unions in the Middle Ages*, Middle Ages Series (Philadelphia: University of Pennsylvania Press, 2012)

Kelly, Kathleen Ann, 'Blue Indians, Ethiopians, and Saracens in Middle English Narrative Texts', *Parergon: Bulletin of the Australian and New Zealand Association for Medieval and Renaissance Studies*, 11 (1993), 35-52

Kłosowska, Anna, *Queer Love in the Middle Ages*, The New Middle Ages (New York: Palgrave Macmillan, 2005)

Kommissionen for det Arnamagnæanske Legat, *Katalog over den Arnamagnæanske Handskriftsamling*, 2 vols. (Copenhagen: Gyldendalske, 1889-94)

—, *Katalog over de Oldnorsk-Islandske Håndskrifter*, 2 vols. (Copenhagen: Gyldendalske, 1894-99)

Krueger, Roberta L., 'Introduction', in *The Cambridge Companion to Medieval Romance*, ed. by Roberta L. Krueger (Cambridge: Cambridge University Press, 2000), pp. 1-9

Larrington, Carolyne, "'What Does Woman Want?'" Mær and Munr in *Skírnismál*, *Alvíssmál: Forschungen zur mittelalterlichen Kultur Skandinaviens*, 1 (1992), 3-16

Lacy, Norris J., 'The Evolution and Legacy of French Prose Romance', in *The Cambridge Companion to Medieval Romance*, ed. by Roberta L. Krueger (Cambridge: Cambridge University Press, 2000), pp. 167-82

Lansing, Tereza 'Post-Medieval Production, Dissemination and Reception of *Hrólfs saga kraka*' (unpublished PhD thesis: University of Copenhagen, 2011)

Lárus H. Blöndal, Grímur M. Helgason, and Ögmundur Helgason, *Handritasafn Landsbókasafns*, 4 vols. (Reykjavík: Félagsprentsmiðjunni, 1947-96)

'Lbs 3941 8vo', *Handrit.is*, National and University Library of Iceland, 2009-15, <http://handrit.is/en/manuscript/view/is/Lbs08-3941> [accessed 30 May 2011])

Leach, Henry Goddard, *Angevin Britain and Scandinavia* (Cambridge, MA: Harvard University Press, 1921)

Lecouteux, Claude, *A Lapidary of Sacred Stones: Their Magical and Medicinal Powers Based on the Earliest Sources*, trans. by Jon E. Graham (Rochester, VT: Inner Traditions, 2012)

Levi, Giovanni, 'On Microhistory', in *New Perspectives on Historical Writing*, ed. by Peter Burke (Cambridge: Polity Press, 2001), pp. 97-119

Lewis, Charlton T. and Charles Short, *A Latin Dictionary: Founded on Andrews' Edition of Fruend's Latin Dictionary* (Oxford: Clarendon Press, 1879)

Lindow, John, 'The Social Semantics of Cardinal Directions in Medieval Scandinavia', *The Mankind Quarterly*, 34 (1994), 209-24

Lyte, Charles, *Sir Joseph Banks: Eighteenth-Century Explorer, Botanist and Entrepreneur* (Sydney: Reed, 1980)

Magnús Gíslason, *Kvällsvaka: En isländsk kulturtradition belyst genom studier i bondefolkningens vardagsliv och miljö under senare hälften av 1800-talet och börgan av 1900-talet*, Acta Universitatis Upsaliensis. Studia Ethnologica Upsaliensia, 2 (Uppsala: Almkvist and Wiksell, 1977)

Malm, Mats, 'The Nordic Demand for Medieval Icelandic Manuscripts', in *The Manuscripts of Iceland*, ed. by Gísli Sigurðsson and Vésteinn Ólason (Rekjavík: Árni Magnússon Institute, 2004), pp. 101-07

Margrét Eggertsdóttir, 'From Reformation to Enlightenment', trans. by Joe Allard, in *A History of Icelandic Literature*, ed. by Daisy L. Neijmann (London: University of Nebraska Press, 2006), pp. 174-250

Marti, Suzanne, 'Hvenær var Tristrams saga snúið? The Origin and Transmission of the *Riddarasögur*', paper presented at the Fifteenth International Saga Conference, Aarhus, Denmark, 7 August 2012

Matyushina, Inna, 'Magic Mirrors, Monsters, Maiden-kings (The Fantastic in *Riddarasögur*)', in *The Fantastic in Old Norse/Icelandic Literature: Sagas and the British Isles*, Preprint Papers of the Thirteenth International Saga Conference, Durham and York, 6-12 August 2006, ed. by John McKinnell, David Ashurst, and Donata Kick, 2 vols. (Durham: Centre for Medieval and Renaissance Studies, 2006), II, 660-70

—, 'On the Imagery and Style of the *Riddarasögur*', in *Scandinavia and Christian Europe in the Middle Ages*, Papers of the 12th International Saga Conference, Bonn, Germany, 28 July-2 August 2003, ed. by Rudolf Simek and Judith Meurer (Bonn: Universität Bonn, 2003) <http://www.skandinavistik.uni-bonn.de/saga-conference/> [accessed 13 August 2010]

Már Jónsson, 'Recent Trends (Or Their Lack) in Icelandic Manuscript Studies', *Gazette du livre médiévale*, 36 (2000), 11-16

McDonald, Nicola, ed., *Pulp Fictions of the Middle Ages: Essays in Popular Romance* (Manchester: Manchester University Press, 2004)

—, 'A Polemical Introduction', in *Pulp Fictions of the Middle Ages: Essays in Popular Romance*, ed. by Nicola McDonald (Manchester: Manchester University Press, 2004), pp. 1-21

McDonald, Sheryl, 'Variance Uncovered and Errors Explained: *Nítíða saga* in the Seventeenth-Century Manuscript JS 166 fol', *Digital Philology: A Journal of Medieval Cultures*, 1 (2012), 303-18

—, 'Some *Nitida saga* Manuscript Groupings', in *The 15th International Saga Conference: Sagas and the Use of the Past, 5th-11th August 2012, Aarhus University: Preprint of Abstracts*, ed. by A. Mathias Valentin Nordvig and others (Aarhus: Department of Aesthetics and Communication, Department of Culture and Society, Faculty of Arts, 2012), pp. 227-28 <http://sagaconference.au.dk/fileadmin/sagaconference/Pre-print.pdf>

McDonald Werronen, Sheryl, 'Two Major Groups in the Older Manuscript Tradition of *Nítíða saga*', *Saga-Book of the Viking Society for Northern Research*, 38 (2014), 75-94

—, 'Transforming Popular Romance on the Edge of the World: *Nítíða saga* in Late Medieval and Early Modern Iceland' (unpublished PhD thesis: University of Leeds, 2013)

McDougall, Ian, 'Foreigners and Foreign Languages in Medieval Iceland', *Saga-Book of the Viking Society for Northern Research*, 22 (1986-89), 180-233

McKinnell, John, David Ashurst, and Donata Kick, eds., *The Fantastic in Old Norse/Icelandic Literature: Sagas and the British Isles*, Preprint Papers of the Thirteenth International Saga Conference, Durham and York, 6-12 August 2006, 2 vols. (Durham: Centre for Medieval and Renaissance Studies, 2006)

Mills, Robert, 'Seeing Face to Face: Troubled Looks in the Katherine Group', in *Troubled Vision: Gender, Sexuality, and Sight in Medieval Text and Image*, ed. by Emma Campbell and Robert Mills (New York: Palgrave, 2004), pp. 117-36

Mitchell, Stephen A., *Heroic Sagas and Ballads* (London: Cornell University Press, 1991)

Mitchell, Stephen A. and Gísli Sigurðsson, 'Virgilessrímur', in *The Virgilian Tradition: The First Fifteen Hundred Years*, ed. by Jan M. Ziolkowski and Michael C.J. Putnam (New Haven: Yale University Press, 2007), pp. 881-88

Mittman, Asa Simon, *Maps and Monsters in Medieval England*, Studies in Medieval History and Culture (New York: Routledge, 2006)

Neddermeyer, Uwe, 'Möglichkeiten und Grenzen einer quantitativen Bestimmung der Buchproduktion im späten Mittelalter', *Gazette du livre médiévale*, 28 (1996), 23-31

Ney, Agnete, Henrik Williams, and Fredrik Charpentier Ljungqvist, eds., *'Á austrvega': Saga and East Scandinavia*, Preprint Papers of the Fourteenth International Saga Conference, Uppsala, 9-15 August 2009, 2 vols. (Gävle: Gävle University Press, 2009)

Nichols, Stephen G., 'Why Material Philology? Some Thoughts', *Zeitschrift für deutsche Philologie*, 116 (1997), 10-30

—, 'Philology and its Discontents', in *The Future of the Middle Ages: Medieval Literature in the 1990s*, ed. by William D. Paden (Gainesville: University Press of Florida, 1994), pp. 113-41

—, 'Introduction: Philology in a Manuscript Culture', *Speculum: A Journal of Medieval Studies*, 65 (1990), 1-10

Nordvig, A. Mathias Valentin and others, eds., *The 15th International Saga Conference: Sagas and the Use of the Past, 5th-11th August 2012, Aarhus University: Preprint of Abstracts*, ed. by (Aarhus: Department of Aesthetics and Communication, Department of Culture and Society, Faculty of Arts, 2012), <http://sagaconference.au.dk/fileadmin/sagaconference/Pre-print.pdf> [accessed 24 July 2012]

O'Connor, Ralph, 'Truth and Lies in the *fornaldarsögur*: The Prologue to *Göngu-Hrólfs saga*', in *Fornaldarsagaerne: Myter og virkelighed. Studier i de oldislandske* fornaldarsögur Norður-landa, ed. by Agnete Ney, Ármann Jakobsson, and Annette Lassen (Copenhagen: Museum Tusculanums, 2009), pp. 361-78

—, 'History or Fiction? Truth-Claims and Defensive Narrators in Icelandic Romance-Sagas', *Mediaeval Scandinavia: A Journal Devoted to the Study of Mediaeval Civilization in Scandinavia and Iceland*, 15 (2005), 101-69

O'Donoghue, Heather, *Old Norse-Icelandic Literature: A Short Introduction* (London: Blackwell, 2004)

Ommundsen, Åslaug, 'Books, Scribes, and Sequences in Medieval Norway', 2 vols. (unpublished PhD dissertation: University of Bergen, 2007)

Parsons, Katelin Marit, 'The Great Manuscript Exodus?', paper presented at the Fifteenth International Saga Conference Aarhus, Denmark, 10 August 2012

Páll Eggert Ólason, *Íslenskar æviskrár: Frá landnámstímum til ársloka 1940*, 6 vols. (Reykjavík: Hið Íslenzka Bókmenntafélag, 1948-76)

—, *Skrá um handritasöfn Landsbókasafnsins*, 3 vols. (Reykjavík: Gutenberg, 1918-37)

'Páll Pállsson stúdent', on *Handrit.is*, National and University Library of Iceland, 2009-15, <http://handrit.is/en/biography/view/PalPal003> [accessed 30 May 2011]

Petzoldt, Leander, 'Virgilius Magus: Der Zauberer *Virgil* in der literarischen Tradition des Mittelalters', in *Hören-Sagen-Lesen-Lernen: Bausteine zu einer Geschichte der kommunikativen Kultur*, ed. by Ursula Brunold-Bigler and Hermann Bausinger (Bern: Lang, 1995), pp. 549-68

Piehler, Paul, *The Visionary Landscape: A Study in Medieval Allegory* (Montreal: McGill-Queens University Press, 1971)

Propp, Vladimir, *Morphology of the Folktale*, trans. by Laurence Scott, 2nd edn. (London: University of Texas Press, 1968)

Putter, Ad and Jane Gilbert, eds., *The Spirit of Medieval English Popular Romance* (Harlow: Longman, 2000)

Quinn, Judy, 'Introduction', in *Creating the Medieval Saga: Versions, Variability, and Editorial Interpretations of Old Norse Saga Literature*, ed. by Judy Quinn and Emily Lethbridge, The Viking Collection, 18 (Odense: Syddansk Universitetsforlag, 2010), pp. 13-37

Rasmussen, Elizabeth, 'Translation in Medieval and Reformation Norway: A History of Stories or the Story of History', *Meta: Journal des traducteurs*, 49 (2004), 629-45

Relaño, Francesc, 'Paradise in Africa: The History of a Geographical Myth From its Origin in Medieval Thought to its Gradual Demise in Early Modern Europe', *Terrae Incognitae: The Journal for the History of Discoveries*, 36 (2004), 1-11

Rider, Jeff, 'The Other Worlds of Romance', in *The Cambridge Companion to Medieval Romance*, ed. by Roberta L. Krueger (Cambridge: Cambridge University Press, 2000), pp. 115-31

Robinson, Peter, 'The History, Discoveries, and Aims of the Canterbury Tales Project', *The Chaucer Review*, 38 (2003), 126-39

Sävborg, Daniel, *Sagan om kärleken: Erotik, känslor och berättarkonst i norrön litteratur*, Acta Universitatis Upsaliensis: Historia Litterarum, 27 (Uppsala: Uppsala Universitet, 2007)

Schach, Paul, 'Some Forms of Writer Intrusion in the *Íslendingasögur*', *Scandinavian Studies*, 42 (1970), 128-56

Schäfke, Werner, *Wertesysteme und Raumsemantik in den isländischen Märchen- und Anenteuersa-gas*, Texte und Untersuchungen zur Germanistik und Skandinavistik, 63 (Frankfurt: Lang, 2013)

—, 'Was ist eigentlich ein Zwerg? Eine prototypensemantische Figurenanalyse der *dvergar* in der Sagaliteratur', *Mediaevistik*, 23 (2010), 197-299

—, 'The "Wild East" in Late Medieval Icelandic Romances – Just a Prop(p)?', in *'Á austrvega': Saga and East Scandinavia*, Preprint Papers of the Fourteenth International Saga Conference, Uppsala, 9-15 August 2009, ed. by Agnete Ney, Henrik Williams, and Fredrik Charpentier Ljungqvist, 2 vols. (Gävle: Gävle University Press, 2009), II, 845-50

Schibanoff, Susan, 'Hildegard of Bingen and Richardis of Stade: The Discourse of Desire', in *Same Sex Love and Desire among Women in the Middle Ages*, ed. by Francesca Canadé Sautman and Pamela Sheingorn, The New Middle Ages (New York: Palgrave Macmillan, 2001), pp. 49-83

Schlauch, Margaret, *Romance in Iceland* (London: Allen and Unwin, 1934)

Scott, Forrest S., 'The Icelandic Family Saga as Precursor to the Novel, with Special Reference to *Eyrbyggja saga*', *Parergon*, 6 (1973), 3-13

Shafer, John Douglas, 'Saga Accounts of Norse Far-Travellers' (unpublished PhD thesis: University of Durham, 2010) <http://etheses.dur.ac.uk/286/> [accessed 1 September 2011]

Sif Rikhardsdottir, *Medieval Translations and Cultural Discourse: The Movement of Texts in England, France, and Scandinavia* (Woodbridge: Brewer, 2012)

—, 'Meykóngahefðin í riddarasögum: Hugmyndafræðileg átök um kynhlutverk og þjóðfélagsstöðu', *Skírnir: Tímarit hins íslenska bókmenntafélags*, 184 (2010), 410-33

Sigfús Blöndal, *The Varangians of Byzantium: An Aspect of Byzantine Military History*, trans. by Benedikt S. Benedikz (Cambridge: Cambridge University Press, 1978)

Sigurdson, Erika Ruth, 'The Church in Fourteenth-Century Iceland: Ecclesiastical Administration, Literacy, and the Formation of an Elite Clerical Identity' (unpublished PhD thesis: University of Leeds, 2011)

Simek, Rudolf, *Heaven and Earth in the Middle Ages: The Physical World Before Columbus*, trans. by Angela Hall (Woodbridge: Boydell, 1996)

—, *Altnordische Kosmographie: Studien und Quellen zu Weltbild und Weltbeschreibung in Norwegen und Island vom 12. bis zum 14. Jahrhundert*, Ergänzungsbände zum Reallexikon der germanischen Altertumskunde, 4 (Berlin: de Gruyter, 1990)

—, 'Elusive Elysia, or, Which Way to Glæsisvellir? On the Geography of the North in Icelandic Legendary Fiction', in *Sagnaskemmtun: Studies in Honour of Hermann Pálsson on his 65th Birthday, 26th May 1986*, ed. by Rudolf Simek, Jónas Kristjánsson, and Hans Bekker-Nielsen (Vienna: Böhlaus Nachf, 1986), pp. 247-75

— and Hermann Pálsson, *Lexikon der nordischen Literatur*, 2nd ed. (Stuttgart: Kröner, 2007)

Spargo, John Webster, *Virgil the Necromancer: Studies in Virgilian Legends* (Cambridge, MA: Harvard University Press, 1934)

Speed, Diane, 'The Construction of the Nation in Middle English Romance', in *Readings in Medieval English Romance*, ed. by Carol M. Meale (Cambridge: Brewer, 1994), pp. 135-57

Springborg, Peter, 'Antiqvæ historiæ lepores – om renæssancen i den islandske håndskriftproduktion i 1600-tallet', *Gardar: Årsbok för Samfundet Sverige-Island i Lund-Malmö*, 8 (1977), 53-89

Stefán Einarsson, 'Heimili (skólar) fornaldarsaga og riddarasaga', *Skírnir: Tímarit hins íslenska bókmenntafélags*, 140 (1966), 272

—, 'Safn Nikulásar Ottensons í Johns Hopkins Háskólabókasafninu í Baltimore, Md.', *Landsbókasafn Íslands Árbók 1946-47*, 3-4 (1948), 157-72

Stefán Karlsson, 'The Localisation and Dating of Medieval Icelandic Manuscripts', *Saga-Book of the Viking Society for Northern Research*, 25 (1999), 138-58

Stein, Robert M., 'Making History English: Cultural Identity and Historical Explanation in William of Malmesbury and Laȝamon's *Brut*', in *Text and Territory: Geographical Imagination in the European Middle Ages*, ed. by Sylvia Tomasch and Sealy Gilles (Philadelphia: University of Pennsylvania Press, 1998), pp. 97-115

Sverrir Jakobsson, 'Centre and Periphery in Icelandic Medieval Discourse', in *'Á austrvega': Saga and East Scandinavia*, Preprint Papers of the Fourteenth International Saga Conference, Uppsala, 9-15 August 2009, ed. by Agnete Ney, Henrik Williams, and Fredrik Charpentier Ljungqvist, 2 vols. (Gävle: Gävle University Press, 2009), II, 918-24

—, 'The Schism that Never Was: Old Norse Views on Byzantium and Russia', *Byzantinoslavica: Revue internationale des Études Byzantines*, 1-2 (2008), 173-88

Sverrir Tómasson, 'Old Icelandic Prose', trans. by Gunnþórunn Guðmundsdóttir, in *A History of Icelandic Literature*, ed. by Daisy L. Neijmann (London: University of Nebraska Press, 2006), pp. 64-173

Tannert, Robert, 'The Style of *Dínus saga drambláta*', *Scandinavian Studies*, 52 (1980), 53-62

Thorndike, Lynn, 'More Copyists' Final Jingles', *Speculum: A Journal of Medieval Studies*, 31 (1950), 321-28

Thoss, Dagmar, *Studien zum Locus Amoenus im Mittelalter*, Wiener romanistische Arbeiten, 10 (Vienna: Braunmüller, 1972)

Tolan, John V., *Saracens: Islam in the Medieval European Imagination* (New York: Columbia University Press, 2002)

Tomasch, Sylvia, 'Introduction: Medieval Geographical Desire', in *Text and Territory: Geographical Imagination in the European Middle Ages*, ed. by Sylvia Tomasch and Sealy Gilles (Philadelphia: University of Pennsylvania Press, 1998), pp. 1-12

Torfi H. Tulinius, 'Íslenska rómansan – fornaldarsögur og frumsamdar riddarasögur', in *Íslensk bókmenntasaga*, ed. by Böðvar Guðmundsson and others, 5 vols. (Reykjavík: Mál og Menning, 1992-2006), II (1993), 218-44

van Nahl, Astrid, *Originale Riddarasögur als Teil altnordischer Sagaliteratur*, Texte und Untersuchungen zur Germanistik und Skandinavistik, 3 (Frankfurt: Lang, 1981)

Veturliði Óskarsson, *Middelnedertyske Låneord i islandsk Diplomsprog frem til Ár 1500*, Bibliotheca Arnamagnæana, 43 (Copenhagen: Reitzel, 2003)

Vésteinn Ólason, 'The Icelandic Saga as a Kind of Literature with Special Reference to its Representation of Reality', in *Learning and Understanding in the Old Norse World: Essays in Honour of Margaret Clunies Ross* (Turnhout: Brepols, 2007), pp. 27-48

—, 'Family Sagas', in *A Companion to Old Norse–Icelandic Literature and Culture*, ed. by Rory McTurk, 2nd edn. (Oxford: Blackwell, 2007), pp. 101-18

de Vries, Jan, *Altnordisches etymologisches Wörterbuch*, 2nd rev. edn. (Leiden: Brill, 1977)

Wahlgren, Erik, 'The Maiden King in Iceland' (unpublished PhD dissertation: University of Chicago, 1938)

Wanner, Kevin J., 'Off-Center: Considering Directional Valences in Norse Cosmography', *Speculum: A Journal of Medieval Studies*, 84 (2009), 36-72

Wawn, Andrew, 'The Post-Medieval Reception of Old Norse and Old Icelandic Literature', in *A Companion to Old Norse–Icelandic Literature and Culture*, ed. by Rory McTurk, 2nd edn. (Oxford: Blackwell, 2007), pp. 320-37

Wenzel, Siegfried, 'Reflections on (New) Philology', *Speculum: A Journal of Medieval Studies*, 65 (1990), 11-18

Wilson, R.M., *The Lost Literature of Medieval England* (London: Methuen, 1970)

Wolf, Kirsten, 'Old Norse – New Philology', *Scandinavian Studies*, 65 (1993), 338-48

Wood, Juliette, 'Virgil and Taliesin: The Concept of the Magician in England', *Folklore*, 94 (1983), 91-104

Woodward, David, 'Reality, Symbolism, Time, and Space in Medieval World Maps', *Annals of the Association of American Geographers*, 75 (1985), 510-21

Würth, Stefanie, 'Historiography and Pseudo-History', in *A Companion to Old Norse–Icelandic Literature and Culture*, ed. by Rory McTurk, 2nd edn. (Oxford: Blackwell, 2007), pp. 155-72

Ziolkowski, Jan M., and Michael C.J. Putnam, eds *The Virgilian Tradition: The First Fifteen Hundred Years* (New Haven: Yale University Press, 2007)

Zitzelsberger, Otto J., 'The Filiation of the Manuscripts of *Konráðs saga keisarasonar*', *Amsterdamer Beiträge zur älteren Germanistik*, 16 (1981), 145-76

Åström, Patrik, 'Manuscripts and Bookprinting in Late Medieval Scandinavian and in Early Modern Times', in *The Nordic Languages: An International Handbook of the History of the North Germanic Languages*, ed. by Oskar Bandle, and others, 2 vols., Handbücher zur Sprach- und Kommunikationswissenschaft, 22 (Berlin: de Gruyter, 2005), II, 1067-75

Þormóður Torfason [Tormod Torfæus], *Historia rerum Norvegicarum*, 4 vols. (Copenhagen: Schmitgen, 1711)

Þórunn Sigurðardóttir, *Manuscript Material, Correspondence and Graphic Material in the Fiske Icelandic Collection: A Descriptive Catalogue*, Islandica, 48 (London: Cornell University Press, 1994)

'Þórður Jónsson', in *Handrit.is*, National and University Library of Iceland, 2009-15, <http://handrit.is/en/biography/view/ThoJon029> [accessed 30 May 2011]

Þorsteinn Jónsson and Halldór B. Kristjánsson, eds., *Eylenda: Mannlíf í Flateyjarhreppi á Breiðafirði*, 2 vols. (Reykjavík: Byggðir og bú, 1996), I: *Ábúendur og þjóðlífsþættir*

Internet Resources

Gudbrand Vigfusson, *An Icelandic-English Dictionary, Based on the MS Collections of the Late Richard Cleasby* (Oxford: Clarendon Press, 1874) <http://www.ling.upenn.edu/~kurisuto/germanic/oi_cleasbyvigfusson_about.html>

Handrit.is, National and University Library of Iceland, 2009-15 <http://handrit.is>

Ordbog over det norrøne prosasprog / Dictionary of Old Norse Prose <http://dataonp.hum.ku.dk>

Oxford English Dictionary Online <http://www.oed.com>

Sverrir Hólmarsson, Christopher Sanders, and John Tucker, eds., *Íslensk-Ensk Orðabók / Concise Icelandic-English Dictionary* (Reykjavík: Iðunn, 1989) <http://digital.library.wisc.edu/1711.dl/IcelOnline.IEOrd>

Index

The Index is divided into an Index of Manuscripts and a General Index. In both of these, page numbers in italics refer to maps and figures.

Index of Manuscripts

General Index

For Product Safety Concerns and Information please contact our EU
representative GPSR@taylorandfrancis.com
Taylor & Francis Verlag GmbH, Kaufingerstraße 24, 80331 München, Germany